SOLDIERS OF THE INTERNATIONAL

CANADIAN STUDIES IN HISTORY AND GOVERNMENT

A series of studies edited by Goldwin French, sponsored by the Social Science Research Council of Canada, and published with financial assistance from the Canada Council.

SOLDIERS OF THE INTERNATIONAL

A History of the
Communist Party of Canada
1919-1929

WILLIAM RODNEY

Department of History
Royal Roads Military College
Victoria, B.C.

∎∎∎∎∎∎∎∎∎∎∎∎∎∎∎∎∎∎∎∎∎∎∎∎∎∎∎∎∎∎

UNIVERSITY OF TORONTO PRESS

© University of Toronto Press 1968
Printed in Great Britain
Reprinted in 2018
ISBN 978-1-4875-8202-9 (paper)

PREFACE

THIS BOOK attempts to trace the origin and development of the Communist Party of Canada (CPC), a small political unit which, since its formation in 1921, has never wielded power or fundamentally affected the order or pattern of Canadian development. While the study makes no attempt to assess the impact of the CPC upon the social, political, or economic life of the nation during the 1920's, its conclusion, inevitably, must be that the party was a failure in those years. It did not gain significant political office, nor did it affect any major issues during a period when Canada was sloughing off the last remnants of imperial control. More important, the CPC failed to create that climate of opinion which its own leaders, as well as those directing the Communist International (Comintern), felt was vital in order to bring about a proletarian triumph in the Dominion.

Fundamentally, the Canadian party's failure to move the Canadian masses must be attributed to Marxist ideology which, based as it is upon class relationships, proved to be an obsolete, ineffective tool. Certainly, the inability of the Canadian component to become an effective political force within the Dominion stems from the Comintern's own misunderstanding of the nature of capitalism in North America, and a gross misjudgement of its resiliency.

Why then write about such a small, obscure party? Inevitably, like the mountaineer's explanation of why he climbs dangerous peaks, the obvious reply is that the Communist Party of Canada is there. But more than that, the CPC is undeniably an integral part of Canada's recent history, and no study of the 1920's and 1930's is complete without taking into consideration the persistent political nagging of the extreme left. Similarly, no account of the part played in the development of Canada by the ethnic groups that came to this land, and whose history is not yet fully written, can ignore the communist movement in the Dominion. In short, the movement from the beginning exercised the attention of a considerable segment of the Canadian community.

Because of the philosophical basis upon which the CPC is premised, as well as its propensity for secrecy, any study of it poses unusual academic and practical challenges. There is the difficulty, for instance, of locating sources, for the party, ex-members, and officialdom are reluctant to make their records available to the researcher. Perhaps the most compelling reason for studying the CPC, however, is to be found in the subordination of the Canadian party to Moscow through what can only be termed moral control exercised at a great distance, surely a fascinating phenomenon, and one of the most extraordinary political relationships of recent times. Through the Comintern the history of the Canadian party, like that of all other communist parties throughout the world, is in a real sense inseparable from the history of the Soviet Union. No other Canadian political party has experienced such direct shaping and control from outside, and no other can trace its origins to that epochal event, the Russian Revolution.

The very smallness of the CPC and its relative lack of importance in the Comintern's scale of priorities during the 1920's did not exempt it from Moscow's control, a condition which it shared with the great parties of Europe which, between them, directed the political outlook and actions of millions of Frenchmen, Germans, Poles, Italians, and other peoples. In their own way the domestic actions of the Canadian party, although tempered to a degree by local conditions, certainly reflected Comintern policy and thinking. What is remarkable is how very little real help the Canadian and other parties received from Moscow. After 1926 domestic quarrels within the Soviet Union began to intrude into Comintern affairs; after 1929 a new force, that of Stalin's personality, radically modified the International's policies and practices. As a result, the Comintern was transformed from the vanguard of the revolution, to use Trotsky's phrase, to being simply another border guard of the Soviet state.

During its first decade the Canadian party, like the Comintern, had its greatest opportunity to build up an effective membership and establish a strong appeal within the country. Its failure to do so was signal, characterized in the process by a leadership struggle which coincided with the advent of Stalin in the USSR. The Canadian party never recovered from that double blow, the impact of which was obscured by the great crash of 1929, by the depression which followed, and by the general ineffectiveness of European political leaders in their attempts to stem the rise of fascism.

In order to facilitate the examination of cardinal aspects of the CPC's development, I have employed what might be termed an impressionistic technique in the structure and organization of this book, and particularly in its time sequence. Hence the separate and distinct treatment of the Canadian party's attempts to gain control of the Canadian Labor Party (CLP), and its efforts to make the Trade Union Educational League (TUEL) the focal point of trade union activity in the Dominion. In daily practice the attention and amount of effort devoted to both policies by party members were by no means so compartmentalized. The difficulties of treating such important party matters may be judged by the fact that the foremost authority on the Communist Party of the United States makes no attempt to deal with the TUEL, an organization that originated in the United States, and upon which the Comintern centred its appeal to the American labour movement. Perhaps the approach employed in this book may be likened to that of a series of photographs taken from the same vantage point with lenses of different focal length. Depending upon the lens selected, the angle of acceptance and the depth of field vary accordingly. To a very real degree the availability and reliability of evidence correspond to the choice of lenses, a choice that more often than not was imposed rather than the result of voluntary selection. In any case, the approach as well as the analysis are matters for which I alone must bear responsibility.

This book could not have been written without the advice, assistance, encouragement, and information given to me by many individuals and organizations. To Professor L. B. Schapiro I owe much. His direction, especially during the initial stages of research, was always firm, clear, and inevitably marked by a gentle humanity that is his own vital characteristic. Mr. Theodore Draper, whose own works on the American party are unrivalled, assisted me sight unseen and made possible interviews which otherwise would have been exceedingly difficult, if not impossible, to arrange. A generous subsidy from the Research Grants Committee, University of London, made it possible for me to overcome the barrier of distance to examine material in various archives and libraries. For their unfailing courtesy and patient assistance I am indebted to the archivists and librarians of the British Museum, the Royal Institute of International Affairs, the London School of Economics and Political Science, the Trade Union Library, the New York Public Library, the Tamiment Institute, the Public Archives of Canada, the Department of Public Archives and Records, Province of Ontario, the University of Toronto Library, and the Department of Labour Library, Ottawa. Mr. W. B. Common, formerly Deputy Attorney General of Ontario, very kindly obtained permission for me to read the transcript of evidence in the trial *Rex* v. *Buck et al.* A good friend, Dennis Healy, and his wife Eileen, were most generous in another way during the early, difficult period of research. I profited much from discussions with Mrs. Jane Degras whose work on Comintern documents is unrivalled, and from many talks with Professor Stuart R. Tompkins, now retired in Victoria, whose knowledge of Russian history after a lifetime of study is profound. The late Professor M. H. Long of the University of Alberta, a man for whom scholarship and courtesy always went hand in hand, was constant in his friendship. To the many others who through either modesty or circumstances do not wish to be acknowledged publicly, my sincere thanks. My thanks too to Professor Kenneth McNaught, formerly editor of the Canadian History and Government series, and to Professor Goldwin French, both of whom have been unfailing and gracious in their advice.

This work has been published with the help of a grant from the Social Science Research Council of Canada using funds provided by the Canada Council. Without their help it would have been impossible to complete this study, and certainly without assistance the book could not have appeared in its present form. Nor could the book have been written without my wife's assistance. She not only typed the entire manuscript in its several variations but throughout the long period of research and writing provided professional advice as well as criticism that was always firm and just. To her more than to anyone else must go the credit for the constant, gentle optimism and encouragement that made completion possible.

Victoria, B.C.   W.R.

CONTENTS

KEY TO PRINCIPAL ABBREVIATIONS

AF of L   American Federation of Labor
Agit-Prop   Agitation and Propaganda [Bureau or Committee]
Arcos   All Russia Co-operative Society [London Office]
CEC   Central Executive Committee
CFO   Canadian Finnish Organization
CLDL   Canadian Labor Defence League
CLP   Canadian Labor Party
CLPA   Communist Labor Party of America
Comintern   Communist International
CPA   Communist Party of America
CPC   Communist Party of Canada
CPGB   Communist Party of Great Britain
CPSU   Communist Party of the Soviet Union
CPUSA   Communist Party of the United States of America
ECCI   Executive Committee of the Communist International
FOC   Finnish Organization of Canada
ILP   Independent Labour Party
IWW   Industrial Workers of the World
KPD   Kommunistische Partei Deutschland
Krestintern   Krest'ianski internatsional [Peasants' International]
MOPR   Mezhdunarodnaia Organizatsiia Pomoschhi Bortsam Revoliutsii [International Red Aid]
NEC   National Executive Committee
OBU   One Big Union
Orgburo   Organization Bureau
Politburo   Political Bureau
RILU   Red International of Labor Unions [Profintern]
SDP   Socialist Democratic Party
SPC   Socialist Party of Canada
TLC   Trades and Labour Congress of Canada
TUEL   Trade Union Educational League
UCPA   United Communist Party of America

ULFTA   Ukrainian Labour Farmer Temple Association
ULTA   Ukrainian Labour Temple Association
UMWA   United Mine Workers of America
USSR   Union of Soviet Socialist Republics
WPA   Workers' Party of America
WPC   Workers' Party of Canada
YCI   Young Communist International
YCL   Young Communist League
YWL   Young Workers' League

SOLDIERS OF THE INTERNATIONAL

And if, in raising this "issue" [party unity] by formation of an opposition faction, Comrade Zinoviev and other comrades laid themselves open to disciplinary measures, then we as loyal Communists and soldiers of the International, rejoice that not even the old guard of our brother party [the CPSU] can endanger that unity with impunity.

Tim Buck in *The Worker*, November 6, 1926.

CHAPTER ONE

THE ROOTS OF CANADIAN SOCIALISM

THE ROOTS of the Canadian communist movement extend back to the early decades of the nineteenth century and the beginnings of organized labour in British North America. From the start the men and, to a lesser degree, the women who attempted to organize the Canadian working population clashed openly and violently with governments and leading Canadian political figures. As one partisan chronicler of the Canadian labour movement has put it: "Urgent measures stoutly put forward in shabby union halls were twisted by politicians and pushed aside by parliaments."[1] From such confrontations and differences arose, in time, a burning desire on the part of a small number of ultra-radical men and women to change the social order in Canada; more specifically, to change it according to the precepts of Karl Marx and, after 1917, to model it upon the new society being forged in Russia.

In the beginning, however, the labour movement in Canada was not infused with any specific ideological concepts. It was concerned instead with the basic matters of working conditions in a new raw land, and the exploitation of a labour force constantly being added to by a stream of immigrants. Accordingly, trade union organization in Canada's early days varied enormously in nature and extent depending, inevitably, upon the degree of industrialization as the settled areas of the country grew in size and complexity, and upon the influx of craftsmen who had experienced a measure of labour orginization and social theory elsewhere. Progress was slow, and the resistance of those in authority considerable. Characteristic of this resistance was an anti-union law in Nova Scotia dating from 1816, reflecting the concern felt by the British colonial authorities as a result of social unrest and agitation which swept over England and continental Europe after the end of the Napoleonic Wars.

Nevertheless, progress in establishing trade unions was made, notably in the larger centres of Upper and Lower Canada. A printers' society, for example, was formed in Quebec City in 1827, followed soon after by the establishment of a similar body in York in 1832. By and large, however, such groups before the Act of Union which united Upper and Lower Canada in 1840, and Confederation in 1867, were few in number, local in character, and conspicuously lacking in influence within their own communities. Indeed, many of the early trade unions in Canada were often secret societies formed clandestinely in the face of the common law. The law itself was based upon precedents and the concept that labour disturbances were criminal conspiracies in which the strikers were considered to be party to an illegal combination in restraint of trade.[2] Such a view stemmed from the Combination Acts, passed by the British Parliament in 1799 and 1800, which, although repealed in Britain in 1824, were never altered by Canadian legislators when the country achieved nationhood.[3] Under the circumstances, the climate of opinion among employers about trade union organization both before and after 1867 was not conducive to the open establishment of bodies specifically prepared to air their grievances, and, if necessary, to take action. In turn, the tradition of secrecy which, in many ways, was the hallmark of the early trade unions, ultimately was taken over and utilized to advantage by the communist movement in Canada.

It was not the restraining hand of authority alone, however, which inhibited the early development of labour organizations in Canada. Two factors combined to restrict the rise of trade unions and to condemn them to remain, for a long time, small parochial units in the undeveloped vastness of Canada. The very nature of the land and its population did not encourage trade union organization. Canada lagged far behind the United States and Europe industrially and consequently did not experience many of the social problems which followed until well after Confederation. As Doris French has noted in her life of the pioneer Canadian trade unionist Daniel O'Donoghue:

Industry was only beginning in Canada. It was still a homesteaders' country. The working population when the census was taken in 1871 divided itself into 385,000 farm workers and only 106,000 "labourers", which included non-farm categories.[4]

The lack of industry was supplemented by the magnetic attraction of cheap land on the frontier; accordingly, "so long as lands were cheap in the west and industry was largely in the domestic stage, there was little stimulus or occasion for labour unions."[5] Only when the shift from the land to the city began in earnest well after 1867 did the demand for shorter working hours and better labour conditions begin to manifest itself on any scale. And only then did strikes become sufficiently numerous to indicate clearly the divergence of interest between employer and employee.

Until Confederation the main influences shaping the nascent trade union movement in Canada came from England. They came in the form of old country artisans such as the stone cutters and masons who had flocked into Ottawa after that "subarctic village," as Goldwin Smith had called it, was chosen by Queen Victoria as the capital of the newly united provinces, Upper and Lower Canada. Such men were not only versed in their trades; they were also acquainted with the theories and practices of trade unionism in the British Isles. In the new country they not only applied their skills, but also became the focus which attracted other skilled craftsmen, many of them native born, who were eager to improve their lot. With the arrival of the newcomers from overseas, Mechanics Institutes and reading rooms soon sprang up in many of the cities of central Canada, and it was in such libraries that many Canadian trade unionists obtained their education, or, like Daniel O'Donoghue in Ottawa, were awakened to the compelling need to learn and to organize.

Despite the link between the British Isles and Canada that grew up in such haphazard fashion, and despite the examples provided by England in the form of trade union development or labour legislation, the connection proved to be of little direct use because labour conditions were so radically different in North America. Consequently, as Canada became increasingly industrialized the trans-Atlantic connections were eroded by time, distance, and the differing social order until they became largely academic. Inexorably, British trade union traditions and experience were replaced by those emanating from the United States. It was, in many respects, a natural development. Doris French rightly points out that

Men of the same craft moved back and forth [across the border between the United States and Canada] in search of jobs, with the logical result that the union card became recognized in both countries.[6]

Because working conditions, as well as the attitudes of mind on the part of the employers and employees, were so similar in Canada and the United States, American trade union practices were taken up with increasing frequency in the Dominion so that eventually, "American movements came to be the stronger, and even the predominant forces affecting labour organization in Canada."[7] The Nine-Hour Movement, for example, spread rapidly from the United States into Ontario, the leading province in industrial development, during the 1860's and early 1870's.

The growth of the new industrialism, accompanied by the formation of new trade unions, did not pass unnoticed in political and official quarters.

From Ottawa [Professor Creighton writes] Macdonald [then Prime Minister of Canada and leader of the Conservative Party] had watched this so-called "Nine-Hours Movement" with curious interest, his big nose sensitively keen for any scent of profit or danger. Montreal, Toronto, and Hamilton were evidently the key centres of working class agitation. . . . [8]

Early in 1872, at the trial of twenty-three printers, members of a strongly organized typographical union in Toronto who were charged with conspiracy for having taken part in a strike, one point emerged clearly: that the legislatures of Canada evidently had never dealt with the subject of trade unions and their work. Professor Creighton continues:

Macdonald seized his advantage at once. He had already concerned himself with industry; now he saw where he could espouse the cause of labour. . . . The circumstances could hardly have been more favourable; the means lay right at his hand. Only the year before, Gladstone had rescued the trade unions of Great Britain from a somewhat similar anomalous position by passing the Trade Union Act and the Criminal Law Amendment Act. All that Macdonald had to do was to re-enact with suitable modifications to suit Canadian conditions, the two British statutes of 1871; and the unimpeachable orthodoxy of Gladstonian legislation would remove all doubts and silence all criticisms. He could confound George Brown [the leader of the opposition Liberal Party and owner of the powerful Toronto newspaper *The Globe*] with William Ewart Gladstone.[9]

The Trade Union Bill (35 Vict. c. 30), a measure of pure political expediency on Macdonald's part, encountered little difficulty during the parliamentary session, and was passed in one day, June 12, 1872.[10]

By exempting unions which registered as such with the federal government from prosecution for restraint of trade, the bill legalized labour organization in Canada and, in effect, gave fresh impetus to the trade union movement. In 1873 the first nationally representative assembly of thirty-one unions met to establish centralized control and direction of organized labour in Canada. Known as the Canadian Labour Union, the new organization urged such moderate reforms as introduction of the nine-hour working day, the use of arbitration in industrial disputes, and the restraint of immigration. The union soon lapsed because of organizational difficulties until it was re-established twelve years later as the Trades and Labour Congress of Canada (TLC).

The Canadian Labour Union's inability to unify the Canadian labour movement, together with the passage of the Trade Union Act, in turn enabled a new force, the Knights of Labour, to make the first real impact upon the Canadian labour scene.

Formed secretly in 1869 in the United States, the Knights were the product of the inflammable social, political, and economic climate prevailing in the United States following the Civil War, in which relations between capital and labour were characterized by the use of force and violence by both sides. Originally the Knights were formed to promote education, mutual aid, and co-operation within labour ranks, but under the given conditions, they found themselves increasingly concerned with strikes and other forms of direct labour action. Nevertheless, the Knights introduced something new in the trade union field. Their secrecy and industrial organization, which admitted labourers in all crafts, set them apart from orthodox trade unions. Another difference from the unions was that the order based its aims and policies on a code of idealistic principles.[11] In all, the Knights of Labour specified twenty-two points in their constitution, and, as the preamble to that set of rules makes clear, their concept of political effectiveness was, to say the least, utopian. Although they favoured intervention to the point of extracting pre-election pledges from candidates they wished to support, the organization declined to accept direct responsibility by campaigning for the men it desired in public office, and made no real attempt to disseminate its views widely or openly.

Unlike the American parent organization, the Knights of Labour in Canada from the start favoured direct and active participation in politics. Indeed, the difference in economic problems of a less industrialized society, in the form of civil government, and in the general temperament of the people, combined in the Canadian wing to bring about a strong move for secession from the American body. This died down, and in the absence of any other effective force, the Knights achieved a considerable following among Canadian working men. At the height of their strength, in 1887, membership totalled 12,253, distributed throughout seven districts and 168 local assemblies.[12] Considering the size of the industrial force in central Canada—there were no industries at the time in Western Canada, which was still virtually unpopulated, and few of importance in the Maritimes—the influence achieved by the Knights in less than a dozen years was remarkable.

Their decline was more abrupt. Difficulties in administration and with the Catholic Church in Quebec, and charges of anarchism levelled at the Knights following the Haymarket riot in Chicago in May 1886, and which radiated over the border, undermined their influence. Also, two new labour organizations, one American and one Canadian, the American Federation of Labor (AF of L), and the Trades and Labour Congress of Canada (TLC), formed respectively in 1881 and 1885, began to attract those members of the Knights who were disillusioned with the order's idealistic ineffectiveness.[13]

The TLC, unlike the AF of L which stressed organization of labour on a craft basis, was an all-embracing federation consisting of representatives from provincial labour organizations, local labour councils, federal labour unions, all of which received charters, and all of which recognized delegates from United States unions such as the American Federation of Labor. The TLC met annually, devoting itself primarily to the promotion of legislation which it judged to be in the interests of the wage earner. With its advent the impact of the TLC upon the Canadian trade unions at the expense of other organizations was swift and dramatic. For example, at the TLC's second convention held in Hamilton, Ontario, in September 1887, 27 of the 43 delegates present represented 22 Knights of Labour assemblies in Canada.[14] The attendance of such a large number of men representing the Knights was, in itself, prophetic of that organization's decline, and simultaneously indicative of the TLC's growing influence.

Of equal significance, the delegates at the Hamilton meeting unanimously supported a resolution which unashamedly declared:

That in the opinion of this Congress the working classes of the Dominion will never be properly represented in parliament, or receive justice in the legislation of the country, until they are represented by men of their own class, and members of this congress pledge themselves to use their utmost endeavours, wherever practicable, to bring out candidates for local and Dominion elections in the constituencies in which they reside.[15]

With the passage of the resolution the concept of the class struggle formally made its belated appearance upon the Canadian labour scene.

Despite the guarded introduction of the class struggle into the TLC's proceedings, the idea received little additional or practical emphasis at the meeting, and subsequently made little impact upon the membership at large. Although the American section of the First International, which was headed by Karl Marx himself, was established in 1869, there is no evidence that the international organization or Marxism in general received any significant notice from Canadian trade unionists. Even the former National Secretary of the CPC, Tim Buck, has not been able to incorporate such a claim into his account of the party's history:

There were Canadian circles of the First International and the continuity of Marxism in our country was illustrated by the fact that among the workers who were associated with the beginnings of the Communist Party of Canada were two who had been members of the First International. It would be erroneous however, to suggest that the development of Marxism [in Canada] proceeded in a continuous upward line. It crystallized in national organization slowly, due to the colonial isolation of the different provinces and the local character of industry.[16]

Little wonder that Friederich Engels who, in the course of a brief visit to North America in 1888, came to Canada, concluded that the working class in America was "still quite crude, tremendously backward theoretically, in particular, as a result of its general Anglo-Saxon and special American nature."[17] Certainly, Engels did not differentiate between the working class in the United States or Canada. If anything, his remarks suggest that Canadian workers were even more apathetic towards organization and socialist doctrines. During a brief stopover in Montreal on Spetember 10, Engels wrote:

It is a strange transition from the States to Canada. First one imagines that one is in Europe again, and one thinks one is in a positively retrogressing and decaying country. Here one sees how necessary the feverish speculative spirit of the Americans is for the rapid development of a new country (presupposing capitalist production as a basis); and in ten years this sleepy Canada will be ripe for annexation. . . . Beside, this country is half annexed already socially—hotels, newspapers, advertising, etc., all on the American pattern. And they may try and resist as much as they like; the economic necessity of an infusion of Yankee blood will have its way and abolish this ridiculous boundary line—and when the time comes John Bull will say "Yea and Amen" to it.[18]

Engels' disappointment at the lack of class consciousness within American, and therefore, Canadian labour ranks however, was scarcely warranted. The first volume of Marx's *Capital* was not published in English until 1887, and Engels' own work, *Condition of the Working Class in England in 1844*, which first appeared in Germany in 1845, was not translated into English until 1887. Under the circumstances, and considering the state of development of labour organization in North America, it is doubtful if more than a trickle of Marxist literature made its way into Canada before the turn of the century. On the other hand, although American trade union practices were becoming predominant within Canada during this period, socialist political theories still largely emanated from Europe. In the case of Canada, left-wing political views originated mostly from the British Isles because the bulk of the immigrants still came from those shores. As a result, during the closing years of the nineteenth century and in the decade preceding the First World War, the political views of men such as Keir Hardie, Ramsay MacDonald, who toured Canada in 1906, as well as others, were radiated most effectively by newcomers to the Dominion, and who became, in effect, the catalysts instrumental in accelerating the spread of socialist doctrines throughout the land. Socialist Leagues patterned after English and Scottish counterparts, for example, were first established in Ontario in the 1890's, and from there quickly spread to other parts of Canada, penetrating as far west as Vancouver Island.[19] As early as 1895 an Independent Labour Party (ILP) was formed in Winnipeg and the west which gradually increased in strength.[20] In British Columbia a Progressive Party came into existence in 1902, and though its activities attracted the attention of the radical American Labor Union centred in the copper-mining town of Butte, Montana, which favoured industrial unionism and which adopted the same platform as the Socialist Party of America.[21] Inevitably, the differences between the theories and practices of the old world and the new soon manifested themselves in the practical matter of trade union organization throughout the Dominion. The American Labor Union's followers, for example, soon became active in British Columbia mining towns, and for a time achieved considerable success in organizing miners and other unskilled labourers. Nevertheless, such successes did not deter or prevent newcomers from abroad from forming their own groups.

In 1905, three years after the formation of the American Labor Union, English and Scottish immigrants in British Columbia, particularly those centred in Vancouver, founded the Socialist Party of Canada (SPC). Although the new party originally intended to be a provincial organization, its example and influence soon spread to other parts of Canada. Eventually, a national executive committee was established and plans for holding a national convention advanced. They proved to be too ambitious. Nonetheless, units of the SPC were established in the prairie provinces and Ontario, but they were too scattered and unco-ordinated to be considered as a national party, and would scarcely merit Tim Buck's claims that as early as 1904 they formed a dominion-wide party organized in five unspecified provinces.[22] How effectively the SPC functioned neither Buck nor any other authority has been able to say. For the more militant members, however, men such as Jack Kavanagh of Vancouver who soon became involved in waterfront and mining strikes, the SPC proved a good training unit. On the whole, and in comparison with other North–American–bred radical developments, British socialism and trade union practices as epitomized in Canada by the SPC were moderating influences.

The contrast between trans-Atlantic concepts and native North American developments is most strikingly revealed by the rapid rise and powerful influence of the Industrial Workers of the World (IWW), the Wobblies, which overwhelmed the embryonic radical groups in Western Canada. Within six years of its formation in Chicago in 1905 the IWW, a frankly revolutionary organization which opposed the craft union, and which rejected both the wage system and the possibility of reform through political action, claimed to have a following of 10,000 members, chiefly among the miners and unskilled workers in the two most westerly provinces, Alberta and British Columbia.[23]

The IWW's appeal was direct and persuasive:

The working class and the employing class have nothing in common. . . . Between these two classes a struggle must go on until the workers of the world organize as a class, take possession of the earth and the machinery of production, and abolish the wage system.[24]

Accordingly, the IWW accepted violence as a natural and inevitable part of organization, and violence, to be sure, was an almost inevitable feature of relations between employer and employee in industries such as lumbering, mining, construction, etc., which used unskilled migratory workers. For the Wobblies strikes were merely skirmishes in an irreconcilable class war, one which could only end when the workers were totally victorious. Accordingly the IWW advocated virtually any policy, including sabotage and, after the outbreak of the First World War, opposition to all militarism which could be employed as an instrument of class warfare.

Despite its promise to create "the structure of a new society within the shell of the old," and its initial spectacular success in Canada, the IWW's progress was short-lived. By the end of 1913 its Canadian membership had dwindled to 1,000, distributed among 13 locals, the majority of which were in British Columbia.[25] The reasons for its failure were basic. The main American body was divided within itself, having been formed in the first place from "a conglomeration of anti-AF of L elements, including those in the American Labor Union, the Socialist Labor Party, and the Socialist Party [of the United States]."[26] Equally important, strikes backed by the IWW had failed to win any immediate demands, and this, together with the changes and shifts going on within the socialist movement in the United States, meant that "there was no longer any need for [the IWW] when the facts changed."[27] As the parent unit declined, the Canadian subsidiary followed suit.

The rise and fall of the IWW reflected the division within the ranks of the labour movement in North America before 1914: the division between socialism and syndicalism. Essentially, the IWW was a North American variety of anarcho-syndicalism which marched forward under such direct-action banners as "the general strike," "sabotage," etc., and which constituted a revolt against the conservatism of the so-called "international unions," particularly the American Federation of Labor, which the IWW contemptuously referred to as the "American Separation of Labor." While feeling against the IWW crystalized on the grounds that the organization was ineffective, the reasons attributed for that ineffectiveness differed considerably between the two extremes within the labour movement. The more moderate orthodox organizations such as the TLC in Canada and the AF of L in the United States, deplored the IWW's use of violence. But more radical individuals then coming to the fore and forming their own groups dismissed the IWW because it was not sufficiently revolutionary. "Their [the IWW's] 'Theoreticians' " Buck writes, "spoke grandiloquently about 'revolution by the tactic of folded arms.' "[28]

While the IWW and the Socialist Party of Canada were in the process of organizing and spreading their gospel, particularly throughout western Canada, the arrival on a large scale of Slav settlers infused a new element into the Canadian radical scene. While the great majority of the 6,804,523 Slavs who came to the new world between 1882 and 1914 went to the United States, a small proportion, less than 5 per cent according to Yuzyk, came to Canada.[29] The great majority of those who came to the Dominion were Ukrainians.* They totalled more than the rest of the Slavic nationalities combined, and it is estimated that by 1914 approximately 100,000 Ukrainian immigrants, mostly from Bukovina and Galicia—territories annexed from Poland by Austria in 1772 and 1775—had entered the Dominion.[30] Most of the new arrivals settled in the prairie provinces, and the majority became agricultural labourers, section hands on the railways, or took up homesteads of their own.[31] Most too, were

*According to Yuzyk the term "Ukrainian" did not come into general use until after the First World War. Until that time only a few intellectuals and one newspaper, *Ukrayinski Holos*, which was established in Winnipeg in 1910, used the designation.

apolitical. A few, however, were acquainted with the aims of the Ukrainian Social Democratic Party, formed in Galicia in 1896, and these (including many of the most literate of the newcomers) settled in Winnipeg where, in 1907, they formed a Canadian variation of the Galician organization.

The programme put forward by the Ukrainian Social Democratic Party in Winnipeg paralleled that of the party in the homeland. Aimed exclusively at the Ukrainian immigrants, the Party, through its newspapers, the weeklies *Chervony Prapor* ("Red Flag") and later *Rabochy Narod* ("Working People"), supported the Second International and ridiculed the Orthodox Church, advocating militant atheism and the class struggle rather than the Christian doctrine and peaceful integration into the communities of the new country. These organs, as Yuzyk notes, found a ready market among the radical minority:

... there has always been ... a vociferous atheist element among the Ukrainian immigrants. In the days before the First World War thousands of young men drifted from place to place in search of work, and having lost all contact with the Church picked up evil habits and ridiculed all forms of religion.[32]

The barrier of language, the tendency of immigrants to settle in national groups instead of dispersing and integrating as in the United States, the problems of settling down in a strange new country, enabled the radical Ukrainian leaders to exploit the frustrations, loneliness, and sometimes bitterness, which inevitably arose. The process was repeated within other language groups in Canada, resulting in the rise of such parallel radical organizations as the Russian Social Democratic Party, the Russian Revolutionary Group, and later the Finnish Organization of Canada.

The flow of radical ideas generated by the rise of the Socialist Party of Canada in British Columbia, the influence of the IWW, and the organization of the Ukrainian Social Democratic Party in Winnipeg soon spilled over into Ontario, the nation's industrial heartland, and the stronghold of the TLC and the AF of L. In 1910, the Social Democratic Party (SDP), a composite organization patterned after British and German models, was formed in Toronto. Many of its members had withdrawn their support from the Socialist Party of Canada because it had failed to emerge from its parochial provincial status. Significantly, the bulk of the SDP membership consisted of "workers who had come from continental Europe."[33] The Ukrainian Party, formed two years earlier, soon became the numerically dominant wing of the new organization. While the SDP was thus stronger than the Socialist Party, and more radical, its role was very different from that of any comparable party in continental Europe or the United States, and it never achieved any real influence in Canada. The outbreak of war in 1914, coming so soon after the SDP was formed, dissipated any chance its leaders may have had of developing it into a potent political force.

In some cases, particularly in contiguous areas of the United States and Canada where similar economic conditions prevailed, the influence of Canadian radical labour organizations penetrated into American territory, redressing, to some extent, the overwhelming and varied influences from the United States. British radical influence, for example, was exported from Ontario and British Columbia "to a number of Left Wing centres in the United States, particularly Detroit and Seattle."[34] Interest in British socialism also was heightened by visits of prominent labour politicians, such as Ramsay MacDonald who toured the country in 1906, with the result that "the various socialist programs of Great Britain, Europe ... Australia and New Zealand were [made] known in Canada and met with some acceptance."[35] But for every such visitor from across the Atlantic there were innumerable radical organizers from the United States—Bill Dunne, the hero of Bloody Butte, who crossed the 49th parallel from Montana to British Columbia "as business agent for the radical electrical workers union," is a good example—who came north to spread the doctrines of labour unity and revolutionary action in Canada.[36]

Radicals like Dunne did more than merely help rally the labouring masses and instil into them the desire to improve their lot by joining existing organizations or forming new trade unions. For the first time on any scale, and at a basic level, they brought the Canadian working force into direct contact with the theories, no matter how crudely interpreted, of Karl Marx. These, for the most part, stemmed from the writings, teaching, and enthusiasm of Daniel De Leon, a lecturer on international law at Columbia University, who headed the Socialist Labor Party in the United States. An eccentric and magnetic personality, De Leon who, according to Lenin, was the only American to make an original contribution to Marxist theory, gave the Socialist Labor Party "an unprecedented theoretical vitality."[37] De Leon felt that seeking higher wages and shorter working hours through unions willing to reform the labour movement was useless. Accordingly, under his direction the Socialist Labor Party took the lead in trying to form revolutionary industrial unions which would be controlled by the party. Through the activities of the Socialist Labor Party and its successor, the Socialist Trade and Labor Alliance, through translations of Marxist classics, sponsored by the Socialist Labor Party, which made their way into Canada on a small scale, and through individuals inspired by the writings of Marx and Engels, plus the added contributions by De Leon and others, Marxism was "relayed . . . [by means of] American channels" into Canada.[38] The impact made by radical speakers and pamphlets was not always confined to the labour ranks. A. E. Smith, a Methodist minister who became a Communist Party member in 1925, recalls his experience:

I remember Jack Johnstone [later a prominent member of the Communist Party of the United States], agitator extraordinary, when he was in Nelson [B.C.]. He held street meetings and talked socialism and unionism. He was eloquent and caustic. . . . I told him I was interested to learn more about the things he was talking about. . . . I learned something of Marxian socialism from him in 1912.[39]

Thus, by 1914, Marxist doctrines had reached Canada, and had impressed many of the radically inclined, most of whom were already closely connected with labour. But, in terms of organization, no single party had emerged which had succeeded in making the teachings of Marx (or of any other socialist school of thought) the basis of its political life, and Buck's claim that "when the First World War broke out Marxism was already a national force in Canada," is at best an overstatement.[40] Radicalism in the Dominion at that time in fact consisted of a series of weak, uncoordinated organizations each striving to make an impact upon the comparatively unorganized labour force: the Social Democratic Party with headquarters in Toronto; its Ukrainian wing with offices and newspapers in Winnipeg; the fragmentary groups of the moribund Socialist Party of Canada, confined mostly to British Columbia; and the rapidly waning IWW.

Relative to the size of the Canadian labour force, however, the orthodox trade union movement was equally weak and unevenly spread throughout the country. In 1913, for example, the 64 organizations which formed the TLC boasted a membership of only 80,801.[41] The geographical imbalance of distribution is equally evident, for in 1912, out of a total of 1,883 locals in Canada, only 653 were found in Western Canada.

The remainder were confined almost entirely to Ontario and Quebec.[42] Canadian labour too was characterized by a general lack of sympathy and understanding between the eastern and western branches caused by the great distance separating the regions, and by the pull of geographic, economic, and social forces. The wave of industrial unionism which caused so much turmoil in British Columbia at the turn of the century, followed by the widespread influence of the IWW throughout the west, never made the same headway in central Canada. The eastern wing of the trade union movement, as exemplified by the TLC and the AF of L, was essentially conservative, and the policy of the TLC which, from 1906 was committed to one of provincial autonomy in labour organization, did not encourage formal nationwide solidarity. Another restraining factor in the development of labour unions and the spread of radical doctrines was the British North America Act, which, under sections 91 and 92, distributed power rather haphazardly among the central government and the provincial authorities.[43] With the responsibility for the protection of property and civil rights clearly vested in the provinces, the BNA Act said nothing about conspiracy, intimidation, violence, illegal boycotting, deportation of aliens, and other related matters, with the result that the problems of regulation and control devolved upon the central authority in Ottawa.

The general conservatism of the population in central Canada was also an inhibiting force which countered the rapid spread of radical thought. The traditions of the United Empire Loyalists coupled with the moderate influence of newcomers from the British Isles who settled in Ontario, the most industrialized region in the country, formed an effective bulwark against radical ideas, while the indigenous French-Canadian population, primarily agrarian and dominated by the clergy, was effectively shielded from socialist doctrines, particularly from Marxism, because it endorsed atheism. Nevertheless, while the general impact of radical, and particularly Marxist thought, upon the Canadian labour population up to 1914 was small, the radical organizers and organizations which had been active in the country succeeded in creating a climate of opinion which the war never obliterated, and which persisted until altered conditions allowed it to emerge in the form of revolutionary organizations.

Whatever shock socialist circles in the country may have felt when European socialist parties endorsed their government's war policies after the First World War broke out was soon superseded by resentment over the Canadian government's action against aliens and radical organizations in Canada. Shortly after hostilities began, Parliament passed the War Measures Act,* enabling the government to carry out decisions rapidly by Orders in Council without the necessity of justifying its actions in Parliament.[44] An immediate result was that German and Austro-Hungarian nationals were ordered to register as enemy aliens. As a result of the order the count of aliens registered in June 1915 revealed 5,088 persons interned and 48,500 paroled. Further legislation—PC 2194 passed on September 20, 1916†—which called for registration of "every alien of enemy nationality residing or being in Canada" emphasized the government's fear of a possible fifth column emerging in Canada.[45] Such actions, however, caused fear and resentment among large sections of the immigrant population, including many who had either not taken out naturalization

*The Act was passed on August 22, 1914, and provided for a fine of $5,000 and five years imprisonment for illegal association.
†Under provision of PC 2194, figures for June 1, 1918, show 2,087 interned and 79,057 paroled.

papers, or who had not been in the country long enough to be eligible for British citizenship. Among those particularly alienated were the Ukrainians, the majority of whom had come from Galicia and Bukovina in order to escape oppression and exploitation by the Austrian authorities. It was therefore difficult for them to understand why they were included in the government orders.

Labour circles remained quiescent for the first two years of the war while the nation devoted its energies to the requirements of the conflict overseas. In turn the authorities, under the provisions of the War Measures Act, curbed formation of new radical organizations as well as the actions of those already in existence before 1914. The conscription issue in 1917 brought the latent resentment caused by the government's arbitary rule, by the high cost of living, obvious profiteering on war contracts, scandals over purchase of food and equipment for the armed forces, and a marked effusion of titles for Canadian businessmen and politicians, to the surface. Following the passage of the Conscription Act on August 28, 1917—it was introduced on June 11—Sir Robert Borden, the Conservative Party leader, and his cabinet colleagues were left in no doubt about the prevailing mood in the country. In addition to French Canada, which strongly opposed conscription, labour circles, too, felt that the measure was not sweeping enough. Left wing trade unionists and socialists throughout the country were, as various associations made clear in letters to Borden, "in favour of conscription of wealth and all resources of the Dominion and the entire Manhood of Canada."[46] The establishment of a Union Government (composed of 10 Liberals and 13 Conservatives) in October under Borden's leadership, followed by the feverish elections of December, reflect the turmoil occasioned in Canada by the conscription issue.

The news that the Tsar of Russia had been deposed, coinciding more or less as it did with the conscription issue, did much to break down the inhibitions against organization and expression within the labour and radical groups caused by the war effort and, more particularly, by the War Measures Act. Canadian newspapers, too, reflected the general enthusiasm triggered by the news of the February revolution and the Tsar's abidication on March 15. "The successful revolution in Russia warrants the liveliest satisfaction," exulted the *Toronto Daily Star* on March 15, 1917. Two days later the same paper went further saying, prophetically, that "nothing compares with it in magnitude but the French Revolution. Its influence may be even more far-reaching." Much of the satisfaction stemmed from the feeling, general among the allied nations, that Russia, despite the upheaval, would stay in the war. Also, the economic potential of Russia's thinly populated eastern reaches occasioned almost as much enthusiasm as did the Tsar's deposition, for many responsible people—and the opinion was not confined to Canada alone—held that with the restraining influence of tsardom removed, large scale development and trade would be possible once hostilities ceased. As an editorial in the *Toronto Daily Star* of March 17 put it:

Population ... increased rapidly and under free institutions we may expect the swift development of the huge area of Asiatic Russia, 6,400,000 square miles. ... We are witnessing not only a political revolution but the opening of a new world.

The expectation was that Canada, with its favourable geographical position, would be able to take advantage of such conditions, and that feeling persisted within business and financial circles as well as in the government until well after the First World War had ended. Indeed, it was basic to the passage of Orders in Council on October 21 and 23, 1918, authorizing the establishment of a Canadian Economic

Commission in Siberia.[47] Typical of the unbounded optimism in business circles were the views expressed by Baron Shaughnessy, President of the Canadian Pacific Railway. On September 13, 1918, he predicted in Regina that: "Canada will find in Siberia and a re-awakened Russia a new market for implements and other manufactured products after the cessation of the war."[48] Neither radicals nor conservatives saw how tenuous were the grounds on which they built their hopes, or how soon they were destined to be disappointed.

CHAPTER TWO

THE YEARS OF UNCERTAINTY AND UNREST:
1917-1919

IN THE TRAIN of events abroad and the anti-conscription feeling at home, Canadian radicals became less timid, and for the first time since 1914 began to reassemble and to speak openly. With Russia in the spotlight, the lead in radical re-emergence was taken by the more revolutionary members of the Ukrainian Social Democratic Party. A few days after the Tsar's abdication Matthew Popowich, one of the most active of the radical Ukrainians and a founding member of the Communist Party of Canada, addressed a public meeting in Winnipeg commemorating the birth of the Ukrainian poet, Taras Shevchenko. He concluded his talk thus:

I am confident that the workers and peasants, our class brothers, will not stop. Now that tsarist autocracy is cracked and Nicholas has abdicated the people will go on from this provisional government forward to government by the working people and thus forward to socialism.[1]

While the precision of Popowich's expression may be queried, it accurately reflects some of the opinions current in many parts of Canada in the spring and summer of 1917. Such views were encouraged and accelerated by news of developments in Russia. Symptomatic was the suggestion made at the annual Trades and Labour Congress meeting held that year in Ottawa that the workers of Canada should follow British precedents and organize an Independent Labour Party of Canada on a basis sufficiently acceptable to trade unionists, socialists, Fabians, co-operators, and farmers alike. The suggestion was quickly carried out, and an executive council was authorized to undertake the preliminary task of organization. As a result, on July 1, 1917, at Hamilton, the Independent Labour Party (ILP) of Ontario was established as a provincial section of the newly fledged national body. Quebec followed suit in November.[2] Although the national body so bravely proclaimed at Hamilton never became seriously active in the Canadian political scene, the party did make an *ad hoc* effort to counter the proposed conscription legislation which became the central issue in the December 1917 federal election by supporting labour candidates across the country who were opposed to the War Times Election Act. Of the forty candidates who received the ILP's blessing only one was elected, while the remainder lost their deposits. Despite such an unpropitious start, provincial ILP bodies comparable to those established in Ontario and Quebec were organized everywhere except in Prince Edward Island by 1919, and it was upon these that most of labour's political activity devolved.[3] Such developments did not occur solely against a backdrop of unremitting hostility on the part of government and employers. Labour organization in Canada, as elsewhere, was given much impetus by the dramatic news filtering out of Russia. Buck's analysis of the interim period between February and November 1917, while written in retrospect as well as from a Marxist viewpoint, underlines the effect almost any information from Russia had upon the radical movement throughout the country:

All across Canada the combination of discontent and democratic anticipation continued to influence wider circles of workers. By the Fall of 1917 it had become a ferment. Slender and distorted though our information about developments in Russia was, enough came through so that continuous discussions in our places of work kept widening circles of militant workers informed.[4]

The impact of the Bolshevik coup in November upon radicals in North America was stunning. Certainly the tiny minority of Canadian Marxists, as Buck points out, was "taken by surprise both by the speed with which victory was achieved in the October Revolution and the enthusiasm with which Canadian workers greeted it."[5] Without knowing the facts which led to the successful assumption of power, with only the haziest inkling of Bolshevik beliefs, Canadian radicals approved the change wholesale even though the great majority, until November 1917, had never heard of Lenin.

The realization that a party of insignificant proportions—the strength of the Bolshevik Party was estimated to be approximately 200,000 in August 1917—could seize and retain power against what seemed overwhelming odds "gave fresh hope to those who had been advocating Marxian ideas, just as it reinforced suspicions of those who had seen socialism never far behind trade unionism."[6] On the strength of its success "the Bolshevik revolution had a dazzling, dreamlike quality, all the more glamorous because it was far away, undefiled by any contact with the more recalcitrant American [and Canadian] reality."[7] Some of the dazzling, dreamlike quality of the revolution and its effect upon the receptive is conveyed in A. E. Smith's account of his reaction upon hearing the news.

The shock of the Russian Revolution was powerful enough to be felt even in Brandon [Manitoba]. ... It is a sad confession to make but I must say that up till 1917 I had not read the Communist Manifesto. I was aroused. I began to seek information. I sent away for a number of books dealing with the teachings of communism. I got the Manifesto. I remember the first time I read it through. It was like a revelation of a new world into which I felt I must enter and to which I seemed to belong. ... I began to preach about the great events taking place in Russia and about the great storehouse of truth I had found. I was only a preacher of truth. ... I saw that Jesus was a Communist. I linked his life with the old prophets, the great preachers of the Old Testament, who were early Communists. Of course they were not scientific but they stood for the principles of communism. ...
I preached sermons dealing in a factual manner with the Russian Revolution—with Lenin's life and teachings, with Stalin's leadership, and with the allied intervention.[8]

While the last line of the preceding passage reflects the date, 1949, when the account was published, and provides a commentary upon the deadening effect of Stalin's influence upon communist parties far beyond the Soviet borders, Smith's recollections nevertheless retain something of the impact made by the Bolshevik's triumph.

Until 1917, however, there was very little Russian influence in the Canadian radical movement; what there was, moreover, was not strictly Russian since the impetus came from the Ukrainian wing of the Social Democratic Party. After 1917, despite distance and the lack of direct contact, Moscow became the dominant influence. The leaders of the Ukrainian Social Democratic Party, despite the traditional antipathy between Ukrainians and Great Russians,

... hailed the establishment of the Soviet Government as the victory of the proletariat and the harbinger of the world communist movement. ...
The Ukrainian Social Democratic party in Canada swung towards bolshevism in November 1917, soon after the Soviet coup d'état in Moscow. The less radical element was gradually forced out of the leadership. The party organ *Rabochy Narod* was converted into a semi-weekly in 1917 and made a mouthpiece of Russian communism.[9]

Such changes within the Ukrainian radical party, and the general ferment in labour ranks caused by the Bolshevik's success may, in Marxist terms, have "inspired the

Canadian working class to a higher stage of development," but the unrest also impinged upon the Canadian authorities.[10] Typical of the concern caused by the renewal of activities by foreign language organizations was that expressed by the Chief Press Censor for Canada, E. J. Chambers, who early in 1918 wrote to his United Kingdom counterpart soliciting advice and up to date information about developments within Russia:

I have found it pretty difficult to know just what to do in dealing with publications printed in Ukrainian, Russian, Lithuanian, Estonian and Finnish languages owing to the peculiar unsettled conditions of affairs. . . . As you doubtless know we have compact settlements of peoples from different parts of Russia in Canada and some of them are disposed to force my hands in one direction or another, writing me drawing attention to what they consider to be objectionable matter in the publications printed in dialects or languages other than their own.[11]

Until such activites began to cause serious concern, however, prosecution of the war and the conscription issue, which created so much unrest in labour circles and divided French Canada from the rest of the nation, occupied most of the government's time and energies. As a result, radical activities in Canada and the magnitude of the changes occurring in Russia in the spring and summer of 1917 caused Canadian authorities little real concern. Equally, lack of knowledge about Russia and the Russian revolutionary movement was not confined to official quarters. The fact that Leon Trotsky, one of the great heroes of the October revolution, had been interned at Amherst, Nova Scotia, for most of April 1917, was, at the time, of no particular significance to Canadian officials—as opposed to the British authorities who ordered his removal from the vessel *Christianiafjord*—and of little or no direct interest to Canadian radicals.[12]

Early in 1918, however, Prime Minister Borden began to receive reports of mounting labour unrest throughout Canada.[13] Soon after, an investigation of the IWW was undertaken, and in his report to the Minister of Justice, the Acting Chief of Police for Canada, while noting that the IWW seemed to be preparing "to become better organized," suggested that perhaps it was

. . . advisable that an Order-in-Council be passed forbidding the holding of meetings in any foreign language during the period of war, also that the Chief Press Censor be empowered to place on the prohibited list all IWW, Ukrainian Socialistic [sic] Democratic Party, and other literature of a socialist nature that when a seizure is made, those in whose possession it is found can be prosecuted.[14]

Nothing came of this suggestion. Later, as unrest continued to increase, Borden wrote to a Montreal lawyer, C. H. Cahan, who had been in contact with British Intelligence representatives in the United States, saying, "it seems desirable that some effective organization to investigate the whole subject [of radical activity] should be established and we [presumably the Cabinet] agree that you should be asked to give us the benefit of your advice and service for that purpose."[15] Cahan accepted Borden's offer, and in the autumn of 1918 formally became the Director of the Public Safety Branch of the Department of Justice. Soon after being approached by Borden, however, Cahan submitted an interim report putting down economic factors, war weariness, and tales of profiteering as the causes of unrest. In particular he noted that

There is considerable mental unrest among the peoples of Slavic origin in Canada, Russian, Ukrainian, and Austrian, which is directly attributable to the dissemination in Canada of the Socialist doctrines, espoused by the Russian Revolutionary element, and more recently by the Bolshevik Party in Russia. . . .[16]

This report was supplemented by a fuller report submitted in September. In the second report Cahan suggested that the Order-in-Council passed on August 5, 1918, which required "every alien of enemy nationality" over the age of of sixteen to register with the police, should be extended to include Russians, Ukrainians, and Finns. His reasons for their inclusion, while overdrawn, are indicative of the incipient effect of the Russian revolution on both radicals and authorities:

The Russians, Ukrainians and Finns who are employed in the mines, factories and other industries in Canada, are now being thoroughly saturated with the Socialistic doctrines which have been proclaimed by the Bolshevikii faction of Russia. . . . Since the outbreak of the present war, revolutionary groups of Russians, Ukrainians, and Finns have been organized throughout Canada and are known as the Social Democratic Party of Canada, the Ukrainian Revolutionary Group, the Russian Revolutionary Group, and others. . . . They are known to hold public or private meetings and to direct revolutionary propaganda . . . . In Toronto the membership of these revolutionary associations is about 1000 to 1200. In Montreal about 700 attended a meeting which was recently raided by the police. . . . Considerable quantitites of literature in the Russian and Ukrainian languages . . . have recently been sent into Canada direct from Petrograd . . . . The Red Guards of Finland are also sending similar [material] to Finns, who are employed in considerable numbers in industrial centres . . . such as Vancouver, Port Arthur, etc. . . . .[17]

The government acted rapidly. Within two weeks of Cahan's submission, and almost entirely on the strength of his reports, an Order-in-Council, PC 2384, was passed on September 27, 1918, banning 14 organizations.*[18]

But the effect of the ban was limited. In Toronto the Social Democratic Party was fragmentized into a number of groups, the more radical of which soon resumed activity. The Ukrainian wing in Winnipeg however, through an unforeseen stroke of good fortune, was able to continue its activities without a pause. Because of the language barrier and the general conditions among Ukraninians in western Canada, members of the Ukrainian Socialist Democratic Party established the Ukrainian Labour Temple Association (ULTA) in 1917. Ostensibly a cultural and educational society, the ULTA "although it included some of the leaders of the suppressed (USD) Party, did not fall under the ban."[19] Organization and propaganda activities, therefore, continued without any real disruption. Ironically, the legislation was instrumental in crystallizing radical thought, for it aroused all shades of labour opinion throughout the country. In addition, the resentment aroused by the passage of PC 2384 so close to the end of the war was exacerbated by two additional factors: dispatch of Canadian troops to Russia, and the wholesale release of men from the services which, coinciding with the general economic recession following the armistice, tended to over-saturate an already swollen labour market.

From the start, intervention was not a popular issue with the Canadian Cabinet or the Canadian public. Indeed, many members, including Borden, hotly resented the British government's interference in the internal affairs of the Dominion, especially the sending of a

. . . telegram to the Governor General [the Duke of Devonshire] respecting expedition Vladivostok without first consulting us. The subject was at the time under discussion here [Borden was then in London for meetings of the Imperial War Cabinet] and [Major General] Mewburn [President of

---

*The organizations were: the Industrial Workers of the World, the Russian Social Democratic Party, the Russian Socialist Revolutionaries, the Russian Revolutionary Group, the Russian Workers' Union, the Ukrainian Revolutionary Group, the Ukrainian Social Democratic Party, the Social Democratic Party, the Social Labour Party, the Group of Social Democrats of Bolsheviki, the Group of Social Democrats of Anarchists, the Workers' International Industrial Union, the Chinese Nationalist League, the Chinese Labour Association.

The inclusion of the Social Democratic Party in the ban was challenged in Cabinet by N. W. Rowell, who wrote to Borden on October 29, 1918. As a result, and despite Cahan's objections, the Social Democratic Party was removed from the list and two other organizations, the Finnish Social Democratic Party and the Revolutionary Socialist Party of North America, were added. It is interesting to note that the background of the ban and the part played by Cahan is not included in Borden's *Memoirs*. At the time that PC 2384 was passed Borden was on holiday in Virginia.

the Militia Council] had already communicated with [Major General] Gwatkin [Chief of the Canadian General Staff] for information of Cabinet. I [Borden] desire that no reply should be sent to British Government's message except through me.[20]

Because of the feeling in Canada during the period July to November 1918 before the armistice was concluded, even military men like Mewburn were concerned about how the public would "view the raising of another Force to be sent to another theatre of war."[21] Despite these considerations and the possibility that Canadian troops in or proceeding to France might have to be diverted, Canada, once the allied decision to intervene became firm, began to raise a force for dispatch to Siberia. With the signing of the Armistice, however, the reasons for the necessity of Canadian forces in Russia (put forward mainly by Lloyd George and Winston Churchill), lost what little validity they may have had before November 11, 1918.[22] Differences in the Canadian Cabinet, which had subsided when the decision to take part in the allied operation had been agreed upon and which had been overshadowed by the conclusion of the struggle in Europe, again came forward and soon widened into a distinct split. T. A. Crerar, the Minister of Agriculture, for one, was "absolutely opposed to sending any additional forces to Siberia . . . I cannot agree that the retention of our forces in Siberia and the securing of further forces there can be justified on the grounds of necessity of re-establishing order in Siberia. The matter of how Russia will settle her internal affairs is her concern—not ours."[23] Crerar's stand, which supported point six of Woodrow Wilson's famous fourteen points, not only reflected the feelings of "many members of Council," notably Ballantyne, Calder, and Reid, but also the general feeling against the dispatch of troops which was particularly evident throughout Western Canada.[24]

Opposition to the Siberian operation revealed itself most clearly in Vancouver and Victoria, the ports through which material was shipped and from which the Canadian troops destined for Vladivostok sailed. For example,

The Longshoremen's union had passed a resolution of sympathy with the [Russian] revolutionaries. One day my father [J. S. Woodsworth] discovered that he was helping load a boat with munitions, to be used against the revolutionaries in Siberia. Without a moment's hesitation he downed his tools and gave up his day's work and pay. The others refused to quit on the ground that if they did, either the Seattle local of the union or the soldiers would be given the job—and the wages for this particular job were good.[25]

While the realities of post-war economic conditions tended at first to inhibit the effectiveness of such isolated demonstrations, increasing unemployment perpetuated discontent, and radical organizations mushroomed.

Almost from the outset the government had been worried about the possible effects of the Russian revolution upon soldiers of Slav extraction serving in the Canadian Army. Field Marshal Lord Ironside, who commanded the allied troops in Archangel, recalls that "when the Russian Army collapsed in 1917, all the Russians in the Canadian Army had been withdrawn to non-combatant units."[26] In the face of increasing propaganda spread by radicals and the general antipathy towards the allied intervention in Siberia, the authorities became very uneasy about the effects of these pressures upon the morale of troops bound for Vladivostok.[27] The upshot of the government's uneasiness was that "35 undesirable Russians" were removed from the Siberian expeditionary force and discharged, the two platoons of Russian-speaking personnel were broken up, and their members evenly distributed among the other infantry battalions.[28] British reports, which Borden received while in London, contributed further to the government's growing alarm.

Reports indicate that the Bolshevik Government of Russia is making very active and to some extent successful propaganda in Germany, Switzerland and Scandinavian countries. Their activities also reach into France, Italy and Great Britain. Very large grants are placed in the hands of their agents. There is reason to believe that the same efforts will be extended to Canada and the United States soon.[29]

Such information, coupled with a mounting volume of protests against Canada's participation in the Siberian intervention, all of which were reported to Ottawa by military and police authorities, supplemented by accounts of public meetings in local newspapers, combined to create an air of continuous uneasiness within the government, a condition that was all too easily transformed into alarm.[30] The protests took the form of resolutions put forward by organizations such as the Vancouver Trades and Labour Council and passed at public gatherings requesting that press censorship be lifted, and objecting to the despatch of Canadian troops to Vladivostok, as well as the distribution of pamphlets published by such bodies as the Lansdowne Lodge (No. 438), International Association of Machinists, in Toronto. Similar resolutions passed by more conservative organizations such as the United Farmers of Ontario (UFO) simply added weight to the protests emanating from radical labour and increased the government's concern.[31]

Throughout the winter of 1918 and the spring of 1919, "political ferment continued to be stirred up by a mixed procession of old and new Marxists, foreign agitators, new fanatics, and idealists [who were] prepared to say their respective pieces into whatever receptive ears they could find."[32] Canada's participation in the intervention provided a target not only for Marxists but also for orthodox politicians, who charged "that troops and equipment were being sent [to Siberia] to protect the investment of capitalists of the Allied Nations."[33] That charge in turn was amplified by a plethora of short-lived radical broadsheets such as *The Soviet*, published in Edmonton, *The Red Flag*, which flourished briefly in Vancouver, *The Searchlight* in Calgary, *The Eastern Federationist* in New Glasgow, Nova Scotia, and the *Western Labour News* in Winnipeg. *The Red Flag*, in its February 15, 1919, issue, reprinted a typical commentary which first appeared in the *Seattle Union Record*.

From every part of Canada the cry goes up: "Bring the boys home." We join in that cry with all our strength. "Bring them home from Siberia." "Bring them home from Archangel." The war that they engaged to fight in is over and done. They must not be used as pawns for the designing money and territory grabbers of Europe. They have done their work; they have suffered enough; they are all democrats who fought to make an end of war and who believe in the self-determination of peoples.

Such comments, as well as descriptions (mostly imaginary) of the way the capitalist armies bolstered counter-revolutionary forces headed by tsarist officers, and financed by Britain, France, and the United States, were stock features of the radical press throughout the country.

The government's prohibition of socialist literature, especially material originating outside of Canada, brought equally strong denunciations from the radicals in the labour movement. One local of the United Mine Workers at Cumberland, B.C. (No. 2299), went so far as to pass a resolution protesting the ban as an unjustified action that deprived Canadian labour of the publications turned out by the Charles M. Kerr Publishing Company, Chicago, a concern described in the *Western Labour News* of January 24, 1919, as "the main source of the classics of working class philosophy." The Cumberland local's concern, which was shared by labour throughout the land, was triggered by the severe sentences imposed upon radicals prosecuted under the government's Order-in-Council PC 1241,* and by the importance the authorities attached to socialist publications, most of them Kerr Company products, seized as evidence for the trials.[34] In turn, the growing volume of radical publications and propaganda did not pass unnoticed in Ottawa. In an attempt to offset it, the Chief Press Censor tried to organize a counter-propaganda campaign spearheaded by the departments of history and political science at Canadian universities. Academe, however, declined to become engaged, on the grounds, as Sir Robert Falconer, President of the University of Toronto, put it, "that the universities would do more harm than good," and that government measures to keep employment up and prices down would be much more effective.[35]

By the spring of 1919, however, the government's uneasiness about the nature and extent of radical activity in the country was transformed into general alarm. The growing concern was exacerbated by official reports about the impact of inflammatory literature, including Russian revolutionary tracts, which were beginning to flood into the Dominion, mostly from the United States, openly as well as "by every secret means ... even to the extent of putting it [prohibited literature] into the linings of clothes."[36] Sir Thomas White, the Acting Prime Minister, cabled Borden, then at the Peace Conference in Paris, expressing the Cabinet's concern over the situation developing in British Columbia:

Bolshevism has made great progress among the workers and soldiers there. We cannot get troops absolutely dependable in emergency and it will take a long time to establish old militia organization. Plans are being laid for revolutionary movement which if temporarily successful would immediately bring about serious disturbance in Calgary and Winnipeg where socialism [is] rampant. We think most desirable British Government should bring over cruiser from China station to Victoria or Vancouver. The presence of such ship and crew would have steadying influence. Situation is undoubtedly serious and getting out of hand by reason of propaganda from Seattle and workers and soldiers.[37]

Despite White's excited and impractical request for a British cruiser—it was quickly and effectively squelched by Borden who suggested utilizing the Royal North West Mounted Police to deal with any emergency—there was, nevertheless, considerable cause for the Cabinet's concern. Radical views, the "Bolshevism" of White's telegram, by then were being propagated widely throughout the country, and with particular effectiveness in western Canada. Apart from the protests over Canada's participation in the Siberian venture, the extreme views then circulating found considerable acceptance on at least two other grounds. First, and most obviously, they provided a datum and offered an alternative, however utopian, to the deadening effects of increasing unemployment. Second, labour grievances in the Canadian west were increased by the distrust which developed after the December 1917 federal elections when conservatives captured 41 of the 43 prairie seats, and after passage of the Union government's repressive measures towards the end of the war. Symptomatic of the feeling in labour ranks was the action taken by delegates from west of the Great Lakes at the annual Trades and Labour Congress of Canada convention which met in Quebec City in 1918. They assembled in caucus and decided to hold a conference of western labour representatives in Calgary early in 1919 in order to co-

*Early in 1919, a Charles Watson was sentenced at Kingston, Ontario, to three years imprisonment and fined $500.00 for alleged radical activities. Among the documents seized from his premises were *The Philosophy of Socialism, What is Anarchism?* and the *Preamble of the Industrial Workers of the World*, all Kerr publications. Arthur Skidmore, President of the Stratford, Ontario, Trades Council, was similarly charged and sentenced, and many of the same pamphlets were used as evidence by the prosecution.

c

ordinate their activities and so escape the domination of the conservative eastern trade unions.[38]

Considerable additional publicity was also given to labour grievances and demands "through the agency of the Labour Church, an organization with branches in a number of western [Canadian] cities."[39] Confined entirely to the west, the Labour Church* was conceived and started early in 1919 by William Ivens, a recently expelled Methodist minister and editor of the trade union paper *Western Labour News*, sponsored by the Winnipeg Trades and Labour Council, which began publication at the end of July 1918. The Church attracted a wide variety of individuals, among them idealists like J. S. Woodsworth. In the spring of 1919 Woodsworth was still in Vancouver labouring as a docker. His daughter writes about the impact of the Labour Church upon her father:

At this point he received an invitation from Rev. William Ivens of Winnipeg to make a speaking tour across the prairies; its purpose was to educate workers' organizations to the need for social change. The tour [was] under the auspices of the Labor Church which Mr. Ivens had founded that year along earlier British lines.
My father accepted the invitation with alacrity. ... Once again he was on the road, doing the work he felt impelled to do, lecturing on a wide range of topics including his views on war and on the peace settlement, his reasons for leaving the ministry, his conviction that only fundamental economic changes could right the wrongs of poverty and injustice. He saw more clearly now that those wanting real change would have to organize along both economic and political lines.[40]

Woodsworth's actions were not surprising. To him the Labour Church stood for a replacement of the selfish scramble for existence by a co-operative commonwealth in which each individual would have an equal opportunity for advancement. It squared too with his wish to secularize religion—to make it part of everyday living.[41]

By the spring of 1919, despite the efforts of Marxists, disgruntled trade unionists, and idealists such as Woodsworth and Ivens whose views by then were appearing in the labour press, no organization or individual had succeeded in welding together the various radical bodies in Canada into a single unit with a precise programme based upon specific aims. Nor did prompting from outside Canada elicit a response or help to unite radicals in the Dominion. Accordingly, when the call from Moscow crackled out over the airwaves on January 24, 1919 announcing the formation of the Third International, no organization in Canada was ready or able to send delegates to the inaugural conference, and only a scattered handful of relatively weak groups were prepared in principle to support the new organization. It is doubtful if any of the leading radicals in Canada, men such as Kavanagh, Midgley, and others who figured in police and military intelligence reports heard the call, or if, even after the March meeting at which the Third International was formed, more than a few were aware of its existence, let alone its aims.[42] Unlike their American counterparts, Canadian socialists had no residents in Moscow who might have put forward a Canadian view.[43]

The chief achievement resulting from the general unrest and dissatisfaction echoed by radicals and labour groups was that it pressured the Borden government into insisting upon Canada's withdrawal from the Russian expedition. Canada's stand, buttressing the United State's views, in turn caused the Allied effort to peter out. When Canada withdrew her troops, any hope that the rest of the Empire, particularly Australia, would lend support was decidedly reduced. Without such support Britain

---

*There were English and American precedents. These included the Christian Socialist movement in Britain started by two Church of England clergymen, Kingsley and Maurice, the Christian Socialist Fellowship begun in Louisville, Kentucky, in 1906, and the Church Socialist League founded in 1911 by clergy and laymen of the Episcopal Church of America.

was too exhausted by her exertions on the western front to continue the action on any scale. In addition, the British Cabinet was very much divided over the policy of intervention in Russia. Only Winston Churchill, the Minister for War, advocated a full scale effort by Britain and the Empire.[44] While the Canadian government was reaching as well as implementing its decision, the "wild talk," coupled with the formation of small units such as the Russian Workers Union in Vancouver, keyed up socialist sympathizers in western Canada to a feverish pitch of excitement which culminated in the prearranged meeting of western labour radicals.

The Western Labour Conference held in Calgary, March 13-15, 1919, and attended by 239 delegates (all but two from the prairie provinces and British Columbia), the majority of whom were consciously moved by the example of Russia which, even then, was considered to be a working model of Marxism, passed resolutions frankly revolutionary in spirit and words.[45] The British Columbia Federation of Labour, for example, presented a resolution (No. 5) expressing open conviction that the Soviet system of labour organization was superior to that of North American trade unions, and that the convention fully endorsed "the principle of 'Proletarian Dictatorship' as being absolute and efficient for the transformation of capitalist private property to communal wealth."[46] To take one example, J. R. Campbell, representing a Vancouver carpenters' local, referred throughout the conference to the central committee of the One Big Union (OBU), which came into being at the meeting, as the "central soviet," while the provincial committees were labelled "provincial soviets," and so on.*

Among the resolutions passed—they included a demand for a six-hour working day and a five-day working week— was one advocating a general strike on June 1, 1919, if Canadian troops were not withdrawn from Russia. Measures such as these, many carried unanimously, and the despatch of fraternal greetings to the Soviet government and to the German Spartacist League, clearly demonstrated the profound respect of many labour leaders for the Russian system of government.† Although their knowledge of that system was inexact, they no longer had faith in orthodox political methods as a means of obtaining what they felt were legitimate concessions. A contemporary appraisal of the principal leaders by A. Bowen Perry, Commissioner of the Royal North West Mounted Police, who interviewed "Messrs. [V.R.] Midgley and [W.A.] Pritchard, two members of the Committee of five‡ . . . in charge of the propaganda," as well as J. Kavanagh of the Longshoremen's Union, in Vancouver, is indicative of the men in the movement and the government's views:

All these men, in addition to being members of different unions, are Revolutionary Socialists. They are intelligent, well read men, and are close students of economic and social literature.

They acknowledged that they were determined to bring about a revolution in social and economic conditions, but protested that they were opposed to force and violence. They stated that the "One Big Union" of labour in Western Canada must first be perfected before they could take a forward step. . . . These men are able speakers, forceful and clear. They are tireless in pursuit of their objects,

---

*The Central Committee consisted of five members, as did each of the four provincial committees, one for each of the western provinces. The OBU grouped its members according to the territories in which they worked. In small towns all workers were organized in a single unit; in large centres separate units were to be formed for each industry.

†The Spartacist League was formed in Germany during World War I and led by Rosa Luxemburg, Franz Mehring, Klara Zetkin, and Karl Leibknecht. By the time of the Calgary meeting Luxemburg and Leibknecht were dead. Rosa Luxemburg held the view that communist parties had to come into being in all countries before a Communist International should be formed, a position diametrically opposed by Lenin.

‡The other members of the Committee were: J. R. Knight of Edmonton, R. J. Johns of Winnipeg, and Joseph Naylor of Cumberland, B.C.

and have all the fervor of fanatics. I am not prepared to say that they are aiming at a revolution in the ordinary sense of that word, but I do say that they are influencing a section of labour in the west, and unchaining forces which, even if they so desire, some day they will be unable to control. . . .

At the present labour is extremely sensitive as to any interference with free speech, and active prosecution should be postponed until the result of the "One Big Union" is known.

The "reds" intend to provoke a general strike which may so develop as to bring about a political as well as an economic revolution. They will readily accept any aid that the foreign [i.e. language groups, rather than assistance from an external organization] societies may give them, and I fear they realize clearly that such assistance may mean riot and bloodshed. If it fails, then the responsibility will be thrown on the alien enemy [i.e. residents in Canada who originated from Germany and the Austro-Hungarian territories]. If it succeeds, they hope to create and control. Their ideas may not be very clear, but they are prepared to profit by any situation.[47]

This appraisal and the assessment of the more revolutionary leaders' intentions was judicious and accurate.

Before the Western Labour Conference broke up it had been agreed to take a referendum to determine the newly-formed OBU's position in relation to the rest of organized labour in Canada, particularly in relation to the Trades and Labour Congress, which in western eyes represented eastern and conservative union domination, and to take a ballot on the subject of a general strike proposed to start on June 1, 1919. But before the result of the OBU referendum was known, and before views about the proposed general strike were completely canvassed, the building and metal trades in Winnipeg went on strike in mid-May, forestalling plans for the proposed greater action. Between 30,000 and 35,000 workers went out in Winnipeg, and despite threats by the government to intern or deport its leaders as the action continued, the stoppage carried on without concessions by employers or employees.

The strike aroused labour sympathy throughout the country and heightened the government's worry about the aims and actions of radical organizations.

Many cities, including Brandon, Calgary, Edmonton, Prince Albert, Regina, Saskatoon, and Vancouver, became directly involved, while strikes as far off as Toronto and Amherst, and Sydney, Nova Scotia . . . were doubtless traceable to the same source.[48]

Quebec alone was unaffected by the labour troubles since the international unions were not so strongly organized in that province as in the rest of English-speaking Canada.[49] Such was the prevailing mood that a few of the more radical labour leaders, using the authority and power implied in their positions, made known their views in a truculent, threatening manner. J. R. Kavanagh, Secretary of the Vancouver Trades and Labour Council, sent the following telegraph message to Borden:

Unless the government recedes from its position in opposition to collective bargaining through joint councils and its determination [to] replace postal workers at Winnipeg [who had walked out in sympathy for the metal and building trades] and other places the workers in this city will declare a general strike.[50]

Alarmed by the likelihood of further strike action and by the general feeling in the east, the government prepared to meet the situation by mobilizing troops and strengthening the federal police in Winnipeg.[51] Borden certainly was prepared "to repress revolutionary methods with a stern hand," and he did not shrink at doing so.[52] His attitude towards revolution and the revolutionaries was not merely the outcome of internal dissension and unrest, but was based equally on information he received while overseas at the end of 1918, and buttressed by a continuous flow of information from the British Colonial Office.[53]

From the start the Winnipeg strike was a period of frenzied activity for all radicals, including the radical churchmen:

preached on the strike. I declared the cause of the strikers to be right and just . . . I helped to prepare the strike bulletins. I spoke at the great open air meetings called by the strike committee in the city parks. I marched at the front of the street parades. My church was opened to the strikers who, on one occasion, marched in as a body.[54]

As the Winnipeg strike progressed, the more extreme elements among the city's radicals, notably members of the Ukrainian Labour Temple Association and the Jewish Social Democratic Party, who espoused what they considered to be the views held by the Bolsheviks in Russia, realized that the dispute provided an opportunity to further their own cause. Accordingly, they attempted to foment as much unrest as possible among the Ukrainian and Jewish people living in Winnipeg. According to one report from the Comptroller of the RNWMP to Borden's private secretary, G. W. Yates:

There [was] a great deal of evidence to show that this man [Jacob Penner, described as a Russian Jew and an influential member of the Jewish Social Democratic Party in the city] and his associates were very much behind the scenes during the recent strike at Winnipeg.[55]

Indeed, during the strike the recently completed Ukrainian Labour Temple served as headquarters for the strikers. The use of the building for such purposes together with the actions of men such as Penner, John Navisivsky, and Matthew Popowich, all of whom later became leading members in the Canadian communist movement, caused contemporary as well as later analysts to conclude, mistakenly, that the strike had been "communist inspired."[56] Sir Robert Borden, for example, in his memoirs, was certain that the action in Winnipeg constituted

. . . a definite attempt to overthrow the existing organization of the Government and to supersede it by crude, fantastic methods founded upon absurd conceptions of what had been accomplished in Russia.[57]

The evidence for such a decided assessment in 1919 or later, however, was and remains, according to the most complete studies of the strike so far carried out, decidedly limited in nature and extent.*

Whatever credence can be given to the charge that the Winnipeg strike was a calculated attempt on the part of the new Soviet government to foment revolution in Canada stemmed largely from rumours which were sparked by an unintentional diversion of "money from Moscow." The subsidy, which originated from Ludwig C. A. K. Martens, the so-called "Bolshevik ambassador" in New York and head of the Russian Soviet Government Information Bureau, was first reported in May 1919 by Jacob Spolansky, a Russian immigrant to the United States, who became a member of the Bureau of Investigation of the United States Justice Department in 1919, and who specialized in unmasking the American communist movement from its earliest beginnings.[58] A further report from American officials in Chicago to British authorities in New York completes the story:

About the middle of June, 1919, Seven Thousand ($7000.00) Dollars were transmitted to F. Charitonoff, who is a well known Anarchist agitator in Canada. The money was transmitted as subsistence for a new publication known as *The New Age*, which was never published, and the money was turned over to the general strike for propaganda purposes. One Fedchenko, a notorious Russian Anarchist of Pittsburgh, Pennsylvania, who is out on bonds [sic], pending deportation proceedings, was making frequent trips in June, between Detroit and Winnipeg carrying money and confidential documents.[59]

---

*D. C. Master's view that the dispute was primarily an effort to secure the principle of collective bargaining is essentially accurate. He fails to take into consideration the efforts of the so-called "Bolsheviks" to take advantage of the strike, and makes no attempt to determine the effect of their efforts in prolonging the action.

Because of the activities of the Lusk Committee and the strong anti-communist feeling in America, the new revolutionary paper intended to be produced in Winnipeg was to be distributed throughout the United States from the Manitoba capital. The unexpectedness of the strike, its relatively short duration, the increasing harassment of the nascent American communist movement, the unorganized state of the Comintern, and the lack of established, reliable means of quick communication with the Soviet Union make it doubtful that further subsidies for strike purposes were either sanctioned or provided by Moscow. Nevertheless, the single infusion of money undoubtedly encouraged Russian-speaking radicals in Winnipeg initially to take a more active role in the strike than they might otherwise have done, and so made them conspicuous and resented.

Because of the anti-foreign feeling which developed in Winnipeg as the strike continued, however, a feeling similar to that which arose during the great steel strike of 1919 in the United States led by W. Z. Foster, the movements and actions of the ULTA and members of other local foreign language groups became increasingly discreet. The War Measures Act was still in effect, and the fear of arrest, intensified by the detention of many individuals with radical affiliations, was strong. Accordingly, as the strike developed, the "Bolshevik's," the designation commonly applied to foreign-language radicals, met in small groups in their homes to discuss the action; they made no attempt to hold public meetings at the well-known labour gathering places.[60] J. S. Woodsworth was convinced that " . . . there was not a single foreigner in a position of leadership, though foreigners were falsely arrested to give colour to this charge. . . . There was absolutely no attempt to set up a Soviet Government." In the main the assessment is accurate. Only in the matter of the origin and the amount of "money which was said to be coming from Russia in large quantities," and which Woodsworth claimed to be "a collection of 250 dollars raised by some miners in Alberta" was he out of focus.[61] At that a single contribution of seven thousand dollars could scarcely be termed lavish revolutionary assistance.

Despite "the hard work of Jews and a few blind Britishers"—the reference is to leaders of the Jewish Social Democratic Party and war veterans with English trade union experience, such as R. E. Bray who was arrested along with other strike leaders* on June 16 and 17, 1919—the Winnipeg General Strike did not lead to revolution.[62] Nor did the unemployed and disgruntled veterans become victims of "Bolshevik" propaganda as was feared by the authorities. Much of the government's continued alarm and Borden's own anxiety was caused by a cable from Milner which read:

Information from what [had] hitherto been trustworthy authority that the Russian Soviet Government has a plan for resuscitating the revolutionary movement in Canada and has put two million roubles in foreign money at the disposal of the communistic sections at Ottawa, Calgary, Lethbridge, Edmonton, Regina, Victoria, Vancouver, Toronto, and Montreal.[63]

With the founding of the Third International in March 1919 such an action may indeed have been contemplated by the Soviets. But, whatever the theoretical intent, in practical terms Moscow and the Comintern, their own difficulties apart, would have been hard put to locate "the Communist sections" referred to in Milner's despatch.

Ironically, the chief victim of the strike was the newly formed OBU, which never

---

*Those arrested were George Armstrong, Bray, F. J. Dixon, Rev. William Ivens, John Queen and Rev. J. S. Woodsworth. They were charged with sedition or seditious conspiracy, and were not tried until 1920.

again exerted comparable influence in the Canadian labour movement. On the other hand, there is no doubt that the strike is unique in Canadian history, and that it was the most dramatic expression of the militant spirit which swept through the country during the years immediately following the October revolution. But, while the action aroused much sympathy throughout trade union and labour circles in Canada and the United States, the communist claim that "the labor movement in Winnipeg and the main body of its members were both in advance of the rest of the country at that time" is not justified.[64] Unquestionably, the most active participants, such as John Queen, Ivens, Woodsworth, and others, were better schooled and better grounded in socialist and Marxist thought than most of the labour leaders and strikers; but the great body of strikers reacted more on the basis of conditions current in the country, particularly in the west: unemployment, the anti-foreign feeling, the charged atmo-sphere created by intervention following the turmoil caused by the conscription issue and blatant wartime profiteering, and labour's general resentment towards the policies and actions of a Conservative government. The strike made orthodox labour conscious of its shortcomings and mistakes and tended to make the trade union leaders more cautions. A. E. Smith's assessment, though Marxist and full of wisdom after the event, is nevertheless valid. He felt that although the leadership from the beginning was afraid of the great power inherent in the strike, the cause of the failure was more fundamental:

There was no working-class party with a conscious understanding of this power and what should be done. ... Yet objectively here was revealed more clearly than by any other event in Canadian labor history the elemental factors of working class power.[65]

For Marxists in Canada the real outcome of the strike was the realization that "the sectarian passivity of the Socialist Party of Canada ... the syndicalist confusion and political sterility of the IWW and the OBU" held out no promise for them.[66] The lead in evolving a truly revolutionary movement shifted to central Canada, and with the displacement eastward Moscow became not only the source of inspiration but also the catalyst which enabled the Communist Party of Canada to be born.

CHAPTER THREE

THE BIRTH OF THE CANADIAN COMMUNIST PARTY

IN CENTRAL Canada, notably in Toronto and Montreal, the Winnipeg strike was followed closely by the more militant members of the Socialist Party of Canada and those organizations banned in September 1918. For a short time after the strike, until the end of 1920, the ground swell of OBU doctrines carried into Ontario and Quebec, but the OBU, moribund after the Winnipeg action, failed to make a lasting imprint on radical ranks. Instead, new forces gradually began to intrude. Despite the War Measures Act and the ferment which followed the Armistice, it was the decision to intervene in Russia which created conditions and provided sufficient cause for the more revolutionary radicals to resume their activities.

Initially, their efforts consisted mainly of small meetings, many of which were held under the cover of the Socialist Party, of language federations ostensibly engaged in cultural pursuits, or under the guise of trade union activities. Information about Russian developments, Marxist theories and socialist thought was spread by whatever pamphlets and books found their way into the country, or through contact with those, mostly immigrants, who had gained some experience of socialist theory and practice in Europe. In this manner, for example, Maurice Spector, a founding member of the Canadian Communist Party, obtained and read such material as Lenin's pamphlet *The Soviets at Work*, various of Marx's writings, and copies of *The New Age*, the tribune of Alfred Richard Orage and the English Guild Socialists.[1] Once printing of radical newspapers and periodicals resumed in the United States, such publications as *The Ohio Socialist*, which featured many articles on the situation in Russia, began filtering into Canada. In addition, through contact with men such as Arthur [Gustav] Ewert, "a tall fat German with a round, red face like the man smoking a cigar in the old Regensburg advertisements . . . in the I.R.T. [Interborough Rapid Transfer] trains" who spent six years in Canada "and . . . helped [to] found the Canadian Communist Party," Tom Bell, Spector, and many others were converted to Marxism.[2] Ewert and his wife, whom Buck incorrectly refers to as "Mr. and Mrs. Everhardt," had taken part in strikes in Toronto, and were ultimately deported to the United States. After spending a year in Detroit they returned to Germany in time to take part in the abortive 1923 uprisings. Ewert, whose influence on Bell and other Canadian radicals is undeniable, ultimately became a member of the German Communist Party's Central Committee and a leading Comintern functionary.

The War Measures Act and the investigations of the Lusk Committee in New York State combined to create a climate of opinion which deterred rapid and open increase in radical activity. However, such official action strengthened the resolve of the more determined radicals to form a truly militant party with revolutionary ambitions. The American investigations were instrumental in causing at least three radically inclined women, Rebecca Buhay, Annie Buller, and Bella Gauld, who were attending the

Rand School of Social Sciences in New York,* to return to Canada.[3] All had been active in the socialist movement while in New York, and one, Rebecca [Becky] Buhay, had extensive contacts with well known radicals including J. B. Salutsky and Scott Nearing. Indeed, as secretary of the Eighth Assembly District Socialist Party group Buhay had corresponded with Ludwig C. A. K. Martens, the unrecognized Soviet representative in the United States.[4] On the basis of their New York experiences, all three women became active in Montreal socialist and labour circles, and their efforts soon were evident further afield.

First and foremost they pressed for the establishment of a Montreal Labour College similar to the Rand School to bring socialist teachings to the Canadian labouring masses. A description published by Annie Buller in *The Canadian Tribune*, March 24, 1952, gives a good picture of the times and the spirit motivating the young idealists.

Soon after our [Buller's and Bella Gauld's] return in 1919 we met with Mike and Becky Buhay and a few others; it was agreed that we organize a Labor College and that we seek support from [the] trade union movement. . . . We managed to get support from a number of active workers around the college . . . .
The College came into being in 1920. We rented two rooms at St. Joseph's Hall, later we bought a building on Jeanne Mance [Street], as two rooms could not accommodate all our students and the Sunday Forum.
The College conducted nightly classes on economics, history, current events. Besides our local teachers like Bella [Gauld], Mike Buhay and the rest of us, we invited for our forum as guest lecturers, Jim Larkin, William Z. Foster, J. S. Woodsworth, Bill Irvine, Scott Nearing and many others . . . .
The Marxists around the college carried on a real ideological struggle against reformism [mostly against the doctrines expressed by the AF of L and the TLC]. Before long they became the founders and leaders of the Workers' Party of Canada [the legal front of the underground Communist Party] in Montreal.

By the end of 1919 a confidential report (accompanying a memorandum from the Minister of Immigration and Colonization) forwarded to Sir George Foster, then acting Prime Minister, noted that

. . . the known "Reds" in Montreal . . . number about fifty, Beckie Buhay, a Jewish girl about twenty-eight or thirty years of age, a sister of Michael Buhay . . . being the cleverest and most outspoken. She is credited with being the leader amongst the English-speaking Radicals, while another woman, Ray Mendelson [*sic*], is the leader of the foreign radicals.[5]

Their militancy was undeniable. Indeed, *The Ottawa Citizen* of June 2, 1919, had noted the arrest of "Mrs. Ray Press Mendelsohn" the previous day in Montreal for attempting to speak at an unauthorized meeting held in Mount Royal. Undeniably, such public action for a time made Montreal one of the major centres of extreme radical activity in the country.

However, it was Toronto which became the main revolutionary centre in Canada after the Winnipeg strike. There, according to Buck, as early as February 1919 the first organized attempt to establish a "Canadian Party of the new type" took place, but the preliminary conference called to discuss the establishment of "an International Workers Association in support of the Russian Revolution and to further the struggle for socialism in Canada" was raided by the police and "John Boychuk, Tom Bell, Mrs. Florence Custance, Mr. and Mrs. Everhardt [the Ewerts], and other leading

---

*The Rand School, which was organized in 1906 as an "educational auxiliary of the socialist and labor movement", gave courses in economics, sociology, trade unionism, English, and public speaking. In 1918–1919 the school's curriculum included lectures in Marxian Philosophy, Elements of Socialism, Principles of Marxism, and a study of socialist classics. The lecturers included Max Eastman, Charles A. Beard, James O'Neal, Scott Nearing, and Alexander Trachtenberg. In 1917 Sen Katayama lectured on the Japanese working class movement while in 1919 Louise Bryant described recent events in Russia.

members of the committee were arrested."[6] Being German, the Ewerts were classified as enemy aliens and deported. Bell, Boychuk, and Custance were charged with being in possession of seditious documents. Bell and Boychuk, who had been tried on the same charge in Vegreville, Alberta, in August 1918, and given a suspended sentence, were sentenced to two years. Both, however, served only a portion of their sentences; Bell, for example, was imprisoned from June until December 20, 1919. While evidence is lacking that an organized attempt was made to form a revolutionary party, the implication is clear that activity was increasing, despite the War Measures Act. Radical activity, however, remained scattered and unco-ordinated. When the ban on radical associations was rescinded by Order in Council P.C. 702, which was passed on April 2, 1919, such activities as holding meetings, organizing new groups, re-assembling old ones, and distributing literature were resumed openly and on an increasing scale. Nevertheless, the War Measures Act, like a Damoclean sword, remained on the statute books.

By the end of 1919, despite such reverses as the February arrests, Marxist groups in Toronto were much more clearly defined than anywhere else in Canada. The flow of literature from across the border had increased considerably, an unintentional by-product of the formation in September 1919 of the Communist Labor Party of America (CLPA) and the Communist Party of America (CPA)*, both of which were competing for Moscow's attention and approval.[7] The American parties provided ideological guidance, and considering the repressive climate prevailing in the United States at the time, a measure of inspiration. Both were anti-AF of L; both advocated militant political action, a policy contrasting strongly with the attitudes of earlier American socialist and syndicalist groups; and both proclaimed the establishment of the dictatorship of the proletariat as a basic political aim. More important, both parties pledged total and unconditional allegiance to the newly founded Third International—the Comintern.

No comparable parties emerged so clearly or so early in Canada. The time lag was inevitable. Through men like Louis Fraina, John Reed, and others, the American socialist groups had been in much closer contact with the Marxist movement abroad, and after the October Revolution, in more frequent touch with the Bolsheviks in Moscow. Moreover, close contact between America and Russia was to be expected since, even in those early days, the United States was recognized by Marxists as the greatest remaining stronghold of hated capitalism. By comparison Canada was an industrial pygmy, and, so far as Moscow was concerned, the country was regarded (indeed, if it were considered at all during the immediate post-revolutionary days) as a British colony. Consequently, the Comintern, early in 1920, sought to fuse the two American groups—a preliminary agreement between the UCPA and the CPA was reached but never put into effect—and Zinoviev, Chairman of the Executive Committee of the Communist International even proposed that

The IWW should take the initiative in seeking the basis for the unification of all unions with a class-conscious revolutionary character such as the Union of Industrial Workers, the One Big Union and a few revolutionary unions in the AFL.[8]

In Canada there were no well-led groups prepared to respond to the call. The IWW

*The CLPA was founded in Chicago on August 31, 1919, with John Reed, Benjamin Gitlow, and Alfred Wagenknecht forming the leadership. The CPA, which was also founded in Chicago on September 2, 1919, was led by Louis Fraina and Charles E. Ruthenberg, with Jay Lovestone a member of the executive.

north of the border had been a spent force since 1914, and Zinoviev, in lumping the IWW, the OBU, and other unions together, displayed the ignorance which character-ized the Comintern's concept of labour organization in North America.

As for the American parties giving the lead to Canadian Marxists, the factors which affected organization and growth in the American republic did not apply north of the border. One of the early complications was that both of the United States parties were driven underground some four months after they were formed.[9] Also, the great strike wave in the United States which swept the country towards the end of 1919, coming as it did hard on the heels of the Winnipeg General Strike, alerted government and orthodox trade union leadership to revolutionary doctrines, and conversely, indicated to Canadian Marxists that the time was not propitious for open organization.

Nevertheless, the influx of some of the CLPA and CPA literature—both parties published their own newspapers, the CLPA's *The Voice of Labor* and *Communist Labor* in New York, and *The Toiler* in Cleveland, and the CPA's *The Communist*—as well as the writings of Lenin, which were becoming increasingly available, together with an occasional bulletin from the young Comintern, aroused much interest in Toronto radical circles. Some of the literature allegedly originated from surprising sources. Buck recalls that

By the summer of 1920 we secured our first copies of the Theses and Statutes [of the Third Inter-national] from Washington. The U.S. government had them translated and printed in a handy pamphlet as part of its anti-Soviet campaign.[10]

While such pamphlets, newspapers, and other literature stimulated Marxists in Toronto, and although information about the American communist movement trickling over the border provided them with examples for comparable action, it soon became clear that a wide gulf separated the active radicals from the Canadian masses. In order to reduce the gap and to prepare the workers so that they would be aware of their power at a propitious time, the more active revolutionaries in the city, led by Florence Custance, a former English school mistress, formed the Plebs League of Ontario. In addition to Custance, the executive of the new body included Max Armstrong and Maurice Spector. The League, modelled after the English organization of the same name, held meetings on Sunday afternoons, and by the autumn of 1920 was well underway with its programme of lectures and discussions. Through Florence Custance, who acted as secretary, the Toronto Plebs organization—its headquarters was at 28 Wellington Street West—got in touch with the English League, and at one point, in October 1920, agreed to affiliate with the latter.* Also, the Canadian League made arrangements to get radical newspapers from the United States, England, Scotland and Ireland.

Initially, the League's activities were limited and cautious, the first phase of a feeling-out process that continued until well after the formation of the Communist Party of Canada. The view prevailing in Toronto was that soap-box oratory had to be carried out carefully since the Plebs League had only one role: to prepare the workers for the coming revolution.

The Plebs League, however, was but a forerunner of and an early adjunct to the Ontario Labour College, which also came into being through the efforts of Custance, Bell, Spector, and Max Armstrong in 1920, and which was backed by two wealthy

*The Plebs League of England was active from at least the beginning of World War I. J. F. Horrabin, a member of the English League's executive, was also editor of *Plebs*, the organ of the British Labour College.

men, J. Sutcliffe, a Toronto accountant, and J. Counsell, a Hamilton lawyer. Classes began in October and included lectures given in a branch established in the nearby city of Hamilton. Through the autumn Armstrong and Bell took turns holding classes in Hamilton, with Spector assisting whenever required. The College paralleled the one in Montreal and, like the latter and the Plebs League, was intended to bring Marxist socialism to a wider audience than was possible through the activities of a small number of unco-ordinated groups. Besides holding formal lectures, the Plebs League distributed and sold at its own meetings or through the Labour College whatever books, pamphlets, or other publications it obtained from various sources. These included items such as Otto Kuusinen's *The Finnish Revolution, The Appeal of the Executive Committee of the Communist International to the I.W.W., The Plebs* from England, and various American radical publications. Perhaps the most important aspect of all these developments was that material was provided for the conversations and endless discussions so basic to the formation of a revolutionary organization. But progress was slow, and in December 1920 the League's membership in Toronto numbered only about 70.

Although the activities of the Plebs League and the educational efforts of the Labour College widened the range of contacts and potential adherents for the militant groups in Toronto, they also accelerated the drift towards the bedrock of revolutionary theory and practice. By the end of 1920 most of the League's leading members had rejected the Socialist Party of Canada, the Independent Labour Party, and the OBU because the organizations were not radical enough. They agreed with Bell and Spector, both of whom felt that although pamphlets, leaflets, and open meetings did a certain amount of good, the time had come to build up a secret underground organization composed of small groups not exceeding ten in number. Each group was to be separate and independent but under the control and direction of a central executive. Backed by general agreement among the Plebs League leaders, the first tentative approach was then made to the communist movement in the United States.

In January 1921 Bell, the most revolutionary and outspoken of the Plebs executive, and who had the added prestige of having suffered imprisonment under the government's Orders in Council, journeyed to New York to attend a secret meeting of the United Communist Party of America (UCPA).* Bell returned to Toronto with the news that the Comintern had ordered the two parties, the UCPA and the CPA, to unite.[11] On the basis of Bell's news, the nucleus of the Plebs League (Bell, Custance, Spector, and others) decided at a meeting held in the home of Florence Custance to affiliate with the former, thus becoming a Canadian underground extension of the United Communist Party of America. Within a few weeks, railway employees and news agents who were members of or active sympathizers with the American party, were carrying illegal literature and messages across the border between Buffalo, New York, and Toronto. In Toronto Florence Custance received most of the printed material, and in this way obtained copies of the publication *Soviet Russia*, the "Russian Constitution," Lozovsky's *The Role of the Labor Unions in the Russian Revolution*, and a weekly paper published by the Socialist Party of America.

Like the American communist movement, the Canadian was unable to avoid rivalry and faction. Within the Canadian group some friction resulted from Bell's taking the initiative in organizational matters without consulting Spector and

---

*The CLPA was eliminated at a secret unity convention held in the woods near Bridgeman, Michigan, during the last week of May 1920.

Custance. Also Bell's extreme revolutionary talk did not accord with the prevailing view of the necessity for caution during the formative period, and caused concern. His penchant for strong language, too, upset Custance who, despite her revolutionary fervour, remained rather prim and straight-laced.

When the Plebs League executive members were seriously considering extending activities beyond the "beginners" stage at which they felt the League operated, a rival organization also dedicated to the awakening of the workers came into being. Under the leadership of John MacDonald, a member of the Pattern Makers' Union, and vice-president of the Independent Labour Party of Ontario, Joseph Knight, an OBU organizer in eastern Canada, and Knight's wife, the Workers' Educational Club appeared on the Toronto radical scene. The Club's meetings, held mostly in a building called Occident Hall, occasioned some anger on the part of leading figures in the Ontario Labour College (especially Florence Custance), since it duplicated the activities of the College and of the Plebs League. Duplication of programmes and activities led in turn to rivalry for the leadership of the ultra-radical groups in Toronto, and to doctrinal controversy. At an open forum meeting held at the Labour Temple on January 23, 1921, Spector, with some bitterness, asked MacDonald, the rival faction's leader, how long the latter had been a communist. Macdonald is said to have replied: "from today." A week later, at the beginning of February 1921, MacDonald, at a Labour Temple meeting, formally and openly severed his connection with the Independent Labour Party. According to *The Toronto World* of February 2:

He strongly defended the dictatorship set up in Russia by Lenin and Trotsky .... He declared that if communism could not be brought about in Canada by legal means it would be brought about by illegal means. The only justifiable revolution was a successful revolution, and the means to the end were of minor importance. Some of the communists [there] would have to go to jail, and some of them would undoubtedly go to jail. He had come out now as a communist, and he hoped to organize groups in Toronto, which would spread until Canada was a communist country.

MacDonald's public conversion to communism did not end controversy or differences within the radical movement. Instead, the Workers' Educational College group, which by then had made contact with the Communist Party of America and had affiliated with it, continued its separate existence. It was a very *ad hoc* existence, for the Canadian extension of the CPA had no fixed headquarters, and during its short life used the Ukrainian Labour Temple for most of its meetings, reflecting unintentionally, the nationalities' differences which split the American movement.

Thus, early in 1921, "before," as Tim Buck notes, "the Communist Party of Canada was founded, many left wingers had already become members of either the Communist Party of America or the United Communist Party of America."[12] What Buck, who acknowledges the development without elaboration, fails to make clear is that the initiative in making cross-border connections with the United States communist parties came from the Canadian side.

While the basis for a Canadian communist movement was being evolved in Toronto, the decline in revolutionary activity in the western half of the Dominion following the Winnipeg General Strike was partially redressed through the activities of Ukrainian revolutionaries. Paul Yuzyk writes:

Since the Ukrainian Social Democratic Party could not very well be revived without rousing public indignation, the leaders rallied around the Ukrainian Labor Temple Association. From Manitoba the organization spread to other Canadian cities where the pro-Soviet Ukrainian elements had sufficient following to undertake erection of labor temples following the one in Manitoba's capital. The first conference of the Labor Temple Association, held in Winnipeg in 1920, decided to form a national organization; by 1923 it had 24 branches.[13]

Under the cover of cultural activities, through organizers who toured western Canada where the bulk of the Ukrainian population had settled, and through the medium of *Ukrayinski Rabotnychi Visty* ("Ukrainian Labour News"), the ULTA was able to build up its membership and its assets substantially before the Toronto groups had emerged from the stream of post-war socialism. Eventually, on October 21, 1924, the organization was incorporated on a national basis under the Companies Act as the Ukrainian Labour Farmer Temple Association (ULFTA).

The views expressed in *Ukrayinski Rabotnychi Visty* after the Winnipeg strike reflected the uncertainty felt by radicals in all parts of the Dominion, and by the Ukrainian revolutionaries in particular; hence the language used was often reminiscent of the Aesopian style adopted by Russian writers and revolutionaries who wished to avoid tsarist censorship. John Boychuk, protesting in *Ukrayinski Zhitya* ("Ukrainian Life") of September 17, 1919, over the arrest of two comrades on suspicion of making revolutionary speeches, expressed himself in such a fashion:

Now you Ukrainian labourers and farmers, consider what is going on around you. Observe and reflect upon your hardships, because you are like those bees who are busy on flowers day by day, from daylight till dark, always working, and you never think, and do not like to hear a voice telling you: "Look at the drone bees, how they destroy your work."

His article, dated Vegreville, Alberta, September 5, was, appropriately, signed with only his initials. By the spring of 1921 uncertainty, fear of official reaction, speaking and writing in guarded forms had been replaced by a distinct air of optimism and direct revolutionary language. In an article entitled "First of May," Matthew Shatulsky, writing in *Ukrayinski Zhitya*, April 30, 1921, reflected the change in atmosphere.

... will we ever celebrate (as in Soviet republics) the first of May? ... Yes we will. ... The ranks of our proletarian fighters are increasing every day ... we will accept their call, as the proletariats did in Russia accept their call to overthrow despotic Czarism ... the struggle will be a hard one, but all our lives have been hard.

Much of the optimism stemmed from the boast that the ULTA had about 5,000 members. Nevertheless, Shatulsky took the precaution of writing under the pseudonym of "Volynec."

A similar development took place among the radical groups which had coalesced among the Finnish immigrants settled mainly in the metal-mining regions of northern Ontario, and the lumbering areas at the head of the Great Lakes. The first Finnish organisation in Canada, the Finnish Society, was formed in Toronto in 1902. It was soon followed by a second, the Temperance and Workers' Society, organized in 1904. Both united in 1905 to form a new body, the Finnish Society, which continued to be politically and socially active in and around Toronto until 1910. That year the Toronto unit took the initiative and succeeded in amalgamating all Finnish societies in Canada into a single national organization, the Canadian Finnish Organization (CFO). In 1911 the CFO, wasting little time, did two things: first, on October 25 it obtained a charter, thus acquiring formal institutional respectability; second, and more significantly, it affiliated itself with the Social Democratic Party of Canada. As the Finnish wing of the SDP, the Canadian Finnish Organization very quickly became a radical force of considerable influence within the Finnish-speaking community in Canada. By establishing its headquarters in the nickel-mining centre of Sudbury, Ontario, one of the principal Finnish communities in the Dominion, and through its newspaper *Vapaus* ("Liberty"), socialist and Marxist doctrines were given considerable currency until the organization was banned for its activities in September

1918.[14] In addition, the movement's leaders—John Werner Ahlqvist was the most prominent at the time—suffered arrest and prosecution for possessing prohibited literature. Such official action contributed further to the prevailing mood of resentment and frustration, and exacerbated the feeling within labour ranks that drastic methods were needed to achieve the worker's rights.[15]

Although the CFO and the Social Democratic Party were banned in September 1918, the CFO was permitted, officially, to resume its social activites on December 18 on the proviso that it would drop its affiliation with the SDP. Soon afterwards the Finnish body temporarily affiliated itself with the One Big Union, but that connection, like the OBU itself, proved to be short lived, and the Finnish radicals rapidly reverted to their previously established pattern of organization and propaganda. The effectiveness of the CFO's efforts is indicated by A. T. Hill, one of the vanguard of Finnish radicals in the Dominion to become active in the Canadian communist movement, who claims that the organization was made up of 60 locals and over 2,000 members before it changed its title and received its charter as the Finnish Organization of Canada (FOC) in 1923.[16] The object of the incorporation was to obtain control of and jurisdiction over the properties of various Finnish branch organizations in Canada in the name of the FOC.

At the end of 1918 the Finnish and the Ukrainian organizations formed by far the largest revolutionary grouping in Canada. All that was lacking was a firm leadership with a common aim and purpose which could bring both under a single authority. From the start, that element of leadership was provided by native-born Canadians and recent immigrants from the British Isles—Bell, Custance, MacDonald, Buck, the two Buhays, Spector, and others—not, as Professor Brady implies, by the most active individuals from among the Ukrainian and Finnish populations.[17] In Toronto, the chief centre for the activites of radical extremists, circumstances never enabled the rival communist parties which emerged early in 1921 to transmute their rivalry into serious physical or ideological action. Both groups knew that the Comintern had ordered the amalgamation of the two antagonistic American parties "because all Moscow considers it to be a matter which is indispensable and which must not be postponed."[18] Such a step automatically included the two Canadian groups once they had established connections, however tenuous, with the United States parties. That the Comintern considered amalgamation of the newly-established groups in North America important is confirmed in its six-point plan for party unity drawn up in 1920.[19] Since the expected fusion had not taken place, Moscow, no longer interested in encouraging the anarcho-syndicalism of the IWW and OBU, as it had been when it addressed its appeal to the IWW, despatched a three-man commission, generally referred to as the Pan-American Agency,* to the United States to ensure that unity was achieved.[20]

Indications of the Comintern's interest in and concern about the American and Canadian developments were embodied in a set of "instructions" signed by Zinoviev and found among papers seized in New York at the end of April. These specified that the "American Council of Communist International" was to appoint "Committees in the United States, Canada, and Mexico, to be known as "The American, Canadian,

*The "American Agency" consisted of three men: the Japanese Sen Katayama, who acted as chairman; the Lettish Communist from Roxbury, Massachusetts, Carl Jansen or Johnson, who represented the United Communist Party, and Louis Fraina who stood for the Communist Party of America. For purposes of travel, convenience, and above all, secrecy, Katayma and Jansen adopted cover names: "Kavki" and "Charles E. Scott."

Latin-American Bureau of the Red Labor Union International."[21] The main object was to secure an adequate representation from North American labour groups to the Red International of Labor Unions' (RILU or Profintern) founding Congress. Equally important, the Comintern did not want two rival United States delegations with marked differences at the Red International's initial meeting. Under the heading "The United States" the instructions recognized that "problems in Canada, although on a vastly smaller scale, approximate those in the United States. The One Big Union must be especially utilized."[22]

As early as April 1921 the proposed amalgamation of the Canadian units was actively considered by both communist-orientated groups in Toronto, for the Comintern had specifically empowered the American Agency on April 2, 1921 to unite the two United States parties by the beginning of June.[23] Such discussions, at first mostly theoretical, assumed a more serious air when Caleb Harrison,* who used the pseudonym "Atwood" during his stay in Canada, came to Toronto in April 1921 as the Pan-American Agency's representative.[24] Harrison's (or Atwood's) arrival marked the end of the scattered revolutionary agitation which up to then had characterized the activities of the Canadian ultra-left radicals. He quickly established contact with the two rival groups, particularly with Bell and others of the UCPA, and brought them together to work out the details of unification. One issue of an underground paper, *The Communist*,† "published by the authority of the Third (Communist) International in Canada" to mark May Day 1921, was produced, the first tangible result of Atwood's presence.[25] From the talks which followed, "standing committees on Program Constitution, Resolutions, Press and Finance," together with a committee of at least three reliables, Harry Reigate, William Moriarty, and George Wiltshaw, were set up.[26] The latter group was responsible for working out the arrangements for the convention: selecting the site, arranging for accommodation and catering, and providing the delegates with money for travel. The convention subsidy, claimed to be "at least $3,000" according to Esselwein's evidence in 1931, came from Comintern funds and was provided through Atwood.[27] Thus the Comintern, through the agency of Atwood, was the catalyst in the fusion which followed. With Atwood's presence the CPC officially attached itself to the Comintern. Formal acknowledgement of Atwood's report to the Pan-American Bureau that the Canadian party had joined the International's ranks did not come, however, until after Scott, one of the Pan-American Bureau's triumvirs, arrived in Toronto in September and sent back his own report to Moscow on the status of the party in the Dominion.

Besides initiating arrangements for bringing the two Toronto groups together, Atwood, as directed, also approved the final selection of a sympathetic OBU member whom the bureau in charge of arranging the first Congress of the Red International

---

*Harrison, one of the few members of the Socialist Labor Party in the United States and one of the American communist movement's early adherents, was sent to Toronto not only because the Pan-American Agency felt that fusion of the Canadian groups was important and should parallel that of the American units, but also because Fraina, one of the triumvirs, was suspect, making it imperative for Scott and Katayama to remain on hand and supervise the amalgamation in the United States.

†Four issues of this paper, which was sub-titled the "official organ of the Communist Party of Canada (section of the Communist International)," were produced under Spector's editorial guidance at a Ukrainian or a Finnish printing establishment. Tim Buck, in *The Worker*, March 9, 1929, states that only two issues were published, but corrects the figure in his book *Thirty Years, 1922–52* (Toronto, 1952), pp. 26–27.

of Labor Unions* wished to attend the meeting. The job of selecting and persuading a suitable person had been channelled through one of the American communist groups, and had been entrusted to Ella Reeve Bloor, then in Cleveland, Ohio. She travelled to Winnipeg, met the OBU Central Labor Council, but was not successful in persuading R. B. Russell (of general strike fame, and the man the Profintern bureau hoped would come) to accept the invitation. Bloor then went to Toronto where she contacted Joseph Knight, the OBU's organizer in central Canada, who had been active on the periphery of the nascent Canadian communist movement. With Atwood's assistance the necessary credentials for Knight were obtained, and he proceeded to New York where, in company with the American Trade Union Delegation (Browder, Bloor, and Foster among them) he embarked for Europe.[28] Knight was sent to Moscow to stress the need for unity among the world's revolutionary labour ranks, and to underline the necessity for the OBU, by then in decline, to coalesce with the Canadian communist movement. Knight thus became the first Canadian delegate officially approved by the nascent communist movement in the Dominion to attend Comintern—he sat as an observer at some of the Third World Congress sessions—and Profintern congresses. Significantly, at the time he was selected and while still en route to Moscow, the Canadian party had not yet come into being.

Deep conspiracy characterized the birth of the Canadian Communist Party. Pseudonyms were adopted; delegates were instructed to travel singly to the convention site; and all were told explicitly whom to meet, when, and where. Spector recalls that although he was one of the principals in the movement he did not know where the meeting was actually to take place. He travelled as instructed, was met by a contact man, and arrived at the convention site at night. His party name was "G. Stanley"; Custance was "Johnson"; and MacDonald used the cover title of "J. Lawrence." Most details were worked out quickly, within four to six weeks—Spector is inclined to think four, because, as he claims, "things moved fast"—and at the appointed time,

... in accordance with the mandate of the Pan-American Council of the Third International to bring about the formation of a Communist Party of Canada, delegates representing the Canadian section of the C.P., the U.C.P. and other Canadian groups,

assembled surreptitiously at night in a small barn on Fred Farley's† farm near the placid agricultural town of Guelph, Ontario.[29] Guards were posted, and strict security measures prevailed throughout the convention.

The place and fashion of meeting, underground and illegal, in themselves denote the great change that the imperialist war and the Russian Revolution have wrought in the conditions of the class struggle even in backward Canada.[30]

At seven o'clock on the morning of May 23, 1921, Atwood, "the representative of the Pan-American Council who acted as chairman," called the convention to order.[31] The Credentials Committee, Bell and Trevor Maguire, reported that 22 delegates, 15 representing the MacDonald-Wiltshaw CPA wing, five the UCPA section headed by Bell, Custance, and Spector, and two especially invited Socialist Party of Canada members, unnamed, were present. With credentials approved, secretaries elected, and

*The first RILU congress opened on July 3, 1921. It was preceded by the Comintern's Third World Congress which was held June 22–July 12.

†Farley was a member of the UCPA wing. Before becoming involved in the Canadian communist movement he was a member of the Socialist Party of Canada and the Guelph Workingmen's Association.

D

greetings from the ECCI and the American fraternal parties* conveyed to the gathering, Atwood, introduced by Bell, addressed the group.[32]

He described how the American parties came into being, revealing that Ludwig Martens, the Soviet government's unofficial representative in New York, had provided financial aid to leading American radicals, and how, because the need for unifying the revolutionary movement in North America had been recognized by Comintern, the Pan-American Agency had been formed before Martens was deported from the United States. Most important, he assured the delegates that the Comintern was prepared to assist the Canadian party financially until it became established. Atwood's address set the tone of the meeting; his authority in turn channelled subsequent discussion and added weight to the convention's decisions.

The real business began after the various committees, appointed before the convention assembled, reported on the results of their work. The programme submitted for approval was essentially the same as that adopted by the Communist Party of America, somewhat modified to suit Canadian conditions. It presented the essentials of the *Manifesto* passed at the First Comintern Congress and a digest of the *Theses* adopted at the Second. It analysed the capitalist economy, capitalist imperialism, and defined "the aims and processes of the proletarian revolution in Canada" as a lengthy process which began with the destruction of the capitalist state and the establishment of the dictatorship of the proletariat, and ended with the transformation of the capitalist system into the "Communist Society."[33] To this end the convention agreed that:

... the Communist Party of Canada [would] systematically and persistently propagate to the working class the idea of the inevitability of and necessity for violent revolution, and [would] prepare the working class for the destruction of the bourgeois state and the establishment of the proletarian dictatorship based upon Soviet power.[34]

This, it followed, would include destruction of all parliamentary institutions. Nevertheless, it was agreed that "while the Communist Party of Canada makes its major campaigns and activities among the working class in their mass-struggles outside of the parliaments, it will participate in elections and election campaigns for revolutionary propaganda and agitation only."[35]

Trade union matters and labour policy provoked the most discussion. That it did so is scarcely surprising. Most of the delegates were practical men who drew primarily upon their experiences in the labour movements in Canada, the United States, and the British Isles. Marxist theory and its Leninist interpretations were sophisticated abstractions that were distinctly secondary in the spectrum of their thoughts. In the end the delegates from western Canada succeeded in having their view accepted that "sabotage by the AF of L bureaucracy, and wartime repression by the State" were equally as important as the industrialists' propaganda in preventing a wider acceptance of socialist views among the working populations.[36] The result of these combined pressures they felt, caused a separation of the advanced workers from the main body, leaving the greater part of the organized working masses more completely at the mercy of the AF of L officialdom than before. The views thus expressed about trade union and other matters at the convention in turn became the basis for determining the party's future policies and actions.

With the adoption of a constitution the party's nature and its role in the Canadian scene were clearly fixed. Article Four unequivocally stated that the newly-formed

*The American parties also united at Woodstock, New York, in May 1921. Until Atwood broke the news the Canadian convention was unaware that the United States groups had been amalgamated.

organization was to be highly centralized, and above all that it was to be "an underground, illegal organization."[37] The latter qualification was made to ensure that no part of the membership would misconstrue the Communist Party of Canada's real character, with the resulting confusion and dissension which marked the American and British parties' experience. There was no point, it was felt, in attempting to reap a short-term gain by making the party's position less precise, since the laws prevailing in Canada would not prevent the authorities, after the prominence given to socialist doctrines during the Winnipeg General Strike, from taking official action against it. At the conference, too

It was decided that it would be foolhardy to declare ourselves [openly] as having organized a Communist Party. So, in spite of the fact that most of the groups which were represented at this conference had functioned in the form of educational societies, international workers' groups and Plebs Leagues ... it was decided that in the interests of the general movement and in order to demonstrate to some extent to a large section of the working class, particularly the organized working class, what were the aims of our Party, we should first, function as a so-called illegal party; in other words, as an underground party.[38]

The convention's most significant act was its affiliation with the Comintern, to which it unhesitatingly pledged its complete loyalty, and its recognition of Moscow's primacy in the world communist movement.

The Communist Party of Canada, Section of the Third International, assembled in its constituent convention in May, 1921, endorses and adopts unanimously, on roll-call vote, the 21 points for affiliation with the Communist International, as binding upon all delegates present and for its entire membership, without any reservations.[39]

In doing so it brought to an end the period of the historic left in which the Canadian communist movement, however briefly, had existed in a world of its own.*

With the election of a temporary Central Committee, which included Custance, MacDonald, Moriarty, and Spector, the meeting came to an end, and the delegates, dispersing quickly and quietly, faced the hard work of carrying out the decisions and suggestions they had approved. All departed as they had come, surreptitiously, exhilarated by their success in forming a party which, in their estimation, not only constituted the vanguard of the Canadian working class, but also was armed with a programme for mass action and prepared for armed insurrection and civil war. The mood of optimism pervaded *The Communist's* first issue. The paper declared:

Ours is an age of revolution versus imperialism. History is with us. Socialism is no longer the possession of a cloistered sect, nor a subject of parliamentary diplomacy. It is a bitter, relentless mass-struggle against the most monstrous coalition of oppression and destruction that history has record of.

Such optimism not only reflects a total acceptance of the revolutionary philosophy, but also the comparative youth of the CPC's leading members. Bell was 25; Buck was 30; Michael Buhay was 31; his sister, Rebecca, 26; Custance was 40; Hill, 24; MacDonald, 33; Popowich, 31; and Spector, the youngest, was 23.†

All were of "proletarian" origin. Buck, for example, was obliged by family circumstances to begin work in a machine shop at the age of twelve. With the exception of Spector, then a student at the University of Toronto, and Florence Custance, who had obtained teacher training in England, none had proceeded beyond secondary school. Indeed, few of the Canadian communist movement's leaders had achieved even that level of education. Again, all, in one way or another, had been brought into early

---

*Although Comintern, ostensibly, was dissolved in 1943 the Canadian Communist Party has never retracted the 21 points for admission or disavowed its primary loyalty to the USSR.
†For biographical details of these persons see Appendix A.

contact with social injustice, and all had become aware of or were involved in labour agitation and trade union organization. Buck, for instance, while still very young, had been impressed by Keir Hardie's oratory and views; similarly, MacDonald was a product of pre-World War I Scottish trade unionism, with all of its overtones of bitterness and hardship. The similarity of backgrounds, together with the mood then prevailing in Canadian labour circles, inevitably attracted such men and women. Their motives for joining the nascent communist movement were buttressed by the experience of economic insecurity caused by the slumps before and after the war, as well as a craving after some ideal which would square with their heightened social awareness, and which would provide a "datum" for their actions within a society that was daily becoming more complicated. In their view the Russian revolution had illuminated the workers' miseries with extraordinary clarity, and although the glowing light of 1917 had passed, the vistas revealed in that blinding flash still remained fresh and vivid: socialism, the classless society, the withering away of the state—all seemed to be on the threshold. In that moment of supreme optimism few, if any, of the Canadian party's founders had any premonition of the hard work, frustrations, and bitterness that were to follow.

CHAPTER FOUR

THE RISE OF THE WORKERS' PARTY

IN THEORY, what emerged from the Guelph convention of May 1921 was a highly centralized organization composed of a disciplined proletarian vanguard whose mission was to destroy the bourgeois state machinery, to establish the dictatorship of the proletariat, and to replace the capitalist system with a communist society.

On paper the structure and organization of the party were clearly laid down. At the base of the pyramid were "Groups," with a membership of between five and ten; any number of Groups up to a maximum of ten formed a "Branch"; and two or more Branches composed a "Local." In turn, Locals were combined to form "Sub-districts" within specified geographical areas (these were not laid down at the convention) with the Sub-districts forming the major components of "Districts."

Each group elected its own "Organizer," with the Group Organizers making up a "Branch Executive Committee." This Committee elected a "Branch Organizer" from within its own ranks, and the Branch Organizers formed a "Local Executive Committee," which in turn appointed one of its members as "Local Organizer." The Local Organizers within a Sub-district then formed a "Sub-district Executive Committee." The District Organizers, who acted as chairmen of "District Executive Committees," consisting of "Sub-district Organizers" and "Language Section District Organizers," were appointed by the party's "Central Executive Committee" (CEC). The annual convention was the supreme party authority, with the seven-member CEC assuming that role between conventions.

The duties of the Group, Branch, Local, Sub-district, and District Organizers were also laid down specifically, but not amplified in detail. Group Organizers, for example, were responsible for seeing that each Group met at least once a week, and for keeping their units posted on Group and party activity. Again, the Branch Executive Council was to meet once a week, the Sub-district committees were to meet twice a month; their organizers were charged with making full reports as well as with transmitting decisions of and carrying out the instructions from the CEC at the local level. In addition, the District Committee was expected to make regular remittances of dues and funds collected in its area, to forward financial statements to the party centre, and to submit weekly reports to the District Organizer. The District Organizers followed suit and reported weekly to the CEC. They were expected also to submit regular financial statements for circulation among the general membership in their areas.[1]

From the start the various revolutionary language groups in Canada, unlike those in the United States, were made "integral parts of the Communist Party of Canada and [were] subject to the absolute control of the party."[2] At Guelph it was specified that, within two months of the secret convention, the language groups—and by language groups the party meant the Finnish and Ukrainian organizations, even though formally in the CPC's eyes language organizations were considered units if their membership numbered 200 or more individuals speaking a given tongue—were to hold their own conventions, and were to submit to the party for approval their constitutions as well as any decisions or by-laws which were passed. Each language organization was to elect a three-man Bureau as well as an editor for its paper. These, together with the selection of a District Organizer, had to be approved by the CPC's Central Executive Committee. Also, the minutes of each language section's Bureau were to be submitted regularly to the CEC. In this way the Canadian party hoped to prevent any feeling of superiority comparable to that which emerged among the Russian members in the American movement and which caused so much dissension throughout the United States party during its formative period.

Translating revolutionary theory into practice, however, was another matter. Nevertheless, within days of the Guelph gathering, Florence Custance, acting for the CEC, addressed a circular letter dated June 9, 1921, to all "Comrades in Canada of the former C.P. and U.C.P. of America," in which she clarified the changes brought about by the amalgamation.

You are all aware of the fact that the convention called by the Pan American Council of the Communist International to form the Communist Party of Canada has come and gone, and that you are officially members of the Communist Party of Canada instead of either of the Communist Parties of the U.S. In about a week you will receive copies of *The Communist*, our official organ, which will give you a detailed account of the convention and its work. After you are familiar with the new constitution and its provisions the C.E.C. of the Party will direct the work of organizing all the groups according to the new laws, after which we expect to conduct an incessant and determined campaign for communism among the working masses of Canada.

Meanwhile, all existing groups were urged to continue their activities much as they had done before the unity convention.

The neat, orderly pattern visualized in the constitution became increasingly remote as the convention delegates returned to the realities of organization in their own territories. The new party was an underground organization; its membership was small and scattered; distances between principal areas where party groups were active were great; resources were limited; and apart from the hard core of dedicated revolutionaries, the Canadian working class was largely apathetic and unorganized.

For the CEC the post-convention period was a busy and exhausting time. First, there was the promised paper to be brought out, and this occupied Spector fully. At the convention and after, Atwood, on behalf of the Pan American Bureau and the Comintern, promised enough money to subsidize an illegal publication. However, most of the Canadian leadership, notably Custance, MacDonald, and Spector, kept pressing for sufficient money to start a legal paper. Bell sided with Scott of the Pan American Agency, who came to Toronto in September 1921, in opposing the idea of an overt publication. This difference was one of the first to arise following unification, and it continued as awareness grew that the small underground party—it numbered 200 in Toronto—was not reaching a wide enough spectrum of the working population. These factors, plus the Comintern's shift to a united front policy at its Third Congress, eventually caused a corresponding shift in outlook within the Canadian party. The change in attitude, however, was not an easy transition for many party members. Secrecy had become almost a way of life, and they clung to the notion that communists had always worked underground. As proof of their contention, they had only to point to the dazzling success of the Bolsheviks. Nevertheless, towards the end of August 1921 the CEC finally agreed that a legal paper, to be entitled *The Workers' World*, should be brought out. The projected publication, the first issue of which was scheduled to appear in September, was never produced. Instead, the paper's name was altered to *The Workers' Guard*, and under the editorial guidance of F. J. Peel, an old, very highly respected socialist and a founding member of the CPC, the first issue appeared early in October.[3]

Other organizational difficulties soon emerged. Factionalism, which made itself apparent before unification and which centred around Custance and Reigate on the one hand, and Bell and William Moriarty on the other, continued, with the former pair and their followers becoming increasingly isolated as the work of consolidating and developing the party progressed. The gulf between the two groups widened gradually, and the differences were exacerbated by Scott who, after his arrival in Toronto, became suspicious of Custance because at one time she had established connections with Madame Kollontai.*[4] Such differences, however, never assumed the importance they achieved in the United States communist movement, and never greatly impeded the Canadian party's development. The remaining Central Executive members, knowing Bell's passion for secrecy and intrigue, attempted to play down the differences, first by allowing Custance to become Secretary of the Canadian Friends of Soviet Russia, a front organization started in October 1921, and later by promoting Bell, first to Branch Organizer and then to District Organizer.

Initially, administrative problems occupied most of the CEC's time. Organizers had to be selected and despatched to relay the Comintern's hot gospel to existing groups and to new ones once they were formed. Communication with Moscow, relayed by the American party, was slow and still difficult, and the time lag frequently rendered some of the views expressed by both sides obsolete. Despite group isolation and distance the initial difficulties of welding together an underground party were often minor, but at the same time the total effect was too often one of frustration. In turn, the great activity at the centre tended to dissipate directly with distance from Toronto. Minor details, dues stamps for example, particularly those sent to party groups in western Canada, were returned sporadically, and yielded low returns, thus inhibiting developments that were dependent upon money. Scott, who made Toronto his Canadian headquarters, continually checked on the party's development, and his presence, no matter how closely or accurately he reflected Comintern policy and thought, coloured the CPC Executive's own views and action. Despite the mystique of his Comintern authority, Scott's advice was not always accepted or followed. For example, he urged MacDonald to go to Moscow as soon as possible after the secret Guelph convention. However, the tenuous condition of the CPC and Mac-Donald's desire to organize the party into an effective political entity militated against the journey to the Mecca of revolutionary power at such an early stage of the Canadian unit's development. Moreover, the decision not to visit Moscow squared with Mac-Donald's propensity to deal with matters such as labour agitation and organization,

*Alexandra Kollontai, the daughter of a tsarist general, toured the United States twice, in 1915 and 1916, lecturing on social and sexual questions. She was a prolific writer and projected a socialist and feminist viewpoint. Before World War I she was a Menshevik; after the war broke out she went over to the Bolsheviks and became a strong supporter of Lenin. When and if Custance contacted Kollontai is not clear. By the time the Canadian party was formed Kollontai had broken with Lenin. Because of Kollontai's activities with the left opposition in Russia Scott's distrust of anyone who had contact with her—Custance for example—was understandable, particularly at that time when secrecy was thought to be of paramount importance by most of the Canadian party members. As the Comintern representative in Canada, Scott not only was aware of the developments in Russia but could not afford to take chances. As it was, there were no contracts between the "Workers" opposition in Russia and the Canadian communist movement.

which he understood, and to leave the niceties of theory and doctrine to others.

In the autumn the commencement of classes at the Ontario Labour College consumed much of the Executive Committee's time. Custance, for example, lectured on "Economics and Economic Geography" in October, while Spector surveyed the period from the French Revolution to the Russian Revolution in strictly Marxist terms. To the CPC's leaders the Labour College was important because it enabled the party to maintain some contact on a broader front than was possible through its underground organizational activities, and because it was felt that the lectures helped to educate the workers for revolution. Through the College revolutionary literature such as *The Toiler* was sold or distributed, and promising new recruits for the party contacted. Both activities were carried out quietly, for official reaction—as shown by the arrest on September 21, 1921 of A. S. Wells, editor of the Vancouver Trades and Labour Council's paper *The British Columbia Federationist*, for printing and selling a translation of Lenin's pamphlet *Left Wing Communism an Infantile Disorder*—was still feared.*[5] Throughout the summer and autumn of 1921 most of the party executive spoke at labour meetings or, like Custance who lectured at the Montreal Labour College as well as in Ottawa in November, went further afield on party business. MacDonald toured as far west as Winnipeg in August and September, one of his chores being to establish firm relations with the Ukrainian revolutionaries in that city.

Despite these concerted efforts it soon became obvious that the newly unified Communist Party of Canada was not making an impact upon the Canadian labour and political scene. Opinions within the party about the CPC's nature and role differed widely, especially after Knight returned from Moscow and reported on the proceedings at the Comintern's Third Congress and the Profintern's initial meeting.

In relation to the American and Canadian parties, the Third Congress was considerably more important than the first two meetings of the International. Within two months of the Comintern-directed unification of both North American parties, the Third International began campaigning for the establishment of open, legal, mass parties, and that campaign, directed particularly at the American delegation, started at the Third Congress. Knight, of course, heard about it. At the Moscow meetings the debates and discussions revolved around the disastrous Ruhr rising in Germany in March 1921, and the growing recognition that the revolutionary wave which Trotsky, Lenin, and other Russian leaders thought would sweep across Europe had receded. The Russian leaders, basing their arguments on the lessons of the German setback and upon the partial but obvious economic recovery in Western capitalist states, insisted that Communist parties outside the Soviet Union give up their immediate revolutionary aspirations and settle down to winning a majority of the industrial and rural workers over to their cause. "To the Masses!," the slogan adopted at the Third Congress, summed up the Russian arguments; the emphasis shifted from small secret parties imbued with revolutionary spirit and doctrinal purity, to large, open organizations.[6] When the Russians told the American delegates to abandon their illegal status and to get out into the open among the working masses, the instruction applied equally and with as much force to the Canadian party.

Knight, besides noting this injunction and reporting it to the Canadian party, also

---

*The case was called to court on September 26 and adjourned until October 10. When it came before the Assize Court on May 12, 1922, the Crown Prosecutor entered a stay of proceedings, which relieved the *Federationist* and Wells of criminal liability.

observed the reluctance of many American members* to abandon their Party's illegal underground status, a reluctance shared by many Canadian party members.[7] Apart from hearing the various attitudes expressed by United States delegates, none of which crystallized into party action or policy, Knight fell in with the general drift of the Russian argument, and his short speech at the Congress foreshadowed the views he expressed to the CPC and the OBU on his return to Canada. Knight's views—he was in complete agreement with Foster, Browder and Batt of the American delegation—countered the anarcho-syndicalist arguments expressed by other American delegates including Gordon Cascaden, the second Canadian representative: notably, that by affiliating with the Comintern, the IWW and the OBU would lose their independence. On July 8, 1921, he declared:

The fear of the domination of the party is absolutely groundless. We do not go into the trade unions and declare that we propose to subject them to ourselves; we subordinate the trade unions to ourselves by working within them, participating in their struggle and winning the confidence of the workers, and finally becoming masters of the situation, to use it for the purposes of the revolution. It is for that reason it is necessary to penetrate into the trade unions, and closely bind them with the party, in order to create a great revolutionary party for the overthrow of capitalism.[8]

In a previous article devoted to the Canadian labour movement, Knight declared that in Canada "the west [was] divided from the East; the western section of the movement being revolutionary and that of the East dominated by the safe and sane petty bourgeois democrats." More important, he stated that there were "enough well-informed and experienced revolutionists to form a real Communist Party and a move in that direction [had] already been made."[9]

Knight returned to Canada as the authorized representative of the Soviet Red Cross, charged by the Comintern and Profintern to persuade the OBU to affiliate with the Moscow labour organization. He reported on his trip to both the Communist party and the OBU, but while his views dovetailed with those held by the Russian leaders and accepted by the majority of the American trade union delegation, they did not necessarily square with those of the OBU. Knight's arguments in favour of openly and promptly affiliating with the Profintern, put forward at the OBU's third annual convention† held in Winnipeg September 26–29, shortly after he returned, were not accepted and the meeting reversed its decision.[10] Knight then gave up his OBU work and instead proceeded to central and western Canada on a speaking tour sponsored by the Canadian Friends of the Soviet Union, to raise money for famine relief in Russia.‡ His regular wage and travelling expenses, together with instructions, came from New York.[11] Occasionally, although he was no longer an OBU organizer, Knight still spoke for that organization.

For the Canadian party the Comintern's decision to establish a united front came as a surprise, and initially many of the leading members were against forming an open, mass party. Steps to launch such a party, however, were taken quickly, first by establishing *The Workers' Guard*, and second, by addressing a call through that organ to all

*Robert Minor of the United States communist movement argued against the idea and tried to make certain that any legal communist organization would be under the unqualified control of the illegal organization. Among the Canadian communists who were loath to give up secrecy of underground activity was the future party leader, Tim Buck.

†Among the delegates were M. Popowich, a leading Ukrainian communist, and J. W. Esselwein, a paperhanger and interior decorator from Regina who was, in reality, an RCMP secret agent.

‡Both Cascaden and Benjamin Gitlow, the former writing at the time, the latter well after he had broken with the American Communist Party, claim that funds ostensibly collected for famine relief were used in reality by the Comintern to finance its work abroad.

socialist, radical, and labour groups for a preliminary conference at which the basic details for such a public party would be worked out.

Delegates to the conference assembled at the Toronto Labour Temple on December 11, 1921. Two days before, a caucus of the underground Communist Party's leading members, supervised by Scott, was held at William Moriarty's house. At the closed meeting the main lines of the conference were agreed upon, and the principal committee members, all trusted party members, were selected. At the public meeting held on December 11, MacDonald, as previously arranged, was unanimously selected as temporary chairman, with Michael Buhay as vice-chairman and Moriarity as temporary secretary.[12] A Credentials Committee of three, including Buck, examined the delegates' qualifications.

MacDonald, in his opening address, outlined the basis of the projected Workers' Party, the name already agreed upon for the public organization. He emphasized the paramount necessity for co-ordination of revolutionary and socialist labour groups in Canada. No national socialist party existed; the SPC was confined almost exclusively to the west, and though it was a useful educational body, it was almost moribund. On the other hand, the Independent Labour Party of Ontario went to the other extreme by claiming that Parliament would emancipate the workers. This argument reduced the workers' militancy and tricked them into accepting parliamentary means as an easy way out of their dilemma. Both organizations had degenerated to mere electoral machines which neglected the workers' needs and struggles. To be successful the Workers' Party had to recognize from the outset its dependence on direct contact with the workers, and active participation in labour struggles such as the capitalist reaction against the campaign for an open shop, then in full swing. Such an innovation, MacDonald felt, threatened to destroy the entire trade union movement in Canada.

Buhay, the vice-chairman, followed the same theme: it was necessary for the new party to participate in all elections to prove the futility of the ballot in bringing about an improvement of the worker's lot, and at the same time, through election campaigns, to establish contact with the greatest possible number of the working class. Inactivity within the new party had to be countered and rooted out. The trade unions, unemployment associations, every strike, had to feel the Workers' Party's presence and support. The party had to work on the twin bases of direct contact and direct action. Florence Custance added a more idealistic note in emphasizing the need for a party of action, one prepared to suffer with the workers in their struggle. Matthew Popowich, speaking for the Ukrainian delegates, told the meeting that the ULTA numbered 3,000, and that the organization was in sympathy with the call to form a national open revolutionary party. A. T. Hill of the Finnish organization claimed a membership of over 2,000, scattered over 60 locals, all of which were waiting for such a public militant party to come into being. He was sure that the entire Finnish membership would come to the Workers' Party.

To provide the conference with guidance and to prepare for the first national convention which was to follow, a five-member By-Laws Committee, which included MacDonald and Tim Buck,* was appointed and a Provisional Organization Commit-

*The other members of the By-Laws Committee included the Ukrainian communist Matthew Popwich, G. Lockhart, and H. Puro, editor of the Finnish paper *Vapaus*. Six points were quickly agreed upon by the Committee and adopted by the meeting. These laid down the size of branches, local executives, dues, and the affiliation of language groups. The Organization Committee included Peel, who was appointed chairman, A. Lyons, M. Buhay, MacDonald, Buck, Florence Custance, J. Boychuk, A. T. Hill, and, as secretary, W. Moriarty.

tee of nine was empowered to carry out organizational work as it saw fit, and to start as many branches as possible. Before the conference closed it approved a *Manifesto* addressed to "Fellow Workers, to Members of the Socialist Party of Canada, to Members of Labour Parties, and to Trade Unionists." The document, in discussing the weaknesses of the workers, pointed out that in the period following the end of the war the workers "neglected to avail [themselves] of the opportunities for consolidating [their] forces," and that they "failed to follow up this example [the Winnipeg General Strike] of what is possible by organized effort."[13] Addressing itself to the trade unionists, the *Manifesto* declared that the WPC sought to prevent attacks on organized labour by the capitalist class by making the unions fighting organizations, by perfecting available trade-union machinery, and by endeavouring to develop the feeling of militancy which would help them to fight back when attacked by the "wolves of capitalism." The *Manifesto* thundered:

Class against class is the order of the day, and we who are the subjected class must learn to fight our battles just as viciously as our oppressors. The industrial weapon is not enough, we must organize our forces so as to take advantage of every weak point in the armour of our oppressors if we are to prosper.[14]

A provisional five-point platform completed the *Manifesto* and summed up the views expressed by MacDonald, Buhay and other delegates who spoke. Number Four clearly delineated the party's nature:

Democratic centralism shall be the guiding principle of the Workers' Party and all members will be required to submit to the direction of the party in all struggles affecting the workers, such as unemployment, wage reductions, open shop campaigns, etc.[15]

One of the declared intentions in the provisional platform was that the party eventually would acquire a party press, to be under the control and direction of the National Executive Committee.

Immediately following the conference MacDonald set out on a tour which took him as far west as Vancouver. His object was to contact party members, to establish groups wherever possible, and to make arrangements for the first formal convention. Before he embarked on the tour, letters were sent by various delegates who attended the December 11 meeting to other radicals whom they considered reliable and who lived at points where MacDonald expected to speak, urging them to form Workers' Party groups, and to make contact with MacDonald. Popowich, the Ukrainian leader, for example, wrote to J. W. Esselwein (the RCMP undercover agent whom he had met at the third annual OBU convention in September) to tell him that a new party, the Workers' Party of Canada, had been formed at a provisional conference in Toronto. Soon after Esselwein received Popowich's letter "an organizer came through and organized branches there [i.e. Regina, Saskatchewan]."[16] The organizer was MacDonald, and with Esselwein's eager assistance two meetings were held in the city, and a party branch formed. At one meeting MacDonald met Malcolm L. Bruce, a sharp-tongued socialist who often spoke at labour gatherings. As a result of the contact Bruce joined the local group formed during MacDonald's brief pause in Regina, and subsequently was sent by the branch as a delegate to the first convention of the Workers' Party.[17]

Some of the *ad hoc* arrangements of MacDonald's tour and the problems besetting initial party organization have been recalled by E. R. Fay, an early CPC member.

In December 1921 Jack MacDonald came through organizing the provincial organization of the Workers' Party. I got him to speak to the Central Council meeting on unemployment, and I had an interview with him later the same night. I told him that if the Calgary Local of the S.P. of C. and the Dominion Committee had taken no action by the time the Inaugural Convention was held in February I would get a group of five together and form an English Language Branch of the Workers' Party in time to have representation at the Convention.

He gave me supplies and stamps and as nothing had been done by the end of January 1 spoke to four who I knew had voted for affiliation. They agreed to form the Branch. ... we met at Goss's Barbershop on Fourth Street East. ... Altogether, we were an international group [it included a Greek, a Ukrainian Jew, an Englishman, and an Irishman in addition to the Anglo-Scottish author] .... We credentialled J. R. Knight as our delegate to the Convention of the Workers' Party (February, 1922), so that we could get a full report of what took place.[18]

MacDonald's public speeches echoed those made by delegates who attended the meeting announced through *The Workers' Guard*, to establish the Worker's Party of Canada. During the tour MacDonald revealed that the initial convention was scheduled for the end of February 1922, and that delegates would then decide if the Workers' Party would affiliate with the Communist International.[19] In realistic terms, there was little doubt about affiliation. Through the selection of delegates, and because the executive was pre-determined, the convention's role was simply one of approving formally and in an outwardly democratic manner what in fact had already been decided. To those considered reliable (Esselwein was included), MacDonald revealed that the Workers' Party was, in reality, the Communist Party's mass movement. Ultimate control, therefore, rested with the Comintern.

In turn Scott, as the Comintern's representative in Canada, also lost little time in exploiting MacDonald's initiative. Within a matter of weeks he too toured western Canada in order to confirm MacDonald's assessment of the feeling prevailing among the country's radicals, and to follow up the more likely contacts established during the latter's journey. Scott's efforts met with variable success. In Winnipeg he tried hard to induce the One Big Union to ally itself with the Workers' Party at the forthcoming convention, but he failed to convince R. B. Russell, the OBU leader, who refused to commit himself. In Vancouver he managed to obtain temporary control over the poverty-stricken radical paper, *The B.C. Federationist*.* In terms of organization, however, as E. R. Fay confirms, Scott's follow-up efforts were more successful: "In a few weeks the [Calgary] Party Branch had grown to 30 members after a visit from Bob Mogridge and Charlie Scott."[20]

The contrast between the two journeys is striking. MacDonald announced his coming and permitted his presence to be publicized;† Scott came and went without fanfare, making his contacts quietly, if not surreptitiously. Between them they succeeded in stirring up considerable interest as well as causing much disquiet among the OBU and some socialist groups. Nevertheless, the degree of optimism expressed by *The Workers' Guard*, January, 14 1922, during MacDonald's western swing, was unwarranted:

Our national organizer, Comrade MacDonald reports that his reception in Winnipeg would revive the spirits of any jaded revolutionist. The secession of the 26 English-speaking comrades of the Soc. [*sic*] Party of Winnipeg Local, who favoured affiliation with the Third (Communist) International, left but four centrists with the Soc. Party of Canada.[21]

According to the same despatch the Workers' Party strength in Winnipeg stood at

---

*The object was to obtain a legal publication for the party in western Canada, and to prevent the paper from falling into the hands of the Socialist Party of Canada, the leading members of which refused to affiliate with the proposed new party.

†MacDonald's itinerary included Timmins, Ontario; Regina, Moose Jaw, and Saskatoon, Saskatchewan; Edmonton and Calgary, Alberta; Nelson and Vancouver, B.C. He spoke in Winnipeg, Manitoba, on January 2, 1922.

290, but the local organizers declared it would reach 400 by the middle of February. And in central Canada, which *The Workers' Guard*, February 14, 1922, asserted was "the present stronghold of the Party," a similar degree of success was claimed: "We have practically entrenched ourselves in all the industrial centres throughout Ontario."

Initial efforts to launch the open party were not as simple or easy as *The Workers' Guard* intimated. Indeed, in the very same issue of January 14, 1922, the paper openly complained that organization work and mass propaganda were being hampered in Toronto by civic authorities who curtailed the party's activities by shutting down meeting places. Moreover, soon after MacDonald began his tour, the thorny question of affiliation with the Comintern began to intrude, and in Vancouver the SPC local declined to approve the link. As a result, those backing the Workers' Party, led by J. Kavanagh, President of the Longshoremen's Union in Vancouver, J. M. Clark, General Secretary of the Lumber Workers' Industrial Union, and A. S. Wells, *The B.C. Federationist's* editor, succeeded in further splitting the already weakened Socialist Party organization.

Much of the suspicion and resistance which greeted MacDonald's proposals stemmed from a lengthy pamphlet, *Shall Unionism Die?*, written by Gordon Cascaden, the second Canadian delegate at the Comintern-Profintern congresses, which gained wide currency in Canadian labour circles. In his account, which was serialized under a different title in *Alberta Labour News*, the official organ of the Alberta Federation of Labour, Cascaden described his experiences in Moscow, and pointed up the Profintern's aims and intentions.[22]

On the basis of his observations Cascaden objected to the policies advocated by communist parties—and the objection was precisely that put forward by most socialist groups and parties—because the communists insisted that a political party took precedence over a strictly trade union or labour-type organization, and that all organizations not submitting to the theories, practices, and discipline inherent in a communist party, must be destroyed:*

Communist political party advocates therefore must try to gain control of these [dissenting] unions to build up their political parties, and if the unions happen to be of a kind favoring labor's control of the means of wealth production, then they must try to win their support until such time as the political party may conquer them and convert them into mere schools for political party communism.[23]

The Moscow meeting, he charged, was clearly rigged, with delegations not committed to a "Labor Union First" programme being given the most votes. Thus, the Russian and Czechoslovak delegations, for example, got 16 votes, while Canada, which was lumped in with Rumania and Azerbadjan, was empowered with eight.[24] Also, Cascaden complained about the chairman's (Lozovsky's) autocratic attitude and actions at the Congress; about the unfair actions of Reinstein, the resident American Communist Party representative in Moscow and Secretary of the Credentials Committee, in seating delegates and in cross-examining Cascaden in an attempt to discover the latter's attitude towards the Comintern and towards the formation of a Canadian Communist Party. In particular, Cascaden was extremely bitter about Knight's opposition to his being given a decisive vote, and for bringing a charge, the nature of which was never revealed, against him. He asked,

Why did Knight, whose pulpit-texts of "Get out of the American Federation of Labor" and "Destroy the American Federation of Labor" [which] were heard from Vancouver to Montreal, vote in Moscow to destroy ... [the] One Big Union, which he represented?[25]

*According to Cascaden it was Bukharin, who made it clear, before the Profintern Congress got under way, that labour unions must be "schools for Communist political party activities."

The accusation was well founded, and indeed, proved an accurate forecast of the fluctuations and uncertainties which subsequently characterized Canadian labour politics. For example, on the strength of Cascaden's report to the Edmonton district of the Lumber Workers' Industrial Union, the Edmonton local refused to affiliate with the RILU. However, at the Lumber Workers' next convention held in Vancouver in January 1922, the union voted to affiliate with the Profintern, and expelled the Edmonton district.[26] More immediately, Cascaden's articles caused many of the less extreme labour groups, especially those which had not committed themselves to any political alliances, to examine the nascent Workers' Party and its subordinate units much more critically.

While accounts of the Moscow meeting, together with varying degrees of resistance from the Socialist Party, the OBU, and other labour groups combined to impede the Workers' Party's initial development, they did not prevent its birth. On balance, MacDonald's tour showed results, and, in addition to Toronto, branches were started in Montreal, Ottawa, Hamilton, Niagara Falls, Guelph, Kitchener, Edmonton, and Vancouver.[27] On February 17, 1922, 63 delegates from these units, together with "a number of fraternal delegates from trade unions and the One Big Union" met at the Labour Temple in Toronto to launch the new party.[28] The distribution of delegates clearly reveals the areas from which the embryonic communist movement drew its strength: forty-two came from Ontario; five from Quebec; and the remainder from the west.*

The presence of non-communist fraternal delegates at the convention re-emphasized the need for the WPC to define its attitude towards existing labour organizations. At the preliminary conference held in December 1921 a committee was appointed to examine the question, but before its report was brought down at the innaugural public meeting, Earl Browder of the American Communist Party and editor of *The Labor Herald*, the Trade Union Educational League's (TUEL) official organ, delivered a forceful, disturbing address. What made Browder's words so significant in the context of the Workers' Party founding convention was the TUEL's own change in doctrinal attitude since its formation in 1920 by W. Z. Foster. Before Foster's conversion to communism the TUEL stood for an easy-going evolution from craft unions to industrial unions, and from industrial unions to labour's ultimate victory and the destruction of capitalism. After the RILU's birth the League added the dictatorship of the proletariat and the defence of the Soviet Union to its programme, and these, together with its opposition to dual unionism, squared with the Comintern's united front policy.[29]

The gist of Browder's talk was that the AF of L was the most reactionary labour body in the world, and that the American revolutionaries had been mistaken in withdrawing from that body in order to form ideal unions of their own. The lesson, he suggested, was that revolutionaries should establish a network of committees in every town, village, and hamlet throughout North America, and at the same time, fuse the many existing trade unions into industrial unions. The final step was to persuade them to affiliate with the RILU. Such a plan formed the basis of the TUEL's programme, and Browder strongly urged that the WPC should begin its existence by

*The convention's business arrangements were put in the hands of four committees. These were: Constitutional, made up of Buck, Hill, and Navis; Programme, Bell, Buhay, and Spector; Resolutions, Blugerman, Lloyd, and a third member, unknown; Arrangements, Bell, Blugerman, and Greenburg. The latter group organized a highly successful and profitable convention dance which was held on Friday, February 17 at Mosher's Arcade, 623 College Street.

following the precedent of working in harmony with the League established by the Workers' Party of America.[30]

Discussion, sparked by Browder's words, became heated over a resolution declaring that the WPC pledge itself to support all efforts made within existing unions towards consolidating the trade union movement by amalgamating related crafts on the basis of one union for each industry. The resolution brought sharp reaction from the OBU delegate, R. B. Russell, who labelled Scott a foreign agitator, and who warned the convention that the new party would fail as a political organization if the measure were adopted. Russell's stand was immediately attacked by MacDonald, the two Buhays, Malcolm Bruce, and Spector, all of whom charged that the OBU was a pure syndicalist movement doomed to irrevocable failure.[31] The resolution itself, however, was approved with little difficulty. By approving it, the convention went on record as being diametrically opposed to the OBU's policies and practices, and in effect, reversed the earlier Comintern directive calling for co-operation under the leadership of existing labour organizations such as the IWW and the OBU. By passing the resolution the WPC, in effect, created a permanent breach between itself, the OBU, and other less revolutionary labour organizations in Canada. In turn, the new party emerged from the convention firmly in the Comintern camp, pledged to follow the labour policies and practices advocated by the TUEL. Indeed, the platform which the convention adopted was almost identical with that approved by the meeting at which the Workers' Party of America came into being in New York, December 23–26.[32]

At the Toronto convention, too, the relationship between the foreign language groups and the Workers' Party was clarified. The Finnish Socialist Organization, represented by J. Ahlqvist, H. Puro, A. T. Hill, and J. Lund, affiliated outright with the WPC, having decided to do so at its convention held on February 16.[33] The Ukrainian Labour Temple Association, through its representative John Boychuk, also accepted the new party's leadership, but divisions within the ULTA precluded the same arrangement which the Finnish revolutionaries followed.[34] These varying arrangements between the WPC and the language groups, which Buck describes as a social democratic form of organization, lasted until 1925.

In addition, the meeting approved a constitution and elected an eight-man National Executive Committee (NEC).* Early in March, soon after the delegates dispersed, the Central Executive Committee (CEC) held its first meeting at which five District Organizers were appointed, party posts allocated, and the party's geographical structure determined. The latter, arrived at by dividing Canada into six districts and by following the pattern evolved by socialist parties in North America, was based upon the provincial divisions,† except where industrial developments such as the mining regions in British Columbia and Alberta made it practical to follow other arrangements.[35] In keeping with the formation of the new party, *The Workers' Guard*

---

*The Committee included John Kavanagh, J. G. Smith of Vancouver; J. MacDonald from Toronto; W. Gilbert from Winnipeg; Malcolm Bruce from Regina; and Michael Buhay of Montreal. W. Moriarty and Trevor Maguire, both from Toronto, were appointed secretary and assistant secretary.

†The Districts and their appointed organizers were: District One (Maritime Provinces), appointment postponed; District Two (Quebec and Ottawa), Michael Buhay; District Three (Ontario, from Port Arthur to Quebec but excluding Ottawa), Tim Buck; District Four (Saskatchewan, Manitoba, and Ontario up to Port Arthur), H. M. Bartholomew; District Five (Alberta, including District 18, United Mine Workers of America), R. Mogridge; District Six (British Columbia, exclusive of District 18), W. Bennett.

was transformed into *The Worker*, and put under the general direction of J. Kavanagh.*
In general however, the transformation was limited. The Central Executive Committee, the real seat of power in the Party, continued to be a reflection of the dominant
personalities who had been in the communist movement from the beginning. Neither
Custance nor Bell was elected to the open party's executive committees,† an omission
stemming from their personal differences and from Scott's lingering doubts about the
political reliability of Custance.[36] Nevertheless, despite such differences, the overt
party was truly launched. Significantly, the main lines of policy and the slates of
elected officers had been settled and approved by Scott at a pre-convention meeting of
CPC members held at 271 Manning Avenue on February 16. Thus, from the outset,
control of the new party remained firmly in the hands of those approved of by
Moscow.

---

*Kavanagh was appointed by Scott. *The Worker* was to be patterned after the American party
paper of the same name published in New York.

†The CEC consisted of: National Chairman, J. MacDonald; Vice Chairman, M. Armstrong;
Executive Secretary, W. Moriarty; Assistant Secretary, T. Maguire; Industrial Director, T. Buck;
Assistant Industrial Director, F. Brown; Editor-in-Chief of *The Worker*, J. Kavanagh; Associate
Editors, F. J. Peel and Maurice Spector.

CHAPTER FIVE

UNDERGROUND OPERATIONS AND THE CPC

FROM THE MOMENT that unity was achieved at Guelph one problem dominated the Canadian communist movement: what was to be the role of the underground party and the relationship between it and any open party which, it was expected, eventually would follow. Indeed, after some initial but fairly stiff resistance, it was never doubted by most of the CPC leaders that an open party ultimately would be formed, and much of their thinking during the months between Guelph and the Toronto gathering held on December 11, 1921, was devoted to that problem. Consequently, by the time that the preliminary conference was held the roles of both the underground and the open parties, referred to respectively as "Z" and "A" parties by the communist leaders, had been determined.[1]

"Z" was to be the driving force. The underground party was to lead the overt party in the direction dictated by the Comintern, and was to set an example of hard, self-sacrificing work, the hallmark of a revolutionary elite. The influence and control exerted by "Z" on "A," it was felt, must be a genuine leadership and not a dictatorial rule; the executives at the most important organizational levels of "A" should include a numerical majority of "Z" members, but not a complete "Z" executive, since that would prevent the conversion of promising individuals to the communist cause and their subsequent education and training in communist principles. The small "Z" group would be able to control "A" more effectively than a large, loosely organized body. It was the duty of every "Z" member continually to assess non-"Z" members belonging to the "A" party with the object of recruiting the most promising for the clandestine body. The underground unit was to pay particular attention to the supply and distribution of suitable literature for the "A" party and, where possible, "Z" members were instructed to do their best to be elected "literature agents" in the overt party's groups. Special attention was to be given to ex-servicemen, especially those who were disillusioned by their experiences during and after the war, since they, the party felt, were an influential portion of the working masses.

From the start, all important matters scheduled on the agenda before "A" party conventions were dealt with at "Z" conventions which always preceded the open party's gatherings. The "A" meetings formally approved the preselected slates of officers, and important policies which the "Z" meetings determined, and dealt with minor matters which were not considered by the underground party.[2] Such was the pattern of events which took place before the preliminary gathering held on December 11, 1921, and the first WPC meeting in February 1922. With the launching of "A," and the establishment of its mouthpiece, *The Worker* (known in this context as "K") during the period following the first WPC convention, it became particularly urgent to form as many new "A" groups as possible. It was equally important to keep

E

promising individuals, as well as the remnants of such radical organizations as the IWW, under observation.

Secrecy was the keynote of this philosophy, since it was imperative that the relationship of "Z" not be disclosed. In turn, any delicate operations were undertaken by trusted "Z" members. For example, the Comintern representative to the United States party, Professor H. Valetski, a Polish mathematician, entered the United States illegally from Canada by way of Niagara Falls in July 1922, after being escorted by a "Z" member of the CPC.*[3] The members of "Z" were known in the underground movement by pseudonyms which were usually kept secret from most of the party. These pseudonyms were known only to the secretary and other members of the Executive who dealt with official correspondence.[4]

The communication chain extended from the "Z" Central Executive to the District Committees, with the District Committees responsible for the distribution of confidential party mail throughout their area. Often directives from the "Z" Central Executive Committee or the party secretary were transmitted in code,† or sent to reliable party addresses.[5] Security was continually emphasized, and any action on the part of the authorities both in Canada and the United States prompted the CEC and the District Organizers to take immediate action. Following the break-up of the secret Communist Party of America convention held at Bridgeman, Michigan, in August 1922, Tom Bell, then the CPC's Organizer for Manitoba and Saskatchewan —District Four of the WPC—warned each party group to take strict precautions. In a letter dated Winnipeg, August 24, 1922, he wrote to the Secretary of the party's Regina branch:

> The American papers are carrying a story of the break up of the "Z" convention last Monday. Seventeen of the delegates were arrested and a search is being conducted for those who escaped including four men from across [presumably from across the Canadian border and possibly even from Russia]. At the same time the offices of the TUEL were raided and all documents taken away. Foster who escaped the first raid has since been arrested. I have wired to stop anyone going to Chicago.
>
> These happenings make it necessary for us to be somewhat careful since the names of comrades on this side may have been seized in the raids. Therefore you will see that comrades who have been in correspondence with Chicago will clean their houses in case there should be any visits from the police. Of course, there may be no necessity for caution but it would be foolhardy to take any chances.
>
> All the stuff of the "A" party will be quite respectable, all "Z" stuff should be hidden or destroyed. Send no letters to the States until you hear that things have been fixed up. Also be careful what you say in letters to the offices of party "A" here [Winnipeg]. Yours, Gregg.[6]

The letter, complete with its "Z" party pseudonym, typifies the attitudes held and the actions taken by the Communist Party of Canada throughout the interval between the first convention at which the public Workers' Party was launched, and the second convention held a year later. Unknown to the sender, the Secretary of the party's Regina branch who received the communication was also an RCMP undercover agent.

With the formation of the overt Workers' Party, Moscow's subsidization of the Canadian communist movement ended. Indeed, little money for organization and similar current expenses was given to the Canadian communist party because, after the initial grant of $3,000 made at Guelph, the Comintern felt that in a relatively prosperous country such as Canada the movement in the Dominion ought to be self-supporting. If support were continued, Moscow argued, it would tend to undermine the party's own efforts to make itself financially sound.[7]

---

*On the basis of interviews, Valetski's escort has been identified as Trevor Maguire.

†According to evidence at the trial of Buck and others in 1931 the code used was of the cipher type based on a specific page in a predetermined publication.

The difficulties in doing so, however, soon became apparent. Inexperience and lack of organization, together with the heavy initial outlay for items such as office supplies, party emblems, dues stamps, membership cards, caused "the inevitable financial troubles of a working class organization."[8] A review of the WPC's finances at the second convention confirmed that monetarily the Finnish and Ukrainian sections were the backbone of the party, but that revenues were insufficient to meet the party's needs.[9] According to the CEC report presented by Moriarty, Districts Two and Three (Quebec and Ontario) were the best organized and fairly sound financially. Party organization had just got under way in District One (Maritimes), while District Four (Saskatchewan, Manitoba, and Ontario up to Port Arthur), despite a preponderance of Finnish and Ukrainian supporters and the appointment of Tom Bell as organizer, was the least well organized. According to the report the Finnish membership, totalling 2,028, contributed nearly $3,200, by far the largest amount collected within the party, while the Ukrainian organization, with 880 members, added nearly $900. Returns from the other districts were in the order of a few hundred dollars, and the total party receipts from all quarters did not exceed $5,300. In the same vein, the convention of the underground Communist or "Z" party, which preceded the WPC convention, confirmed that the "Z" section had helped to subsidize *The Worker*, and provided funds for special organization work. Such assistance, it was felt, was consistent with the "Z" party's chief task, that of strengthening "A" and transforming it into an open mass communist party.[10]

The Canadian communist movement's financial problems did not end when its two wings, the overt Workers' Party and the underground Communist Party, merged into a single unit in the spring of 1924. On the first day of the Workers' Party Third Convention, held on April 18–20 at the Labour Temple, Toronto, MacDonald, in his capacity of Secretary, presented a statement of the Party's financial standing for the period February 1923 to March 31, 1924. During that interval the WPC received $13,045.63 from membership dues, sale of literature, supplies, and special assessments. Payments for office equipment, wages, organizers travelling costs, 1923 convention expenses, literature, and "sundry" expenditure totalled $10,522.42. Apart from the surplus, which was quickly devoured by convention costs, loans to District Three, and a small contribution to *International Press Correspondence*, the figures listed by MacDonald indicate the limited scope and scale of the communist movement's activities during its early days. Significantly, the proportion of income given over to "sundry" expenses—which were never explained—totalled $2,883.03, roughly a quarter of the total expenditure for the period.[11] Whatever the party's needs, money was always in short supply and hard to obtain, a condition that worsened throughout the decade.[12]

Soon after the Communist Party of Canada emerged into the open under that title a delegation, led by Buck, attempted to obtain a Comintern subsidy for the CPC. However, O. A. Piatnitsky, a pre-revolutionary Bolshevik and the Organization Bureau's (Orgburo's)* indefatigable watch dog, turned down the request on the

*The Orgburo was established at the Fourth Comintern Congress held in November-December, 1922. Although its functions have been at best vaguely defined, E. H. Carr describes it as the most important of the new organs provided for in the Congress. The Orgburo's functions consisted of looking after the improvement of the organization of communist parties, supervising and controlling the Comintern's illegal activities. After the Fifth Congress held in July 1924, Piatnitsky was named to the Comintern's budget commission. No proceedings or reports of that body's activities have ever been published, just as nothing has been published about the financial aid given by the Comintern to its member parties.

grounds that the CPC was getting along reasonably well, and that other Communist International sections were in greater need of assistance. Indeed, on the basis of interviews and reports of meetings it is clear that the CPC received proportionately less assistance from Moscow than, for example, did the American party.*[13] The reasons for the Comintern's stand are clear. The Canadian party was one of its less important components, and this was a major factor in determining the nature and extent of Soviet assistance. At the same time, however, the CPC was also one of Comintern's more self-sufficient units. Piatnitsky's refusal, of course, did not mean that the Canadian Party was left solely to its own devices for raising money, particularly money required for confidential Comintern work. In general, all expenses incurred in such missions were charged to Moscow, which usually paid the expected expenses in advance or, if the party had put out its own money, refunded the costs after a strict accounting. The amount of Comintern aid to the CPC thus not only fluctuated, but at the best of times it was never sufficient to spare the Canadian communist movement from an almost continuous financial crisis. One result was that full-time party workers such as Buck, MacDonald, and Spector were continuously called upon to make sacrifices of time and money to meet the party's needs, and it was as much in the interests of efficiency as anything else that the request for a subsidy was made.[14]

The scale of pay for party organizers in 1922–23 provides a valuable glimpse of party life and party finances. Remuneration ranged from a minimum of $15 per week to $30 per week for leading members of the Central Executive Committee. While an organizer was travelling away from his operational base the party covered all travel and living expenses. For trips abroad the CPC made special collections to defray the delegate's expenses as far as the Soviet border. Once inside the USSR the Comintern covered all costs. Expenses for delegates not only included the funds required to travel abroad, but also payments for dependent's remaining in Canada. Spector, for example, received over $300 from the party to attend the Comintern's Fourth Congress in 1922, while his dependents received a $65 subsistence allowance. MacDonald's wife received $280 during her husband's absence, an amount equalling that given to MacDonald to enable him to reach Russia.[15]

That the Canadian party's request for assistance was made to Piatnitsky was not accidental nor unusual. Nor did it indicate a particular channel of communication to the centre of Comintern influence, for Piatnitsky, as Benjamin Gitlow makes clear, was a power to be reckoned with within the Comintern, and as head of the Orgburo, the logical person to approach for money and any other assistance special problems required.

His department [the Orgburo] took care of the finances, the passports, secret service work, and kept check on all the Communist parties of the Communist International ... with the exception of the Russian Party, which was a power unto itself and the real boss of the International.[16]

The Canadian delegation's approach simply followed an established procedure.

They [the Comintern] have a meeting of the executive committee of the Communist International at which requests for funds are made by various parties. They have a special committee that handles it,

---

*In this context it is worth noting Theodore Draper's assessment of the nature and volume of assistance received by the United States party from Moscow. "There is little doubt", he writes, "that American Communism received considerable outside financial aid in the first fifteen years of its existence. At minimum this aid in all its ramifications probably totaled half a million dollars. This money was generally allotted for special purposes rather than as a means of existence."

generally headed by Piatnitsky . . . . That committee brings in a report to the executive, and the executive approves the report. Then the money is voted and it is transmitted to the various parties.[17]

While the Canadian delegation's approach for money proved unsuccessful, the connection with Piatnitsky and the Orgburo was firmly cemented. The contact was the natural outcome of the Canadian party convention's decision "to continue with an underground apparatus but to do away with the payment of dues etc.,"[18] That decision in turn squared with the third of the Twenty-One points, which insisted upon all parties maintaining a secret underground wing.[19] Until the Fifth Congress the Comintern was continually organizing its departments and, of course, applying its experiences in dealing with member parties. Up to the time Buck, Bruce, and Hill arrived in Moscow the connection with the CPC for confidential tasks was not precise nor firmly fixed. There is little doubt that as a result of their presence in Moscow the main details of confidential work which the Comintern required in Canada were settled, and that in the process Buck became one of the key figures for such tasks within the CPC.

At the same time the Canadian party became an important component in the prosecution of clandestine communist activities in North America. *The Report of the Royal Commission* (1946) makes clear that from 1924 there was "an organization at work in Canada directed from Russia and operating with Communist sympathizers in Canada" because secret operations for North America could be carried out more easily and conveniently from the Dominion.[20] Montreal, because of its geographical situation and because it was an international port, became the convenient point of entry or exit for Comintern agents and representatives seconded for duty to the American party. Valetski reached the United States by way of Montreal and a route through Ontario, while in 1925 Green (Gusev), the most important Russian representative to come to North America, returned to Russia by way of Canada.[21] On the other side of the country, Vancouver was also used by the Comintern as an entry and departure point for its agents and couriers. Jan Valtin tells about Michel Avaton, the Comintern's Lettish agent bound for Vancouver who, during the voyage, "volunteered no information about his assignment there."[22]

Canada and the Canadian party also became important in another respect, for the CPC was able to furnish the American party and the Comintern with passports which enabled United States party and Comintern agents to travel abroad with little or no trouble. The apparatus required for, and the method of obtaining a Canadian passport was, as Gitlow makes clear, quite simple.

We had, at the time [1927], a set-up in Montreal, Canada, an agency for the purpose, and it was centred in an . . . export-import house . . . that had very excellent connections with the passport bureau of the Canadian Government and which also did work for the Soviet Union in that respect. . . . we would go through Canada to make out the [passport] application in Canada. Then the application was mailed to Ottawa, and then [the acquired passport] was mailed [by the CPC] to us in New York and we used it in New York to board ship for Europe and into the Soviet Union.[23]

Gitlow himself used the alias "James Hay" in the Canadian passport he obtained by such means in 1927.[24] According to Gitlow, the American party leader, Jay Lovestone, was among those who made use of falsely acquired Canadian travel documents. He also notes that at the time of the raid by Scotland Yard on the headquarters of the Soviet trading organization in London, the All Russia Co-operative Society (Arcos), a number of United States Communist Party leaders were travelling under assumed names on Canadian passports "obtained by a Canadian communist, an OGPU [the

Soviet secret police] contact in Montreal engaged in the import and export business."[25]
The import-export business was headed by Nathan Mendelsohn, a relative of Mrs.
Ray Press Mendelsohn, who was arrested in 1919 for radical activities.*

Undoubtedly too, the establishment of a Soviet trade mission, the equivalent of
Arcos, in Montral in 1924, materially facilitated such discreet operations as obtaining
Canadian passports for Comintern use, or passing along instructions to the Canadian
and American parties.[26] During the three years that the Soviet agency remained in
Montreal its premises at 212 Drummond Street were frequently visited by MacDonald,
Spector, Buck, Custance, Michael Buhay, and other leading Canadian party members.
According to British authorities the seizure of Arcos documents by Scotland Yard in
the spring of 1927 clearly established that the Soviet society's quarters in London had
been used "as a centre of military espionage and Communist activities both in the
United States [and], the Dominions," and that among the seizures was a list of secret
addresses for communication with Communist Parties in North America.[27] Among
the names and addresses discovered in the London raid were those of MacDonald,
Spector, Tim Buck and his wife, who was listed as Alice Ayres, Mrs. Mary Sutcliffe,
and E. Pirtinnen.[28] One result of the Arcos raid was that the Soviet mission in
Montreal was forced to close, thus eliminating a facility of considerable usefulness to
the Comintern and its Canadian ancillary.[29] The collection of information and the
acquisition of passports and other Canadian documents thus was shifted elsewhere.

A Canadian passport was particularly useful because it "was good for 5 years and
could be renewed for another 5 years," thus saving the recipient the trouble of getting
another document for a period of 10 years.[30] Genuine or "legitimate" passports—
according to Gitlow "illegitimate" passports were documents which were forged at the
Comintern's two "passport factories" located in Berlin and Moscow—eventually
found their way "into the hands of the OGPU where exact duplicates were forged
which, together with the originals, were supplied to its agents and spies for their
personal use in travelling over the world."[31]

As the CPC developed, such activities became an inevitable corollary of the party's
link with the Comintern. At best, however, only a small minority of the Canadian
party were ever directly involved in the conspiratorial tasks set by Moscow, and the
majority of the membership remained unaware of the confidential work carried out on
the Comintern's instructions by the select group. In turn, the CPC devoted the bulk of
its efforts to gaining mass influence by means which were conspicuously non-conspira-
torial. Class warfare was projected openly upon the Canadian public by agitators and
lecturers, newspapers and periodicals, but to little or no avail, for the working man,
in terms of party membership or endorsing the communist viewpoint at the polls,
remained indifferent throughout. Handicapped as an effective political organization
by its numerical weakness and by its polyglot character, the Canadian party, despite
its greatest efforts, remained almost totally isolated from the Canadian scene.

*See Chapter Three.

CHAPTER SIX

THE CPC AND THE FOURTH COMINTERN CONGRESS

WITH THE FAILURE of the Canadian communist leaders to co-opt the OBU into the Workers' Party fold at the first WPC convention, the party leaders embarked upon a concentrated effort to organize and publicize the new body. In effect, the set back was a failure to bring about a united front from above through co-operation with OBU and other labour leaders in the Dominion. In turn, and as a reaction to failure, a concerted attempt to create a united front from below under exclusive communist leadership was initiated through the party press, and tours by leading Canadian party members.

In May and June 1922, Buck covered Ontario, then proceeded west before travelling to Chicago to attend the first TUEL convention.[1] MacDonald, meanwhile, covered the Maritime provinces. Early in April a Women's Bureau, headed by Florence Custance, was formed with the express object of educating women to take a greater part in the revolutionary struggle, and to organize themselves in order to avoid exploitation and being driven into prostitution.[2] A short time later Custance, as Secretary Treasurer of the front organization, the Canadian Friends of Soviet Russia, went abroad to attend a meeting of the International Workers' Aid (MRP)*[3] Conference in Berlin. More important, during her absence she was selected to be the Canadian party's extra delegate to the Fourth Comintern Congress, a move calculated to win her over to the CEC, and so end any factionalism still existing within the party's inner circles.[4] Originally, J. Kavanagh was selected to attend as a third delegate,† but that decision was countermanded because the party could not afford to have experienced organizers away for a comparatively long period at such a crucial time in the public party's life.[5] In July, too, the Workers' Party established the Young Workers' League (YWL) with Trevor Maguire as Secretary, which aimed "to create a more sympathetic interest in the affairs of labor; to teach the young workers of Canada that they [were] distinctly subject to the influences of Canadian capitalistic development."[6]

Soon after completing his organizational tour, MacDonald, with Spector, (both had been designated by Scott to attend the Comintern's Fourth Congress), set out for Russia.[7] The two delegates travelled together via New York, England, and Berlin, leaving Toronto at the end of September. Before they left, a meeting of the underground Communist Party's Central Executive was held in Winnipeg at which the movement's progress was reviewed, and where the two delegates received instructions on the points the party expected them to raise in Moscow. These were brought into clearer focus by communications from Florence Custance, already in Berlin at the

*The MRP (the initials stand for the Russian designation Mezhdunarodnoi Rabotnichi Pomoschii) was established in Berlin on September 12, 1921, under Muenzenberg's chairmanship.
†At the time of the WPC convention Scott also proposed that Bell should be a delegate.

MRP conference. She confirmed that virtually no material about the Canadian party or Canadian politics, economics, or labour development, had reached the Comintern, so that little was known of the Communist Party of Canada or its open counterpart, the WPC. At the same time she emphasized how much importance the German Communist Party (KPD) attached to the united front programme promulgated by the Comintern, as well as the German party's efforts to establish Workers' Councils in factories, and its work in spreading popular slogans such as "equal pay for women" as widely as possible.[8] At the Winnipeg meeting the CEC approved what Scott had been pressing for from the time the Canadian party came into being: "that the party should send fraternal delegates to the [Fourth Comintern] Congress." The reasons publicly put forward for so doing were highly idealistic:

It was felt that the interests of the Party could be served by showing our sympathies with the principles of the Third International in this manner. It was further felt that by so doing we would indicate that the Workers' Party was a definite part of the world movement of the working class, and as such could justly claim that we are moving along the paths of International Association which will eventually establish the proletarian dictatorship.[9]

MacDonald, who was also delegated to attend the Profintern's Second Congress (November 19—December 2, 1922) as the TUEL's (Canadian Section) representative, and Spector, backed by the Canadian party, supported by Custance's reports from Germany and financed through collections "made by individual approach since circumstances would not permit a public appeal," left with the firm resolve that they would press for Comintern recognition that the two Canadian communist parties, underground and public, were separate, independent entities from the American parties, and that they should be treated as such by the Comintern. Their case, as a *Report* written by the delegates on their return to Toronto indicates, was thoroughly prepared and detailed:

The International delegates went to Moscow with long and complete reports of every phase of the activities of "Z" and "A". These reports were prepared by C.E.C. and addressed to the Presidium. . . . Care was taken to report statistics as exactly as possible. The figures of "Z" and "A" were tabulated district by district. In addition, these reports contained the policy of "Z" as an open party, as adopted at the Underground "Z" conference of last year. That policy was to transform "A" as rapidly as possible into an open "Z" party and to transform "Z" into an emergency apparatus of the open "Z".[10]

For the last year, the *Report* continued, the CPC had exerted every effort to transform the "A" party, described as the "legal apparatus of the underground party," into an open communist party which would be the only section of the Comintern in Canada:

Over this policy there has been no factional dispute, nor has there been any question of "mechanical control", such as agitated the American Movement. In accordance with our policy we ceased publication of the underground organ [*The Communist*], and we published all documents of the Comintern in the Organ of the "A" Party [*The Worker*]. The program of the "A" Party had already [included] the principle of proletarian dictatorship for the past year.[11]

Thus prepared, MacDonald and Spector set out for Moscow. Before they left, various rearrangements were made within the party organization. Tom Bell took up his post as District Organizer in Winnipeg, thus removing one of the chief disruptive elements from the party centre, while arrangements were concluded to have Malcolm Bruce come to Toronto from Regina to become editor of *The Worker* during Spector's absence.[12]

The *Report*, which MacDonald and Spector carried to the Fourth Congress, covered the communist movement's development in Canada since the Guelph convention, and reflected a certain measure of optimism. Unity had been achieved with a minimum of disruption and friction within the party; in keeping with the Comintern's injunction to make contact with the working masses an open party complete with a women's section and a youth league had been launched publicly; and overtures to the Canadian Labor Party and to the dissident miners in Nova Scotia seemed full of promise. Indeed, while both men were en route to Moscow, MacDonald was given his credentials as the official delegate selected to represent District 26, UMWA, at the Profintern Congress,* and empowered to affiliate the District with the RILU.[13] In addition, for a party which had come but lately into the revolutionary movement its progress in relation to most other parties, notably the American and British, gave the three delegates cause for considerable satisfaction. The Report of the Credentials Committee at the Fourth Comintern Congress noted that "the C.P. of Canada has 4,180 members", while figures elsewhere in the same document put the strength of the United States party at 8,000, and that of the British party at 4,116, only half of which constituted paid-up membership.[14] The Canadian party's showing proved a powerful point in its case for independence from the American party's influence which manifested itself in many and varied ways. The United States party, for example, claimed that it was through its efforts that further secession of the OBU type in the North American labour movement was prevented, and that it was primarily responsible for the UMWA District 26's (Nova Scotia) revolutionary solidarity. In practice, it had very little direct influence in the Canadian OBU movement or within the labour movement in the Nova Scotia coal fields.

In fairness to the Comintern, Moscow's inability to differentiate between matters concerning the American and Canadian parties was not only the result of ignorance and a characteristic lack of interest. Reports from the Canadian communist movement initially were forwarded through New York, and the American party simply included them with its own. Since there was no Canadian party representative resident in Moscow, there was no effective counter to the dominant American influence, and no-one to differentiate beween the activities of the parties north and south of the American-Canadian border. For a time, however, American predominance was offset by Scott's prolonged stay in Canada. The argument for Canadian party independence was used in particular and with great effect by Florence Custance who, by obtaining early passage on a vessel carrying supplies from Stettin to Petrograd, reached Moscow well before MacDonald and Spector despite trouble with German and Polish officials.[15] To some extent too, the deficiency in publicizing the Canadian party's activities was rectified by the inclusion of an article on Canadian labour organization and attitudes written by MacDonald, which appeared in *Internationale Presse-Korrespondenz* just before the Congress opened.[16]

The Comintern's Fourth Congress opened in Petrograd "on the day of the fifth anniversary of the greatest historic event of our time" with a splendour and impressiveness which surprised MacDonald, Spector, and Custance.

There was a wonderful demonstration at the depot; the whole city seemed to have turned out to welcome the delegates. We marched to the Smolny Institute where the Petrograd workers treated us in real style. . . . Comrade MacDonald talked at two gatherings of soldiers, about 4,000 at each meeting. . . . In the evening the Congress was officially opened in the Opera House . . . .[17]

---

*The Comintern's Fourth World Congress and the Second Profintern Congress overlapped. The former ran from November 5—December 5, 1922; the latter from November 19—December 2, 1922.

Any feeling of satisfaction over the Canadian party's progress was quickly dissipated as the Congress settled down to business on its resumption in Moscow, for MacDonald and Spector soon discovered that the Comintern was only mildly interested in North America, and that most of that interest was centred upon the American party. Eberlein, of the German party, who reported for the Credentials Committee, made it clear

... that the number of invitations [issued] was based not merely on the actual membership of the parties. The distribution of credentials also took into account the political and economic situation of the given country, and finally, the degree of illegality of the party and the extent of its oppression by the enemy.[18]

Initially, the Canadian party received only one invitation and was assigned one vote, which was pre-empted by MacDonald who, as Secretary, spoke on behalf of the CPC.[19] After reaching Moscow, however, Spector and Custance were given consultative votes.[20] The Canadian party's position was further enhanced before the three delegates left Moscow through their success in establishing direct communication with the Comintern, and Custance obtained a recognition that the party front organization, the Canadian Friends of the Soviet Union, was an entirely separate body from its American counterpart. She also met Krupskaya and a Vladimir Lvov, whom she described as "the former representative of the Czar in the Holy Synod," experiences which formed the basis for subsequent public talks on subjects such as "The Living Church in Soviet Russia."[21]

Although the Fourth Congress did not pay much attention to the North American communist movement, and while none of the Canadian delegates spoke at the open recorded sessions—Canada was discussed once at a session of the Executive Committee of the Communist International (ECCI)—the meeting proved to be important in the Canadian party's development. The real work was done through private meetings with Russian leaders and with other delegates, in the course of which Spector and MacDonald quickly discovered the Comintern's views on many matters which, despite Scott's presence and advice, had puzzled and perplexed the Canadian leaders. They soon found that open communist parties did not have separate underground parties or apparatus which paralleled those in the United States and Canada. Through private talks, and through the formal resolutions which were discussed and passed by the Comintern and Profintern congresses, the Third International's leaders made it clear that every effort was to be made to establish an open communist party. The issue was discussed in particular by the American Commission, a luminous body under the chairmanship of Otto Kuusinen and including Bukharin, Lozovsky, Radek, and Valetski, the Comintern's representative who had passed through Canada en route to the United States earlier in the year, which was established on the second day.[22] Zinoviev, speaking in Moscow on November 9, recognized that the greatest difficulty existing in the American communist movement—the same applied to the one in Canada—was the problem of "combining together legal and illegal work."[23] In setting up the American Commission, and by reaching the conclusion that mass, legal parties were desirable, the Comintern Presidium, so the Canadian delegates felt, essentially endorsed the policies initiated by the CPC. Their confidence was further increased by the views expressed during discussions of North American problems at both congresses, that the united front in both the United States and Canada meant intensifying the party's efforts among the trade unions.

In both countries there was a comparatively large trade union movement, and it was the duty of the communist parties in North America to create labour parties based on the trade unions. The point was taken up in greater detail by Lozovsky both within the American Commission and at the Profintern Congress. Speaking on November 20 at the sixteenth session of the Congress, he asked:

What is the role of the Communists in the States [and Canada]? They must work within the trade union movement upon the platform of the ... Trade Union Educational League. What is the League's program? Simply the program of the R.I.L.U. ... The program of the Trade Union Educational League of America is of course, less clear, less definite, less specific than the program of the Communist Party of America [or Canada]. But it cannot have this precise character in as much as it aims at uniting all the opposition elements. Our task in America is to assemble the forces of the entire Anti-Gompers opposition. The party must show the greatest persistence in aiding the work of the League, seeing that within a very brief period the League has been able to develop tremendous energy in its organizational work. Our task in America is to help the League to rally its forces to induce sympathizers with communism to give their active support to the League. ...

The same views were expressed at the Profintern's general sessions, and were incorporated in the resolutions and decisions passed by the RILU.[25] In particular the TUEL was instructed to bear in mind "that there is a great number of organized left wing workers outside the American Federation of Labor, and that the great majority of the American proletariat is outside any organization."[26]

At the Congress Katayama, drawing upon his experiences as a member of the Pan American Commission and his work in Mexico, noted the need for increased co-operation between communist parties in adjacent territories, and accused the American party of never looking beyond its national border.[27] The charge was not altogether applicable to the relationship between the American and Canadian parties: the Canadians felt the Americans too often intruded but seldom co-operated. However, Katayama's words on November 30 underlined the type of problem which the Canadian delegates brought before the Comintern executive, and helped them achieve independence from United States interference.

MacDonald, Spector, and Custance returned to Toronto with the Comintern's approval to work for the establishment of a fully open and legal communist party whose policies were to be based upon co-operation with the trade unions. On February 15, 1923, soon after returning, MacDonald wrote in *The Worker*:

The Comintern is satisfied that the Workers' Party of Canada is doing good work for Communism. I am satisfied that the Party, while having many shortcomings, measures satisfactorily with other parties of our age and strength with, perhaps, the exception of Australia's. I am convinced that we should take steps to make ourselves still more definitely Communist, at least in name. There may be nothing in a name, but it will at least distinguish us from reformist and pseudo-revolutionary organisations.

This proved an accurate forecast of subsequent Canadian party developments.

Unknown to the three delegates, the very first congress which they had attended was the last at which discussion was comparatively uninhibited. After Lenin's death, as hope that a further revolutionary wave might roll across Europe receded, as Russia gradually reassumed her position as a great power, and as the prestige and authority of the Bolsheviks became virtually unchallenged, disputes within the CPSU had marked repercussions within the Comintern. Discipline rather than adherence to principle became the touchstone of relations between the parties outside the Soviet Union and the Comintern, which, as time went on, became increasingly dominated by the Russian party.

CHAPTER SEVEN

THE CPC AND THE UNITED FRONT

SOON AFTER MacDonald, Spector, and Custance returned from Russia, a bulletin was sent to communist party branches throughout the country as part of the preparations for the second WPC convention, for which tentative plans had been made before the three delegates' departure. The circular, signed by G. Howard (the party name used by Trevor Maguire), noted that the three delegates had presented their *Report* on the Congresses to the Central Executive, and that the Comintern approved "one hundred per cent of the Party policy."[1] *The Report*, the bulletin added, would be sent out through "A." The main purpose of the circular, however, was to elicit information.

The resolution on the political situation [in Canada] and the tasks of the Party adopted at the last National Conference [February 1922] stated that the policy of the Party would be developed towards the formation of an open "Z" party with an underground apparatus. The CEC wishes to have the opinion of the membership as to whether the time has not arrived for taking this step, and desires the group members to discusss the following points.
1. Shall the next convention "Z" come out as an open "Z" party, changing the name from "A" to "Z"?
2. Shall the present "Z" party, as a party be liquidated, in event of an open "Z" being established, and be substituted by an underground non-dues-paying apparatus?
3. Shall open affiliation with the C.I. [Communist International] be applied for after the next convention?
Immediately on receipt of this bulletin the gp. sy. [group secretary] will call a special meeting of his groups to discuss the above. He will make a note of the discussions and forward same through Party channels to the district office, which will summarize reports and forward to the national centre.[2]

Within the Central Executive opinion on the question was sharply divided, with Moriarity and Maguire leading the opposition to the creation of a legal communist party, backed by Boychuk and Hill, the Ukrainian and Finnish representatives.[3] The Ukrainians in particular opposed the idea because they feared their connections with a party openly labelled as communist and affiliated with the Comintern would enable the authorities to confiscate their considerable property holdings.[4] These views came out at a CEC meeting held early in February 1923 at which Custance, MacDonald, and Spector gave personal accounts of their experiences at the Moscow Congresses. By the time the Workers' Party Convention was held at the end of the month (preceded as before by that of the underground Communist Party) it became clear that the majority of the "Z" party members agreed that transformation of the Workers' Party into an open communist party was desirable. Against the weight of approval from the field as well as Moscow's sanction of the proposal, the dissident voices faded, though some opposition to the disbanding of the "Z" party lingered for a time, stemming from a romantic feeling that an underground party would guarantee that the proposed open party would, indeed, remain a revolutionary one.[5] Such views were undermined by the hard facts of organizational work, together with the Comintern's insistence, through Scott, that the policies laid down at the Fourth Congress were to be implemented as soon as practicable.

The first step was taken at the Communist Party's convention held at the WPC's headquarters towards the end of February 1923. There, the 28 delegates—only half of whom were able to vote—representing all but one district, discussed "the most important article on the agenda . . . the question of liquidating the "Z" party and the coming out into the open."[6] According to MacDonald's appraisal, the "Z" party had grown steadily during the year, and during that period the CEC had attempted to co-ordinate the organization of the legal and the illegal parties and to reduce duplication of effort as much as possible. The *Report** emphasized that:

Party members will recognize that owing to the rapid progress made by "A" during its first year of existence, it has been imperative that the majority of our most active and responsible members devote their whole time to this work. This has resulted in building up a party which, in all but names, is an open "Z" Party. The year's experience has proved, without possibility of contradiction, that open "Z" activity is the only practicable method of carrying our message to the masses with any measure of success.[7]

Reports from every party district and section confirmed the increasing need and desire for an open "Z."

Discussion of a motion by the convention secretary (Buck) went on at great length to the effect that, since the Workers' or "A" party was an established Communist or "Z" party in all but name, the underground be liquidated as a party and replaced by an apparatus, the organization of which should be worked out by the new Central Executive Committee. All of the delegates agreed that the WPC should become an open communist party, but they were sharply divided over the time and methods required to achieve such a transformation. To avoid the dangers of future dissension and misunderstanding, and to resolve the discussion, a committee of seven representing all shades of opinion brought forward a resolution which not only reaffirmed the party's policy, but also included practical recommendations for implementing it. These stated that within six months the CPC should:

(a) dissolve the dues-paying underground organization;

(b) substitute for it an emergency apparatus with technical responsibilities, to be created and controlled by the Central Executive Committee;

(c) make "A" the only dues-paying political Communist organization in Canada;

(d) change the name of "A" (the Workers' Party) to that of "Z" (the Communist Party) at the end of six months;

(e) make these changes the responsibility of the new Central Executive Committee. The resolution was passed unanimously. Any remaining business was felt to be of minor importance, and was left for consideration at the Workers' Party convention scheduled to be held a few days later.

The meeting confirmed that the "Z" or Communist Party had helped to subsidize *The Worker*, or "K" as it was referred to in underground ranks, and that, whenever necessary, financial help was given to the Workers' Party, notably for special organization work. Such direct assistance, it was felt, was consistent with the "Z" party's chief task, that of strengthening "A" and transforming it into a mass Communist party. Apart from such financial obligations, the convention felt that the Canadian communist movement's great achievement was in finding the means for sending three delegates to the Comintern's Fourth Congress. Moscow's call, like that of

*The report of the proceedings was signed by "J. Page," the pseudonym used by Tim Buck.

Mecca, was loud and clear. Indeed, so strong was its attraction that discussion at the meeting centred on the increasing number of party members and sympathizers in the Ukrainian and other language ancillaries who were returning to the Soviet Union. As a result the convention decided that in future all party members who wished to return were first to obtain permission from the CEC.[8] Finally, the underground meeting confirmed that CPC membership was roughly one quarter of the total (4,810) listed for the Workers' Party in the Comintern's *Bulletin of the Fourth Congress*. An incomplete return put membership at 702, most if not all of whom were also Workers' Party members.

The underground convention, like the Fourth Comintern Congress, was an important watershed for the Canadian communist movement, for it marked a major change in attitude and policy. The key figure in this charge of attitude was the Comintern's representative, Charles E. Scott, who controlled the convention, using the international delegates' report as a guide for his actions.[9] By shepherding discussions and by intervening at opportune moments, Scott virtually dictated the convention's programme and, in the selection of candidates for party positions, he either drew up or criticized any suggestions for the slate of officers. Certainly, anyone who did not meet with his approval had little chance of being elected to any position within the underground Communist Party or the open Workers' Party. Indeed, during the CPC's brief life the power of the Comintern representative's word had been clearly demonstrated, for it was Scott's suspicion of Florence Custance which was responsible for her exclusion from the party's Central Executive after the February 1922 convention. Her election to office on both the underground and the open Workers' Party executives in 1923 in turn was approved by Scott only because her efforts in Moscow on the Canadian party's behalf had raised her in his estimation.

While the underground Communist Party convention dealt with policy at the highest party level, the second Workers' Party convention, held in Toronto on February 22–25, 1923, dealt with the less important issues, those which were either not considered at the secret meeting or which already had received the Communist Party's tacit approval. Thirty-six delegates,* including fraternal representatives from other sympathetic though non-communist organizations, assembled from all six districts established by the WPC after its first congress.[10] Discussion at the meetings centred upon the Canadian communist movement's relations with labour organizations in the country, and Moscow's views about the nature of that relationship. In addition to relying upon the experience and advice of the recently returned delegates, MacDonald, Spector, and Custance, and upon Scott's influence, the Comintern made known its views on a majority of the subjects scheduled for discussion by the convention, for the agenda had been forwarded to Moscow in advance for comments and approval. These, in turn, revealed the extent to which the Cominterns' views had

*The party districts were represented as follows: District One, J. B. McLachlan, H. M. Bartholomew, J. S. Wallace; District Two, M. Buhay, A. Gauld; District Three, M. Bruce, Tim Buck, Florence Custance, W. Hart, W. Killigrew, Joseph and Mrs. Knight, J. Oksanen, and M. Spector; the Finnish unit was represented by A. T. Hill, J. W. Ahlqvist, D. Aho, J. Lund, J. Wirta, and E. Kussela; the Ukrainian group sent M. Kivari and Zaradowski; District Four, T. J. Bell, H. Jameson, J. W. Esselwein, Leslie Morris, and G. Barron; District Five, J. Lakeman, W. Long, and G. Maki.

The fraternal delegates included Earl Browder, who represented both the Workers' Party of America and the TUEL. In addition, the Ukrainian and Finnish delegations were supplemented by John Boychuk, a member of the WPC's Central Executive, and H. Puro, the editor of *Vapaus*. J. B. McLachlan was also credentialled as a fraternal delegate from District 26, United Mine Workers of America. All delegates received one vote, except those from District Five, who were given two. Malcolm Bruce and W. Moriarty were elected convention chairman and secretary.

been coloured by the Canadian delegates' representations in Moscow, and by reports from Scott, its field representative.

Canada and the Canadian worker, the Comintern felt, were becomingly increasingly important to both Great Britain and the United States "in the future developments of world capitalist imperialism."[11] The Comintern's letter, dated Moscow, January 29, 1923, and signed on behalf of the ECCI by Bukharin and Kuusinen, strongly urged the Workers' Party to continue its efforts in the labour field "with great intensity . . . and [to] apply yourself to the extending of active party groups in every trade union branch and section" because this phase of its programme was "one of the most important tasks in preparing for the coming victories."[12] In particular the ECCI approved the Canadian party's attitude toward the Canadian Labor Party (CLP):

We think you appreciate at their true value such affiliations and look forward to a continuation of this policy in the future. The true political party of the working class should not only be the party in the vanguard of the army of emancipation, directing the advance by its proclamations, but should also, through the activity of its membership, direct all the other organs of working class expression in action. This can only be done by Communists working as disciplined units in a strongly organized Communist Party.[13]

The party leaders had some measure of satisfaction from these words, since the Quebec section of the CLP had approved affiliation with the WPC if the latter's members abided by the Labor Party's constitution and paid dues before the Quebec section's Fourth convention ended.[14] More recently, and before the Comintern's letter had reached the WPC, the CLP's Ontario section had followed the Quebec precedent at its fourth annual convention, held early in February.[15] The Workers' Party gathering thus had some cause for optimism, for the two CLP sections represented the most highly populated as well as the most industrialized areas in the country. These facts presented a tantalizing background to the Comintern's recently enunciated united front policy.

The Comintern's letter also reminded the convention that it was essential to establish a strong, well-directed, and thoroughly controlled party press because such a press was vital in directing and consolidating the forces of the working class and for fixing party members' ideas. On the basis of the letter and Spector's lengthy report on the decisions endorsed by the CI's Fourth Congress—a summary appeared in *The Worker*, March 15, 1923—the Workers' Party convention ran its course, a route largely predetermined by the underground party, approved by the Comintern in Moscow, and implemented through the presence of Scott.

The work of orienting the Canadian party to the Moscow-approved course was not without its difficulties. Organizational deficiences, which were ever present, and which were not simply the result of inaction by party organizers, were highlighted by the Convention. While Custance, MacDonald, and Spector were away, the work proceeded at a steadily accelerating pace. During the autumn of 1922 the Industrial Organizer, Buck, again proceeded to tour western Canada, attending district party meetings in Edmonton and in Vancouver in January 1923, as well as the Alberta Federation of Labour convention. Similarly, Trevor Maguire, then party secretary and *The Worker*'s business manager, went to the Nova Scotia coal fields to consolidate the advances made there by MacDonald before he went to Moscow. Activity went beyond the trade unions. Beckie Buhay, taking advantage of a mining dispute in Edmonton to decry capitalist exploitation, instigated a march by women to the city hall to demand that the strike be settled, and to highlight women's rights.[16]

Such efforts, while tightening up party organization and stimulating interest in the WPC, were offset by the high cost of travelling over vast distances, and by a comparatively low yield on the investment of time, effort, and money in terms of increased membership, effective influence within existing labour unions, or increased efficiency within the party's own groups. Nevertheless, considering the difficulties inherent in launching an open party dedicated to revolution within a hostile, apathetic society, the WPC had some cause to feel pleased. Party membership, while small, totalled 4,808, a figure well up on the Comintern scale.[17] That figure, of course, included the "Z" membership, as well as those of the Ukrainian and Finnish ancillaries.*

The new party's difficulties were many. Despite the Finnish organizers' strenuous efforts and that section's steadfast financial support, the convention revealed that the Finnish comrades had not responded to the WPC's call for increased trade union activities. This was particularly true for the Finnish lumber workers who, because they were scattered thinly throughout Ontario's forests, presented the party with a difficult organizational problem.[18] Similarly, the Ukrainian section faced problems of comparable magnitude, the greatest being opposition to the communist cause within the Ukrainian population in Canada, which was sparked, so the claim went, by "left baiters" from the U.S.A. Organizationally, however, the Ukrainian communists had made considerable progress. The Ukrainian Labour Temple Association (ULTA) at its annual convention, which preceded that of the WPC, endorsed the Comintern's united front tactic and the WPC's trade union policy, including the matter of affiliation with the Canadian Labor Party.

The party leadership reported the greatest and most obvious progress in the field of party publications. Although publishing *The Worker* entailed a severe drain on party finances—the cost of printing and mailing was estimated at over four cents per copy, and each copy sold for five cents—as well as upon the Central Executive Committee's time, the circulation of 4,500 copies was sufficiently impressive for the convention to approve weekly publication of the paper from the beginning of April.[19] The decision, indeed, accorded with the party's call for a weekly publication which had been voiced throughout the autumn of 1922. The convention's press committee's report, too, resolved that definite space should be allocated in the paper for reports about the Young Workers' League activities and party work among women. A suggestion that propaganda leaflets should be written or translated into French for circulation among French-Canadian workers marked the party's growing awareness of its neglect of that section of the Dominion's population, but little stemmed from the recommendation, nor did the added suggestion that the TUEL should be pressed to publish its literature in French come to anything. The problems of publishing, distributing, attempting to increase circulation, and of collecting payment from the party branches for the bundles of *The Worker* which each group received were enough to curb attempts at expansion, no matter how theoretically logical or desirable such schemes might have seemed.

Both the Finnish and Ukrainian section press also reported comparable progress during the interval between conventions. The semi-weekly *Ukrayinski Rabotnychi Visty*, for example, had published *The Workers' Party Program and Constitution*, and had made tentative arrangements to distribute the first volume of Marx's *Capital*, which was to be translated into Ukrainian and printed in Berlin. Similarly, the Finnish

---

*The Finnish organization numbered 2,028 members, organized into 59 branches, the majority of which were located in District Three (Ontario).

section reported that *Vapaus* had succeeded in establishing itself financially and that its circulation numbered 2,700, a significant figure since the paper was published thrice weekly. The Finnish section had also published various party pamphlets, including *The Workers' Party Program and Constitution, Science and Revolution,* and *Theses of the Third* [Comintern] *Congress.*[20] These efforts met the party's call for increased propaganda, and dovetailed with what had been attempted in the English-language press by the Central Executive.

With the conclusion of the convention the Workers' Party began the hard work of implementing the policies which had been approved by the Comintern and endorsed at the Toronto meeting. Preparations to publish *The Worker* weekly were concluded during March, and party organizers were despatched across the country to kindle interest and to step up party activity. As encouragement, the first issue of *The Worker* as a weekly appeared on April 2.

Two features of party development and activity for this period stand out. Immediately before Spector set out to tour the west he summed up the work of the Comintern's Fourth Congress in *The Worker*. In his article in the first weekly issue he pinpointed the principal issues confronting the Canadian party: the need to win over a majority of the workers to the side of communism, and to establish a united front of all labour forces, including even the reformist and backward workers; the problem of influencing the farmers; and the need to make Canada completely independent from Britain. Although the article dealt primarily with domestic problems, Spector also attempted to justify the Soviet's New Economic Policy (NEP) and stressed the importance of maintaining contact with the Comintern and following its lead in all matters.[21]

Spector's general analysis was soon followed by a series of articles in *The Worker* dealing at length with what the party considered its two most important problems: the united front and its relations with the Canadian Labor Party (CLP).[22] Pitched down to reach the entire Workers' Party membership, undeviating in their Marxist orthodoxy, and in complete accord with the Comintern's freshly proclaimed united front policy, the articles, printed while Spector toured western Canada, formed the basis for his meetings during April and May 1923. They provide a revealing glimpse into the CPC's attitude towards the leading issues of the day, notably towards the Canadian Labor Party, and at the time same they compress the arguments then being put forward to the general membership by party organizers in both public and private meetings. It was by far the longest and most closely-knit argument written by a party member, and added considerably to Spector's reputation as the party's leading theoretician.

While unrest in the Nova Scotia minefields was building up to a climax in 1923, the WPC's executive, in keeping with the Comintern's united front policy, made its first real incursion into Canadian politics. John MacDonald and Malcolm Bruce were sanctioned by the party executive to stand for office in the Ontario provincial election of June 1923. Their nominations, however, were neither formally nor directly backed by the Workers' Party. Both men were endorsed instead by the unions to which they belonged. Both were nominated as candidates for Toronto South West by the Labour Representation Political Association, an *ad hoc* body in Toronto composed of affiliated trade unions, women's organizations, and political parties such as the Independent Labour Party (ILP) and the Workers' Party.[23]

Significantly, leading Communist Party members held a number of important posts in the Association. Buck was vice-chairman, Joseph Knight served on both the

F

executive committee and the press committee, while William Moriarty was one of the body's two auditors. Under the circumstances the manifesto issued by the Association revealed the extent to which MacDonald and Bruce had managed to infuse the campaign with the communist movement's views. The campaign repudiated the old Conservative and Liberal parties, and stressed the need for labour to have its own representatives in the provincial legislature. Capitalism was condemned outright for its oppression of the working class, and the workers were warned that they could not hope to find security so long as it continued. Instead, the manifesto advocated a new economic system, a new society

... where economic rivalries as wars will be the forgotten relics of Capitalism, where greed, the basis of our present system, will be replaced by service, where human exploitation will be no more.[24]

The Toronto party branches immediately threw themselves wholeheartedly into the campaign, and for the moment other party problems receded into the background.[25]

The ballot results were profoundly disappointing to both the WPC and to the Canadian labour movement as a whole. Of the eleven labour representatives who had sat in the provincial legislature prior to the election, only one was returned. Of the labour candidates in the Toronto area, Bruce headed the poll with a mere 2,812 votes, MacDonald receiving 2,211. Although the election wiped out the gains labour forces had achieved following the war, it did not fill the communist leaders with undue pessimism. They regarded their entry into the political arena as merely the first skirmish in an expected series of pitched battles. More specifically, on the basis of the election campaign the WPC felt that

... the experiences of the United Front should now be made the basis for the extension and strengthening of the Canadian Labor Party, and the drawing together into CLP Central councils of all affiliated bodies in every locality.[26]

Some comfort could also be drawn from the fact that Bruce and MacDonald had waged "a spirited class fight" during the campaign, a campaign which the Workers' Party regarded as another useful opportunity for stirring up the workers to a realization of their true plight under the capitalist system.

At the same time, the Conservative landslide in Ontario not only shattered labour representation in the provincial legislature, but also destroyed the United Farmers of Ontario (UFO), an association of rural interests under E. C. Drury which had swept into power in 1919.[27] From the communist standpoint the fall of the UFO cleared the air, ostensibly creating conditions in which the differences between capitalism and socialism henceforth would be clearly differentiated.* Such conditions, they felt, could only redound to the Workers' Party's ultimate advantage.

*The advent of the UFO in Ontario was paralleled by the rise of the National Progressive Party under the leadership of T. A. Crerar, who resigned from the Union government in 1919. After the First World War the Progressives managed to obtain 66 seats in the House of Commons. Despite their name, the Progressives never contemplated extensive social reforms. They merely undertook to secure such objectives as a reduction in freight rates, tariff revision, and a re-allocation of the national income in favour of the farmer. The defeat of the UFO in 1923 presaged the fall of the Progressive Party, which was, to all practical purposes, killed in the 1926 federal election. The legacy left by the Progressives militated against any dramatic advance in building a revolutionary movement among the Canadian farmers, a point which neither the CPC nor the Comintern grasped.

CHAPTER EIGHT

THE EMERGENCE OF THE
CANADIAN COMMUNIST PARTY

THROUGHOUT 1923, while the communist movement in Canada attempted to reconcile and develop its "economic and political wings," events in Germany increasingly commanded the Comintern's attention. In turn, this concentration of interest on Germany soon made itself felt within all parties of the International. From the time that French troops entered the Ruhr on January 11, 1923, an action which triggered off a protest campaign organized by the Comintern (and to which the Workers' Party of Canada responded by issuing a manifesto on the "Menace of the Ruhr Invasion"), and throughout the ensuing great debate on the united front between the Communist Party of Germany's (KPD) right and left wings, overtones of the doctrinal split in the German party intruded into the Canadian party's inner life.[1] An increasing number of articles on or about Germany, some written by Radek, appeared in *The Worker* throughout the spring and summer of 1923 and kept the party membership abreast of developments. Such public news was supplemented by additional information which filtered through to the CPC over the Comintern's secret channels of communication. "On the Way to the German Revolution," which appeared in *The Worker* on May 30, is typical, and was of particular interest to the Canadian party since it was written by Arthur Ewert, who was described in an editorial note as being "well known to many Canadian workers."* Ewert, the note added, "was deported from Canada to Germany where he is at present filling an executive position in the Communist Party."[2] While news of an expected revolution in Germany caused some speculation within the Canadian communists' upper echelons, the majority of the CEC were too engrossed in their own problems to give the German situation much attention. Maurice Spector, *The Worker*'s editor, alone became increasingly absorbed in the possibilities of revolution in Germany, and the prospect of a further extension of communist rule, this time in an advanced, industrialized country. He felt the German situation would lead to an uprising, and concluded that taking part in such an action would prove of immense value when the revolutionary wave ultimately reached North America. Spector therefore determined to go to Germany for first-hand experience, and approached one of the party's "angels," J. L. Counsell, for the necessary subsidy. This secured, and with party approval, he went to Berlin in the autumn of 1923. While in Berlin Spector was put up for a time by Hertha Sturm,† the most active member of the International Women's Secretariat, a Comintern front organization whose headquarters were then in the German capital. The contact with Sturm was significant,

---

*For details of Ewert, see Chapter Three. Ewart returned to the United States as a Comintern representative and attended the American party's Fifth Convention in 1927. He travelled under the pseudonym "Grey."

†Spector recalls that Sturm's apartment was filled with a large quantity of arms.

for she was an active, outspoken woman of considerable abilities who always maintained that Russian conditions did not approximate those in the West, and that therefore the lessons of the Russian revolutionary experience were not entirely applicable within the political conditions which prevailed in most Western countries.[3] Sturm's views struck a responsive chord in Spector, but one which did not manifest itself until much later.

When the German uprising in October failed, Spector, disappointed, went to Moscow in January 1924 for consultation with the Comintern. He received his travel documents from Jacob Mirov-Abramov, the Comintern representative in the Press Department of the Soviet Embassy in Berlin until 1930. While still in Berlin, however, Spector summarized and analysed for the CPC Executive the underlying causes of the German communists' failure to spark a full-scale uprising. Considering that his role in the action had beeen negligible, that he had little direct experience of the KPD's internal politics or of the prevailing conditions in Germany, and that his own bias tended to favour the left, his report was a surprisingly accurate and succinct appraisal of the prevailing views and of the causes underlying the October fiasco. To some extent, his report to the Canadian party offset the views of the KPD right wing which, because they were approved by the Comintern, tended to find their way into the party press more readily than those of the German left opposition. At the same time, in levelling the charge that the KPD right wing, through lack of revolutionary courage, had betrayed the German revolution, Spector anticipated the identical thesis put forward by Trotsky in his Introduction to "Lessons of October," which appeared in a collection of essays entitled *1917* in the autumn of 1924, about the time of the seventh anniversary of the Bolshevik seizure of power.[4] Unknowingly, Spector had become one of the Western hemisphere's first Trotskyites.

Spector's novitiate in the Trotsky order, begun in Germany, was completed in Moscow. Besides discussing Canadian party problems with the ECCI, he attended the Second All-Union Congress of Soviets—amongst other things it ratified the USSR Constitution—as a privileged observer.[5] There he soon became very aware of the differences within the Russian party, differences which openly manifested themselves at the Thirteenth Party Conference (January 16–18, 1924) in a resolution—virtually unopposed—condemning Trotsky and his opposition to the all-powerful secretaries and party apparatus. Lenin's death immediately following the Conference did nothing to still the ferment, and Spector, arriving in Moscow at that time, was exposed to all the rumours and cross-currents of opinion within Comintern and Russian party circles.* Spector's growing awareness of Russian party differences, coupled with his German experiences, caused him to have reservations about the Comintern's approach to general problems and to other communist parties. He kept his thoughts to himself, but the kernel of doubt remained.

While in Moscow, Spector's discussions with the ECCI revolved around three main points: the question of Canadian trade union autonomy; the attitude of the WPC to the Canadian Labor Party; and the activities of the WPC Central Executive Committee.[6] All were considered at some length, but no specific Comintern opinions were put forward until after Spector returned to Toronto. During his stay in Moscow, however,

*Interestingly enough, while Spector was in Moscow the British Labour Party, which took office on January 23, 1924, established *de jure* diplomatic relations with the USSR on February 1. Canada, following the British lead, also recognized the Soviet Union in 1924. As a result, a Soviet trade delegation, headed by A. A. Yazikoff, came to Canada and established itself at 212 Drummond Street, Montreal. See Leslie Morris' recollection in *The Canadian Tribune*, April 2, 1962.

he got some insight into Comintern thinking and learned of the "bolshevization" campaign which was to be pressed so firmly during the next year. In an article published in *International Press Correspondence* (Inprecorr), and an ECCI resolution adopted by the Russian party's Central Committee to mark the twenty-fifth anniversary of the party's foundation, it was stated that the German experience had shown clearly that the organizational basis on which the Russian party was formed could be applied successfully to Western European parties before a revolution had actually taken place.[7] The shift from the geographical organizational basis implicit in district committees and local cells to the establishment of factory cells to which non-industrial party members would be attached was foreshadowed in another way, since the Comintern's Organization Bureau (Orgburo) headed by Ossip Piatnitsky, a veteran Russian bolshevik, began to function in January 1924. Spector returned to Toronto towards the end of March and immediately plunged into preparations for the Workers' Party Third Convention scheduled to start on April 18.

The upshot of his discussions in Moscow appeared in the ECCI's report to the Canadian party following the meetings of the Comintern's enlarged Executive held in the Soviet capital in April. In condensed form the Comintern's report covered the WPC's main activities during the previous year: affiliation with the CLP; the TUEL's attempts to become the guiding spirit of the miners' and steel workers' strike; and the party's active attempts to organize the unemployed workers into unemployed councils under the slogan "work for full maintenance."[8] The report, dated Moscow, May 5, 1924, showed that in the interval between ECCI meetings the Canadian party had been discussed six times: three discussions centred on political questions; two dealt with organization matters; one was unspecified.[9] By contrast, the KPD had been discussed 75 times, and the American 41. Aside from the main European parties and the United States party, the Workers' Party of Canada was discussed more than any other except the Australian. The ECCI *Report* stated that the party press was "pretty well organized," and that "bearing in mind the prevailing conditions the party as a whole [was] working satisfactorily."[10]

Essentially, little had changed in party policy or practice during Spector's absence. Joseph Knight, one of the early Canadian communists, left the party early in the new year, emigrating to the United States, and his departure, while serious in the sense that it deprived the party of an experienced organizer and speaker, removed one source of conflict within the central core. On the party's flanks, the Ukrainian wing experienced the uncomfortable glare of publicity during a court case heard in Port Arthur in December 1923, dealing with an alleged seizure of property from a non-communist Ukrainian cultural group, Prosvita, by the Ukrainian Labour Temple Association (ULTA) in Winnipeg.[11] Following the disclosures made at the trial, *The Manitoba Free Press*, a liberal Winnipeg newspaper, conducted an investigation of ULTA activities. The resulting series of ten articles put the party on the defensive, eliciting replies from both MacDonald and the Ukrainian leaders, all of whom took the stand that the charges directed at the Ukrainians were but another attempt to smash the workers' movement in Canada.

The *Free Press* articles made four charges: first, that the ULTA was merely a branch of the WPC; second, that no fewer than 800 Ukrainian farmers in western Canada were members of the ULTA and therefore members of the WPC; third, that 40 children's schools with an enrolment of over 1,200 had been established by the ULTA and were teaching revolutionary theories; and last, that the growth of the

Ukrainian organization had been due to the successful application of the "boring from within" tactics.[12] MacDonald, in a long letter in *The Worker*, January 12, 1924, addressed to *The Manitoba Free Press*, denied the claim that the ULTA was a branch of the WPC, basing his stand on the legal position that the two bodies were separate organizations. In reality, of course, the party never considered the two units to be separate, independent entities.

Such background matters, together with commemoration meetings following Lenin's death and calls to double *The Worker*'s circulation, occupied MacDonald and the CEC during Spector's absence. Simultaneously, preparations for the forthcoming convention continued. These included holding district conventions, choosing delegates, and formulating recommendations and resolutions which were then "forwarded to the National Office so that they [could] be considered in the convention order of business."[13]

The decisions taken by the Workers' Party Third Convention*, which was held on April 18-20 at the Labour Temple in Toronto, hailed as "perhaps the most momentous gathering since the party was organized," were determined by two factors.[14] First, and most conclusive, was a letter from the Comintern† determining the WPC's main policies; second, Spector's experiences in Germany and Moscow paved the way for the Comintern's instructions, and were instrumental in shaping the CEC report to the convention. In its instructions to the Canadian party the ECCI took up the three points raised and discussed with Spector during his visit to Moscow. Trade union autonomy, however, was dismissed briefly; "it [had] been decided to discuss it in all its aspects at the next Congress of the RILU."[15] But the party was cautioned to spare no effort in combatting attempts to split the miners in both the Nova Scotia and Alberta mine fields following the defeats sustained at the hands of the UMWA. It was reminded that Canadian workers needed education and training to consider matters from a point of view broader than that of local and provincial issues.

In addition, the ECCI posed an awkward question: why, despite the tremendous fighting spirit displayed by the Nova Scotia miners and apparent revolutionary potential within District One, was nothing heard of party activity in that province? Indeed, the Comintern complained, the ECCI did not know whether the party was growing or advancing its membership there.

The ECCI was equally pointed in its criticisms and suggestions concerning the WPC's attitude towards the Canadian Labor Party. It detected that some Canadian communists apparently were willing to jettison their connection with the WPC without being forced to do so by reactionaries within the CLP. To correct any misconceptions and to avoid further confusion, Moscow stressed that the WPC was, at all costs, to avoid leaving the impression that the Canadian Labor Party was the sole standard bearer for Canadian labour. Such an impression left little room for manoeuvring and was exceedingly hard to repudiate.[16] At the same time the Comintern letter suggested that, on the basis of the WPC's experience and existing conditions in Canada, the CLP be developed as a labour and farmer party.

To make the Canadian Communist Party a more effective force in the country's

---

*Forty-two delegates representing a total of 45 votes, were seated. Seven members of the CEC had a voice in the proceedings but no vote. Five delegates from Districts One (Manitoba), Five (Alberta), and Six (British Columbia), received two votes each. The strongest contingent, 22 in all and including nine Finns controlled by A. T. Hill, came from District Three (Ontario).

†The letter, undated, was signed by the Comintern's General Secretary, W. Kolarow.

political life, Moscow further suggested that the CEC should in future make greater efforts to clarify issues for its members and "inaugurate centrally directed campaigns that [would] reach all parts of the country."[17] As an example, the ECCI singled out the Nova Scotia miners' dispute, making the point that the WPC ought to have launched a nation-wide appeal for the imprisoned workers (McLachlan and others), and to have sent that appeal to the British miners and to the Labour government under Ramsay MacDonald. The Canadian party leadership, the Comintern implied, lacked imagination and initiative.

In analysing the Central Executive's actions during the interval between conventions, Moscow's tone was perceptibly sharper. "From your minutes [these were always forwarded to Moscow]," the Comintern remarked, "we note that there is hardly any discussion and decision on the policies to govern the activities of the party as a whole." What, for instance, Moscow asked, was the stand and policy of the CEC on the Nova Scotia strike the previous summer? The letter went on:

We fail to find anything in the minutes of the CEC about this. It is true that the CEC sent its representatives there [MacDonald and Bruce] in addition to its two members [McLachlan and Bell] who are there steadily, yet the strike was not properly initiated, neither was it skillfully conducted. And we do not know whether the comrades there were pursuing the policy and line of action, as laid down by the CEC or not.[18]

On the basis of this criticism the Canadian party was asked to keep in touch with Moscow more regularly. The communique ended with the suggestion that the party should produce and disseminate pamphlets on various questions dominating the Canadian political and economic scene.

The Comintern letter did not go unchallenged—Bruce heatedly asked where the ECCI got the information on which to base its criticism of the Nova Scotia strike—but it typified the manner in which Moscow attempted to keep tight rein on the Canadian party's policies and actions. Until the formation of the Comintern Orgburo, direction and control of foreign parties were exercised through dedicated individuals who, like Chekhov's "Three Sisters," constantly turned to Moscow for inspiration. The Canadian party leadership too, turned tropistically to Moscow for direction, not only because Moscow was the source of financial and material support (indeed the Canadian party, as already noted, received little direct assistance after its formation) but because it was the Grail of the Revolution. Through the mystique emanating from Russia, through representatives like Scott, through the actions and efforts of convinced leaders like MacDonald and Spector, through journeys of leading members to Moscow, the Canadian party swung into line with the Comintern on all major issues. After 1924, supplemented by the work of its formal control apparatus, the Orgburo, Moscow's control manifested itself increasingly in an attempt to impose a new organizational structure upon all parties—a process summed up in the term "bolshevization."

Essentially, "bolshevization" meant that the Canadian party, like the other parties which made up the Comintern, would have to modify its structure and organization and, in the process, stiffen party discipline. Unquestionably, the model which provided the only acceptable datum was the CPSU. Professor E. H. Carr writes:

The years 1924–1926 saw much attention given to the organization of Comintern and of the relations of its central organs to the constituent parties. . . . The Russian party must take the lead in questions of organization, as in all other questions. It must not only occupy the central place in Comintern, but its forms of organization must provide the model for those of other parties. This was the key note, implicit at first, but soon openly and emphatically expressed, of all Comintern discussions on organization. The emphasis on questions of organization was part of the broader campaign for "The Bolshevization of the sections of the Communist International" proclaimed at the fifth congress.[19]

The Comintern's letter to the Canadian party, arriving as it did during the interim period before the attempt at implementing bolshevization was fully or openly under way, clearly indicated Moscow's shift towards a more mechanical form of control. It also revealed the ECCI's misconceptions which had proven so disastrous when the Comintern forced the repudiation of Senator La Follette and the American Communist Party's role in the Farmer-Labor movement.[20]

The convention's two most important reports, one covering organization, the other political matters, were delivered by MacDonald and Spector, the latter replacing Bruce who was originally scheduled to deliver the political affairs summary. According to MacDonald, general conditions in Canada during the party's financial year militated against a numerical increase of party membership. The Finnish section had shown a marked increase, the Ukrainian had maintained itself, but in other branches* there was falling off, so that the total membership stood at approximately 4,000.[21] MacDonald attributed the "slight decrease in membership" to the large emigration of Canadians, some of whom were faithful party members, to the United States. His summary of the party's actions at the Trades and Labour Congress (TLC) convention and in Nova Scotia avoided any of the critical points raised in the ECCI's letter. Instead, he contented himself with presenting the best assessment possible in both cases. From the TLC meeting he took comfort in knowing that despite lack of representation from the Nova Scotia and Alberta mining districts, and the efforts of reactionary labour officials, the communists were able to coalesce a solid left-wing vote ranging from 20 to 40 per cent of the delegates.[22] The party's most important achievement, he claimed, had been the building up of the CLP and the crystallization of the left wing in the trade union movement. MacDonald declared:

We are desirous of building up a real mass political party of the Canadian working class; of presenting a united front to the enemy; of drawing larger masses into the struggle. But we are not desirous of building up a reformist labor party. . . .
    There is the imminent danager . . . of forgetting in our United Front Policy, that our chief task is the building up of a fighting communist party; of organizing the revolutionists into a disciplined political party.[23]

Similarly, he warned, the work in the trade unions carried out under the auspices of the TUEL had created the impression among some sections that a left-wing block was all that was required in the labour movement. This idea, of course, had to be resisted and combatted.

Only in the matter of the party's relations with and policy towards farm organizations did MacDonald admit a decided deficiency. There was little contact between workers and farmers, especially in eastern Canada, though some progress, largely through the efforts of Ukrainian radicals, was evident in the western provinces. At the September 1923 meeting of the Enlarged Executive Committee held in Edmonton, the CEC agreed that the party should give all possible assistance to the farmers, but nothing had been attempted to bring about organizational unity. This, however, did not preclude publicizing the slogan of "A Workers' and Farmers' Government" which, MacDonald felt, should be given greater publicity than in the past.

*In the CPC's annual submission to the Department of Labour it put its membership at 4,500, and listed its organization as follows: District One (Nova Scotia), six branches; District Two (Quebec), eight; District Three (Ontario), 70; District Four (Manitoba and Saskatchewan), 22; District Five (Alberta), 20; District Six (British Columbia), 13. Total, 139 branches.

Spector, in his report on the political situation, dealt in detail with the issues raised by MacDonald and in particular, with the economic and political crisis of the farm population in Canada. Although the farmer was getting considerably more for his produce than in 1914, he was forced to pay even more for his essential requirements than he earned. As a result, farmers had become the slaves of banks, mortgage houses, insurance companies, manufacturers, and other capitalist interests. The way out of this situation, Spector urged, was to bring to power "a real Workers' and Farmers' Government, not the sham 'Farmer-Labour' wreck of the Drury and Dunning type [the reference is to government leaders in Ontario and Saskatchewan]."[24] On the basis of MacDonald's and Spector's words, the convention passed a resolution in favour of working for the broadening of the CLP into a Canadian Farmer-Labor Party. Spector, writing in *The Worker*, after the convention made it clear that the party's next step was to line up the labour and farmer movements, and that endeavour was to be one of the chief tasks during the following year.[25]

The convention moved forward with discussions following the lead set by MacDonald and amplified in the political, industrial, press, and women's section reports delivered by Spector, Buck, Bruce, and Florence Custance. One matter, however, brought a ripple of opposition to the convention surface. MacDonald, in his opening address, touched briefly upon changing the Workers' Party name to that of the Communist Party of Canada because the WPC "had at least advanced so far in our political life, to warrant distinguishing ourselves, if only by name, from other sections of the labor movement who not unfrequently like to pose as communists."[26] This decision, to complete what in effect had been determined during the prolonged debate over merging the "A" and "Z" parties at the previous convention and confirmed by the party's experiences during the interval, had not been taken lightly. The Executive had consulted the Comintern to determine its views. When the proposed change of title came before the convention, MacDonald "read a cable from Comrade Johnson [Scott, then on the staff of the Profintern's American section in Moscow] to the effect that the Comintern did not recommend [nor] did they object."[27] Bell, one of the delegates with a double vote, alone opposed the proposal on the grounds that politically there had not been enough change in the country to warrant the alteration. In the end, the proposal was endorsed with only two dissenting votes, those cast by Bell.

The decision "to break new ground by changing our name to that of the Communist Party" was hailed throughout the party as a major step forward.[28] It was especially approved by Charles Emil Ruthenberg, Secretary of the Workers' Party of America, who attended the Canadian party convention as a fraternal delegate.* Ruthenberg, ever since his release from prison in the spring of 1922, had led the fight against the underground existence of the communist party in the United States. He saw no reason for the continued existence of an underground communist party which served merely to control an overt Workers' Party.

In making the change, the Canadian party recognized the necessity and logic of so doing. Despite Bell's opposition, the Canadian communist movement was never faced with the weight of dissension which prevented the American movement from doing the same, without qualifications, until 1929.[29] Nevertheless, "it was decided to continue with an underground apparatus but to do away with the payment of dues etc."[30] The decision to maintain a clandestine section of the party was neither

---

*The American party altered its name to the Workers' (Communist) Party of America in September 1925; it changed its title to the Communist Party of the USA in March 1929.

surprising nor unexpected, for it was in accord with Article Three of the 21 conditions for admission to the Comintern adopted in 1920, and squared with the resolution of the Third Congress held in 1921, which insisted that all members of the International, even legal parties, be prepared for revolutionary insurrection, for armed struggle, and underground activities. With the establishment of the Orgburo at the Fourth Comintern Congress in 1922, control of illegal activities was transferred from the inner circles of the International's Executive Committee to a new body, the Section of International Communication or OMS (Otdeleine Mezhdunarodnoi Svyazi).[31]

Ruthenberg, in his address to the Canadian convention, stressed that the problems confronting the communist movement in Canada were the same as those which beset the American.[32] Since Canada and the United States were part of the same industrial order, it followed that both parties should and must establish the closest connections, and co-operate fully with each other. In describing the attempts to bring about the united front in the American republic, Ruthenberg told how, in Minnesota, the National Executive had instructed every Workers' Party of America candidate in the federal elections to declare themselves communists, and to speak directly for the communist election slogans. He believed that the American party had succeeded in finding the way in which to build up a Farmer-Labour Party, and suggested that the Canadian communists, because of the similarity in conditions, could follow the same policy. He also suggested that the Canadian party, in light of the Comintern's criticism of its handling of the Nova Scotia strike, should consider the establishment, after the American party's counterpart, of a political committee divorced from all organizational problems. It was vital, Ruthenberg felt, for the Executive Committee to be in a position to give party members a definite lead on every question, and to be able to formulate policy on every issue. The Canadian communists, however, did not follow Ruthenberg's advice, for Canadian conditions, they held, differed from those in the United States. As it transpired, the American party's policy and actions proved disastrous, shattering any possibility of building up a strong agrarian-labour alliance in the United States.[33]

Apart from Bell's opposition to changing the party name and his contention that a real victory had been won in Nova Scotia because the miners had saved their union, a point he felt should have received more stress in Spector's political report, the convention proceeded smoothly. Any tensions existing within the leadership were well masked, except for one incident. This occurred when Malcolm Bruce, The Worker's editor, aired some of the frictions within the CEC while giving his report on the party press. He accused the rest of the Central Committee of attempting to create a united front without the labour rank and file. He directed his attack primarily against MacDonald and William Moriarty, The Worker's business manager, labelling the latter MacDonald's rubber stamp! The charge was a pale variation of a similar debate which had divided the German party, with Bruce, in the CPC context, representing the left wing favouring a united front from below, and MacDonald and his supporters favouring a united front from above. The attack, with its personal overtones, failed to disrupt the convention's course or to dislodge the MacDonald-Moriarty-Spector machine. But it was instrumental in preventing Bruce's re-election to the Central Committee,* a development resulting from his inability to organize support from the strong Finnish delegation.[35]

*The elections were held on the last day of the Convention. Bruce was defeated by two votes, 21–19; Hill, a MacDonald man, swayed the Finnish delegates sufficiently to ensure Bruce's defeat. The CEC elected on April 20 consisted of Bell, Buck, Custance, MacDonald, Moriarty, and Spector.

In spite of the setback, Bruce's star in the party did not wane appreciably; indeed, within a few weeks he was despatched to Moscow as one of the Canadian party delegates to the Comintern Fifth Congress. Bell, on the contrary, although elected to the CEC, felt himself increasingly isolated from the main stream of party development following the convention. The Comintern's criticisms of the party's actions in Nova Scotia reflected adversely upon him, and his stand during the discussions about changing the party name ran counter to the CEC's views. Realizing that his opportunities of gaining primacy within the party were slight—his reputation for intrigue and factionalism, his failure as Organizer of District Four, and his penchant for drink militated against him—because the MacDonald faction was clearly too well entrenched to be dislodged without a powerful and carefully organized opposition, Bell decided to leave the Canadian communist movement. In July he resigned* from the party and, like so many other Canadians, emigrated to the United States.[35] His place on the CEC was taken by Malcolm Bruce after the latter's return from the Comintern's Fifth Congress.

Before dispersing, the convention endorsed MacDonald's suggestion that the holding of Enlarged Executive Committee meetings should be abolished for the better interests of the party. He buttressed his case by pointing out that the last gathering, held in Edmonton, had cost over one thousand dollars, and that "the treasury of the party has never been in that condition [which] would give the CEC the necessary confidence to go ahead and spend money on organizing work."[36] Emergency meetings, it was felt, could be called if really important matters required such gatherings. The convention also confirmed an earlier CEC decision to set up a Jewish Propaganda Committee of five members, one of whom would sit on the CEC. "There is no reason," MacDonald told the convention, "that with a little work there should not be sufficient number of Jewish workers enrolled in the party to form a Jewish section."[37] It was also proposed to issue a monthly Jewish organ to promote interest in the new section, and the new publication, Der Kampf ("Struggle"), a monthly printed in Yiddish, appeared for the first time in November 1924.

On the day following the CPC convention, the party's youth wing held its own gathering, the second in its history, and also modified its title to the Young Communist League (YCL). After its first convention in February 1923, the Young Workers' League (YWL)† as it then was, received a letter from the Young Communist International in which Moscow charged the Canadian youth wing with the task of "showing the working class of Canada the way out of wage slavery and political disenfranchisement" by recruiting exploited youth and training them "for the struggle of the proletariat."[38] From this rather broad and general directive the junior section, like its parent body, turned to specific issues. At the YCL convention‡ the youth section

---

*Bell's resignation was accepted at the monthly CEC meeting held on August 10. Both Browder and Spector recalled that Bell became active in the American party. Browder remembered that Bell was a proof reader for the Daily Worker in Chicago in 1924. In 1925 Bell wrote a 48-page booklet entitled The Movement For World Trade Union Unity, which was published in Chicago by the American party. With the opening of the Lenin School, Bell was sent to Moscow as a member of the American party student group. J. T. Murphy, the British party representative at the Comintern in 1926, subsequently met Bell in Moscow. Bell also wrote a commentary on the Sixth Comintern Congress, Nakanune Epokhi Novykh Voin, which was published in Moscow in 1928.

†Leslie Morris, who ultimately became General Secretary of the Canadian Communist Party, was made national secretary of the YWL, and in that capacity attended the convention of the American party youth wing held in Chicago in May 1923. At the CPC convention Morris was seated as an official delegate and given a vote.

‡The National Executive elected at the convention consisted of Morris, A. T. Hill, Louis Steinberg, C. Frear, and W. Toukanimi.

faithfully mirrored the policies adopted by the main body, pointing up the transformation in party structure and approach which the ECCI had laid down at the beginning of the new year. They were assisted in the task by Tom Bell and Michael Buhay, the fraternal delegates from the adult party.[39]

With the end of its convention the adult party quickly turned to the tasks laid out at the historic meeting. A series of rapid internal changes were made in an attempt to translate the convention's decisions into realities. The newly-elected CEC, as one of its first moves, selected three delegates, Tim Buck, Malcolm Bruce, and A. T. Hill, to represent the Canadian party at the Fifth Comintern Congress scheduled for June.[40] In order to enable Bruce to attend, Spector took over as editor of *The Worker*, and his stewardship made itself apparent at once.[41] Spector, in his first editorial, "On the New Tasks," made his own sense of mission clear:

We must not prove ourselves unworthy of the Workers' confidence. The change of name has committed us to achieve greater initiative, greater endurance, greater efforts, greater wisdom and greater militancy.[42]

These words reflected more the man than the party, but throughout his initial editorial the party and its tasks were held squarely before the rank-and-file members. Spector's editorial continued:

We have pledged ourselves to broadening out the labor party movement into a Labor-Farmer movement. We will aim at a Canadian Farmer-Labor Party. We will strive to make the slogan of a Workers' and Farmers' Government[*] not some dim and distant ideal of a program but an immediate aim . . . But, the very work is the building up of our own Communist Party, which we mean to be the soul and inspiration of all this movement and action. . . . If the Communist Party were to succumb, the whole labor movement would receive a set-back, the extent of which is unthinkable. . . . Every worker, every farmer of Canada should, in the next year, be made familiar with the work and aims of our Communist Party.[43]

On this enthusiastic note and with these brave words, the retitled CPC, led by MacDonald and Spector, set out to project a true communist party before the Canadian working public.

*The slogan "a workers' and peasants' government," amended to "farmers" for North American usage, was first enunciated at the Third ECCI Plenum, June 12–23, 1923, at which Charles E. Scott represented the Canadian party.

CHAPTER NINE

BOLSHEVIZATION AND THE CANADIAN PARTY

BOLSHEVIZATION, the Comintern's call to its members to reorganize on the basis of the Russian party's factory nuclei in order to become "revolutionary" mass parties, was first formally proposed at the Third International's Fifth Congress in 1924. The move was not entirely unexpected, for rumours of impending change were circulating when Spector was in Berlin during the late autumn and winter of 1923. These rumours were confirmed in January 1924, when the ECCI adopted a resolution (passed earlier by the Central Committee CPSU to mark the party's 25th anniversary) which stated that the German experience had shown clearly that the organizational basis on which the Russian party was formed could be applied to western European parties before a revolution had actually occurred.[1] The shift from a geographical organization marked by district committees and local cells to that of factory cells to which non-industrial party members would be attached was thus clearly foreshadowed. That the change would not be long delayed was stressed by the creation of the Comintern's Orgburo, which was established "for the improvement of the organization of communist parties and the supervision of illegal activities," and which began functioning in January 1924.[2] Spector, armed with the points covered during his discussions with Comintern officials in Moscow, with German party members in Berlin, and with the views, opinions, and gossip which characterized life in the rooms of the Hotel Lux, returned to Toronto towards the end of March 1924.[3]

From the moment reorganization was mooted, the idea of bolshevization was resisted by the Canadian party. But while the CEC doubted the feasibility of reorganization on the Soviet pattern in Canadian conditions, it did not express the view openly. Instead, at the party's Third Convention, held in April 1924, the CPC paid lip service to the concept of factory nuclei as the correct basis for communist party organization, but did not take further action. Much the same attitude prevailed within the American communist movement.[4] In neither party were any steps taken to implement the change until pressure was exerted from Moscow.

Although discussions about the German party dominated the Comintern's Fifth Congress, individual party problems were taken up in detail at the operative level of the newly-created Organization Bureau. Because of the similarity of their structure and organization, the difficulties of reorganizing the Canadian and American parties were considered together. During the discussions both the American and Canadian delegations—the latter consisting of Buck, Bruce, and Hill—expressed their reservations about the Comintern's proposal. Buck cited two extenuating conditions prevailing within the Canadian party. Few CPC members, he pointed out, worked in heavy industry or in large factories because Canadian industrial development was still limited in scope and scale. Also, about 80 per cent of the party members could not speak English.[5] Such specific arguments failed to sway Comintern officials. Piatnitsky insisted that there could be no exceptions in the Comintern's plan for bringing all its member parties into conformity with the Russian party's particular pattern for organization. Indeed, both the American and Canadian delegations were ordered to begin immediate activity among the English-speaking workers employed in factories, mines, and other industrial enterprises to put the decision into effect.

Once Moscow made its attitude on bolshevization clear, few delegations continued to resist the idea, and most rapidly reconciled themselves to the necessity of modifying their party structure and organization. After its initial resistance, the Canadian delegation, too, quickly swung into line with the Comintern. Indeed, Buck, early in the Congress, made it clear that the CPC unequivocally endorsed the Comintern's views. Speaking during the discussion on the "ECCI's Report and the World Situation," Buck drew upon the CPC's experiences to refute Arthur MacManus of the British party,* who had argued that achieving a united front and bringing about a workers' and peasants' government were more important than building a mass party. Speaking at the Fourteenth Session on June 26, 1924, Buck replied:

The Canadian party had been working in the Trade Unions etc., influencing and controlling their actions tactically, but this had produced no ideological effect, i.e., it was not revolutionizing the masses. If we are to build up the united front, we must base our activities on the workshops. . . . The solution of the united front problem in Canada, the United States and Great Britain, meant basing the organizational activity of the parties on the factories and workshops.[6]

It was one thing, however, for the three Canadian delegates to accept the Comintern bolshevization programme on behalf of the Canadian party, and quite another for the party to put it into effect. First, members had to be made aware of the true meaning and import of the decision to make every factory a fortress of communism, and here *The Worker* became the prime instrument of instruction, supplementing the efforts of party organizers. In the October 25, 1924, issue of the paper, Buck explained:

Shop nuclei or factory groups must be the basic units of the party; each one of them functioning as a branch, holding meetings, collecting dues, accepting new members, initiating and developing their own activities, sending delegates to the city central committees, and building up within the shop or factory wherein they are employed a definite unit of the communist party: organizing, educating, and leading the workers of that concern, and bringing them through their daily struggles, to an understanding of the other wider and deeper struggle for working class power.

Such major details as the size of the party, the nature of its organization, and the extent of its power within the nation's industrial scene were easily and conveniently brushed aside by invoking Moscow's authority. In the same article Buck continued:

To the argument that we in Canada cannot organize on this basis because of the smallness of our numbers, the comrades of the Organization Bureau of the Comintern reply that we are standing the question on its head. We do not build up mass Communist Parties so as to organize them on the basis of factory mass parties.

In practice, any attempts to bring about a transition to the factory nuclei by the Canadian party immediately following the Comintern's Fifth Congress were negligible. The only areas where such change was possible were in the country's two largest cities, Montreal and Toronto, and even there the scheme was impractical and premature. Nevertheless, the CPC faithfully trumpeted the Comintern policy for the remainder of 1924 and throughout 1925, hoping, in the process, to increase both its membership and prestige.

*He could criticize the British delegate with some assurance, since the CPC's membership was proportionately greater than that of the Communist Party of Great Britain (CPGB). Figures listed at the Congress showed 4,000 members for the CPC and 3,700 for the CPGB.

The Comintern's insistence upon bolshevizing its sections reached a climax at the ECCI's Fifth Plenum, which met from March 21 to April 6, 1925. Most parties were discussed at that gathering, and at the Organization Bureau's meeting which opened on March 15.[7] Most sections by then had been given an inkling of what Moscow expected from reports brought back by delegates who had attended the Fifth Congress, and this general airing had been reinforced by the Organization Bureau's draft model statutes for communist parties which were brought out and circulated in January 1925. These made abundantly clear the Comintern's intentions and desires to bring the parties which made up the International into conformity with the structure and organization of the Russian party. On the basis of the reports from the Profintern and Comintern Congresses of 1924, and from subsequent developments, the Canadian party despatched William Moriarty, *The Worker*'s business manager, to the Fifth Plenum.

To the Comintern, "bolshevization" represented the logical culmination of changes which had been taking place from the time the Third International was launched in 1919. To the Canadian and American parties the shift to shop units as the basic form of communist party organization proved difficult and was certainly less effective than the party presses of both suggested. In Canada the reorganization was never put into effect on any scale, largely because MacDonald and Spector tended to regard "bolshevization" as impractical. Nevertheless, because the change had been decreed by the Comintern and emphasized at the Fifth Plenum, the CPC, despite its leaders misgivings, had to implement the policy as best it could.

Ostensibly, reorganization proceeded throughout 1925, but with very little success. Only in Montreal, as the CEC's report to the party's Fourth Convention conceded, had any factory nuclei been formed. Because of external pressures, however, the slow rate of change which marked the initial period could no longer be tolerated. Following the failure of the German and Bulgarian Communist Parties to take advantage of the revolutionary situations which developed in those countries in 1924, the bolshevization of Comintern sections, in Moscow's eyes, became doubly urgent. With the partial stabilization of capitalism (which did not eliminate the inherent contradictions and antagonisms of capitalism and capitalist imperialism) and in the face of liquidatory and revisionist tendencies current everywhere, so the argument ran, it was more necessary than ever to reaffirm the Comintern's bolshevik basis. In his report to the party membership, MacDonald stated:

Bolshevization for the Communist Party of Canada means therefore (a) intensive Marxist-Leninist education, (b) building up of a real and organized left wing minority movement in the trade unions to campaign for amalgamation, national autonomy, international trade union unity, (c) party reorganization on a shop-group basis, (d) building the Labor party as a mass movement based on the trade unions and under the leadership of the Communist Party, (e) alliance of the poor farmers with the workers in a Farmer-Labor Party, (f) greater political activity through the propagation of a program of action for the masses to demand the nationalization of the basic industries under workers' control and without compensation, a Workers' and Farmers' Government, and Canadian Independence.[8]

As MacDonald's summation makes clear, the Canadian party leaders by then had virtually ceased emphasizing the TUEL, and had started to think of labour organization in terms of working within the labour movement, much in the fashion of the Communist Party of Great Britain's Minority Movement.

The party's proposals to reorganize the CPC which were incorporated into a separate resolution by the party's Fourth Convention in September 1925, were buttressed by advice from Piatnitsky in Moscow. Apart from emphasizing the necessity for the Canadian party to prepare itself in accordance with the decisions approved by the ECCI's Fifth Plenum and the Fifth World Congress held in Moscow in March and June 1925, Piatnitsky's word on the position of the language groups is illuminating.

With respect to the Workers' Party of America the ECCI has decided to reorganize the language federations gradually and systematically in order to enable the party to become a united and centralized organization. As the Canadian Party is mainly in the same position, you will receive additionally an extract from the letter to the W. P. of A. [Workers' Party of America].9

Piatnitsky's directive aimed at curbing the comparative independence which the communist language federations in North America enjoyed, and in the long run, made it possible for Moscow to subject the communist parties in the United States and Canada to greater control. As it turned out, Piatnitsky's policy proved difficult to implement, for bolshevization never succeeded in wiping out the foreign language problems which beset the Canadian and American communist moments.

Nevertheless, one of the earliest effects of bolshevization in the CPC was the gradual erosion of the language groups' autonomy. Before the reorganization programme was put into effect, the Finnish and Ukrainian units had supported the party like flying buttresses, visible and distinct, yet still part of the Communist Party's structure. The arrangement, however, was considered to be social democratic, and therefore not acceptable to a truly communist party.10 After bolshevization began, the language groups gradually lost their structural identity. In the process of absorption, however, the CEC inherited each group's difficulties so that it was forced to take action on a variety of Finnish and Ukrainian problems which previously had been dealt with at lower levels by the language federations. At the time of the CPC's Fourth Convention (September 1925), the feeling of optimism which still pervaded the party countered serious consideration of long-run problems. Nevertheless, while the Canadian "bolshevization" convention never required the presence of a Comintern representative, such as Sergei Gusev who presided over the comparable American gathering held in August 1925, it marked the beginning of a new phase in the party's history, for once it was over the CPC never regained its former individuality and independence.

Through the autumn of 1925 the CPC continued the task of reorganization. As a first step, the number of administrative districts into which the party had been divided was increased from six to nine. Ontario, where the party's influence and membership were the greatest, was split into three new units:* Southern Ontario, which became District Three; North Bay-Timmins, which became District Four; and Port Arthur-Kenora, which was designated District Five.11 November saw the beginning of a drive intended to convert the CPC into a truly mass party by recruiting 500 members and by adding 1,000 new readers to The Worker's subscription list. "Red Month," as the campaign was styled (it was extended to December 15) failed to attract the militants in the numbers hoped for, and in fact did not offset a small loss of members through application of the bolshevization theory. MacDonald, in his annual return to the federal Department of Labour, put the party strength for 1925 at 4,600, a figure which did not change substantially for the next two years.12

*As a result the party's administrative divisions were: District One (Nova Scotia), six branches; District Two (Quebec), nine branches; District Three (Southern Ontario), 19 branches; District Four (North Bay-Timmins), 13 branches; District Five (Sudbury-Sault), 18 branches; District Six (Port Arthur-Kenora), 23 branches; District Seven (Manitoba-Saskatchewan), 22 branches; District Eight (Alberta), 23 branches; District Nine (British Columbia), 14 branches.

With the increase in the number of administrative districts and the launching of the "Red Month" recruiting drive, the CPC began its reorganization on the factory and street group basis in earnest. Initially, the CEC dealt with the problem with extreme caution, first by issuing a carefully prepared statement forwarded to all party units; second, by specific instructions sent out from the party's Organization Bureau. These advised a thorough registration of party members which, it was felt, would reveal the most promising comrades who would then, regardless of language, form a series of nuclei. The party members forming the nuclei in turn would proceed, through discussions, to work out the programme which the group would follow. "No Nucleus," it was emphasized in *The Worker*, November 7, "must be set up without it having some immediate tasks ahead of it, and the tasks must include some at least which will enable the Nucleus to function right away." If the preliminary conditions were carefully observed, the argument ran, the reorganization would both strengthen the party and extend its influence. Reorganization too, it was hoped, would assist in recruiting suitable new members.

Theoretically, the scheme was sound, but in a vast and varied country such as Canada its application posed endless problems. The first and most obvious danger was that of a mere mechanical splitting up of territorial districts and branches. In communities such as Sudbury, Ontario, where almost the entire communist membership in the district was Finnish, reorganization simply resulted in dividing the large existing branch into several smaller groups. In such cases the CEC felt that division was immediately useful, and that it constituted an advance on the old form of organization because it brought more members into active party work. More became group functionaries or took on the duties of representatives on the city committees. Country regions and smaller centres with one predominant population posed a lesser problem and were quickly reorganized on the nucleus basis. In such centres and areas where the membership was homogeneous—that is, in Finnish and Ukrainian districts— transition from the old style of existence to the new caused very little disruption to party life because no language problems resulted from the change.

But large industrial centres were more difficult to reorganize. Because various nationalities were suddenly brought together in the new units, it was almost impossible in some cases to conduct group business in the normal operating language, English. This led eventually to the Comintern suggestion that the party should begin language classes.[13] Throughout the interval between the Fourth and Fifth Conventions (some twenty months), difficulties such as the language problem forced the CEC to improvise as the bolshevization programme proceeded. The results, as MacDonald revealed at the Fifth Convention in 1927, were uneven. Only Toronto was considered to be completely reorganized on the pattern of the original plan. Winnipeg communists, who were the first in the party to declare themselves reorganized, still retained a large Ukrainian branch with a membership ranging from 70 to 90; Edmonton, during 1926, reverted to the previous system of separate language units; while in Vancouver the party membership was divided into three large units without any consideration of street or area grouping, the very essence of the original reorganization plan. Similarly, the party members outside any of the listed groups were coalesced into miscellaneous branches, with some railway shop groups forming an "international" branch.

Confusion over the character and meaning of the decreed change in party structure and organization continued throughout 1926, and very few of the new units, including the shop groups, functioned as the leadership had hoped. Communist-produced shop

G

papers, a few of which had begun to appear before bolshevization of the Canadian party was inaugurated, soon disappeared, and the situation became sufficiently chaotic for the CEC to review the results in October 1926, and to sanction various modifications.[14] The most important of these permitted a revival of the purely language territorial group in particular cases, a step directly resulting from the Ukrainian problem in Winnipeg.

From the earliest days of the communist movement in that city, Ukrainian party leaders, Matthew Popowich, John Navis, Matthew Shatulsky, and others claimed that the CPC leadership had not given sufficient credit to the Ukrainian wing for its contributions to the revolutionary cause. Bolshevization, in centres with large Ukrainian populations such as Winnipeg, served to further diminish the Ukrainian communists' importance within the party. This appeared all the more unjust after Popowich's good showing in the Winnipeg civic election of 1925. The Ukrainian grievance was thus fundamental to the CPC's eventual modification of the bolshevization of the Canadian party. It was offset, too, by posting Popowich to Toronto early in 1926—he replaced Bosovitch in March—to represent the Ukrainian communists on the party's national Agit-Prop Committee, and by the inclusion of Mac-Donald and Spector as the CEC representatives on the party's Finnish and Ukrainian committees.[15]

Despite the concessions on organization made for the Ukrainian party members, the Ukrainian problem was not eliminated. Indeed, before the changes sanctioned by Toronto could make an impact, the communist movement in Winnipeg was further split by the selection of W. N. Kolisnyk to stand for civic office. The non-Ukrainian communists objected to Kolisnyk on the grounds that he was too conservative, that he was more interested in demonstrating to the public that Ukrainians were capable of holding public office and professional posts. Kolisnyk's subsequent election as alderman mollified criticism within Winnipeg party ranks for a time, but the issue was not completely resolved until it was brought before the Comintern at the Sixth Congress in 1928.[16] At the same time, Kolisnyk's victory at the polls once again served to focus attention upon the Canadian communist movement and its political intentions. *The Manitoba Free Press* of December 1, 1926, immediately dubbed the new alderman "the local officer in the Bolshevist army which marches under the red banner," and proceeded to dramatize Kolisnyk's success:

The Communist assault on the city council has gone on for years. It became notable in 1923 when Mr. Popovich, a brilliant Winnipeg Bolshevist, polled 1,408 votes in ward three. The line was being formed and the ranks put in order. In 1924 Mr. Popovich got a total of 2,144; the red tide was rising higher. In 1925 he got 2,025; a slight ebb, but in that election he got 90 second choices. In 1926 Mr. Popovich is away, Mr. Kolisnyk takes his place and the trench is captured and the flag stuck up on the parapet; 2,073 votes in all, and of these 198 are second choices.

For the Canadian communist movement the electoral success was a brief, bright moment during an otherwise difficult time.

The Canadian party's experiences in attempting to carry through bolshevization were of considerable interest to the Comintern. Accordingly, when Buck and Popowich were despatched to the ECCI's Seventh Plenum held in Moscow from November 22 to December 16, 1926, one of their most important charges was to explain the CPC's problems connected with reorganization, and the issues raised among the language groups by the attempts to bolshevize the party. These were explained and gone over at length in the American Secretariat and the Organization Bureau, and after many protracted discussions the Canadian delegates succeeded in convincing the Orgburo that the ECCI's impressions of the Canadian party's progress, particularly in reorganization among the language groups, were not accurate. Buck and Popowich both objected to the view that the Canadian party could profit from the American party's experiences with language groups during reorganization because conditions in the two countries were different. Both made it clear that the CPC did not wish to depart from the party's original plan for reorganization, but suggested that local conditions had to be considered in any attempt to bolshevize the Canadian party.

While Buck and Popowich were in Moscow, their arguments seemed to prevail. After their departure there were second thoughts within the Comintern's Orgburo, and the instructions forwarded to Toronto from Moscow again referred the CPC to the United States party's experiences as a model for its actions. Popowich, who reported on these matters to the CPC Fifth Convention, made it clear whom he and Buck considered responsible for the Comintern's muddled thinking about the Canadian party's problems. "Evidently," he commented, "the United States comrades who were left in Moscow after our departure, and the representatives of the Organization Department in particular, succeeding in defeating our efforts."[17]

The incident illustrated the difficulties of convincing the Comintern that its information was not always accurate and that its views were not always valid. It underlined, too, the difficulties confronting a small party lacking a representative of standing in Moscow to put its case in the Comintern's committees and departments. Stewart Smith, then at the Lenin School, was very young, comparatively inexperienced, and lacked the necessary mandate from the Canadian party. For its part, the Comintern, in its desire to impose organizational and structural unity upon all of its sections, could not accept the Canadian delegates' plea that any deviations from the original instructions for reorganization were carried out in order to minimize loss of membership.

MacDonald, in his review of the CPC's progress at the party's Fifth Convention, made it clear that the policy had raised as many problems as it had solved.[18] Some sections reorganized more successfully than others, and of these, a few freely criticized the party, saying (as did the Sudbury Finns, for example) that they felt the party centre was insincere in its declared desire for reorganization.[19] Despite the party's earlier experience with Moscow, the CEC, to make the reorganization process continue more smoothly, permitted the formation of pure language groups composed solely of party members who were troubled with language difficulties. This modification, however, was quickly criticized by the ECCI's Orgburo, which regarded the step as retrogressive. MacDonald, speaking for the CEC, did not agree, saying that since the preceding convention the party had learned by experience "that a mere mechanical reorganization [gets] us nowhere, but results in retreats in certain quarters which tend to make future reorganization more difficult."[20]

The disagreement between Moscow and Toronto over interpretation was considered by the CPC to be of sufficient importance to warrant sending A. G. Neal, editor of the Finnish newspaper *Vapaus*, and John Navis of the Ukrainian Labour Farmer Temple Association (ULFTA) to the Comintern's Sixth Congress in 1928 to discuss bolshevization of the Canadian party, and to determine the role of the two main language groups within that programme. Leaders of both the FOC and the ULFTA felt that they were unable to comply with the requirements laid down by Moscow because of the particular circumstances of language, economics, and geography. By the time the Congress met, further bitterness and dissention had developed among Finnish and Ukrainian members, and Popowich appealed to the Ukrainian communists to be patient until the matter had been taken up by the Comintern.[21] On its return, the Canadian delegation brought back a resolution from the Anglo-Russian secretariat saying that the chief object of all language organizations was to transform themselves into mass organizations which would draw the foreign-born workers into the general stream of the Canadian labour movement and such communist front organizations as the Canadian Labor Defence League (CLDL).[22] At best, however, Moscow's advice only succeeded in mollifying the Finnish and Ukrainian groups; it did not succeed in solving the Canadian party's organizational difficulties.

Publicly, of course, the party was presented as a trouble-free, smooth-working apparatus. Maurice Spector, quoted in the *Quebec Chronicle Telegraph* of June 25, 1927, certainly presented the CPC as such after the attempt to bolshevize the party had been under way for a considerable time:

The unit of the party organization is the group. There are area groups, so-called because those who make them up live within the same neighborhood, or "area" and the shop groups, which are made up of individuals working in the same factory.

Each group has a secretary and sends a delegate to the central committee of the city in which it is located. This central committee is the standing body and each group delegate serves simultaneously and constantly in his own group and on the central committee.

These central committees are linked up within a given district by a district executive committee which is elected at a convention.

The executive committee of each district calls a convention before each national convention is held and delegates are chosen to represent the district at that national convention. There, the Central Executive is chosen to manage the national affairs of the party. All delegates who have been at least two years in the party are eligible for offices on this executive.

It was an accurate summary of what in theory the party organization should have been. In practice, it was decidedly otherwise.

Despite the CPC's efforts and the Comintern's injunctions, bolshevization of the Canadian party during the first decade was never fully or successfully accomplished. The failure to implement it stemmed, in the first place, from the Comintern refusal to recognize the validity of local and regional conditions which were always such important factors for the Canadian and American parties. Much more serious, as E. H. Carr has pointed out, was the Comintern's lack of political logic.

The attempt of Comintern, in Western Europe and the United States [North America, in fact], to insist on forms of organization suitable for underground parties in revolutionary conditions had been a direct challenge to democratic and parliamentary traditions which were deeply rooted in those conditions, even among the workers. It was also difficult to reconcile with the policy simultaneously inculcated by Comintern on those parties of the peaceful penetration of other left-wing parties, of the formation of united fronts with them and of the ultization of democratic and parliamentary procedures to further their aims.[23]

Certainly, MacDonald, Spector, and other party leaders were never wholly convinced that bolshevization was a practical proposition for the CPC. Accordingly, after 1926, the attempt to reorganize the CPC by substituting factory nuclei for territorial units, gradually lost its impetus.

Although factory cells were continued in certain industrialized areas, the territorial basis for the Canadian party, as Spector's public summary made clear, remained in effect. Indeed, the same arrangement held true for all of the major parties within the Comintern, none of which successfully made the transition. MacDonald, in 1929, was taken to task by the ECCI for his reservations over bolshevization, and the party leadership as a whole was criticized for its failure to modify the CPC structure and organization according to Moscow's wishes.[24] Spector's defection to Trotsky's side in 1928, too, in the Comintern's eyes, dramatically emphasized the latter point. But in both cases Moscow's reaction was more one of denigration and an opportunity to divert attention from an obvious policy failure. After MacDonald's demotion in 1929, the new CPC leadership was again strongly urged by the ECCI in a letter dated October 3, 1929, to carry out a systematic reorganization of the party. Moscow's firm stand, however, was more in the way of an order to the Canadian party to rid itself of undesirable elements, and to tighten up its organization. At the same time it re-emphasized the CPC's failure to prepare itself for revolution during the five years which had elapsed since the Comintern first enunciated its bolshevization policy.

CHAPTER TEN

THE INTERIM YEARS: 1924-1925

EARLY IN May 1924, after the CPC emerged from the Third Worker's Party Convention as an openly proclaimed communist party, Tim Buck, Malcolm Bruce, and A. T. Hill secretly left Canada to attend the Comintern's Fifth Congress. Buck travelled under his party name of "J. Page," while Bruce adopted the pseudonym "F. J. Masson." Hill, his place as the FOC's representative in Toronto temporarily taken by A. G. Neal, the editor of *Vapaus*, travelled under his own name, using funds supplied by the Finnish organization. They paused in Berlin* only long enough to pick up their documents for travel within Russia.[1] On arrival in Moscow they were met by Charles E. Scott, the former Comintern agent in Canada, then a member of the Profintern's American Section, and like the majority of other representatives were housed in the Hotel Lux.[2] Scott, besides his official duties, also acted as guide, showing the three Canadians over the historic revolutionary landmarks still bullet-scarred from street fighting, and pointed out where Lenin and John Reed were interred. The Canadian delegates' experiences and impressions were subsequently embodied in letters from Buck and Bruce to the Central Executive, portions of which eventually appeared in the Canadian party press.[3]

The Fifth Congress,† the first to be held after Lenin's death, was dominated by discussions of the dispute within the German party and the abortive October 1923 revolution in Germany.[4] Briefed on the background of the dispute by Spector, the Canadian delegates witnessed the spectacle of Zinoviev's attack on Radek, who had defended the right deviationists, exemplified by Heinrich Brandler. A contemporary account of Comintern, written in June 1924, describing the position and role of delegates from abroad, affords a revealing glimpse of the nature of the International's meetings and the dominant position of the Soviet party. It applied with startling precision to the Canadian party and its three representatives.

That the Communist Party of the Soviet Union should take such a lead [in the direction of Comintern business] is natural enough. The "foreign" delegates are not, for the most part, the leaders of their home parties which are fighting on the home fronts. And the home parties are after all only "parties", very often very weak parties, bound to their respective Parliament, even though they are careful to make it clear that they do not like parliaments, and prefer dictatorships of the proletariat. These foreign representatives live close to the active controlling centre of the Russian Party, but without exerting any great influence upon it. Through them, however, Moscow exerts a continuous influence, as critic and mentor, on their homes parties. The representatives in question live a half Bohemian life, each with one, perhaps two, rooms in hotels which have been emptied for their use—the "Hotel Lux", for instance, which is still called by its former name though it has been rebaptized as "The Soviet House".[5]

---

*Bertram Wolfe, then a member of the Mexican Communist Party and also enroute to the Comintern Congress, recalls meeting Bruce and Buck in the German capital and joining them in a meal of bread and sausage.

†Reports about the number of delegates vary, ranging from 406 to 510. Of the total, 117 represented the Russian party.

While discussions and developments in Germany held the delegates' attention and dominated the gossip and talk between Congress sessions (which took place from June 17 to July 8, 1924), more prosaic business still required attention.

Accordingly, Buck represented the Canadian party on the Agrarian Commission and served on a committee dealing with the communist women's movement, while Bruce was made a member of bodies dealing with propaganda and colonial affairs. Hill, representing the YCL, held discussions with the Young Communist International's secretariat, and attended sessions of the Comintern and the Third Profintern Congress which followed. Like Bruce, he did not speak at any of the sessions.[6] Neither Canada nor the Canadian party were discussed at any of the formal Congress sessions. Any references to the dominion and the CPC arose during discussions of other questions—of the ECCI report and the general world situation for example—and took the form of asides rather than direct examination of the Canadian party's problems and experiences. On the other hand, Canadian labour problems were specifically and quite fully discussed at the Profintern Congress which followed that of the Comintern.

At the operative level of the Comintern's Organization Bureau, however, the organizational problems confronting the CPC were aired fully and without inhibition. The Canadian situation was taken up in conjunction with the American party's difficulties, and the issue which aroused most controversy was the Comintern's call for all parties to reorganize on the basis of the CPSU's factory nuclei. At the WPC Convention held in April 1924, the Canadian party, to be sure, had paid lip service to the concept of factory nuclei, but within its inner circles strong doubts persisted. Through Piatnitsky, the Comintern made it clear to the Canadian delegates that it expected bolshevization to be put into effect.

After the Comintern and Profintern Congresses Buck, Bruce, and Hill returned individually to Toronto via New York. They reached Canada in late August and early September after pausing for a week or so in Berlin to get some first-hand impressions of the German situation. During the months they were away in Russia, the party had clarified its stand on Canadian trade union autonomy, emphasizing that "the Trades Congress must become a real centre of power" in order to attract the great bulk of Canadian workers, over half of which were not affiliated with the TLC. In addition, as Spector had pointed out editorially in *The Worker*, May 17, 1924,

The Canadian "ends" of the Internationals [such as the United Mine Workers of America] must be given complete economic and political autonomy in Canadian affairs. We have our "own" injunctions, laws, thugs, and troops to cope with. . . . The movement for Canadian autonomy is a movement within the International unions. It starts out from the premise that national secession is bad. But in the interests of freedom of development and action of the Canadian unions, the Internationals, the A. F. of L. must recognize that Canada is no mere state of the American Union whose workers form a State Federation of Labor. . . . The trade unions in this country recognize the importance of international affiliation. But they can no longer be held in tutelage.

The CPC's attitude towards labour formed the background to the international delegates' return, and determined their immediate activities. Bruce was despatched at once to Nova Scotia where, besides lecturing on his observations and experiences in Russia, he was directed to shore up the CPC's organization following Tom Bell's departure to the United States. To the party this had become particularly urgent because of the counter activities of an OBU organizer, Ron Legere, who had begun organization work among the coal and steel workers in Cape Breton. The party's reaction to the OBU—described as a voice from the graveyard—challenge was sharp and certain. OBU policies were bankrupt, the union's leaders were warped, and it was the IWW story all over again.

Beginning as a revolutionary union it [the OBU] has become a yellow pacifistic organization whose bureaucracy and press are distinctly counter-revolutionary. . . . Lenin specifically devoted himself to urging the rebels to WORK INSIDE THE REACTIONARY UNION.[7]

This, Spector urged, was the true programme. Even W. Z. Foster had come to such a realization, and became a communist instead of remaining a syndicalist. Interestingly enough, the same view had been put forward at the beginning of August by J. B. McLachlan, in *The Maritime Labour Herald* of Glace Bay, Nova Scotia.

Both the party leadership and Moscow took the OBU incursion into what each considered to be a stronghold of Canadian communism with great seriousness. Lozovsky, the Profintern's General Secretary, and Kalnin, Secretary of the International Propaganda Committee of Revolutionary Miners,* cabled MacDonald urging him to take all possible steps to prevent splitting the existing union organization in Nova Scotia.[8] The message was printed forthwith in *The Worker* of September 6, 1924 in an attempt to counter the OBU's sudden and unexpected interest in the Nova Scotia miners and steel workers.

Comrades, to split and withdraw District 26 from the UMWA would surely play into Lewis' hands and would surely result in demoralization of your union, seriously weakening whole miners' movement. We therefore call upon you and all other true revolutionists and our adherents to immediately take stand against splitting policy and to reject vigorously all proposals to withdraw your district from UMW of A. On with the fight against the [John L.] Lewis gang. Down with disruption and secession. Hail solidarity and unity of the UMW of A.

Although no split occurred and OBU efforts soon petered out, communist influence within the UMWA in Nova Scotia did not increase correspondingly. Instead, orthodox labour throughout the Dominion began to take a long, hard look at the revolutionary party and the TUEL, and resistance to the blandishments of the united front quickly increased, a resistance which became more apparent as the nation's prosperity increased.

During the autumn of 1924 the CPC contented itself with amplifying the Comintern's programme through its press, and its organizers, including Bruce and Hill, who remained on extended tour. At the party centre Spector, besides editing *The Worker*, gave a Marxist education course; MacDonald spoke at the labour forums and toured Ontario giving local communist groups advice and encouragement; in Montreal the Labour College, and the newly organized Jewish groups, formed the basis for party activity. *The Worker* fulminated against Ramsay MacDonald's Labour government in Britain, discussed the Chinese situation following the ECCI's manifesto on China,† and filled its columns with comments about the "faked" Zinoviev letter.[9] The Manitoba branch of the CLP was formed in October and the annual meeting of the Quebec section held in November gave communist members such as Mike Buhay an opportunity to present resolutions and put forward their views on the convention floor.[10] The leadership also derived some satisfaction from the showing made by Matthew

---

*J. B. McLachlan also received word from the Profintern warning him against the efforts of what were termed "dual unionists" to persuade the Nova Scotia miners to seceded from the UMWA.

†The ECCI, in collaboration with Red International of Labor Unions (Profintern) bureau, started a "Hands Off China" society in 1924, but branches were not formed immediately in Canada. Instead, the CPC focused attention on the imperialist actions in Canton and on the mainland. The communist criticism of the MacDonald government was sparked by the Labour Party's decision at its annual conference not to accept the British Communist Party in affiliation or to endorse any communist as a Labour Party candidate in elections.

Popowich, one of the CPC's pioneer Ukrainian leaders, in the Winnipeg civic elections.[11] The outcome, according to party thinking, was a defeat for labour as a whole, though the 2,005 first-choice votes Popowich received were taken as an indication that the communist movement was gaining ground.

But party leaders recognized and allowed the party press to publicize the need for Canadian communists to do more to bring the French-Canadian working class into the revolutionary movement. The language barrier and the lack of French Canadians who knew anything about Marxist theory or practice were cited as principal reasons for the gap in revolutionary organization in Canada.[12] In practice this deficiency was never rectified, despite various half-hearted attempts. As a result, the communist groups organized in Montreal by the Buhays and the French Canadian, St. Martin, remained isolated in a sea of English capitalist and French-speaking clerical reactionaries.

With the advent of 1925, Cape Breton continued to hold the CPC's attention. The labour situation there remained acute, and was exacerbated when the miners' agreement with the British Empire Steel Company (BESCO) expired and the company began to campaign for a further wage cut of 10 per cent. The Canadian party reacted at once. The Central Executive called upon Nova Scotia miners to down tools, and castigated the Liberal government, headed by MacKenzie King, for its failure to cut through the constitutional morass of the British North America Act and bring relief to the destitute area. Spector voiced the party's views in a sharply-worded article in *The Worker*, February 21, 1925, on the Privy Council's Judicial Committee declaration that the Industrial Disputes Investigation Act, popularly known as the "Lemieux Act,"* violated the provisions of the British North America Act and was therefore *ultra vires*. He declared:

A class-conscious leadership of trade unions would have fought this scheme to hamstring the workers' will to action [i.e., the passage of the Lemieux Act in 1907], but the trade union bureaucracy only made a few feeble protests and adapted themselves to the "enlightened" liberal form of sabotaging the labour movement by arbitration. . . . Although the Lemieux Act was absolutely against the class interests of Canadian workers, the repeal of the British North America Act destroying the sovereignty of British Imperialism over the Dominion and making for the Dominion's centralization would be in the interests of the workers, even though certain sections of the Canadian bourgeoisie desire these things too. . . . we may expect this latest decision of the Privy Council to loosen still further the bonds of the Empire.[13]

Loosening the bonds of Empire through abolition of the BNA Act, thus bringing about Canadian autonomy, became at this time one of the Communist Party's rallying cries, and squared with Comintern views on British imperialism. Indeed, the early spring of 1925 saw the Comintern attitude towards imperialism, British imperialism in particular, increasingly expressed in *The Worker*.[14] According to the Comintern the dominions were becoming more and more industrialized and therefore less dependent on British industrial power for goods and services. Thus they were less prone to accept Britain's decisions and actions in foreign policy. Also, the United

*The Lemieux Act was drafted in 1907 by MacKenzie King when he was Deputy Minister of Labour, and made provision for a three-man conciliation board to investigate a strike or a lockout before the dispute could be declared in effect in what was considered a public utility. Under the Privy Council's ruling, a federal conciliation board could have no authority and the Nova Scotia provincial government was reluctant to interfere in the dispute and so offend the coal and steel directors. The Nova Scotia dispute occupied by far the greatest amount of space in *The Worker* and other party organs throughout the first half of 1925, and took up most of the CEC's time. Spector's arguments were echoed in parliament by J. S. Woodsworth who, though not a party member, still contributed a column to *The Worker*, and in turn, drew many of his arguments and ideas from it.

States was becoming steadily more powerful, and it was essential for Britain to remain at peace with her. Such views, put forward mainly by Radek and Trotsky, were attacked by Zinoviev at the Fifth Plenum of the ECCI, held in the spring of 1925, on the grounds that the Anglo-American rapprochement would result in a combined Anglo-American imperialism which would be sufficiently powerful to eliminate the political and economic contradictions prevailing in Europe. The articles appearing in the Canadian communist press, however, gave no hint of the mounting attack upon Trotsky then beginning within the Russian party. Instead, the party organs were concerned more with domestic issues, and the Comintern's interest in completing the shift to factory cells as the basic party unit.

Throughout the autumn and winter of 1924–25 *The Worker* also devoted much space to the apparent drawing together of British and Russian trade unions following the visit of a British delegation to the Russian unions' sixth congress in the autumn of 1924, and the increasing importance of the Minority Movement* within the British party.[15] Two additional pages in many issues of *The Worker* enabled Spector to print more material, and he availed himself of a wide variety of articles and commentaries from Comintern sources. Articles ranged from Piatnitsky's reiteration of factory nuclei as the best basis for communist organization, to R. Palme Dutt on "Empire Socialism," and the impressions of A. A. Purcell, leader of a British trade union delegation which visited Russia, and President of the Amsterdam International, who wrote on "The Truth About Russia." Because of the importance attached to the need to educate the Canadian working man, the paper increased its volume even though the financial drive to raise $5,000 failed, realizing only $1,600 after four months.[16]

Whatever disappointments the Canadian communist movement suffered during 1924, it could always look to Moscow for an explanation and a new guideline. The shifts and turns of analysis and policy often fluctuated considerably. To take one instance, the Fifth Congress, with Zinoviev its chief spokesman and supported by Eugene Varga, the Comintern's economist, resolutely declared in mid-1924 that world stabilization was out of the question, and confidently predicted a severe American crisis which in turn would cause economic deterioration in Europe in 1924–1925. At the Fifth Plenum, March 21 to April 6, 1925, the ECCI belatedly recognized that Western capitalism had recovered substantially, but labelled it a passing phenomenon, a partial and temporary stabilization. On the basis of this fresh analysis the Plenum unanimously adopted the ECCI's report which, besides stating that the events which transpired since the Fifth Congress had confirmed the analysis made at that time, also called upon all parties to carry out more vigorous compaigns for trade union unity.

After the experiences of the Canadian delegates to the Fifth Congress, the CPC, in order to present its own views more effectively and to determine Comintern thinking, despatched William Moriarty to the Fifth Plenum. At Moscow the American Commission, headed by the Finnish communist leader Otto Kuusinen, examined problems which had continued to plague the American party for so long.[17] In the process, the

---

*The Minority Movement was organized initially by Willie Gallacher to persuade the revolutionary minorities of workers which existed in many British trade unions not to secede from those bodies but to remain and become increasingly active. Management of the Movement was taken over by Harry Pollitt after the preliminary organization work was completed in 1924. The Movement was subsidized by the Profintern, at least for a time, because Moscow considered it a part of the united front tactic.

Commission also dealt with Canadian party matters. For the CPC and William Moriarty, the American party's disunity was of secondary importance. Nevertheless, it was the American Commission's recommendations which had a direct bearing on Moriarty's discussions with the Orgburo, and on the problems and tactics facing the Canadian movement. The Commission recommended that the American party should not attempt to form a labour party patterned after the British example, urging instead the development of the moribund TUEL into an active left-wing labour opposition. Also, the Commission pointed out that the language groups in the American party tended to concentrate too much on their own special interests, which were counter to bolshevik organization principles.[18] The impact of these criticisms and recommendations upon the Canadian party were two fold. First, they confirmed that the CPC's drive to gain control of the Canadian Labor Party was the correct tactic in the Canadian setting; second, the reorganization recommended for the United States party's language sections* was put into effect in the Canadian party, though on a much smaller scale.[19]

While in Moscow, Moriarty also experienced at first hand the controversy over Trotsky which had convulsed the Russian party, and which by then was beginning to make itself felt throughout the Comintern.[20] Bukharin, in one of the longest reports to the Plenum, strongly indicted Trotskyism, and after he finished, none of the speakers who followed defended Trotsky.[21] In the face of such a devastating attack, and with a clear indication that the tide of feeling, at least in Russia, seemed to be running against Trotsky, Moriarty, in order to determine the Canadian party's attitude, cabled the CEC in Toronto to ask for their views on Trotskyism.

Before replying, the CEC canvassed its members for their views, and some doubt and wavering soon became apparent. Spector, for one, openly confirmed his sympathy with Trotsky's views. Buck, who was then in western Canada on party organization work, was contacted for his opinion. He replied saying that he was prepared to back any stand made by the Executive Committee members at the CPC national headquarters since he did not have any hard and fast views on the Trotsky issue.[22] The variations in views and emphasis were implicit in the party's cabled answer, which was, in effect, more of a reproof of the Comintern than a forthright denunciation of Trotskyism. The cable, dated April 8, 1925, ran:

The Executive Committee is not convinced on the basis of evidence obtained, that the Comintern is actually menaced and confronted with a system constituting Trotskyism. Notwithstanding Trotsky's mistakes prior to 1917 and during the course of the revolution, we are unconvinced that the implications of the "permanent revolution" theory attributed to him are actually entertained by Trotsky and that he contemplates revision of Leninism. We are of the opinion that the prestige of the Comintern has not been enhanced here by the bitterness of the anti-Trotsky attack. No request from leading elements or party membership for discussion in the Party press.[23]

Unquestionably, Spector, who drafted the communication,† was the key man in formulating the CEC's stand and in establishing the Canadian party's position, since MacDonald was not interested in Russian party matters. But even at that the incident

---

*According to Buck, the CPC until 1925 was social democratic in organization, "and our party was organized on the basis of language branches and language sections." The American party had 13 language units; the CPC was really concerned with only three: the Finnish, Ukrainian and Jewish, though other smaller and less important groups existed.

†The cable was published in *The Worker* on August 1, 1925. There is no direct evidence to confirm why publication of the cable was so long delayed. The decision to make it public, however, may have been dependent upon Moriarty's return from Moscow, his account of the Plenum proceedings, and his impressions of the feeling prevailing in Comintern circles.

indicated the attitude of comparative independence prevailing in the dominion's communist movement. In the welter of current party work, Spector's outlook and Buck's willingness to follow the majority stand were brushed aside. In the long run, however, neither was forgotten. In the end, too, bolshevik discipline prevailed: all Comintern parties supported the Russian party, and secret reservations remained the prerogative only of individuals such as Spector in Canada and James Cannon in the United States.

Before returning to Toronto, Moriarty spent some time touring Russia,* partly in company with Bill Haywood of the American communist movement.[24] En route to Canada he paused in Britain to attend the British party's annual convention, held in Glasgow on May 31 where, as a fraternal delegate, he both represented and spoke for the CPC. He returned to Toronto early in July, in time to assume some of the responsibilities usually held by MacDonald and Spector, both of whom had gone to represent the Canadian Labor Party and the CPC at the British Commonwealth Labour Conference in London, England, at the end of the month.[25] After the excitement and stimulus of the Soviet scene he found Canadian party affairs rather flat, and the comparative emptiness of the party's till, after Piatnitsky's refusal of funds, alarming. Neither dejection nor the CPC's impoverishment, however, were in themselves unusual; both were characteristic of persons and parties serving in the Comintern's ranks.

*His stay in Russia was reported by *The Ottawa Citizen*, July 13, 1925, and the *Toronto Daily Star*, July 18, 1925. In the *Citizen* Moriarty disposed of the rumour that Haywood had left the USSR. In the *Star* he claimed that he had interviewed Trotsky in company with a Russian-speaking delegate from the British Communist Party. Trotsky, he declared, was "the nervous restless leader who would not adapt himself so readily as others to changing conditions demanding new policies."

CHAPTER ELEVEN

THE CPC AND THE CANADIAN LABOR PARTY

AFTER THE COMINTERN issued its initial call for a united front in December 1921, and as the first WPC convention drew to an end in February 1922, two possibilities for achieving Moscow's desires in the Dominion became increasingly obvious to Canadian communist leaders.[1] These were: (a) to collaborate with the Canadian Labor Party (CLP) which had been formed in August 1921, and which attempted to model itself after the British Labour Party; and (b) to promote the Trade Union Educational League (TUEL), especially in economically depressed areas where labour unrest made the situation ripe for communist exploitation.[2]

At the time the CLP consisted of four loosely organized provincial sections; Nova Scotia, Quebec, Ontario, and Alberta. Manitoba, Saskatchewan, and British Columbia were in the process of being organized. At the local level each section was composed of affiliated political parties, trade unions, labour councils, and co-operative societies. Provincial conventions were held annually at which provincial executives were elected, and from which representatives for the national executive were appointed. The latter body was headed by a president, vice-president, and secretary-treasurer.[3]

Immediately following the WPC convention, therefore, MacDonald attended the CLP's Ontario section's third annual convention in Stratford, Ontario, on February 26, 1922. As a fraternal delegate from the newly formed Workers' Party, he described the WPC's aims and organization.[4] That formal contact with the CLP's strongest section was quickly followed up at the organization's highest level when MacDonald, supported by Spector and Buck, put the WPC's case before the CLP's second national convention in Montreal at the end of August. Although the communist delegation was denied the privileges of the national convention until the WPC was accepted as a member of the CLP's Ontario section, the groundwork for affiliation was completed.[5] Once made, the Communist Party's contact with the CLP was never broken.

The communist leaders' efforts to affiliate the WPC with the Canadian Labor Party were soon rewarded. Before the end of the year the CLP's Quebec section approved affiliation on the basis that the WPC's members would abide by the CLP constitution and pay their dues before the provincial unit's fourth convention ended.[6] Early in February the CLP's Ontario section followed the Quebec precedent at its fourth annual meeting.[7] Since the two sections represented the most highly populated as well as the most industrialized areas in the country, the WPC leadership felt that the developments represented a tangible advance in the Canadian party's efforts to achieve a united front within Canadian labour.

From the beginning the Comintern, through Scott and the ECCI, approved the Canadian party's policy towards the CLP. In a letter dated Moscow, January 29, 1923, and signed by Bukharin and Kuusinen (then Secretary), the International made its position clear and explicit:

We think you appreciate at their ʳrue value such affiliations and look forward to a continuation of this policy in the future. The true political party of the working class should not only be a party in the vanguard of the army of emancipation, directing the advance by its proclamations, but should also, through the activities of its membership, direct all the other organs of working class expression in action. This can only be done by Communists working as disciplined units in a strongly organized Communist Party.[8]

Although the communists' efforts to solidify Canadian labour politically meant co-operating with all shades of labour opinion, it did not mean, as Spector quickly took pains to point out at the WPC's second convention, that the Workers' Party would sink its distinctive aims, principles, and organization as a communist party. In *The Worker* of May 1, Spector wrote:

On the contrary it regards the maintenance of its aims and principles, its freedom of criticism and agitation and its identity as an organization to be the guarantee of further progress to the Labour Movement.

At the same time, the party leaders felt that there were no reasons why the CLP should not express the political and industrial aims of the class struggle. After the WPC's second convention, Spector noted:

There is no reason why we should not profit from the mistakes of labor parties in the past and fashion the Canadian Labor Party into an organ of real action capable of reflecting whether on the floor of the House [of Commons] or in the street the spirit of such struggles as those of the Winnipeg strike or of the Nova Scotia and Alberta coal miners.[9]

The communist movement, therefore, stood for a Labor Party which would reveal the utter fraud of capitalism, democracy, and the harsh realities of wage slavery. Spector, in particular, left no doubt that what the Canadian communists wanted was a labour party organized and prepared to carry out a proletarian programme of socialist reconstruction, and it was on that basis that the CLP became the focus of the communist movement's quest for a united front.

Throughout 1923 the WPC, with MacDonald and Spector in the leading roles, pleaded the case for the CLP. At the annual Trades and Labour Congress (TLC) meeting in Vancouver, it was the communist delegation which presented a resolution which sought to endorse the CLP as labour's authorized political voice.[10] The first real opportunity for the CPC to elaborate the communists' views about the Canadian Labor Party occurred at the second annual convention of the CLP, held in Montreal, November 10-11, 1923.* MacDonald, representing the WPC, spoke at some length on the first day of the meeting.

He outlined the different ideas of the right, centre and left wings, and showed how a united front could be created by all those who were sincerely interested in fighting the common enemy, captitalism, without any unit losing its political identity. ... He reviewed the European situation, particularly that of Germany, showed how the German workers had tried both the right and centre tactics as well as capitalist government and were now faced with two alternatives, either a Fascist dictatorship of capitalism or a working class dictatorship. Our labour movement could learn much from these events ... and it was necessary for us ... in Canada to build up both the economic and political wings of our movement so that in the near future the strength of our movement would lead to the formation of a Farmer-Labor government.... [11]

The views expressed by MacDonald were not only representative of the Canadian communists' thoughts on the united front, but were initiated and approved by the Comintern. Moscow stipulated that on joining the CLP, the Workers' Party was to reserve the right of free criticism and, above all, to maintain its organizational identity.[12] Many of the subsequent resolutions passed at the Quebec section's meeting

*The convention was attended by 88 delegates representing 27 different organizations.

were therefore openly introduced, or were communist inspired. All reflected the WPC's basic programme: amalgamation of all craft unions into industrial unions, and recognition of the USSR by the governments of Canada and Great Britain.[13] To have these views endorsed by the Quebec section represented, in the party's eyes, a considerable advance in bringing its programme before a wider audience.

Developments at the Nova Scotia Independent Labour Party's (ILP) fifth annual convention* a fortnight later gave the communist leaders even greater cause for satisfaction. The ILP affiliated itself with the CLP, and the resolutions passed by the convention amplified and coloured those expressed earlier in Montreal. More important for the communists was McLachlan's election as president of the ILP, although he was absent in prison. Joe Wallace† became vice-president and Tom Bell was placed on the executive committee.[14] The successes in central Canada and in the Maritimes were supplemented by the news that the Manitoba Independent Labour Party was actively considering affiliation with the CLP.[15]

The optimism generated within the Workers' Party by these developments was tempered by the awareness that while the CLP had grown considerably, it had not yet taken on the character of a real mass movement. Spector, for one, realized this, and made no effort to conceal the problems ahead. For him the most vital and interesting aspect of the CLP movement was the question of an alliance with the farmers.

It is a question that should be thrown open for discussion in the Workers' Party, the [Canadian] Labor Party and the farmers' organizations, whether a united front in the form of a Canadian Labor-Farmer Party does not meet the requirements of Canadian conditions more than a strict-Labor Party, modelled after the British example. The Farmers' Movement in Canada is politically in a state of flux and even disintegration. . . . In this state of flux and even dissatisfaction inside the farmers' movement, it is possible to bring about an alliance between workers and farmers, with advantage to the Labor movement. In these manoeuvers it goes without saying there is a danger that the Workers' Party might be swallowed up.[16]

Spector concluded that it was imperative for the WPC to develop greater initiative than it had shown hitherto.‡ That meant increasing the party's industrial membership, strengthening its own organization, and raising the general educational level of its members, while bearing in mind that "the leading role of the Workers' Party as a Communist Party must be continually kept in view."[17]

Throughout the early months of 1924 the Workers' Party and the communist press focused attention upon the CLP and the need for working class political solidarity. From the communist viewpoint, their efforts met with considerable success when MacDonald was elected vice-president of the CLP's Ontario section at its fifth annual convention held on March 22, 1924, at Hamilton.§ In addition, at that meeting MacDonald and Moriarty were designated delegates to the next CLP national convention, a further indication that the communist drive towards achieving a united front—and ultimate control of the CLP—was making tangible progress.[18] What pleased the communist leadership most was that the advance had been achieved

---

*The convention, which was attended by 33 delegates, was held at Sydney Mines on November 24, 1923.

†Wallace became an early member of the CPC and his "proletarian" poetry has been one of the main cultural features of the Canadian party press since the 1920's.

‡Spector had in mind the American party's disastrous experiences when it attempted to forge an alliance with the Farmer-Labor movement led by John Fitzpatrick during the spring and summer of 1923, followed by the United States communists' ill-starred support of Senator La Follette's attempts to create a third party in the United States.

§103 credentialled delegates, of which 24 represented eight Workers' Party branches, attended.

despite opposition led by James Simpson, an old-time Toronto labour leader who was secretary-treasurer of the CLP's national executive.

Notwithstanding the communist leaders' obvious successes, the WPC's policy towards the CLP was not universally approved of within the party. Tom Bell, writing immediately before the Third Convention, warned that the main danger lay in the WPC's enthusiasm for the united front. If it were not carefully controlled, he warned, the party would degenerate to a point where the communists would be indistinguishable from "labourites" who fully believed in a "constitutional" solution of the class struggle. Indeed, Bell claimed that it was becoming more evident daily "that our members are being turned into political Jeckyls [sic] and Hyde—they were good Labourites at one time and good Communists at another."[19] This, he claimed, was happening because the party had not threshed out its problems related to the CLP. If the communists were going to challenge the reformists for control of the CLP, he felt it was essential for the Workers' Party to remain in the CLP as an independent party and fight to have its programme accepted by the workers. To be thrown out of the CLP was, in his opinion, a lesser evil than being allowed to remain inside the organization at the expense of abandoning principles.

While not representative of party thinking, Bell's reservations were echoed by the Comintern. Like Bell, the ECCI detected in some Canadian communists an apparent willingness to sink their identity with the WPC without being forced to do so by reactionaries in the CLP. In order to avoid confusion, however, Moscow, in an undated letter signed by the Comintern's secretary, Kolarow, made it clear that it was

... a matter of [the] greatest importance in the political struggle in Canada that the CLP should be developed .... Nevertheless, we [i.e., Comintern] must not fail at all times to point out the insufficiency of the CLP and the absolute necessity of the WPC. The role and the importance of a communist party in the class struggle and in the Proletarian Revolution is a lesson that the radicals and revolutionaries of Canada should still be taught to grasp and understand.[20]

The ECCI also raised the question of whether the CLP should be converted to a Labour and Farmer party. In doing so, it noted that despite the difference between Great Britain and Canada—Canada's population was half agrarian, comparable to that of the United States—the CLP was patterned after the British Labour Party. The ECCI suggested therefore that the Canadian party discuss the question thoroughly, particularly through the communist press which, Moscow felt, did not explain the differences between a true workers' and farmers' government and a well-to-do and "corrupt" farmers' government such as the post-war United Farmers administration in Ontario. It was of prime importance, the Comintern felt, that the Canadian communists should begin a campaign to create a cleavage between "the well-to-do farmers and the poor tenant farmers," and to link the latter with organized labour.[21] Prompted by the Comintern's views, Spector and MacDonald raised the issue at the WPC's Third Convention—the convention at which the party adopted the title of Communist Party of Canada—which responded by endorsing a resolution in favour of broadening the CLP into a Canadian Farmer-Labor Party.[22]

The possibilities of doing so were increased materially when MacDonald was elected president of the CLP at its national convention held in London, Ontario, directly after the TLC had finished its annual deliberations.[23] Up to that time the communists, despite their successes in Ontario, Quebec, and the Maritimes, felt that as a national entity the CLP had developed indifferently. The emphasis had tended to be on provincial rather than on national development. With MacDonald's election the CPC felt that the provincial sections would have to restrain themselves "until we see if the new [national] executive will shake off the laissez-faire methods of the past."[24] It soon became evident that action to shape the CLP into a national party more in keeping with the CPC's concept was not going to be quickly or easily accomplished. Since each provincial section was autonomous, and since the Canadian Labor Party was simply a loose association of provincial sections, the CLP's national executive had little effective power. Within the national executive, too, opposition to the communists' drive for domination, headed by James Simpson, soon began to manifest itself. Accordingly, MacDonald, Spector, and the CPC leadership reverted to the provincial sections as the most effective bodies through which they could hope to achieve control of the CLP.

That such an approach was sound was demonstrated at the CLP's Ontario section convention held in Toronto April 10–11, 1925. Spector struck the keynote of the CPC's aims when he declared

... that his party considered that the Labor Party could only be a success if it were an effective instrument of the class struggle and if it followed the lead of the Communists and the Left Wing. The unity that the Communists call for is the unity of the international trade union movement, the united front is for the purpose of the class struggle, international solidarity is of the kind manifested by Soviet Russia . . . .[25]

Outnumbered four to one—194 delegates representing 66 affiliated bodies attended —the communist delegates, led by MacDonald, Spector, Bruce, and A. E. Smith, acting as a unified caucus, succeeded in obtaining the convention's approval of several controversial resolutions. These included approval of the Profintern as the medium for unifying the international trade union movement on a world scale, and one which voiced the convention's admiration for Lozovsky's cabled offer of $5,000 on behalf of the RILU and the All Russian Miners' Union to J. B. McLachlan, for miners' relief in Nova Scotia.[26]

Apart from making their influence felt on the convention floor, the communist delegates succeeded in influencing the gathering sufficiently to have A. E. Smith* elected president, MacDonald vice-president, and four of the five delegates to the CLP's national convention selected from their ranks.[27] The convention also approved MacDonald and James Simpson as the CLP delegates to the British Commonwealth Labour Conference scheduled to be held in London during the summer.

Using the same tactics, communist delegates—seven out of a total of 85—to the second annual British Columbia CLP convention held in Vancouver on May 2–3, had resolutions reflecting the CPC's point of view on immigration, non-contributory national unemployment insurance, and capitalist wars endorsed by the meeting.[28] The Toronto and Vancouver successes in the CPC's avowed purpose of transforming the CLP into a militant political entity directed and controlled by a communist minority did not go unnoticed. The two conventions alerted labour leaders across the Dominion, and opposition to the CPC, nominal until then, began to stiffen. Before it became marked, however, MacDonald and Simpson, as the CPL representatives, proceeded to England for the oft-postponed Commonwealth Labour Conference.

Spector too attended the conference. Although he obtained his credentials from the CLP at the latest possible moment, the CPC's decision to send him was not an

---

*In his autobiography Smith admits that his election to the CLP Ontario presidency was "quite unexpected." He won by two votes. By the time of the CLP convention Smith had formally joined the CPC.

H

unpremeditated last-minute development. He attended the London meeting because the Comintern had instructed the CPC to get at least one party member to the conference, for the British Labour Party did not permit communists to hold membership in its ranks. Spector was to make contact with British communist leaders, and at the conference, to intervene whenever possible to help bring out the communist viewpoint.[29] MacDonald, as an official CLP representative and the known leader of the Canadian party, felt it prudent to exercise a certain measure of discretion. Nevertheless, in keeping with the instructions laid down by the CLP's Ontario section convention, he spoke at the meeting, taking the opportunity to voice what was, in effect, Comintern's stand on imperialism and Canadian independence.[30]

Opposition to the communist tactics and policies within the CLP did not appear immediately after the CPC's successes in Ontario and British Columbia. At the CLP convention,* which, in 1925, preceded the TLC convention, MacDonald indeed was returned as president of the organization by acclamation.[31] The storm broke in the autumn when the CLP's Quebec section, meeting on November 28, 1925 at Quebec City, expelled the Communist Party units within its ranks by a small majority.[32] Mike Buhay blamed the action upon the delegates representing the Brotherhood of Railway Carmen who, he claimed, had packed the convention and, on express orders from their leaders in the United States, forced the expulsion through.

To the CPC's Central Executive Committee the expulsion was a serious matter. It quickly issued a lengthy statement deploring the actions of "the reformists and reactionaries" at Quebec.[33] It also took pains to counter the charge that the "red" delegates were attempting to lead the CLP into the arms of the Third International saying that the CLP was a federated party. While the statement rested its case with a plea for labour political unity, it also struck a defiant note.

The expulsion of the Communist Party from the Quebec section will not liquidate the communist branches there. Neither will it keep the communist party from participating in elections or other activity. We will carry on. We offer and accept the united front of the Canadian workers on the basis of a fight for the demands immediate and partial of the Canadian workers.[34]

To offset the effects of the expulsion the CPC immediately initiated protest movements through its members in other CLP provincial sections which continued during the remainder of 1925 and throughout 1926. But the tide against the party within the Canadian labour movement had definitely turned.

At first, the CPC's efforts to retain its initiative within the CLP proved successful. At the Ontario section's convention held in London on April 2-3, 1926, the party persuaded the convention to approve a resolution urging the Quebec section to rescind its action against the communist units in that province. More important, the 50 communist delegates, through careful briefing by MacDonald and Spector, and by acting as a disciplined unit, managed to avoid a repetition of the Quebec development. A resolution sponsored, as in Quebec, by the Railway Carmen, urged the CLP to exclude the CPC from affiliation with the Ontario section. The convention's Resolution Committee, in a majority report, concurred, but MacDonald quickly countered by presenting a minority brief which recommended the defeat of the resolution on the grounds that a federated party such as the CLP could not exclude any working class organization. After a sharp debate, the majority report recommending the CPC's

*Only 15 delegates representing the CLP in Quebec, Ontario, Saskatchewan, and British Columbia attended the meeting which was held on August 30, 1925, in Ottawa.

expulsion was defeated.[35] The communist victory* was an important one, for Ontario was the lynch pin in the country's industrial development and, in the party's eyes, control of the CLP's Ontario section was basic to its ultimate aim of controlling the country's political labour movement. However, the London meeting was the last at which the "principle of unity" was applied.[36]

From the CPC standpoint, comparable successes were registered at the CLP Alberta convention, held at the same time as the Ontario meeting, and later, at the British Columbia convention held in Vancouver on May 22–23, 1926. Once again the communists' tactics proved effective, and minority delegations were able to introduce a variety of resolutions subsequently endorsed by both meetings.[37] But the germ of resistance, first manifested at Quebec, began to multiply, and the CPC's appeals to the Quebec section and to the national CLP convention failed to lift the ban on the party in the French-Canadian province.[38] By the spring of 1927, the communists in the Ontario CLP section were faced with what Spector, writing in *The Worker* of April 30, termed "the open sabotage of the Right Wing." Until then those opposed to the communists contented themselves with threats of withdrawal from the CLP, but the opposition had never been organized. The effectiveness of the Quebec section's action, however, encouraged the less extreme labour men to express themselves more forcibly, and the communists, for the first time, were squarely challenged at the Ontario section's convention in Hamilton on April 15–16, 1927.

The passage of a number of revolutionary resolutions at the CLP Ontario meeting, engineered by the minority group of Communist Party members acting in caucus, reinforced the growing opinion within that body that CPC hegemony could not continue. On the last day of the convention non-communist delegates met to discuss how to prevent the communists from further exploiting their gains and from extending the scope and scale of their manoeuvres.[39] That informal meeting, with James Simpson taking a leading part, became the nucleus of an opposition which resulted in the formation of an anti-communist labour party.

The challenge was not ignored by the CPC, which, Spector made clear, would not "sit idly by and watch a set of class collaborationist politicians hankering for the fleshpot of parliament, destroy the work of many years towards the upbuilding of a united front."[40] The party's intention of transforming the CLP into a communist instrument was also clearly expressed by MacDonald at the CPC's Fifth National Convention. According to the leadership's analysis, the CLP's slow growth was attributed to two factors: increasing bitterness and hostility on the part of union and TLC officials towards the CLP; and the dulling effect of the Liberal government's legislative programme on the Canadian working class which, they felt, had created the illusion among the politically backward workers that the federal government was sympathetic towards labour.† Hostility to the communists and the CLP was not confined to central Canada alone. The Independent Labour Party in Manitoba,

*The motion was defeated by 116 votes to 57, with 42 delegates abstaining. The gathering also adopted various communist-inspired resolutions, including one which demanded that the federal government should refuse to ratify the Locarno treaty. A. E. Smith was re-elected President. In addition, 5 of the 13 members of the executive committee, including Florence Custance and J. W. Ahlqvist, were CPC members.

†This outburst was caused by the Liberal government's enactment of the Old Age Pensioners Act, originally turned down by the Senate, which provided for the payment to any co-operating province of one half the cost of such pensions. The maximum pension was to be $240 per annum to British subjects of 70 years or over who had been resident in Canada. The CPC later tempered its hostility and instructed its members in the CLP to press for its acceptance by each province.

headed by A. A. Heaps and J. S. Woodsworth, led the attack on the party.[41]

To offset the growing opposition to the CPC's policies and actions within the CLP, the party at its fifth national convention in June 1927 urged its members

. . . to intensify the organizational and political work of the provincial sections of the CLP by increasing propaganda and agitation; regular organizational contact and communication through bulletins, leaflets etc., developing organization campaigns through all trade union locals, stressing the need for independent political action by the workers for social legislation . . . .[42]

The recommended antidote, MacDonald felt sure, would prove effective. In his report to the CPC's Fifth Convention, he pointed out:

The strengthening of our influence in the trade unions will offset the attempt being made at present to organize a political party of reformists based on individual membership. This must also be combatted with greater recruiting activity on the part of our Party units.[43]

At the same time, MacDonald took the opportunity to criticize the party's Quebec members for not showing more determination in their efforts to get communist units readmitted into the provincial CLP.[44] Since the Comintern approved the CPC's policy towards the CLP, the Canadian party leaders were confident and uninhibited in their approach to the problem.

In its attempts to counter the growing hostility against it within the Canadian labour movement, the CPC, from the first, seized the initiative. Until the Ontario CLP's spring meeting, and until the TLC annual convention, the communists' efforts had taken the form of increased organization and propaganda moves. Once the opposition became clearly delineated however, the CPC soon took action. In the autumn Spector, in a biting editorial in *The Worker* of September 17, for the first time openly and bitterly attacked James Simpson, the veteran labour leader who had been one of the CLP's founding members and its national secretary-treasurer. The basis for the attack was that Simpson, by accepting the TLC's vice-presidency after his election to CLP office, had proven that there was not a single fundamental issue dividing him from the reactionary Congress leadership. Spector intoned:

The way of Simpson is the way of Hicks, Purcell, Swales, and Herbert Smith [British trade union and labour leaders]. They are radical and use Left Wing phrases when that is safe and implies no action, but when, sooner or later, they have got to stop "left-winging" and make a definite choice between the revolutionary class struggle and reformist class-collaboration, they [Hicks etc.] choose to betray the miners and the general strike and international trade union unity.

The editorial closed with an appeal for unification of all left-wing forces in the Canadian labour movement.

Events moved swiftly after Spector's initial salvo against Simpson and the TLC. Simpson, from his position of strength within the trade union movement, reacted quickly by putting forward an amendment to the Toronto District Labour Constitution at a regular local TLC meeting held early in October. It proposed that delegates who supported organizations other than those affiliated to the TLC should be expelled. Without being specific, it was unmistakably directed at the CPC and its front organizations. Despite the communists' bitter opposition to what they labelled a threat to trade union democracy, the measure was passed with the required two-thirds majority on October 20, a fortnight after it was first proposed.[45]

Almost immediately the CPC shifted its focus back to the Canadian Labor Party, calling for a national convention for the spring of 1928, and expressing the hope that the Quebec section, scheduled to meet before the end of the year, would return to the united front by readmitting communist delegates.[46] One reason for the quick return to the CLP was the announcement that an opposition Labour Party would soon be launched in Ontario, an organization which Spector and MacDonald knew would aim at nothing less than the disintegration of the communist-controlled CLP Ontario section. To the communists the policies which the new party was expected to follow would be similar to those pursued by the Independent Labour Party of Manitoba under the leadership of J. S. Woodsworth. In the CPC's eyes, the ILP and Woodsworth were reformists and class collaborationists bent on deliberately sabotaging the Canadian Labor Party.*

With the launching of the anti-communist "Independent Labour Party of Ontario" at the Toronto Labour Temple on November 7, 1927, Spector and MacDonald made a last desperate effort to recoup their party's position by again turning upon Simpson. Within a week, at a meeting of the Toronto Central Council of the CLP, Spector, on behalf of the CPC, moved a motion expressing lack of confidence in Simpson's ability to head a united front ticket in the forthcoming Toronto civic elections, and proposed Simpson's removal from the CLP slate. One of Spector's most telling arguments was that Simpson, by accepting the office of secretary in the newly-formed Independent Labour Party, was condoning "dual unionism," a position which he had previously opposed. Seconded by MacDonald and Buck, both of whom repeated the charges made by Spector, the motion was approved, and Simpson's name did not go forward.[47]

The communist victory was of short duration, for it led to Simpson's resignation as secretary-treasurer from both the CLP dominion executive and its Ontario section. With Simpson's resignation, and with the corresponding increase in opposition which followed his exit, the CLP quickly lost its significance in the Canadian labour scene. The Quebec section, meeting in mid-December 1927, refused, after protracted discussion, to readmit the Communist Party units in that province.[48] The revolutionary resolutions sponsored by communist delegates and passed at the annual CLP conventions in Ontario and British Columbia in February and April 1928 were not sufficient to counter the effects of the party's failure in Quebec and of Simpson's withdrawal. Simpson's resignation from the CLP was fatal for it spotlighted the CPC's aim to transform the Canadian Labor Party into a mass communist front organization, and in doing so, effectively isolated the Communist Party from the mainstream of Canadian labour and political movements.

Against the wider canvas of the Comintern and Russian party policies, the CPC's misfortune with the CLP was a small parochial problem which never impinged upon Moscow, or affected any other party. In the context of Canadian labour politics, however, the disruption within the CLP caused by the Communist Party's attempts to obtain control and to transform that body into an instrument for revolution (a policy fully approved by the Comintern), arrested the development of an embryonic national left-wing party in Canada. Whatever progress had been made in that direction by the CLP was halted, and the initiative for the creation of a socialist

*The CPC's attitude towards Woodsworth is most strikingly revealed in a short article entitled "Evolution of a Labor Statesman," in *The Worker*, October 29, 1927. Kenneth McNaught, in his biography *A Prophet in Politics* (Toronto, 1959), does not deal with the CLP or the disenchantment on the part of both Woodsworth and the communists following the 1926 federal election, and only mentions that Woodworth's writing often appeared in *The Worker*. Woodsworth's daughter, Grace MacInnis, in *J. S. Woodsworth: A Man to Remember* (Toronto, 1953). makes it clear that her father's sympathies never extended to the CPC but says little about his contacts with the communist movement. Spector, in interviews, felt that Woodsworth either never understood the nature of class government, or refused to face up to the realities of a revolutionary upheaval.

party shifted to Manitoba where it was taken up by J. S. Woodsworth and the provincial Independent Labour Party. Delay and suspicion caused by the CPC's policies and actions within the CLP, together with Woodsworth's leadership, ultimately resulted in the formation of the Co-operative Commonwealth Federation (CCF), a socialist party patterned after the British Labour Party. That development, however, did not occur until 1933, well after the great depression had cast its shadow over the country.

CHAPTER TWELVE

THE CPC AND THE TRADE UNION EDUCATIONAL LEAGUE

IN ITS EFFORTS to achieve a united front in the Dominion the Canadian Communist Party's failure to make the Canadian Labor Party its own political creature was paralleled by a corresponding failure to make the Trade Union Educational League (TUEL) a major communist element in the Canadian labour movement. Lack of success in both attempts, however, certainly was not due to lack of effort. If anything, failure in the case of the TUEL resulted from the party leader's inaccurate assessment of the TUEL's importance within Canadian trade unions, and its potential as a force for change within the labour movement. For the rest, the causes of failure are to be found elsewhere: in the policies of Comintern and Profintern and the directives which emanated from their congresses and offices in Moscow, and in the pervading influence of the parent American organization.

The TUEL movement in Canada began inauspiciously with "the first several groups perishing from inanimation."[1] Soon after the WPC was launched in February 1922, the party inaugurated a campaign calling for the acceptance by labour of the policies and leadership of the TUEL, with Buck, the WPC's Industrial Organizer, touring Ontario in May and June in order to arouse interest in the movement.* In July, most of the CPC executive and selected members of the WPC national executive attended a meeting at Winnipeg, at which W. Z. Foster spoke on the tactics required by the contemporary labour situation and the TUEL's willingness to work with all left-wing trade unionists.[2] The same month Buck travelled through western Canada again attempting to interest labour groups in the League. There, according to Buck, "the philosophy of action aiming towards amalgamation spread like wildfire."[3] The statement epitomized the mood prevailing within the party. In reality it was premature and overly optimistic. Throughout his tour Buck studiously avoided any controversial or revolutionary issues, confining himself to details about the TUEL's structure, organization, and aims, and promoting the sale of pamphlets concerning the League. These included one entitled *The Trade Union Educational League*, and Foster's *The Railroaders' Next Stop*. This was easy enough and in keeping with the TUEL's policy —really Foster's policy—which was intended not to offend the susceptibilities of organized labour and which urged a nationwide pro-amalgamation campaign.[4] As a result of these efforts several TUEL groups were formed in Ontario, one emerged in Montreal, and one began in Edmonton.

From the start organized labour in Canada, exemplified by the TLC,† denounced

---

*See Chapter Four.

†Buck, MacDonald, and Spector attended the annual TLC convention held that year in Montreal at the end of August. At the meeting MacDonald contended that the WPC was the only organization on the right road to emancipation of the workers in Canada. He lashed out violently against the TLC's president, Tom Moore, who rebutted MacDonald's arguments equally forcefully.

both the League and the WPC, particularly after MacDonald had toured the maritime provinces in June urging the miners to break away from their international affiliation with the United Mine Workers of America (UMWA) and to affiliate instead with the Profintern.[5]

The communist's interest in the Nova Scotia troubles was not accidental. Scott, the Comintern representative, was intensely interested in the unrest among the coal miners of Nova Scotia, Alberta, and British Columbia, and he personally investigated the latter areas in order to determine if it would be possible to exploit the situation in revolutionary fashion. The most promising possibility, it seemed on analysis, was in the Maritimes. There, J. B. McLachlan, Secretary Treasurer of District 26 United Mine Workers of America, and an outspoken protagonist in the Nova Scotia strikes, had been contacted by MacDonald and, as a result, had joined the WPC. Embittered by the plight of the miners in his district,* swayed by the unrealistic concept of what had been accomplished in Russia by violent means, attracted by the programmes advocated by the Workers' Party and the TUEL, McLachlan persuaded the UMWA District 26 convention held in June 1922 to declare that it stood " . . . for the complete overthrow of the capitalist system and capitalist state, peaceably, if we may, forcibly, if we must, and we call on all workers, soldiers, and minor law officers in Canada to join us in liberating labour."[6] The convention approved a proposal to apply "at once for membership in the Red International of Trade Unions and that a delegate† be appointed from this convention to represent us at the next convention of the Red International of Trade Unions to be held in Moscow."[7] The convention's stand alarmed UMWA leaders and provincial authorities, but it drew nods of approval from both American‡ and Canadian communists.[8] From the WPC and TUEL standpoints, the outlook seemed full of promise.

Although the WPC campaign to persuade Canadian labour to accept TUEL leadership and policies had been carried out from the time that the party formally came into being, no formal link between Chicago and Toronto had been established. This, in part, was caused by Foster's reticence to announce his communist affiliations. Nevertheless, the connection was soon established, for on completing his western tour in August, Buck proceeded to Chicago as an official WPC delegate to the first TUEL convention, scheduled for August 26–27, 1922, since the League was formed in 1920.[9] At the gathering he reported on the progress made in organizing TUEL groups in Canada, and outlined the existing labour situation in the Dominion. Foster in turn suggested that a Canadian section of the TUEL should be established following the convention, since the need to co-operate in cross-border fashion was important. Such a move, he urged, was the most effective way of paralleling the existing trade

---

*On April 27, 1922, McLachlan cabled Lenin asking if the Soviet government would guarantee repayment of a $15 million distress loan by the Canadian government, the money to be spent in Canada for the purchase of seed and food which would be distributed by the Nansen agency.

†The delegate appointed to attend the second RILU Congress was McLachlan. He could not attend and the District credential was given to MacDonald who attended the Fourth Comintern Congress and the Profintern meeting. A statement to this effect was published in *The Maritime Labour Herald*, November 11, 1922. The proposed affiliation with the RILU was considered subsequently by the UMWA's executive board, and a special committee was appointed to report on the matter. The committee recommended that the proposal be withdrawn, and this was approved by the executive board. The District 26 executive board eventually decided to comply with the UMWA's International executive's decision.

‡Earl Browder, for example, in a letter dated August 3, 1922, wrote to congratulate the District 26 miners on their stand, signing himself as Joseph Dixon, the American representative of the RILU. Dixon was Browder's party name.

union movement in Canada without running contrary to any established national developments in the labour field. An official Canadian TUEL section did not mean, Foster argued, a separation of the Canadian groups from Chicago. However, nothing formal was done to bring about the arrangement visualized by Foster.* Buck simply returned to Toronto, reported the proposition to the communist leadership, and resumed party work in the trade union field.[10]

Further afield the efforts of the American and Canadian communist parties to establish themselves within the North American labour movement were carefully monitored by the Comintern and, after its founding, the Profintern. Accordingly, the trade union policies and programmes of both the United States and Canadian parties were reviewed at the Fourth Comintern Congress. Lozovsky, speaking in the American Commission on November 20, 1922, emphasized that in both countries there was a comparatively large trade union movement, and that it was the duty of the communist parties on both sides of the border to create labour parties based on trade unions.[11] Similar views were expressed at the Profintern Congress sessions, and were incorporated in the resolutions and decisions passed by the RILU.[12] Resolution number 38 specifically charged that the TUEL should strive against disruption and that it should attempt to win over trade unions without organizational fetishism. The TUEL was instructed to bear in mind that there were a great number of organized left-wing workers outside the AF of L, and that a great majority of the North American proletariat were outside any organization.† They were noted by MacDonald and Spector, and were taken up at the national party level soon after the Canadian delegation returned to Toronto.

The first opportunity to air the WPC's trade union activities occurred at the party's second national convention, held in February 1923. Again, the discussion which preceded the passage of a resolution on labour policy was sparked by Earl Browder's address, in which he urged the party to increase its efforts to develop the TUEL in Canada. The impact of Browder's views, together with those expressed by MacDonald, Spector, and Custance, which were based upon their experiences in Moscow, became evident in the resolution approved by the convention. Trade union work, the meeting recognized, was a basic and fundamental preparation which "alone [could] build up the necessary power leading to the establishment of the Workers' Republic."[13] The party therefore called upon its members to support and to participate in the TUEL's activities, and to keep the Canadian movement firmly united in one uniform movement covering the entire continent. "The fate of the Canadian left wing is entirely bound up with that of the United States. National autonomy," the resolution declared, "is an illusion; international unity is the need."[14] Such a view, of course, dovetailed with Foster's concept of communist activity in the American trade union movement, and in turn was approved by the Canadian party leaders.

The convention also pledged itself to support "all real organization campaigns to organize the unorganized," and in particular called upon "our foreign born members to take hold of this work with vigor."[15] Achieving cross-border unity between the

---

*Shortly after the meeting the TUEL's offices were raided by police, and Foster and Browder were arrested. News of the arrests prompted Bell to warn Canadian party members to take security measures. See Chapter Five.

†At the end of 1916 only some two per cent of the Canadian working class was organized. In the years immediately following the end of the First World War the situation did not change materially. See Martin Robin, "Registration, Conscription, and Independent Labour Politics, 1916–1917," in *Canadian Historical Review*, XLVII, 2 (June 1966), 117.

American and Canadian left wings, and fusing the foreign-born and native Canadian workers, however, obviously necessitated a systematic education campaign, and the convention charged the communist press in the Dominion with that task. One of the immediate results was that preparations to publish *The Worker* regularly each week were concluded during March, and party organizers were despatched to various parts of the country to step up party activity on all fronts.[16]

While Knight, Spector, and other party members fanned out across the country on organization work, another highly significant move also took place. Scott, the Comintern representative, quietly left Canada and returned to Moscow by way of Berlin.[17] With his departure the Canadian communist movement, for the first time since it had coalesced in May 1921, was left to work out its own destiny within the limitation imposed upon it by the Comintern.

On his return to the Soviet Union Scott, using the name Johnson, represented the WPC, one of the two "sympathizing parties"—the other was the United States Workers' Party—at the Third Enlarged Plenum* of the ECCI.[18] Unquestionably, Scott's return to Moscow was one of the prime reasons for the Comintern's heightened interest in North America, and why its focus on trade union affairs became much more precise. Indeed, on the basis of his stay in the new world Scott was appointed the Profintern's American representative.[19]

At the time of Scott's departure from Canada the most promising area of revolutionary ferment was Nova Scotia, where the coal miners and steel workers in Glace Bay were at loggerheads with their employer, the British Empire Steel Corporation (BESCO). Unrest and resentment stemmed from a variety of causes: pay claims, unionization and the adoption of the "check-off" system for collecting union dues, and, not least, the fact that J. B. McLachlan and Dan Livingstone, respectively the president and secretary-treasurer of District 26 UMWA, were active members of the Workers' Party. Both the overt and the covert wings of the communist movement in turn supported McLachlan and Livingstone as much as circumstances permitted. Tom Bell, for example, was shifted from his post as District Organizer at Winnipeg to become business manager of the *Maritime Labour Herald*, the outspoken radical paper edited by McLachlan. Bell took up his post towards the end of March 1923, and his influence soon became apparent in the strident revolutionary tone and content of articles which appeared in the *Herald* and in *The Worker*. The most important feature of the Nova Scotia situation, however, was that by holding official positions in UMWA District 26, while simultaneously holding membership in the WPC, McLachlan and Livingstone ostensibly provided proof that a united labour front was possible.

Optimism within the communist ranks did not decline when the UMWA's international committee compelled District 26 to withdraw the application for affiliation presented to the RILU by MacDonald. The decision instead prompted the Profintern

---

*The ECCI plenum met from June 12–23, 1923, and dealt mainly with the dispute between Russia and Britain following French occupation of the Ruhr. The ECCI's report covered the period December 1922 to May 1923, and Scott undoubtedly reported on the WPC's second convention as well as on the party developments which had taken place since MacDonald, Spector, and Custance's return from the Fourth Congress. Scott, using the name Johnson, confirmed in a cable to MacDonald that Lenin had died. Scott's stay in Canada is notable both for its duration and the fact that he was the only Comintern representative to be detached for duty with the Canadian party, a feature which contrasts strongly with the stream of advisers which were sent by Moscow to settle differences within the American party.

to write to McLachlan clarifying the District's position as well as Moscow's attitude on the matter.

We do not counsel District 26 to unite formally as a trade union district, with the RILU if such action would mean their expulsion from the UMWA. We do not demand that units of labour organizations, which are not nationally affiliated with us, should officially affiliate as labour bodies. . . .

The task of District 26 is to remain steadfastly loyal to the principles of the RILU, and also to the organization of the UMW of A, while carrying on an educational campaign within their fellow members [sic] of the UMW of A in other districts in favour of the RILU.[20]

The letter thus not only reaffirmed the Comintern's united front, but at the same time clearly specified the Canadian party's course for trade union action. Essentially, it was a reiteration of TUEL policy.

The Profintern's advice, however, did not prevent the WPC from attempting to take full advantage of the labour dispute in Nova Scotia. In the spring of 1923 Malcolm Bruce, editor of *The Worker*, was despatched to Glace Bay. His arrival resulted in a series of meetings notable for their bitterness and outspoken emphasis on force and violence. Indeed, the bitter and vitriolic way in which Bruce aired his views led to his arrest on the charge of seditious utterance.[21] He was acquitted for lack of evidence on June 6, 1923, and returned hurriedly to Toronto in order to take part in the WPC's Ontario provincial election campaign.

This encounter with authority and the law had the effect of causing McLachlan, Livingstone, and other leading communists in Nova Scotia to take the Profintern's advice and to drop their attempts to affiliate District 26 with the RILU. Their argument for doing so was based on the grounds that the district was almost 100 per cent organized, and that any split, which undoubtedly would follow a formal linking up with Moscow, would be ruinous to the Canadian labour movement.

The Nova Scotia leaders' decision, taken in June, was looked upon doubtfully by Bruce and other members of the WPC's national executive, and as a result MacDonald himself proceeded to Nova Scotia to investigate the situation. He had scarcely arrived in the district when, on July 6, McLachlan* and Livingstone were arrested and charged with seditious libel and conspiracy.[22] Within a fortnight—the date was July 21—MacDonald† too was arrested by provincial authorities and charged with seditious utterance.[23] Any hope of the communists maintaining or extending their position in Nova Scotia through McLachlan's and Livingstone's position in the District 26 organization was completely shattered when John L. Lewis, the UMWA president, revoked the District's charter and disowned the local officers.[24]

That the Canadian communists failed to convert the Nova Scotia miners' dispute to any distinct advantage was painfully clear. In an article of unusual candour, Spector admitted that the party had been "caught somewhat unprepared for the struggle" even though trouble had been brewing for some time in the region. He continued:

The Party Executive played little part in the question of calling the strike and its breaking off, in spite of the fact that the strike leaders were Party members. Nor, it must be admitted, did the Party on account of its unpreparedness, develop a sufficient campaign on the political and industrial issues which the Nova Scotia miners raised for the whole of Canadian Labour.[25]

Instead, the strike and its sorry conclusion for the party raised the question of Canadian trade union autonomy, a point illustrated by the interference of American

*McLachlan was convicted on October 17, 1923, and sentenced to two years.
†He was acquitted on October 31, 1923.

trade union bureaucracy. At the same time, the episode made it clear that it was imperative to stem any further attempts at "splitting away 'at the border' or seceding from the AF of L."[26] Such a view conformed with the policy advocated by the TUEL since its inception.

While the Maritime fiasco was still drawing to a close, the WPC, in its desire to consolidate its labour policy and efforts, convened a "conference of Eastern Sub-District Canadian Section, of the Trade Union Educational League,"* the first of what it hoped would become regular annual gatherings.[27] According to Buck, the significance of the conference was "that for the first time there [was] a definite organization and clear cut program of action for every militant unionist."[28] Since the delegates as a whole agreed with the communist analysis that the trade union movement in Canada was declining in membership and power, that reactionary union officials (exemplified by John L. Lewis and his UMWA supporters in Nova Scotia) deliberately stood aside while employers proceeded to smash all unions across the country, the meeting took the line that it was up to the TUEL to preserve the unions "against the disruptive and decadent influence of the officialdom."[29] The convention devoted the greater part of its time therefore to settling details of definite organization work: setting up political amalgamation committees, appointing organizers and correspondents, and dealing with the problems of specific industries, notably the railroads, the needle, metal, and building trades.

In addition, the conference also formally endorsed a proposal to hold a similar meeting of the TUEL's western section in Edmonton, Alberta, on September 22–23. The decision to do so was carefully calculated to enable WPC leaders to attend the second general TUEL convention in Chicago, scheduled for the first two days in September, before proceeding to Vancouver for the Trades and Labour Congress' annual meeting.† At the same time a meeting of the WPC's Enlarged Executive was announced to coincide with the TUEL western conference.[30] Accordingly, Buck and Bruce sent to Chicago before continuing to Vancouver, while MacDonald, fresh from his arrest in the Maritimes, travelled west, speaking at Ottawa, Winnipeg, Saskatoon, and Edmonton.

At the TUEL's Chicago conference Buck, as the Canadian secretary, reported on the League's progress north of the border. The TUEL, he submitted, had become an established factor in the Canadian labour movement. Buck claimed that:

In popularizing amalgamation and by their advocation of the building up of an all inclusive Dominion-wide Federated Labor Party, adherents of the TUEL have done much to place Canadian Unionism in the forefront of the American movement.[31]

In his report Buck singled out the militant efforts of the needle-trade workers, as well as the miners in Alberta and Nova Scotia, for particular praise, saying that the latter had long been "in the forefront of the rebel movement in Canada."[32] It was from these groups that the TUEL had received its greatest support, and from which the League expected to draw even greater support. At Chicago Buck was elected to the TUEL's national committee, thus completing the formal connection between the American and Canadian parties in their attempt to achieve a united front in the labour field.[33]

---

*The conference, held in the Toronto Labour Temple August 4–5, 1923, was attended by 36 delegates representing TUEL groups from an area ranging from Nova Scotia to western Ontario.

†Moreover, the delegates were able to save the party considerable money by taking advantage of the railroads' cheap excursion rates for workers going to western Canadian harvest fields.

The TUEL western meeting,* which followed the annual TLC convention, claimed to represent the Canadian labour movement from Winnipeg to Vancouver. Not unnaturally, the discussions, while dealing with organization problems in the building, mining, needle, railroad, and lumber trades, centred mainly on the "Progressive Miners' program." The party's experiences in Nova Scotia and in Alberta (District 19 UMWA) had "brought the miners to a realization of the absolute necessity of a unified movement throughout the entire Mine Workers of America."[34] The emphasis on unification was underlined by a cable from Lozovsky, head of Profintern, who warned the conference of international reaction against left-wing labour, and urged them to follow the united front programme advocated by the Comintern. The conference did so by adopting a "whole-hearted endorsement of the Canadian Labor Party as the means for mass participation of the Canadian labour movement in the political struggles of the workers."[35]

To the WPC the western meeting was highly significant, for it marked the completion of the organization of the Canadian TUEL section on a national basis. As a result, so the party felt, the League's tasks were clarified and its programme was brought "in line with the great movement sweeping the entire continent."[36] Such a claim was premature and at best, wishful thinking. The Vancouver TLC meeting in fact crystallized opposition to communist action in the trade union movement, and although that opposition did not take on the excesses which characterized the AF of L's stand in the United States following its Portland, Oregon, convention (which made the TUEL in the United States virtually an underground movement in every American trade union), it was consistent enough to prevent the League from making any further headway in the Canadian labour movement.[37] The Canadian communist movement therefore voiced its outrage at the expulsion of communists from American unions and simultaneously shifted a good measure of its attention to the political field, underlining the point that communist trade unionism existed at the mercy of communist politics. As it turned out, the eastern and western TUEL meetings proved to be the first and last of their kind, stressing that the League's national organization existed more on paper than in practice.

The party's efforts among the Canadian trade unions also posed ideological difficulties. MacDonald, speaking at the WPC's Third National Convention in 1924—the convention at which the WPC openly declared itself as the Communist Party of Canada—warned the delegates that communist endeavours in the trade unions carried out under the auspices of the TUEL had created the impression among some party sections that a left-wing block was all that was required in the labour movement. Such thinking, of course, had to be resisted and combatted.[38] Nevertheless, the goal of a united front remained unchanged.

The apparent consolidation of TUEL organization in Canada was, in actuality, a local prelude to the adoption of a programme of action for the League in the Dominion and the United States as put forward at the Profintern's Third World Congress held in July 1924. The Canadian programme was specifically qualified. The Profintern recognized that while the general programme adopted for the TUEL applied for the whole of North America, the economic differences and organizational problems in the Dominion made it necessary to work out additional details which took those

---

*The conference was held in the Edmonton Labour Temple September 22–23, 1923. Before it met, Buck, MacDonald, Spector, and Bartholomew criss-crossed Alberta (District 5 WPC) attempting to arouse interest in the party and the TUEL.

factors into account. Moscow's plan, in effect, amplified the premises endorsed by the CPC's Third Convention. It called for a greater degree of autonomy for the Canadian trade union movement; for a strengthening of the TLC in order to combat the AF of L's narrow restrictions; for greater efforts to organize the unorganized; and for more concerted efforts to build up and consolidate the Canadian Labor Party into an effective mass organization. Through combined action the Profintern felt sure that:

... the solidarity of the left-wing trade union movement organized by the TUEL, and the revolutionary political movement organized by the Communist Party of Canada [i.e., the party's efforts within the CLP], shall be ideologically and organizationally consolidated for the purpose of the general development of the revolutionary movement aiming at the conquest of power by the working class and the establishment of the proletarian dictatorship.[39]

The concessions to the CPC made by Moscow were achieved because Buck, who presented the Canadian case, was backed by Scott, the former Comintern representative in the Dominion.

Buck's election to the RILU Bureau,* with its aura of prestige for the Canadian party, marked the Comintern's approval of the CPC's desire for as much independence in working out its policies as membership within the International permitted.[40] After its experiences with John L. Lewis in Nova Scotia, the CPC, through the TUEL, began to stress Canadian trade union autonomy.[41] In the long run, that policy developed into a marked difference of interpretation of labour matters between the American and Canadian parties. In the immediate context of Canadian labour organization, however, the CPC leaders pressed for a united front at every given opportunity, including standing for election† in the Trades and Labour Congress (TLC).[42]

Following his return from Moscow and his attendance at the annual TLC convention, Buck proceeded to Chicago, where he discussed TUEL matters and the Comintern and Profintern congresses. The upshot of the talks, together with the injunctions embodied in the Profintern's programme, resulted in the publication of a monthly bulletin, *The Left Wing*,‡ under the control of the Canadian TUEL organization and in co-operation with the League's Chicago executive. Tim Buck was appointed editor of the new publication. "This bulletin," stipulated Moscow, "should contain manifestoes and decisions of the RILU, and should deal specifically and intimately with the needs of the Canadian left wing."[43] Buck, in the first issue, justified publication of the journal on the grounds that:

The left wing movement within the trade unions of Canada has developed during the past two years from a few groups scattered throughout the country to a widespread movement embracing thousands of active rank and filers, and promising to become the dominant factor in Canadian unionism.[44]

In reality, TUEL progress and activities scarcely justified such unqualified optimism.

At the Comintern level, the TUEL's progress in Canada was again reviewed at the Fifth ECCI Plenum held in Moscow in March 1925, at which William Moriarty represented the CPC. The ECCI once more reiterated that it was the CPC's duty to

---

*The Bureau included W. Z. Foster and W. F. Dunne as the American representatives, with Earl Browder and Charles E. Johnson (Scott) named as the alternatives.

†Buck and MacDonald were nominated for president and vice-president of the TLC in 1924. Out of 200 votes cast Buck received 44. MacDonald, in the course of three ballots, received 56, 45, and 39 votes. Before the Congress met, the communists singled out the TLC executive for its lack of leadership; after the convention the party cry was that the TLC had retained its reactionary character.

‡The paper ceased to exist in August 1926.

give its full support to the TUEL, and to transform it into a mass organization of the trade union movement's left wing. At the same time Moscow cautioned the CPC that it was also its duty to form special communist factions in all trade unions and not confine its efforts solely to the TUEL. The latter, according to the ECCI's Canadian Commission, was to be separated formally from the CPC, and every effort made to have it affiliated with local unions and trade councils. Such was the lesson Moscow read from the Canadian party's experiences with the UMWA in Nova Scotia and the TLC. Simultaneously, the Comintern stressed that the CPC's domestic trade union work was not to be emphasized at the expense of international trade unity. The Comintern's commission recognized the difficulties inherent in the Canadian trade union scene, and that the position was complicated by the cross-border affiliation with the American Federation of Labor (AF of L). Accordingly, Canadian communists belonging to AF of L unions were instructed to campaign for the autonomy of Canadian trade unions.

In October 1925 Canadian communist labour policy received its longest and clearest enunciation in a pamphlet entitled "Steps to Power," written by Tim Buck and issued under the imprint of the Trade Union Educational League. Its thesis was simple and was put forward immediately: "History has demonstrated the futility of secession [from existing labour organizations] and the communist faces the fact squarely that what is required is not merely a perfect constitution, but mass organizations with revolutionary policies."[45] The question was: how to create such mass units reflecting revolutionary policies? The rest of the work was devoted to illustrating how it could be done, a process which involved the formation of shop committees and the nationalization of industry. Not unnaturally, it incorporated the latest Comintern views. More than that, "Steps to Power" was the most specific exposition of the TUEL's role relative to the CPC, a role which in turn was dictated to the American and Canadian parties by the Comintern.[46]

The chief obstacles which prevented the CPC, through the agency of the TUEL, from consolidating itself in the Canadian labour movement were the growing intransigence of the TLC which, in the communists' eyes, epitomized "Trade Congress Bourbonism" by turning down all party resolutions and proposals, and growing hostility within the CLP.[47] At the Comintern's Seventh Plenum (held in Moscow, November 22–December 16, 1926) too, the Canadian delegates, Buck and Popowich, ran into unexpected opposition from the American party which, through Browder, objected to the CPC's support for Canadian trade union independence.[48] The Canadian delegation rebutted Browder's criticisms with persistence, skill, and considerable fervour. After much discussion in the Comintern's American Secretariat and its Trade Union Commission, the Canadian view was conceded to be correct by other delegates present: J. T. Murphy of Great Britain, M. N. Roy* of India, Duncan, Browder, and Reinstein of the United States.[49]

Despite the Canadian success in Moscow, trade union affairs throughout the Dominion were, from the CPC's standpoint, far from satisfactory, a condition which Buck made clear at the Party's Fifth National Convention in 1927. The period of prolonged strikes and apparent progress in Nova Scotia and Alberta had been followed by apathy, exhaustion, and collaborationist policies not only within the radical miners' unions, but throughout the whole of North American labour. Buck

*Roy qualified his view by suggesting that the CPC should take greater steps to expose capitalist parties in the dominion, attack the Senate, and strengthen its position within the TLC.

made it clear that the CEC had been disappointed in its attempt to transform the TUEL in Canada into a broad minority movement similar to that in Great Britain.[50] As a result, the CPC, following the convention, set up a trade union department* headed by Buck, and which, in addition, included MacDonald, Mike Buhay, and two unnamed non-CEC members.[51] While the broad basis of the CPC's trade union policies remained unchanged, the creation of the new body emphasized the party's failure to make any real headway within the Canadian labour ranks. In a further attempt to give its approach new vigour, the CPC, in January 1928, began publication of a new periodical, *The Canadian Labour Monthly*, designed to replace the defunct Canadian TUEL journal, *The Left Wing*.[52] Edited by Spector, the journal aimed to rally the workers and to give a broader, more coherent socialist outlook to the Canadian labour movement.† The united front advocated by Comintern remained very much the kernel of the CPC's trade union policy.

That policy ended in the spring of 1928 when the Comintern abruptly abandoned its united front policy and practices.‡[53] Its implications for the communist movement in North America were made clear when Lozovsky, at the Profintern's Fourth Congress, March 17–April 3, 1928, called for the TUEL to become the nucleus of a new organization for the workers in organized industries, while at the same time remaining the focal point for the left-wing members of "reformist" unions.[54] In effect, the new approach advocated dual unionism, a policy which had been resisted fiercely by both the American and Canadian Communist Parties from their earliest days. Mike Buhay, who represented the CPC at the Profintern meeting, reported the shift on his return to Toronto.[55] Although the full import of the shift to a "class against class" policy was reiterated and clarified at the Comintern's Sixth Congress held in July and August 1928, its extension into the Canadian party's trade union work was delayed by the ferment caused within the party by Spector's expulsion in November. By the end of 1928, the Canadian party, with Buck and Stewart Smith taking the initiative, began to take steps to implement the Comintern's new policy.

The Profintern, early in 1929, made it very clear what those steps should be. According to the Anglo-American Secretariat, the CPC was directed to establish a new organization which would become the focal point of all left-wing elements in the Canadian labour field, replacing the TUEL which, by then, was dead in all but name. "The name of this opposition movement," the directive,§ dated February 15, 1929, stipulated, "must be decided at the inaugural convention, but we suggest that it should portray the character of the movement and make reference to unity."[56] Accordingly, a party circular dated March 1, 1929, announced plans for launching the new organization: "It has been decided by the Trade Union Department of the Communist Party of Canada to convene a conference for the consideration of trade union and industrial programs, and for the organizational consolidation of the left-

---

*The department was created at the first CEC meeting held on June 26, 1927, following the convention.

†The first issue contained articles by Spector, MacDonald, Buck, Lunacharsky, A. Vaara, and J. M. Clarke. They dealt respectively with Canada and the Empire; the future of the CLP; the TUEL; Lenin's personality; the miners' problems in northern Ontario; and the Canadian farmer in "prosperity."

‡The theoretical justification for the change was formulated in the resolutions of the ECCI's Ninth Plenum held in February, 1928. The switch from "united front" to "class against class" inaugurated the so-called "third period" in Comintern history.

§The Profintern letter followed the submission of a report on trade union work submitted earlier to the "Anglo-American group" by the CPC.

wing movement, immediately after the Party Convention."[57] The announcement formally signified the end of the TUEL.

In reality, the organization had been moribund since 1924, for it failed to make any headway within Canadian labour following the communists' successes in the Nova Scotia and Alberta coal fields. Fundamentally, the TUEL's failure to achieve hegemony in North American labour stemmed from the bolshevik leaders' belief that the revolution in Russia was but a prelude, that revolt would soon spread to other countries, and that it was necessary, through the agency of the Comintern, to provide revolutionary leadership for the supposedly revolutionary masses. The masses in Canada and the United States were not revolutionary. In addition, once the CPC and the TUEL had tipped their hand their efforts were quickly countered by action such as that taken by John L. Lewis in Nova Scotia, or by the outspoken hostility of the TLC. Even when the possibilities of success in specific areas such as Cape Breton were considerable, the CEC failed to exploit the situation, a failure which the party admitted, and which underlined both the barrenness of the Comintern's policy as well as the CPC's own lack of planning, organization, and general preparedness.[58]

CHAPTER THIRTEEN

CANADIAN PARTY LIFE: 1925-1926

SHORTLY AFTER Moriarty's return to Toronto in July 1925, the CEC circulated the text of a resolution drawn up by a Canadian Commission—the title given to the discussions Moriarty had with Piatnitsky and the Orgburo in Moscow—to all party units. Divided into eight sections, the resolution, together with a covering letter from Piatnitsky, clarified what the ECCI considered the most important issues confronting the Canadian party. The Comintern's views in turn formed the core of discussion and the decisions endorsed at the CPC's Fourth Convention, scheduled for September. Starting with the ECCI's diagnosis of the "Canadian question," the resolution considered Canadian independence, Canadian communists and politics, communists and the Canadian Labor Party, the farmer-labour party concept, work among trade unions, and the CPC's attitude toward the American Federation of Labor.

Essentially, the "Canadian question" in Moscow's eyes may be summed up thus: the First World War had loosened the Dominion's ties with the British Empire; because of Canada's industrial development British colonial exploitation was made more difficult, and this condition was reflected in the greater independence Canada had shown in foreign policy matters. At the same time, the slackening of British imperialist exploitation coincided with increased exploitation on the part of the United States, so that economically Canada was becoming more and more an extension of the United States. Consequently, the argument ran, "the two most powerful imperialist systems of the world play battledore and shuttlecock with the people of Canada."[1] Repression and exploitation by British and American imperialism created an independence movement in Canada headed by the petty bourgeois, farmers, and intellectuals. Under such conditions, however, the complete independence of Canada was in the working class interest, and the resolution urged the Canadian party to make the most of the independence question. Indeed, the resolution stressed that "the CPC should understand that the question of Canadian independence is the central question of the entire political strategy of our Party."[2] The main struggle, it advised, should be directed against British imperialism, the British monarchy, and the British bourgeoisie, with abrogation of the British North America Act one of the immediate objectives.

The resolution was not entirely uncritical. The Canadian party, it continued, was too politically passive.

It is not enough for the Canadian Party only to participate in the international campaigns of the Communist International; it should, on the strength of a careful study of the Canadian situation, and the class conditions, carry on political campaigns and issue political slogans immediately arising from the life of the Dominion.[3]

The CPC's main task, therefore, was to transform the party through bolshevization into a Marxist-Leninist political party. Nevertheless, it was commended for affiliating with the Canadian Labor Party, and was urged to make even greater efforts to weld the CLP's provincial sections into a national mass labour party. The Canadian Labor Party "must be enforced," the instructions declared, to take a stand on all political issues and economic disputes in the class struggle.

Because of the improvement in the Dominion's economy since 1924 the Comintern advised the Canadian party to give up its farmer-labour party slogan advocating a "Workers' and Farmers' Government"—it was enunciated at the Third Convention in 1924—and instead to aim at forming a labour party bloc with the farmers' organizations. Piatnitsky, in his letter, advised the party to proceed cautiously when carrying out active fraction work in such organizations. Dealing with trade union matters, however, the resolution made it clear that the ECCI considered it the party's duty to support the TUEL in order to develop it into a mass organization of the trade union movement's left wing. At the same time Moscow cautioned the CPC not to forget that its duty also was to form special communist factions in all trade unions as well as in the TUEL. The latter, the Canadian Commission felt, was to be separated formally from the party, and every effort made to have it affiliated with local unions and trade councils. As a continuing background theme, international trade union unity was to be stressed at all times. The Moscow Commission nevertheless recognized that the Canadian trade union position was complicated by the cross-border affiliation with the AF of L. Canadian communists within the AF of L were therefore instructed to campaign for the autonomy of Canadian trade unions.

The heart of the resolution was the Commission's censure of the Canadian Party Executive for its stand on the Trotsky issue, and for its failure to reorganize on the factory nucleus basis. The communication ran:

We are compelled to say that considerable ideological confusion is noticeable in our Canadian brother party. The central committee of the party expressed itself in favour of Trotskyism. It did not understand the international importance of the Trotsky discussion in the Russian Communist Party and in the entire international; it even prevented the publication of discussion articles in the Canadian Party Press.

The Executive of the Communist International places on record that by this attitude towards Trotskyism, the Central Committee of our Canadian brother party has completely isolated itself in the Communist International. . . . we urge the Central Committee of the CP of C to publish in the Party Press the decisions of the Communist International and also explanatory articles on the question of Trotskyism-Leninism, and to explain to all party members the Comintern attitude to this question by organizing discussions on it in the party organizations.[4]

Essentially, the Commission's censure was a rebuke to both Spector and MacDonald: to Spector because the Canadian party's stand on the Trotsky issue was largely Spector's own creation, and to MacDonald because he had never been completely convinced that the Russian party's experiences were applicable to Canadian conditions. The Commission's resolution also noted that the CPC was backward in its structure and organization, and that very little had been done in reorganizing the party. It called for continuous and increasing centralization of the party organization, with the language groups allotted "only agit-prop work" as their responsibility. Detailed advice on the party's organizational tasks was put forward in a separate, special resolution which, together with the Commission's injunction, was buttressed by Piatnitsky's own additions in his covering letter. The communication stressed the points Piatnitsky felt required the most attention in the Canadian party. He took particular care to make clear that in reorganization factory and street nuclei were to be formed, that the position of the language groups was to be modified, and that the

CPC, in order to achieve success, must transform itself into a mass party. The hectoring nature and tone of the letter are unmistakable.

Ideological preparation is essential for a reorganization of the party as made incumbent on all sections by the January resolution (1924), the decisions of the Fifth World Congress and of the Organization Conference of the ECCI (March, 1925). The ideological preparation is to be achieved through articles, pamphlets, leaflets, etc., and through bringing up these questions at party meetings, regular conferences, and also special conferences on organization, which can be convened on a town, district, and national scale.[5]

For the CPC, however, Moscow and Piatnitsky were far away. Of much more immediate importance to the party was its Fourth Convention.[6] Taking its cue from the Comintern directive circulated by the CEC, the meeting found that the Canadian economy had improved, that the agrarian and industrial crisis of the previous sixteen months had partially subsided. On the basis of the improvement, the Convention's analysis continued, the capitalist parties had taken the opportunity to spring a general election upon the Canadian people. After much discussion, the Convention went on record as pledging itself to use all its energies in presenting the party's programme to the masses. The communist programme, embodied in a political resolution, called for a capital levy and cancellation of all bonds valued at over $5,000; the nationalization of all basic industries without compensation and underwriters' control; abolition of the Canadian Senate; establishment of a minimum wage on the basis of an eight-hour day and a five-day week; recognition of the USSR; and the abolition of the use of troops in industrial disputes.[7] The most important part of the political resolution discussed and approved by the delegates dealt with Canadian independence and it was agreed, following Moscow's lead, that the British North America Act must be repealed while at the same time any secession movements within the country had to be resisted. The resolution also revised the CPC's agrarian policy.

Our Party has demanded a Farmer Labor Party as a means of organizing the farmers and workers against capitalism. But the temporary improvement in the position of the farmers, the rapid decline of the Progressive Party and other factors make this impracticable. Our Party will continue to work towards a Farmers' and Workers' Republic, but the first step is to build up the Canadian Labor Party; and to assist in organizing a mass Farmer Party on the basis of the class struggle.[8]

The change of policy was directed by two factors: the obvious failure of the Communist Party to make headway within the Canadian farming community except, to a minor degree, among the Ukrainian homesteaders in western Canada who sympathized with the ULFTA and read its newspapers; and conversely, the apparent success the party had achieved through the Canadian Labor Party. The CEC, notably Mac-Donald and Spector, were optimistic over their chances of obtaining complete domination of that organization, and were largely responsible for the shift in emphasis revealed to the delegates at the convention. Above all, abandonment of the farmer-labour slogan accorded with the Comintern's analysis, and with its express orders as laid down in the Canadian Commission's resolution.

Trade union matters which formed the core of the CPC's industrial policy, did not depart drastically from the policies and practices laid down and followed in the period between conventions. It was imperative, Buck submitted, that a left-wing minority movement composed of all radicals within unions should be created and maintained. To support this he cited the success achieved at the British Trade Union Congress held at Scarborough by the CPGB's National Minority Movement. Too many Canadian party members, he complained, did not yet appreciate the importance of trade union work. Buck insisted:

Union work must be treated as a serious party activity rather than as merely left-oppositional activity
. . . . Party members in co-operation with close sympathizers such as are at present grouped around
the TUEL must take the initiative in organizing definite "minority movements" in the more
important industries. These must be more than mere opposition blocs. They must be living fighting
movements, with complete programmes for each industry. . . .[9]

The convention reiterated the CPC's repeated demands for amalgamation of craft
unions into industrial unions, Canadian autonomy for unions, nationalization of key
industries, and international trade union unity, all of which had been approved by
Moscow.

The political resolution, mostly Spector's work, stressed that the temporary
stabilization of the Canadian economy had been accompanied by the centralization
and concentration of capital in Canada through mergers. Most distressing and
dangerous of all was the increasing penetration of the economic life of Canada by
American imperialism—at least 500 million dollars had been invested during the
previous year—a point greatly emphasized by the ECCI.

From the CEC standpoint, however, the outstanding feature of the convention was
the delegates' adoption of the bolshevization policy, the implementation of which, as
already noted, caused the party so much difficulty.

Despite its superficial unanimity, the Fourth Convention was not without elements
of dissension. Choice of the Central Executive brought most of the dissident currents
to the surface, and required an all-night session before agreement was achieved.[10] Few
changes however, were made: MacDonald continued as Secretary, and Spector as
Chairman of the CPC. Moriarty was made National Organizer, his place as *The
Worker*'s business manager being taken by Annie Buller, while Florence Custance
remained in charge of women's work.* For at least one member, Malcolm Bruce, the
convention demonstrated the slight chance of displacing MacDonald and Spector
from the party leadership, and this realization caused him to leave the CPC in the
autumn.† But dissension was neither so deep nor so widespread as that which affected
the American party, and never required the presence of a Comintern representative
such as Sergei Gusev‡ who presided over the comparable American gathering held
in August 1925.[11]

Much of the argument and discussion at the convention centred on the Trotsky
issue, on the ECCI's pointed remarks about the CPC's failure to reorganize after the
fashion desired by Moscow, and on its political timidity. The resolutions subsequently
approved by the delegates incorporated, in the main, the points raised by the Comintern's communication, thus, in theory at least, bringing the Canadian party into line
with Moscow's wishes. Only in the matter of Trotskyism did the convention fail to
make a specific stand, and that omission was the one which mattered most to the
Russian Party and the Comintern.

That the failure to declare against Trotsky and to keep the controversy out of the
party press was deliberate is unquestionable, for, as long as MacDonald and Spector
retained power the imposition of silence was easily accomplished. MacDonald had
sufficient prestige to keep any questioning member in line; Spector, as editor of *The*

---

*Annie Buller's name first appeared on *The Worker*'s masthead in the issue dated October 3, 1925.

†Bruce left the party in the last week of October 1925, though his disengagement was less pre-
cipitous. En route to western Canada he spoke on subjects such as "Empire, Imperialism, and War,"
in Winnipeg, Regina, Saskatoon, Calgary, and Vancouver early in the new year. He then went to
California.

‡Throughout his stay in America, Gusev—he adopted the pseudonym of "P. Green"—never
dealt with Canadian party affairs; he merely passed through the country when returning to Russia.

Worker, the party's main organ, determined editorial policy and decided upon the paper's content. Between the two it was a simple matter to put their policy into practice. At the time too, Trotskyism did not loom large on the Canadian party's horizon; distance from Moscow and the immediate tasks confronting the CPC diminished the importance of the schism within the Russian party. Spector alone, of the Central Executive Committee, realized the issues at stake, but even he was not certain of the grounds for his doubts, so he kept most of them to himself as the Comintern's insistence on conformity increased. In the months immediately following the Fourth Convention, however, the controversy did not prevent the CPC from printing excerpts from Trotsky's writings, or such items as favourable reviews of his recent books—*Literature and Revolution*, for example, in *The Worker*, December 12, 1925.

September also saw the formation of the Canadian Labor Defence League (CLDL), one of the major membership fronts established by the Communist Party of Canada during the 1920's.* It represented the most mature expression of a front achieved by the communist movement up to that time, and resulted from a combination of the party's experiences in the Nova Scotia and Alberta miners' strikes,† and from the example of the International Labor Defence which the American party fostered at the end of June 1925.[12] The League's object was "to fraternally unite all forces willing to co-operate in the work of labour defence into a broad national organization that will stand as an ever-willing and ever-ready champion for the defence and support of the industrial and agricultural workers . . . who are persecuted on account of their activity in the struggle for the class interests of the industrial and agricultural workers."[13] Initially, six branches were established, three in Toronto, of which one was Ukrainian, with the remainder in Windsor, Hamilton, and Montreal.‡ Operational control remained in Communist hands from the outset, largely through the National Secretary, Florence Custance, and the Vice-Chairman, J. L. Counsell, K.C.,§ the wealthy fellow-traveller who had financed Spector's trip to Germany and Russia in 1924.[14] The League never became the butt of faction, as did its American counterpart, but at the same time, the causes it supported tended to be much more parochial than those given aid and comfort south of the border. It was left for the CPC to give a clear lead, as in the Sacco-Vanzetti case; otherwise, the CLDL confined itself to providing aid for individuals, such as "Kid" Burns,** who, according to the communist viewpoint, were victimized during trade union and industrial disputes.[15]

Once the Fourth Convention was over—another did not take place for 20 months

---

*The need for a permanent labour defence league which would provide legal aid for radicals who were arrested and imprisoned was first mentioned in an editorial in *The Worker*, August 8, 1925.

†A. E. Smith toured the Alberta coal fields during the miners' strike which continued from June through September 1925. On his return to Toronto he attended the conference which resulted in the formation of the CLDL. Among those present he mentions Florence Custance, Annie Buller, and Malcom Bruce.

‡Individual members were charged 10 cents per month, while affiliated organizations paid an agreed monthly sum. After its formation the League, in a circular letter dated October 8, 1925, appealed for support to trades and labour councils and other influential organized labour bodies, but received little encouragement.

§In addition to Custance and Counsell, the chief officers were: Chairman, John A. Young, president of the Toronto District TLC, with A. E. Smith and other party members in the immediate background.

**"Kid" Burns, alias Lewis MacDonald, was charged with assaulting W. Sherman, the District 18 UMWA president, in 1925. He was sentenced early in 1926 to two years' imprisonment. A. E. Smith spoke at a mass meeting on Burns' behalf in Drumheller, Alberta, and noted the petition campaign organized by the CLDL urging his release.

—the CPC turned its attention to the forthcoming federal elections scheduled for the end of October. In line with its convention declarations, the party issued an election manifesto calling on Canadian workers to break with the old capitalist parties, and instead, to launch themselves "on the road of independent political action" after the example of the British working class, by supporting candidates nominated by the Canadian Labor Party.[16] The manifesto, which itself was published in *The Worker* on October 17, castigated reformist elements such as the Manitoba Independent Labour Party which, the CPC claimed, merely gave lip service to the united front but in reality was deliberately sabotaging the Canadian Labor Party. It reiterated the Fourth convention's demands for nationalization of basic industries without compensation, recognition of the USSR, etc., adding a demand for abolition of the $200 deposit required of candidates. Out of a total complement of 21 labour candidates, two, J. B. McLachlan,* who stood for Cape Breton South, and A. E. Smith, ran in Port Arthur-Thunder Bay, were open CPC members. Both, together with James Simpson, National Secretary of the CLP, were overwhelmingly defeated and lost their deposits.[17]

During the spring of 1926, while the CPC was battling to retain its hegemony in the Canadian Labor Party and was in the throes of reorganization on the basis of Comintern's policy of bolshevization, two widely-separated events occurred which subsequently impinged upon the Canadian party's development. The more important of these, the Comintern's Sixth Plenum, took place in Moscow from February 17 to March 16, 1926. No Canadian delegates attended, but the American party, divided as ever, was represented by a majority of its top leadership: Ruthenberg, Foster, Pepper (the Hungarian bête noire of the American party), Bittleman, and later Earl Browder.[18] The Sixth Plenum was notable for two changes. At its meetings some of the divisions within the Comintern were given their sharpest expression by Bordiga of the Italian party who, together with the Germans, Maslow, Ruth Fischer, and their followers, became the targets for heavy attacks. They represented the "ultra-left," which, in Comintern eyes, had become the International's greatest danger.[19]

For the Canadian leadership, and for Spector who, in particular, had supported the Maslow-Fischer group in Germany, the change in line was pregnant with embarrassing implications. Together with the Canadian party's stand on Trotskyism it meant that the Canadian leadership was out of step with the Comintern on two major counts, both epitomized by Spector. The second change, which reorganized the ECCI, took place immediately after the Sixth Plenum had concluded its sitting. Eleven national secretariats, each to be headed by a member of the Executive Committee with a staff which was to include representatives of the communist parties in the countries covered, was set up on March 24, 1926. Canada was included in the secretariat with the United States and Japan.[20] The ECCI also confirmed that the Lenin School—it had been proposed in a resolution at the Fifth Comintern Congress held in June–July 1924—originally scheduled to open in the autumn of 1925, would begin classes before the end of the year.

Reorganization of the ECCI and the launching of the Lenin School both directly affected the Canadian party. By including Canada in the same secretariat as the

---

*McLachlan received 3,617 votes out of a total of 17,678; Smith, 1,363 out of 9,477. The total vote cast in the 22 constituencies was 337,906, of which labour candidates received 62,080. Matthew Popowich, who later stood for office in the Winnipeg municipal election in December 1925, missed being put into office by 79 votes. Such a small margin was considered to be a real victory.

United States, the Canadian party was bound to feel the effects of closer linkage with the American Workers' Party, notably in matters concerning labour and trade union work. By fulfilling the Comintern's directive to send a party member to the Lenin School, the CPC was inevitably drawn more fully into Comintern controversies, for the Lenin School student inevitably, in the absence of a permanent representative such as the larger parties maintained in Moscow, was called upon to assist in dealing with Canadian party problems handled by the ECCI secretariat. Clearly, much depended upon the candidate selected by the party.

The selection, in fact, had already been made by the CEC in September 1925, after the Canadian party had been allocated one place at the Lenin School. It fell to Stewart Smith, the Secretary of the YCL and the son of the Rev. A. E. Smith, who had joined the party in the spring. Smith, despite his youth—he was not yet eighteen—was highly regarded by MacDonald, who nominated him for the course, and by Buck, the party's industrial organizer. As part of his preparation for the Lenin School the CPC's candidate toured the Nova Scotia mining districts, speaking in the process, at Glace Bay. Then, armed with a letter of identification supplied by MacDonald, and with enough money to cover his fare from New York to Britain, young Smith sailed for Southampton in May 1926. Before continuing to Moscow, Smith visited the Welsh coal mining areas, and spoke about conditions he had observed in Nova Scotia. After pausing in Berlin in September, where he described his experiences in the Welsh coal districts in *Rote Fahne* ("Red Flag," the KPD's official organ), he went to Moscow.[21] His arrival had been heralded by Buck who, because of his TUEL connections, had written to Earl Browder who had remained in Moscow as the League's representative to the Profintern after the Sixth Plenum had ended. The object was to have someone of experience to give the young Canadian communist assistance and guidance. Once in Moscow, Smith* found that the lack of suitable teachers, study material, and facilities at the Lenin School gave him plenty of time to make up his deficiences in languages and reading.[22]

Smith's over-inflated appraisal of the School, written in 1947 or 1948, is interesting for what it reveals of the man, and for its lack of information about curricula and instructors:

The Lenin Institute in Moscow may be compared as an institution of learning to the London School of Economics. Extension courses and special lectures were available to foreigners. The Communist Party of Canada, as other Communist Parties, from time to time gave some Canadian communists an opportunity to go to Moscow and take such lectures.[23]

More important, Smith's arrival in Moscow enabled him to take a hand in Comintern affairs concerning Canada, responsibilities out of proportion to his age and party experience.

*At the Lenin School Smith used the pseudonym "John Sims," but he travelled under his own name to Moscow via Berlin and Riga. At Riga he received money and assistance from Tom Bell of the British party, which enabled him to get to Moscow. In addition to Browder, the Lenin School numbered on its staff when it opened at the end of 1926, Li Li-San, Chou En-Lai, Walter Ulbricht, and Marcel Thorez, as well as Ladislaus Rudas, who had fought with Bella Kun during the Hungarian uprising in 1919. Pupils at the school took courses in Marxist-Leninist theory and combined it with such practical activities as observing and taking part in trade union, collective farm, or industrial work. The general lack of materials, equipment, and preparation for the influx of students at the Lenin School in the autumn of 1926 is corroborated by J. T. Murphy, at the time the British party representative at the Comintern, and George Aitken (Levack), who was selected by the British party to attend the course. Both knew Smith. Smith himself recalls his difficulties with his heavy trunk of books, for he reached Southampton on the S. S. *Olympia* in the midst of the 1926 general strike.

While Smith was en route to the USSR, the Communist Party of Canada learned at first hand the changes in Comintern policy crystallized at the Sixth Plenum. At an enlarged Central Executive Committee meeting held in the Alhambra Hall in Toronto on June 5, 1926, C. E. Ruthenberg of the American party, who had been elected to Comintern's Executive Committee at the Plenum, gave an account of the Moscow meeting. With Spector in the chair, and in the presence of about 100 party members drawn from the national and local Agit-Prop committees, the Toronto city committee, and the national and city YCL committees, Ruthenberg described the chief problems discussed by the Plenum, and outlined the decisions it reached. According to his account, the Plenum agreed that the partial stabilization of capitalism had continued, but emphasized the temporary character of that stabilization. According to Comintern analysis there were indications that the stabilization was nearing its end, and that a new, important period of revolutionary struggle was about to begin. Germany, Ruthenberg cited, was a good example. British and American capital under the Dawes plan had temporarily overcome the economic crisis, but the country had been shaken by an industrial crisis marked by an unemployment figure of two million.

Only one country, the United States, was excepted from the general analysis that capitalism everywhere was weakening. There the trend was upwards, and the Comintern realized that the United States had become the bulwark of world capitalism.

On the basis of Ruthenberg's address and his talks with the CEC, the Canadian party plenum passed a resolution approving the Moscow decisions, welcoming the Comintern's emphasis on the necessity for mass activity, and promising to take concrete action to bring about a united front in order to win the workers for communism. The party went on record* to endorse the Comintern's energetic struggle "for the liquidation of the ultra-left sickness of our German Party, which had in a greater or lesser degree spread to other parties of the Comintern."[24]

The resolution brought the Canadian party into line with the Comintern's revised policy, a shift considered important enough to bring Ruthenberg to Toronto to explain it in detail. His visit also reflected the reorganization of the ECCI in Moscow, and the fusion into one secretariat of the American and Canadian parties. It did not however, modify the CPC's stand on the Trotsky issue, though the drift towards accepting the actions and denunciations against Trotsky and, by then, Zinoviev, had started.

The first indication of this appeared in *The Worker*, a little more than a month after the Canadian plenum, with the publication of a despatch from Moscow which broke the news of Zinoviev's censure by the Russian party's Central Committee, his expulsion for fractional activity, and his replacement on the Politburo by Ia. E. Rudzutak.[25] But in the main, MacDonald and Spector continued to hold out against the rising tide of Trotsky baiting, and, as long as they agreed on that, it was not difficult to play down the differences within the Russian party. Both men stood not only for Canadian autonomy in relation to Britain and the trade union movement in North America, but also for as much independence as possible within the Comintern. Until the ECCI's reorganization that attitude, because of the strategic positions both

*The resolution also condemned the right deviationists in the French Party and approved the Comintern's continuous struggle against them, as well as the ECCI's call to the American party to end its factionalism. In turn, the CPC pledged itself "to strengthen the Left Wing Minority Movement in the Canadian Trade Union Movement; to further the CLP's development as a mass movement; to support the Canadian Labor Defence League; to work out more specific ways for applying the united front in the class struggle."

men held in the CPC, could be translated into practical measures; after the ECCI secretariats began functioning, and with Stewart Smith in Moscow, it became increasingly difficult to maintain.

When Ruthenberg visited Toronto, and during the months following, the CPC was too much occupied with its own affairs to devote much attention to the doctrinal in-fighting taking place in the Russian party and the Comintern's upper echelons. Party activity, heightened by its summer electoral campaigns—precipitated by the Governor General's (Lord Byng) refusal to dissolve Parliament when requested by the Prime Minister, Mackenzie King—continued at an accelerated pace throughout the Autumn. Becky Buhay began a long tour of western Canada on behalf of *The Worker* in an attempt to stimulate interest in the paper and indeed, the entire communist press; Moriarty went to Alberta to check on party reorganization; Spector, after pausing in Montreal, toured Nova Scotia.

While Spector was away from Toronto, the first public intimation of the struggle for leadership within the CPSU appeared in the Canadian communist press. Buck, in an attempt to clarify the issues and to pinpoint the misdeeds of the "opposition" in the Russian party, brought the dispute before the CPC in the pages of *The Worker*. Until Buck's article appeared, the sole indication openly acknowledging differences within the CPSU had been confined to the single report in *The Worker* which told of Zinoviev's expulsion from the Russian party's Central Committee. Ruthenberg's visit, Spector's absence, and the general drift of Comintern news which appeared in both communist and non-communist sources, combined to make conditions propitious for such an account to find its way into the CPC's main organ. The news that Zinoviev had joined forces with Trotsky was treated with some sceptisicm by Buck and unquestionably reflected the views of the other CEC members who were still in Toronto. "This latest spasm [of news about the differences in the Russian party] had varied from previous ones in that Zinoviev's name is now linked with Trotsky's (very intriguing), but so far as the capitalist press is concerned, that is virtually the only difference that exists."[26] With so many varying reports it was quite understandable, Buck admitted, for the workers to be confused over the true situation in Russia. "The point of divergence between the [Russian] party executive and the minority—or, as it has been termed, the opposition block—is primarily the question of relations with the peasantry."[27] In 1924, he continued, Trotsky had been denounced for his desire to build up industry at the expense of agriculture. In 1926 the Zinoviev group was opposed to the policy advocated by Stalin, Rykov, and Bukharin, of making concessions to the peasantry on the grounds that it encouraged the village kulak, and so constituted a recrudescence of capitalism. They (Zinoviev and his followers) advocated carrying the class war into the villages against the kulak. Thus the Zinoviev group found itself in "a temporary liaison" with the old opposition. The differences, Buck pointed out, had come to the surface at the Fourteenth All Russian Party Conference [April 27–29, 1925], and had been fully debated before the majority view was upheld. What made the Trotsky-Zinoviev alliance so heinous a crime was that they formed a definite faction in opposition to the party executive, and it was this which had brought the disciplinary measure of removing Zinoviev and Kamenev from the Revolutionary War Council and from the Central Committee, and Lashevitch from the Politburo, not the differences of opinion over agricultural policy. Factionalism, however, jeopardized party unity, and if, Buck concluded,

... in raising this "issue" by formation of an opposition faction, Comrade Zinoviev and other comrades laid themselves open to disciplinary measures, then we as loyal Communists and soldiers of the International, rejoice that not even the old guard of our brother party can endanger that unity with impunity.[28]

Buck's article* grossly oversimplified the differences within the CPSU. Under-estimating the peasants was but one of the heresies attributed to Trotsky and his supporters. The article contained no hint of the doctrine of permanent revolution or the more fundamental view that the ultimate success of the Russian revolution depended upon the outbreak of revolutions in other countries, especially the advanced industrial European nations. The subtleties implicit in these doctrinal differences in any case would have been lost on the rank-and-file Canadian party members, while the state of communications between Moscow and Toronto, together with Mac-Donald's and Spector's aloofness from the subject, combined against any full elaboration in the CPC's organs.

The most important aspect of Buck's revelations lay in his readiness to accept the charges and decisions against the opposition group. His summary of the Russian party differences assumed a more significant meaning in the subsequent reports in *The Worker* covering the CPSU's Fifteenth Conference.† Neither of the two despatches carried the news that Zinoviev had been ousted from the Comintern,‡ nor that Trotsky had been removed from his seat in the Politburo.[29] In a sense Buck's enunciated stand formed a prophetic prelude to the Seventh Plenum, for it was only after he and Popo-wich had reached Moscow as the CPC delegates that *The Worker* carried news§ of the dismissals.[30]

*In the article Buck erroneously claims that Zinoviev presented a minority report on the role of the peasant in the Soviet Union at the Fourteenth Conference held in April 1925, when agricultural policy formed the main subject of the discussion. What Buck probably had in mind was the discussion, in part caused by two theoretical works published by Zinoviev (these had added to the conflict during the summer and autumn of 1925), and the anti-Zinoviev statements in *The Daily Worker* [New York] on July 31, and October 6, 1926, signed by the CEC of the American Workers' Party, the latter one by Ruthenberg.

†The Fifteenth Conference was held October 26–November 3, 1926. The Fifteenth Congress was held December 2–19, 1927. *The Worker* designated the Fifteenth Conference as Congress in its issue of November 20, 1926.

‡The decisions had been made at the plenary meeting of the Central Committee CPSU held on October 23–26, which preceded the Fifteenth Party Conference. *The Worker*, November 13, 1926, also carried the agenda for the Seventh Plenum. Seven points were listed for discussion: the world situation and the Comintern's immediate tasks; the situation in the All Union Communist Party; lessons of the British General Strike; the Chinese Question; Communist work in the trade unions; work among peasants; and questions affecting various sections. The first listed was to be covered by Bukharin and Kuusinen; the second, by Stalin. Zinoviev's omission and Stalin's presence on the agenda were not without significance.

§The news was tucked away in an article by Rykov on the results of the Fifteenth Conference. It was followed by a long article in *The Worker*, December 25, 1926, by Stalin, the first to be published in a Canadian communist paper, giving his version of the controversy, which dealt with socialist principles in the Soviet Union and the differences with the opposition. At the Fifteenth Conference Stalin put forward his answer to the left-wing opposition programme: socialism in one country.

CHAPTER FOURTEEN

THE SEVENTH PLENUM, COMINTERN PROPOSALS, AND CANADIAN PARTY POLICIES

AT THE SEVENTH PLENUM Buck, Popowich, and Stewart Smith witnessed the great debate on "socialism in one country" which spilled over from the Russian party into the wider arena of the Comintern forum. The days following their arrival in Moscow were filled with incidents which, in time, impinged upon all parties. Although Trotsky, Stalin, Zinoviev, Bukharin, Kamenev, and Rykov held the spotlight, events at lower, less important levels, and for the Canadian party in particular, were no less dramatic.

For the first time in its history, Canadian party problems were included on a Comintern plenum agenda. In summoning the Canadian delegates the ECCI had requested that the CPC representatives come prepared to discuss the Comintern's many problems, and not merely to obtain and pass on information, as had formerly been the case. The Canadian delegates in fact were specifically asked to clarify five points: (a) the CPC's attitude regarding Canadian independence; (b) the development of the Canadian Labor Party and the CPC's work in relation to it; (c) the party's trade union policy; (d) its organization problems; and (e) the party's desire for a clearer lead in agrarian work. As it turned out, none of the problems were discussed in plenum because of the great number of questions on the agenda, and were taken up instead in a series of sessions by the American Secretariat, the Trade Union Commission, the Comintern's Organization Department, and Krestintern, the Peasants' International.

From the Canadian party's standpoint the most important discussions occurred in the American Secretariat and the Trade Union Commission where Buck and Popowich encountered opposition not only to the CPC's trade union policy but also to its struggle for Canadian trade union independence. The most stubborn and serious opposition came from Earl Browder, who had been in Moscow as the American Workers' Party representative at the Profintern since the Sixth Plenum held in the spring.[1]

This opposition illustrated the difficulties confronting a small party lacking a representative of standing in Moscow to put forward its case in the Comintern's committees and departments. Stewart Smith was too young, inexperienced, and lacked the necessary mandate from the Canadian party. He learned quickly, however, and his stay at the Lenin School was marked by a continually increasing influence which made itself evident in Comintern directives to the CPC. By the time he left, Smith was imbued with loyalty to the Comintern, an overriding allegiance which proved to be one of the decisive factors during the subsequent divisions within the CPC in 1928 and 1929.

In a wider, more important sense, the Seventh Plenum made clear that the CPSU was *primus inter pares* within the Comintern. And it was from the Seventh Plenum that Buck emerged a convinced Stalinist, joining the growing band of youthful communist leaders—Neumann, Togliatti, and Browder are other examples—who recognized their dependence upon the Russian party, and accepted the concept of "socialism in one country" without critical reservation. "The C.P. of Canada," Buck declared two days after hearing Trotsky on December 9, 1926, "unequivocally repudiates the proposal of the Opposition bloc and stands in complete unity with the CPSU in their great historical task."[2] On behalf of the CPC he unreservedly approved the decisions made at the CPSU's Fifteenth Conference and, in company with the majority of other delegates, attacked Trotsky and Zinoviev for their various proposals.* Thus, singlehandedly, Buck brought the Canadian party into line with the rest of the Comintern, a position which had been resisted and put off from the moment the Russian controversy first began to impinge upon the International.

Buck and Popowich returned to Canada late in March 1927, and one of Buck's first actions was to present his report on the Seventh Plenum to the Central Executive which met in Toronto on April 3. The report fell into two sections: the first dealt with the analysis of the Canadian situation and the CPC's tasks which the delegates had presented at Moscow, together with a review of the discussions provoked there by that analysis; the second consisted of a report on the Plenum's sessions, with particular regard to the controversy within the Russian party and to the position of the "opposition," its theories, tactics, and methods. It was the fullest exposition to be put before the CPC executive, and resulted in the passage of a resolution accepting the decisions reached at Moscow, and rejecting the Trotsky-Zinoviev bloc's claim that building socialism in the USSR was not possible. The resolution followed the same main points Buck made in his speech to the Plenum on December 11, 1926.[3] At public meetings Buck, by contrast, reported great progress in the USSR.[4]

On The Worker's pages, the CEC's resolution gave the impression of unanimity, but behind the scenes it was a different matter. Spector refused to recognize the report Buck and Popowich brought back from Moscow, and offered to resign. His offer was turned down by MacDonald who considered that Canadian problems were more important than those primarily concerning Russia, a view which, in all probability, was unprecedented in the Comintern. As a mark of his continued confidence in Spector, and as an indication of his prestige within the party, MacDonald's view prevailed.† Spector therefore continued as party chairman and editor of The Worker, and was commissioned to present the Executive's report on the political and economic situation in Canada at the forthcoming Fifth Convention.[5] By supporting Spector, MacDonald preserved party unity.‡

---

*Buck spoke at the 24th session on December 11, 1926. He attacked the opposition bloc for their proposal that Russian trade unions should withdraw from the Anglo-Russian Committee which had been set up in 1925; for the proposal that Chinese communists should withdraw from the Kuomintang; for Trotsky's and Zinoviev's opposition to Stalin's policy of "socialism in one country," and Zinoviev's apparent acceptance of Trotsky's theory of permanent revolution despite his attempts, in Buck's eyes, to disassociate himself from it.

†Spector in interviews stressed that two factors unquestionably contributed towards MacDonald's attitude. First, MacDonald was primarily a labour man, with his chief interests centred on labour politics; and second, he paid scant attention to Comintern publications and literature, much of which was printed in French, German, and Russian, languages MacDonald did not understand. Spector's contention is that his own knowledge of languages, German in particular (he did not know Russian) enabled him to keep abreast of the Comintern material on Trotsky.

‡MacDonald was given the task of presenting the CEC's report. Buck was to report on the Seventh Plenum and Trade Union work in Canada; Florence Custance was to deal with women's work; Spector and Buller were to cover the press; and Oscar Ryan to report on youth work.

The end of 1926 and the first few months of 1927, hailed by the CEC as the turning point for Canadian labour, saw the CPC in the throes of continued reorganization.[6] The new year too saw the beginning of an intensive campaign in the communist press, led by *The Worker*, to support the Comintern policy* towards China.[7]

Against the varied background of the CLP's Hamilton meeting (April 15–16, 1927) and the Comintern's Chinese policy, the CPC's Fifth National Convention,† the first in over twenty months, gathered as usual in Toronto in June.[8] Spector, who presided, delineated the convention's tasks and placed it into the context of wider events. The picture he presented was sombre, for there was nothing, he reminded the delegates, to celebrate.

Low wages, unemployment, rotten housing, undernourishment, exploitation, and imperialistic war was the lot of the workers and farmers. We [i.e., the communists] shall have something to celebrate when we have overthrown the capitalist system and established a Workers' and Farmers' Government. Meanwhile it is the task of the convention to combat the danger of a second world war, signs of which could be seen in the attack on the trades union movement, on the workers' wages, in the war on China, the encirclement of Soviet Russia, and the attacks on the Communist Party [of Canada]. Ten years of the Soviet regime has seen the Union of Socialist Soviet Republics make wonderful advances. The Soviet Union is a standing menace to the capitalist class and the Tory die-hards are fomenting the second world war to crush the labor movement at home as well as the Soviet Union. There will be no 1914 for the communists because we will declare war on the war makers. This may be called sedition, but it will only be the workers defending their rights.[9]

The most important feature of the Fifth Convention was the CEC's report presented by MacDonald, the party secretary. In it he outlined what had been accomplished towards bolshevizing the CPC. The CEC report showed that the party had made little real progress in advancing its programme. The education campaign had failed to make any impact upon the membership, and very few groups or individuals had taken advantage of the Agit-Prop department's courses or the CEC's recommendation of Bukharin's and Preobrazhensky's *The A.B.C. of Communism* as a basic text. "In quite a few centres," MacDonald complained, "fairly successful classes were organized, but in many others nothing was done. Our comrades are too prone to use the excuse that they have no competent comrade to conduct an educational class."[10] Trained comrades, he pointed out, were necessary for party work, but the delegates and all party members should realize that such men would not appear by magic formula. To offset the acknowledged lack of properly educated men, the CEC, during the interval between national conventions, had considered organizing a Central School for from two to four weeks to which each party District would send its best men. Nothing had come of the idea because the CEC could not find a suitable course

*Bukharin, at the CPSU's Fifteenth Conference held in October and November 1926, had said that the fight against foreign imperialists, meaning the British and American interests, was the communists' main task, and that therefore the united front with Chiang Kai-shek's nationalist Kuomintang had to be maintained. That view, which was supported by Stalin, was approved by the Comintern's Seventh Plenum, and soon all sections began campaigns which followed suit. In Canada the CPC called upon all labour and farmer organizations "to join in a united movement for the formation of 'Hands off China' committees to organize mass protests against intervention by British imperialism." Throughout the remainder of that winter and the spring of 1927 China became the main subject of talks and discussions sponsored by the CPC or sympathetic labour groups across the dominion. When Chiang Kai-shek massacred Chinese communists in Shanghai his actions were denounced bitterly by Comintern. The denunciations were dutifully echoed by the CPC and printed in the party press.
†The convention, which met in the Alhambra Hall, was held June 17–20, and was attended by 75 delegates. It was preceded, as usual, by District conventions at which delegates for the national convention were selected. The main feature of all meetings was a reiteration of the views and wishes expressed by the CEC.

director. "Our first task was to get a suitable instructor and we approached Comrade Scott Nearing for this task.* Unfortunately, he was unable to come at that time [MacDonald did not specify the time] and the matter was allowed to drop."[11] Instead, because of the difficulties in carrying through the educational programme, the CEC decided to issue monthly bulletins which would deal with the outstanding events within the party and the Comintern, to the CPC units. Finances had made it impossible to maintain a party member as a full time Agit-Prop director, and the bulletins were designed to take his place. Only two, however, were issued, and MacDonald ended this portion of his report to the convention with the plea that all city and district committees were to exert themselves more strenuously in order to make Marxism-Leninism percolate down to the lowest party unit. Bolshevization of the party, and the CPC's trade union work had made equally little advance.

Turning to the progress in what the CEC report termed agrarian work, MacDonald emphasized the essential correctness of the party's decision to abandon the slogan of the Farmer-Labor Party taken at the previous convention. Farming conditions in western Canada had steadily improved with a consequent move to the right by farmers' organizations. Of the Progressive Party, only a small "ginger" group, representing farmers in Alberta, remained in the House of Commons, and even that group had shown distinct signs of losing its militancy since the western Progressives had gone into coalition with the Liberal Party.[12] On the basis of that analysis and a directive from the ECCI which impressed upon the Canadian party the necessity of making a serious effort to establish an English paper devoted specifically to the farmers, the CEC recommended that *The Furrow*, a left-wing paper devoted to rural problems which began publication at Saskatoon in 1925, should be supported by the CPC.[13] The convention subsequently agreed to support *The Furrow* financially and to co-operate with the provincial secretaries of the Progressive Farmers' Education League, a front organization which paralleled the TUEL and which was just being organized. Up to that time, communist propaganda directed towards the farming population in Canada had been carried out almost exclusively in the pages of the Ukrainian communist papers *Ukrayinski Rabotnychi Visty* and, after 1925, *Farmereske Zhitya* ("Farmers' Life").[14] The CEC report appealed to the party to combat the reactionaries' tendencies in the farmers' organizations, and at the same time, to carry out recruiting work among the poorest farmers.

Not all of the CEC report was pessimistic or critical. The CEC acknowledged the effective work of the Jewish party members, first for starting the Yiddish newspaper *Der Kampf*,† and second, for publishing it weekly since January 1926. The organ, MacDonald felt, had proven a valuable medium for transmitting communist views which had helped to consolidate the left-wing in Jewish workers' organizations and trade unions, mostly garment unions in Montreal and Toronto, in the fight against the reactionary right-wing in such organizations.[15]

It was the "Hands Off China" campaign, however, which occasioned the most satisfaction. Since its inauguration, MacDonald reported, the campaign had resulted

---

*Throughout the 1920's Scott Nearing, a socialist economics lecturer who had achieved a certain wartime notoriety by his dismissal from the universities of Pennsylvania and Toledo, and who joined the American Communist Party sometime after 1925, was a frequent lecturer at the Toronto and Montreal Labour Colleges. He also toured western Canada several times.

†Indeed, the CEC felt that the newspaper was making such an impact that it had taken the unprecedented step in March of contributing a maintenance grant of $25.00 to *Der Kampf*, for an unspecified period of "several months."

in the formation of many local councils in the country's chief industrial centres. At the time of the convention, a National Council designed to co-ordinate the local council's efforts was being organized in Montreal, the city in which the campaign had been most successful. Thus the CPC, the report claimed, had made valuable connections with many branches of the Kuomintang in Canada, and had secured new readers for its press. "No more important work," it contended, "confronts the sections of the C.I. at present than the full and whole hearted support of the Chinese revolution."[16] In other words, the CPC accepted wholesale the Comintern's policy toward China as enunciated at the ECCI's Eighth Plenum.[17]

Two additional features marked the CEC's report to the convention. The party leaders acknowledged that the communist movement among the French-Canadian population was still weak and ineffective, and that Buck had discussed the problem of organizing effectively in Quebec with the French Comminust Party delegates at the Seventh Plenum. As a result of the talks French party literature became available from France, but it was of a general character only and did not fill the CPC's specific needs in the province. The party, MacDonald told the convention, could not afford to maintain a full-time organizer in Quebec, and would not do so until sufficient progress had been made by party members there to warrant it. Creation of a mass non-party organization for French-Canadian workers—the CEC report did not specify exactly what kind of organization it had in mind—was felt to be an essential first step. In this connection the party had supported a non-communist left-wing publication, *L'Ouvrier Canadien*, from its first appearance early in 1927. The paper, the party felt, provided a base for valuable propaganda work among the Quebec working population, and certainly the CPC's support was in keeping with its united front manoeuvres in the trade union and labour political fields.

The CPC's approach to Scott Nearing, together with the contacts with the British and French Communist Parties, stressed once more the desperate shortage of top calibre propagandists and organizers in the Canadian party. It also indicated the lengths to which the party was prepared to go in its efforts to transform the CPC into a more effective communist party. In this respect the CEC was less inhibited than most leadership groups in other parties.

Lack of literate leadership material was felt in many ways. The CEC report acknowledged that "our connections with the Comintern have not been as close as they should be."[18] MacDonald admitted that the preparation of periodic reports of work carried out by the party, detailed analysis of the political and economic situation in Canada, and the party's tasks in relation to such analysis, entailed much time and effort on the part of leading CEC members. To a party of such proportions and means as the CPC, such work often seemed "less important than the immediate internal party work."[19] The party's immediate tasks were discussed in detail, he went on, while Buck and Popowich were in Moscow for the Seventh Plenum, and from the talks it became apparent how vital it was "to maintain closer connections with the Comintern and Profintern in the future."[20] Clearly, the reorganization of the ECCI was beginning to make itself felt within the Comintern, and the days of virtual autonomy which the Canadian party had enjoyed since Scott left were almost at an end.*

---

*The statements bear out Spector's contention that he and MacDonald had paid as little attention as circumstances permitted to many Comintern directives, particularly the "bolshevization" call. He claims, and the claim tends to be substantiated by available evidence, that MacDonald was very prone to discount Moscow's demands and quarrels, and instead, to get on with the tasks in hand.

Perhaps the most significant item in the CEC report, one the convention endorsed without reservation, placed the CPC firmly on the side of Stalin and Bukharin in the CPSU quarrel.

The Central Executive Committee of the Party in resolution unanimously and unreservedly support the position of the "majority" of the C.P. of the U.S.S.R. in its attitude towards the "opposition bloc", and condemns the fractional activity of that bloc. The C.P. of C. rejects the claim of the "opposition bloc" that the building of socialism is impossible in the U.S.S.R. and solidarizes with the C.P. of the U.S.S.R. in declaring that given a sufficiently long period of peace, the development of industry and agriculture into one harmonious balanced economy, completely excluding the private capitalist is possible.[21]

On paper, unanimity within the central limb of the party remained unaffected, for Spector did not persist in openly supporting Trotsky in the CEC meetings, thus making it possible for MacDonald to report unanimity.[22]

As a review of the CPC's activities during the long interval between the Fourth and Fifth Conventions, MacDonald's report was the key item, for it charted the party's progress and highlighted its tasks. The latter were decided upon by the CEC in the light of Comintern instructions and suggestions transmitted by letter, and on the basis of the reports given by Buck and Popowich on their return from Moscow three months earlier.

In Spector's report on the Canadian political and economic conditions, the analysis followed the general tenor of views expressed during the months between conventions in *The Worker*, and fell into line with the Comintern's outlook on the general world situation. The main point of his report was the observation that the period of acute depression in Canada prevailing during the 1924–1925 period was well past. An economic revival had occurred whose chief danger was that it might strengthen democratic illusions among the workers. On the other hand, he pointed out, economic revival offered opportunity for a renewed wage offensive by the working class. It was therefore one of the Communist Party's chief tasks to organize the workers to avail themselves of the prevailing situation to get the maximum in the way of political and industrial advantage.[23] It was a sound but innocuous analysis, alienating no one and easily integrating itself into Buck's long review of the party's trade union policies and plans.

Before dispersing, the convention also approved resolutions condemning imperialist intervention in China, the severance of trade relations with the USSR by both Britain and Canada, pointing up in the latter case that it was a demonstration of colonial subservience on the part of the King government to have followed the precedent set by the Baldwin government in Great Britain. Never, claimed the CPC, had the case for Canadian political independence been more urgent. The views embodied in these and other resolutions repeated the main points which had been continually pressed upon the party through its press and its organizers.*

Similarly, the election of party officers showed little change. Spector remained Party Chairman; MacDonald retained the key post of General Secretary; Florence Custance continued to head the women's section, while Buck headed that of the trade

*The convention also declared its attention to wage a determined struggle against imperialist aggression on the USSR, adding the slogan "Hands Off the First Workers' Republic" to that enunciated for China. The party unreservedly aligned itself with the CPSU and the Comintern in the defence of the Soviet Union, a declaration fostered by the British government's severance of diplomatic relations with Russia following a police raid on Arcos, the Soviet Trade delegation's offices in London in May 1927, which was claimed to have produced evidence of communist subversive activities against Britain, and which caused a war scare.

K

union.*[24] A Political Committee of the CEC, a sort of inner cabinet, included Mac-Donald, Spector, Buck, Popowich, Hill, Custance, Buhay, Halpern, and Moriarty. All except Buhay were resident in Ontario. Of more significance than the Political Committee was the appointment of a four-man secretariat: MacDonald, Spector, Buck, and Hill. Upon the Secretariat fell the bulk of the work connected with direction of the party. In turn, membership in the Secretariat enabled each individual, depending upon his interests and ambitions, to focus upon the party's inner affairs, a factor of inestimable value during internal disputes.† The convention also authorized Districts Two, Three, Four, and Five to name a member to the Central Executive Committee, which was enlarged to 15 for the purpose. Its meetings were to be held at least twice a year. This change was carried at the convention through the election of Mike Buhay from District Two, Roberts and Menzies from District Three, and Alhqvist from District Four.[25] Designed in part to unify the CPC in accordance with the tenets of bolshevization, the measure fell short because it excluded representatives from the western districts, an exclusion dictated by distance, expense, and because the increased membership did little to offset the dominant influence of MacDonald and Spector, Buck, Custance, and Moriarty, all founding members, and all resident in Toronto.

As soon as the CPC Fifth Convention concluded, the Young Communist League held its own national meeting, the fourth since its foundation in July 1922.[26] Like the parent party's convention, that of the YCL marked a turning point in its existence, for it too decided to press forward more quickly with reorganization on the basis of shop nuclei and area groups according to residence.‡ Initially, during its first four years, the YCL had consisted of a few locals loosely connected with each other and with the National Executive. Between the YCL's Third and Fourth Conventions—a period which coincided with Stewart Smith's tenure as Secretary—a network of units was established across the country, and beginnings made in carrying out active work in trade unions and among farm youth. In the years following its Fourth Convention, the League never succeeded in achieving any of its declared aims. Instead, the YCL became the preparatory school from which most of the Canadian party's future leaders were drawn. This was as much the result of the Comintern's expressed will as to any particular farsightedness on the part of the CPC leaders. Until 1927 the

---

*The remainder of the Central Executive Committee consisted of J. W. Ahlqvist and A. T. Hill, both representing the Finnish Organization; John Boychuk and Matthew Popowich, the Ukrainian communists; Mike Buhay and P. Halpern, put forward by the Jewish party members; and W. Moriarty, L. Menzies, and H. Roberts. Spector and Annie Buller were reconfirmed respectively as editor and business manager of *The Worker*, while Buck was made party representative to the YCL, replacing A. T. Hill.

†In 1929 the emergence of Buck as party leader occasioned some surprise within the CPC. The key to his success was threefold: his membership in the Secretariat; Moscow's confidence, which he enjoyed because he handled the delicate jobs assigned by the Comintern and Profintern to the Canadian party; and lastly, through his trade union work, which gave him a wide range of contacts within the party at large. The parallel to Stalin's rise to power, though slight, nevertheless cannot be discounted.

‡The convention was held in Toronto, June 22–23, 1927, with 25 delegates, including a fraternal delegate from the American party's Young Workers' League, present. Buck attended as the CPC representative and delivered a key speech on the aims and duties of the YCL. At the time of the convention the YCL claimed a membership of 850 in 45 local units throughout Canada. Almost one-quarter of these (10 to be exact) were located in Toronto, Montreal, and Winnipeg. The children's section, the Young Pioneers, had 600 members and 60 branches. In addition, the YCL turned out a weekly paper, *The Young Worker*, and also a mimeographed bulletin, *The Young Comrade*, for the Pioneers' movement, at irregular intervals. Considerable YCL material was also published in *Der Kampf, Vapaus, Ukrayinski Rabotnychi Visty*, and *L'Ouvrier Canadien*, though it was generally a repeat of articles, etc., which first appeared in *The Worker* or *The Young Worker*.

prevailing opinion within the CPC was that as soon as a YCL member attained a degree of political maturity and organizational experience, that member should be transferred to party work.* The classic example of such a transfer is Stewart Smith.[27]

*Among those who entered the CPC after serving their apprenticeship with the YCL were Sam Carr and Fred Rose, both of whom were important in the "spy trials" of 1946; Oscar Ryan, Leslie Morris, and Charles Sims. The last two were later sent to the Lenin School. Morris ultimately became leader of the Canadian party.

CHAPTER FIFTEEN

THE RISE OF CANADIAN TROTSKYISM

DESPITE ITS impressive resolutions the Fifth Convention did not revitalize the Canadian party, nor bring about an immediate modification in its structure and organization. On paper the party's policies conformed more closely than ever before with those of the Comintern; in practice, those policies failed to make any substantial impact upon Canadian labour or politics.

While the clash between the CPC, the Canadian Labor Party, and Simpson was developing, the Canadian party press began devoting an increasing amount of space and attention to developments within the Russian party. For the first time *The Worker* commented editorially upon "the opposition vs. Party in [the] U.S.S.R.," and published the communique* issued by the Central Control Commision in Moscow on June 26, 1927, in which Trotsky and Zinoviev were accused of carrying out factional work, printing factional literature, and of advocating "Thermidorism"—that is, counter-revolutionary activity.[1] The bulletin raised the question of removing Trotsky and Zinoviev from the Central Committee CPSU. With classical communist conformity *The Worker* editorial concluded that the measures proposed by the Control Commission were not only necessary but overdue. Throughout August and September *The Worker*, whose example was followed by the Ukrainian and Finnish communist press, reprinted extracts from Comintern and Russian sources dealing with the opposition in the CPSU.[2] In December Trotsky's expulsion from the CPSU, the approval of the action by the Russian Party's Fifteenth Congress, and the main points from Trotsky's and Zinoviev's speeches were printed, without comment, in each issue of *The Worker*. During this period the paper also printed questions put to Stalin by a workers' delegation, together with his answers. The paper also carried the full report of Stalin's speech at the CPSU's Fifteenth Congress, and accounts of the Congress business.[3]

Lack of editorial comment was not without significance, for it reflected Spector's uncertainty and doubt about the events which had taken place within the CPSU, as well as his power to withold at least some comment because of his position as editor of the CPC's most important mouthpiece. At the time it was possible for Spector to do so because the turmoil within the Canadian party caused by Simpson's resignation from the CLP had not yet subsided; because MacDonald and Buck were concerned with TUEL affairs (and were also in the midst of their campaigns for office in the Toronto civic elections scheduled for the end of the year);† and equally because MacDonald, at the best of times, was never very interested in the cross currents of the Soviet Party's

*The bulletin was the result of a decision reached on June 24, 1927.

†Buck and MacDonald attended the Third National TUEL conference held in Chicago on December 3-4, 1927. They also ran unsuccessfully under the CLP ticket for seats as aldermen in the Toronto city council. Earlier in December, Matthew Popowich, Leslie Morris, and J. Kahana, under CPC colours, tried unsuccessfully for civic office in Winnipeg.

internal affairs.[4] The result of these varying factors was that Spector, throughout the autumn and early winter, was not assailed about his views on the events in Moscow. Under such propitious conditions he kept his views largely to himself, a reticence he was able to maintain because of the relative absence of factional struggle of the American party variety.

An opportunity to express his feelings, however, arose unexpectedly soon after the new year when, as the CPC fraternal delegate, he attended a plenum of the American Workers' Party Central Committee held in New York. There, during a visit to the American front organization, International Labor Defence, Spector learned from Martin Abern and Max Shachtman, both closely associated with James Cannon, the American party leader, that Cannon was disturbed about the turn of events in Russia.* From what they had said, and from Cannon's silence at the party plenum, which was marked by a prolonged denunciation of Trotskyism, Spector surmised that Cannon might be sympathetic to his views.

One evening, he [Spector] managed to get together alone with Cannon, with whom he had never before talked at length. Before long, Cannon recalls, they were "frankly discussing our doubts and dissatisfactions with the way things were going in Russia". Spector spoke openly of Trotsky's great contributions and the Comintern's internal crisis. Beyond expressing his own dissatisfaction with Trotsky's exile, Cannon responded cautiously and made no commitment. Yet they understood each other and knew that some bond had brought them together.

The evening ended inconclusively. Neither knew what to do next. Cannon again bottled up his misgivings, and revealed the tenor of his discussion to no one.[5]

Spector, too, did the same.

At the American plenum he carefully avoided getting himself embroiled in the Trotsky issue, and instead confined himself to an analysis of conditions in Canada, which faithfully echoed the CPC views.[6]

Keeping aloof from the controversy and upheaval within the CPSU was not too difficult for Spector. Within the CPC his intellectual prestige, his position as chairman of the party and editor of the country's leading communist journal, combined with the day-to-day business, diffused whatever interest there was among the leadership in such far-off issues. Nevertheless, it was an anomalous position which could not continue indefinitely.

Throughout the remainder of that winter and the spring of 1928 Spector concerned himself increasingly with the editing of and writing for *The Canadian Labour Monthly*. A campaign for increasing *The Worker*'s circulation, together with preparations for the annual meeting of the Ontario section of the CLP, both of which occurred in April, occupied Spector's full attention. It was a period of intense activity for all the party leaders, with MacDonald and Spector attempting to shore up the Canadian Labor Party, while Buck and Custance concerned themselves with trade union problems and the difficulties of shaping the Canadian Labor Defence League into an effective organization in the Canadian communist galaxy.[7] During this period, the CPC received considerable publicity through an inconclusive debate on the communist movement in Canada held in the Senate in March, and through the expulsion of Tim Buck† from the International Association of Machinists for his affiliation with the party.[8] The ferment within the party was further increased by the discovery of a

---

*The United States party plenum was held during the first week of February 1928. By then Trotsky had been exiled to Alma-Ata.

†Buck, a member of lodge 235 of the union in Toronto, appealed, but the expulsion was sustained.

police agent within its inner circles.[9] The agent, under the name J. W. Esselwein,* had been a member of the party in Regina from its earliest days. During his under-cover career he had been transferred to Winnipeg and to Toronto for party work, had suffered arrest for taking part in a Sacco-Vanzetti demonstration organized by the CPC, and had become a good friend of many of the party's leading personalities, notably Buck, Bruce, and the Comintern representative, Charles E. Scott.

While domestic matters and internal affairs occupied the party, the Central Executive during this period was called upon to select delegates to represent the CPC at the Sixth Comintern Congress. Early in the year, too, the CEC had delegated Mike Buhay to attend the Fourth Congress of the Red International of Labor Unions held in Moscow March 17 to April 3.[10] MacDonald and Spector were selected almost auto-matically, but it was only after some thought that two additional delegates, A. G. Neal, editor of Vapaus, and John Navis, representing the Finnish and Ukrainian party members, were included. Navis,† one of the original Ukrainian communists, was already in Russia.[11] As delegates, both men were empowered to discuss at first hand with Comintern leaders the role of the language groups within the CPC under reorganization necessitated by the bolshevization policy.

Feeling had begun to modify the relationship between MacDonald and Spector so that by the time they left for Russia—they travelled via France—the two men were scarcely on speaking terms.[12] En route Spector had hoped to represent the CLP at the second British Commonwealth Labour Conference, but his application was rejected by the TLC executive.[13] The refusal underlined the split in the various CLP provincial sections, and it was further stressed by the rejection of MacDonald's credentials for a seat at the annual Trades and Labour Congress while he was absent. These develop-ments added to the differences between Spector and MacDonald.[14] Unquestionably, part of the difficulty was caused by Spector's view that the CPC had not made suffi-cient progress in its development as a communist party, and that it ought to redouble its efforts to present a clear-cut programme more to the left than that which the party had followed hitherto. The same view was expressed by Annie Buller, Beckie Buhay, and Sam Carr, who, during the early months of 1928, formed a ginger group within the party. It was offset by an anti-Spector group headed by Stewart Smith in Moscow, and Leslie Morris who later went to the Lenin School. Buck, at the time, remained out-side the pale of controversy.[15] The factionalism never developed into anything stronger than an internal protest movement, and was never carried to the Comintern for arbitration. Nevertheless, the dissatisfaction with MacDonald's leadership was clearly established. With the removal of the two principals to Moscow for the Sixth Congress, the differences subsided until MacDonald, Spector and Smith returned to Toronto.

The Sixth Comintern Congress—the "corridor" congress, as it is described by both Spector and Lovestone—formed a prelude to the full Stalinization of the Comintern.‡ More than anything else, it caused the struggle in the Russian party to be disseminated

*Under his real name, John Leopold, Esselwein was the chief witness during the trial Rex v. Buck et al, heard by the Ontario Supreme Court in 1931.

†Navis proceeded to the USSR to arrange for the distribution of supplies for flood victims in Galicia. Two Ukrainian relief committees had been formed in Canada, both with headquarters in Winnipeg. One was nationalist, the other communist. The Communist committee collected a con-siderable sum, over $21,000, and Navis was selected by the ULFTA and the Workers' Benevolent Association (WBA), a Ukrainian front organization, to supervise the relief programme. He left via New York towards the end of November, 1927.

‡The Sixth Congress was held in Moscow from July 17 to September 1, 1928.

throughout the Comintern, making the conflict truly international in scope and character. From the rostrum Bukharin, through his long speeches analysing post-war development and pinpointing the right wing in all parties as the Comintern's chief danger, ostensibly dominated the congress. In the conference halls, corridors, and in the foreign delegates' quarters, however, Stalin's aides, led by Neumann of the German party and Lominadze of the Russian, undermined Bukharin's prestige and position by encouraging speculation about his "theses," by spreading gossip, and by identifying him with the CPSU's right wing. The Canadian delegation was not exempt from the overtures, for Neumann tried to arrange a meeting between Spector and Stalin, and had also contacted MacDonald.[16] The result was that most delegates were confused and, lacking knowledge of the divisions within the CPSU, were uncertain of their attitudes and affiliations.*

The Canadian delegation was not entirely immune from the pressure of Stalin supporters, or from doubts of Bukharin's fitness for Comintern leadership, but these did not reveal themselves in public expression at the Congress. MacDonald and Spector spoke (the latter twice) during the discussion on Bukharin's report. Navis and Neal confined their efforts to lobbying, and Neal served on a committee which drew up a series of proposals for discussion by the American Commission and the final draft for endorsation by the Congress.[17]

MacDonald, as General Secretary of the Canadian party and leader of the delegation, endorsed Bukharin's analysis, saying that the three periods outlined by the latter—intense revolutionary crisis, the partial stabilization of capitalism, and the current one of capitalist reconstruction—had been "thrown into bold relief in the development of Canadian capitalism."[18] Bukharin, in his speech, had made the point that Canada was co-operating more and more with the United States, thus assuring American economic hegemony in the Dominion. MacDonald countered this assertion by pointing out that the problem was not quite so simple. Despite the overwhelming preponderance of American investment in the country—he listed the figure at over three billion dollars—British capital still played an important role buttressed by an aggressive ideological campaign waged through organizations such as the Imperial Order of the Daughters of the Empire, army cadets, etc. Since 1924, therefore, the CPC had realized that it had to regard the Canadian bourgeoisie, as represented by the Liberal government headed by MacKenzie King, as a partner of British imperialism. Unquestionably, therefore, owing to the contradictions which existed within the framework of Canadian capitalism, Canada would experience a deep governmental crisis whether war, led by Great Britain, broke out against the Soviet Union or whether instead there was an imperialist war between Britain and the United States. At the same time, Canada was becoming increasingly important in relation to the Pacific because because of its position and its exports to China and Japan.

The CPC's main work in Canada, MacDonald declared, lay in the organization of the unorganized workers. More, he felt, had to be done for the defence of the USSR. Canada had yet to send its first workers and trade union delegation to the Soviet Union, though during the famine relief campaign Canadian workers had sent more per capita than any other section of the Comintern. Small as the party was, he concluded, the CPC intended to travel a revolutionary Leninist road.

*Spector claims that at the time, and in the face of such obvious opposition to Bukharin, he was (and still remains) surprised that Lovestone supported Bukharin for so long. That support proved fatal, for Lovestone was labelled right wing, and eventually expelled from the American party.

Later, in *Pravda*, August 24, he amplified the party's role in relation to war and the USSR.

It is very necessary to pay more attention to Canada which will take an active part in any war against the USSR. The Communist Party of Canada is doing everything possible to defend the USSR including the sending of some workers [to the Soviet Union] for training and to organize and train the friends of the USSR.

But it was left to Spector to make the most brilliant and acutely analytical assessment of the Canadian party's development and policies. He did so in great personal doubt about the issue of Trotskyism which still hung heavily over the Congress.

In his first speech he made the point that the partial stabilization of capitalism opened up the prospect of another world war, of a struggle for mastery between the Soviet fatherland and the surrounding hostile capitalist world. Such a concept was fundamentally opposite to that of a fresh, organic development of capitalism on the basis of a new industrial or technical revolution, and the growing power of trusts throughout the world, trustification, which was being put forward by the German and British socialists (Hilferding, Bauer, Ramsay MacDonald) and their satellites in every country. Spector also said:

The role that America plays in the general crisis of capitalism today is obviously different from that of Europe. But America and Europe are the two complements of one world picture which is the general crisis of world capitalism today. I emphasize this because there is undoubtedly a tendency in Canada on the part of some comrades to consider that this analysis of stabilization does not apply to North American conditions generally, nor to Canadian conditions especially. This view is disseminated by the Social Democracy in Canada among the wide masses and it is a view that we must emphatically combat.[19]

It was a prophetic assessment, for Spector pinpointed the views later expressed by Lovestone and MacDonald. On the basis of Bukharin's draft theses he felt that one of the Canadian party's chief tasks was to emphasize the relative character of the current economic expansion in Canada as well as to prepare the minds of the workers for the coming struggle.

The most striking portion of his address, however, came when he proposed that it was "absolutely necessary that the C.I. should intervene directly in the Party Life of the Communist Party of Canada to an extent that has not been done before [i.e., with financial as well as ideological assistance and direction]."[20] Spector concluded his address by saying that Bukharin did not refer to Canada in his proposals because Canada did not hold such an important position as did Germany, France, the United States, etc.

In his second speech to the Congress Spector elaborated on the war danger, agreeing with Bukharin that the Canadian communists, like most other sections of the Comintern, had underestimated the imminence of war. Outside of a few leaflets and manifestoes distributed on revolutionary anniversaries or when important international events such as the Arcos raid took place, the CPC had not done the necessary work to prepare the masses for mobilization against war. The task of the party therefore was to get the TLC and other labour organizations to focus their attention on the problem. He felt that it was "necessary for the Canadian Communist Party and the Communist Party of the United States to co-operate more than they have in the past in working out a common manifesto and a common programme of action for these two countries in connection with the war danger."[21] It was an old plea applied to what the Comintern considered to be a new situation.

Despite his differences with MacDonald, despite his past Trotskyite indiscretions, despite Stewart Smith's animosity, Spector, through his performance at the Congress and his prestige as the CEC's outstanding theoretician, was put forward by the Canadian delegation for a seat on the Executive Committee of the Comintern.* He was duly nominated and elected to the Comintern's highest body, the only Canadian party member to have achieved that position.[22] No comments or extracts of either MacDonald's or Spector's orations were reproduced in the Canadian communist press.[23]

Spector's views about the CPC as expressed in the Congress sessions were genuine expressions of his thoughts on non-controversial subjects, but they differed radically from those which he secretly harboured, and which were dramatically precipitated by an accidental occurrence. In Moscow Spector made contact once again with James P. Cannon, a contact facilitated by their appointment to the Programme Commission, a large body of 60 members from 40 different communist parties.[24] One day both men discovered among the documents issued to them as members of the Commission, a translation of the bulk of Trotsky's paper entitled *The Draft Programme of the Communist International: A Criticism of Fundamentals*. The work, dictated by Trotsky in exile at Alma-Ata, was originally intended as a criticism of the Comintern's proposed programme. It turned out to be, instead, a summary of his thoughts on the most important questions which had arisen within the Comintern during the preceding five years. Trotsky, on completion, sent the document to the Sixth Congress, where it was distributed, on a limited basis and in unfinished translation, to the members of the Programme Commission. It was never discussed, although a report of its contents was passed to the Senioren Konvent. By including it among the issued documentary material, the Comintern officials, perhaps unwittingly (for the possibilities of a deliberate insertion cannot be ruled out), eliminated the uncertainties which up until then had divided Spector and Cannon, and filled in the gaps in their knowledge and understanding of Trotsky's views.

Once Cannon and Spector began to read Trotsky's contribution, Congress proceedings became matters of secondary importance:

We let the caucus meetings and the Congress sessions go to the devil while we read and studied this document. Then I knew what I had to do, and so did he. Our doubts had been resolved. It was clear as daylight that Marxist truth was on the side of Trotsky. We made a compact there and then —Spector and I—that we would come back home and begin a struggle under the banner of Trotskyism.[25]

To raise that banner and to pass along the revealed word, Cannon and Spector decided that it was imperative to smuggle Trotsky's critique back to North America, a dangerous undertaking since it was marked for return to the Comintern secretariat. Nevertheless, both men eventually took their copies out of Russia.†

Initially, however, they were uncertain about their immediate course of action. Together with a group of Cannon's supporters among Congress delegates and American students at the Lenin School, Spector and Cannon discussed the situation. Both men were faced with the choice of taking their chances of rising to positions of

*The ECCI membership was 59, with 43 alternatives. The full members included Bukharin, Foster, Gottwald, Lovestone, Molotov, Pieck, Rykov, Stalin, and Thorez.
†Spector left by way of Leningrad. Before doing so he said that he was questioned by the GPU. The document was about 30 typewritten pages long. Cannon, in *The History of American Trotskyism* (New York, 1944), suggests that a "slip-up" enabled Spector and himself to see Trotsky's critique. On the basis of the scale of distribution to the Programme Commission as well as subsequent events, the suggestion seems unwarranted.

greater importance within their respective parties, or with spreading the doctrines of Trotskyism in the knowledge that such a course would lead to certain expulsion. Spector reached his decision alone. MacDonald, the only Canadian with whom Spector might have discussed the problem in Moscow, and who in the past had been tolerant of his views, was not ready Spector felt, to break with the CPC. After some hesitation Cannon and Spector determined to project Trotsky's cause in North America, but to go about it initially with care and caution. In the light of these developments Spector's election to the ECCI was a sound tactical, although ironic, success.

Events moved rapidly when the Canadian delegation returned to Toronto. Within days of their return an Enlarged Executive meeting was called to hear their report on the Congress, and to approve the decisions reached at Moscow.* The decision to hold a meeting so soon caused Spector some discomfort. He wrote to Cannon:

Like yourself I would have preferred more time to manoeuvre in. The endorsement of the decisions of the Sixth Congress is certain to be on the agenda and the logical step for me would be to register my criticism of the Congress and my solidarity with the platform of the opposition.[26]

At the meeting, however, Spector avoided controversy. MacDonald, who delivered the main report, followed the general run of the argument embodied in the long series of theses passed by the Congress, and summarized the Comintern's views on the international situation, the war danger, colonial problems, the situation in the USSR, and the work of the Canadian delegates at the meeting. Referring to the Canadian question, he stated that the delegates had agreed in Moscow on a new programme which clarified the CPC's stand and corrected "a certain vagueness and deviation that had characterized our propaganda for independence."[27]

The delegation also returned with a resolution approved by the Comintern on the Ukrainian question, which MacDonald hoped would become the basis for overcoming the differences which had arisen within the CPC. The meeting also agreed to hold the next party convention around the beginning of April 1929.

After the meeting MacDonald began arrangements for a tour of party units across the country, while Spector spoke at a public meeting on the "Soviet Union and the War Danger." Describing his talk in a letter to Cannon, Spector made clear the problems inherent in pursuing a difficult and dangerous course.

But my evasiveness nearly went for nothing as a result of a public meeting arranged for me at the Alhambra Hall on "Soviet Union and the War Danger." I not only spoke of the success of the USSR but gave a sober economic analysis of what led up to the grain crisis, stressing the role of class differentiation in the village and the mace of the Kulak [i.e. brutal exploitation]. Many who came chiefly to cheer went away to think.[28]

With its unmistakably critical overtones the speech caused a mild sensation in Toronto party circles. A. E. Smith, a not unbiased observer, corroborates the impact made by the address:

I remember a mass meeting of party members was held in the Spadina hall, subsequent to the return of our delegation from an important congress of the Communist International in Moscow. M. Spector was the speaker of the evening. The address occupied well over an hour. It consisted of a calculated array of slanders against the Soviet Union and its leaders. The speech left everyone cold with astonishment.[29]

According to Buck, "the content of his [Spector's] report was such that, following the meeting, a number of party members headed by Beckie Buhay, demanded of the

*Spector reached Toronto on October 9, 1928. The Enlarged Executive meeting took place October 13-15.

Chairman [Spector] that the matter be dealt with by the Political Committee of the Party." The next day, he continued, and to the surprise of other members of the Political Committee, "Jack MacDonald, the general secretary of the party, anticipated the discussion by moving that an emergency meeting of the Central Committee be convened immediately to investigate the 'political position of Comrade Spector.' "[30] Confronted by a wave of suspicion, Spector was unable to acquire the mailing lists for *The Worker* and *The Canadian Labour Monthly* as Cannon had urged him to do.* The lists, he complained, had been kept under lock and key virtually from the time he had returned to Toronto.[31]

Within days, and before the CEC meeting occurred, events in the American party conspired to bring Spector's real views into the open. At a caucus of American party leaders, Cannon, together with Martin Abern and Max Shachtman, were expelled from the ranks when each took a different stand on a motion condemning Trotsky. After a lengthy party committee investigation the three signed a statement avowing their support of Trotsky's opposition movement. The Political Committee of the American party unanimously expelled them on October 27, 1928,† though the public announcement of their expulsions was held up for three weeks until the presidential campaign, in which Foster and Gitlow ran for president and vice-president, was concluded.[32]

Following these events, the CPC was asked by the American party to endorse the expulsion of Cannon, Abern, and Shachtman. When the motion of support was put at a meeting of the CPC's Political Committee on November 5, Spector refused to endorse it. The Committee then asked if Spector believed that Trotsky's ideological position was correct, and whether he, Spector, was prepared to carry on an aggressive campaign against Trotskyism as well as against the comrades who had been expelled from the Workers' (Communist) Party of America for supporting the Russian opposition. Spector declined to do so. The next day, in a long letter dated November 6 to the Political Committee, he made a frank and dramatic declaration of his support for Trotsky, and recapitulated the main arguments put forward by the opposition.

Since 1923 [the year of his trip to Germany and Russia] I have had reservations about the line of the Communist International, but I have always relegated my own doubts into the background in the interests of Comintern and Party discipline and unity. I was not fully convinced that the discussion of the Lessons of the October "Catastrophe" in Germany had been carried on in a way it would have been while Lenin was an active participant in the life of our International. I was not satisfied that the estimation of the international situation made by the Fifth Congress was correct. In my view the fight against the Russian opposition dating back from 1923 was confused, by the unreal issue of "Trotskyism". The concept of Bolshevization was mechanical.[33]

Spector candidly admitted that on his way back from the Sixth Congress he had come into possession of the opposition's suppressed documents. A careful study of the material resolved his doubts and brought him to his unequivocal position.‡

*Cannon's suggestion that Spector should obtain lists of party members was one of the "practical" measures calculated to help them press their case.

†News of the American party's investigation and the ultimate conclusion undoubtedly filtered to Canada, probably to MacDonald through Lovestone, and formed the basis for MacDonald's call for an investigation of Spector's political views.

‡Spector, of course, learned of Cannon's expulsion before the Political Committee meeting. The day that the Canadian party committee met to discuss and endorse the American party's action, Cannon wrote to Spector giving his view of what course Spector might adopt. "We thought in view of *your position on the E.C.C.I.*, your most effective entry into the situation would be in the form of a letter of protest to the E.C.C.I. against our expulsion which we could publish and which would be the signal for your openly joining forces with us in the publication of the paper. This will give the appearance of the fight spreading on a wider front and *should have a valuable moral effect*." The

Continued at foot of next page

On the surface the admission that he had acquired opposition documents was startling. Within the CPC's Central Executive, however, Stewart Smith, who had just returned to Toronto after two years at the Lenin School, and who assumed the role of chief prosecutor against Spector, revealed with an accuracy smacking of the GPU, that Spector had been in contact with Urbahns, editor of *Fahne des Kommunismus*, who was one of the chief opposition supporters in Germany.[34] Urbahns, Maslow, Fischer, Korsch and others had been expelled from the German party in 1926. Spector had also been in contact with the French opposition during one day in Paris, but found it divided, and nothing emerged from the encounter.

Spector's letter brought an immediate reaction from the Central Executive Committee. Within five days, during which he appealed the CEC's decision, Spector, on November 11, was summarily expelled from the party.[35] At the age of 30, after almost eight years in the Canadian communist movement, he found himself in the twilight of what until then had been an exciting and, within the context of party life, an influential career.*

News of Spector's dismissal, which did not appear in the party press for almost a fortnight, was first announced publicly in the initial issue of *The Militant*, the bi-monthly opposition journal started by Cannon on November 15, 1928. Any further possibilities of a rapprochement were ruled out by Spector's comments in the interval upon reports describing counter-measures taken against the wealthy peasants—the Kulaks—in the Soviet Union. Spector's views, enunciated in the "bourgeois" Toronto paper, *The Globe*, provided little comfort for the CPC, particularly since the news of his expulsion had not been made public.[36] When it was, it created a sensation within labour ranks.†

The party lost little time rebutting Spector's charges. Led by Stewart Smith, the CEC's action was endorsed and Trotskyism strongly condemned at a general meeting

---

*Buck's recollection of the events centring around Spector's ousting are inaccurate. He gives no dates, and he blurs the issue. In *Thirty Years 1922-1952* (Toronto, 1952), pp. 64-65, he states: "When the emergency meeting of the Central Committee convened, MacDonald sprang another surprise by producing copies of correspondence between Spector and the leaders of the Trotskyite organization in the United States elaborating plans to split the Communist Party and establish a Trotskyite organization in Canada. Exposed, and refusing to repudiate the activities that he had carried on secretly until then, Spector was suspended by the Central Committee." Buck's blurring of the events is basic to his denigration of MacDonald, whom he accused of deliberately withholding the copies of correspondence between Cannon and Spector.

Spector first aroused suspicion by his Alhambra Hall speech on October 26, 1928. Cannon, Abern and Shachtman were cast out of the American Party on October 27. The CPC Political Committee did not meet to consider its actions over Cannon's expulsion until November 5. Spector submitted his stand next day and was himself expelled on November 11. Cannon's flat was not burgled until December 23, 1928, and MacDonald published in *The Worker*, January 19, 1929, extracts from correspondence between Cannon and Spector, copies of which had been forwarded to him by Lovestone. Spector was replaced as editor of the paper by M. Buhay, whose name first appeared on the masthead in the issue announcing the CEC's action.

†*The Globe*, November 18, 1928, was the first newspaper that carried the news of Spector's expulsion from the CPC. According to the report Spector admitted on the previous day that he was no longer with the party. The communist press did not release the news until *The Worker*, November 24, 1928, stated that the move was justified on the grounds that it was the duty of all communist parties to wage the class struggle not only on the political and economic fronts, but also on the theoretical and ideological fronts in order "to maintain Marxist-Leninist clarity."

---

italics are MacDonald's, who published the extract in his article "A Renegade Travels Fast," in *The Worker*, January 19, 1929. By the time Cannon's letter reached Toronto, Spector's action had obviated any possibility of following the suggested plan. MacDonald, needless to say, did not mention the time factor, the day that the Political Committee met, nor the date of Spector's letter to the Committee.

of the CPC's Toronto membership, held on November 23.[37] Smith's hand was clearly evident in a long statement which counter-attacked the charges made by Spector in his letter to the CEC.[38] In it the CEC freely recognized that the "right mistakes," which included slogans on the abolition of the Canadian Senate, the theory that the Canadian bourgeoisie was a suppressed colonial bourgeoisie which needed to be pushed into a more aggressive action against British imperialism by the Canadian workers, and the interpretation of the call for a Workers'-Farmers' government in a parliamentary independent Canada. While admitting its fallibility, the CEC shifted most of the blame to Spector who, the statement claimed, had "played the role of an 'intellectual revolutionary' out of contact with the daily party problems and out of contact with the masses of workers throughout his party career." Spector was not only accused of being the chief exponent of the right errors in relation to the Canadian conditions, but also of aligning himself with the "right opportunist errors of the Brandler-Radek leadership of the revolution against the [Comintern] line." And he was taken to task for his reservations about bolshevization. The statement then countered at length the points raised in Spector's letter to the CEC: the unreal issue of Trotskyism; the Chinese revolution; the international situation; and his alliance with the American Trotskyites, Cannon, Shachtman, Abern, and Max Eastman.

The CEC statement was Stalinist in sentiment and expression, a reflection of the changes which had taken place within the CPSU and the Comintern. It also illustrated the impact of the ideological conditioning Stewart Smith had undergone at the Lenin School.*

At the end of its tirade against Spector, the CEC pinpointed the main danger in the Comintern and in the Canadian party as coming from the "right," and that the CPC faced a struggle on two fronts. The first peril came from the Trotsky faction; the danger from the "right" within the party took the form of underestimating the danger of war; of insufficient sharpness in combatting trade union bureaucracy and the reformist social traitors [the reference unquestionably meant Simpson, J. S. Woodsworth, and their followers]; of insufficient energy in organizing the unorganized; and lack of precision in the communists' line towards mass organizations. Unity against Trotskyism and the danger from the "right", constituted the party's watchwords. Alerted though the party was, Spector's stand began a chain reaction of events from which it never fully recovered.

Spector, too, met with difficulties. Those who had indicated their support within the party before the rupture failed to come forward in the time of crisis. After the break, Trotsky's appeal, as voiced by Spector, failed to make an impact upon dissidents within the party or in the Canadian labour movement. That this was so is not surprising, for the critique of the draft programme of the Comintern concerned itself with issues which were primarily theoretical and international, the sort of things which appealed to and interested Spector. Moreover, the tract concerned itself with the struggles within the Russian party, and these were of passing interest to all but a handful of Canadian party members. Trotskyism, too, called for a return to Leninism, and Spector found that appeal a compelling one, though it failed to make any impression

*According to Spector, the Lenin School between 1926 and 1928 was disorganized and rife with faction, and Smith, whom Spector thought was opinionated to begin with, received his education during the worst period in its history. Spector claims that among the reasons for Smith's antagonism towards him was that he, Spector, had been educated at a "bourgeois" institution, the University of Toronto.

on those less well-versed in Marxist-Leninist writings. Spector soon found himself isolated and without a following, and before long joined Cannon in New York. His role became that of a critic, but it lost its effectiveness through distance and the general apathy to the crisis within the CPC.[39]

CHAPTER SIXTEEN

NORTH AMERICAN EXCEPTIONALISM AND THE TRIUMPH OF STALINISM IN CANADA

UNTIL SPECTOR'S DEFECTION, the Canadian party had "always been what Zinoviev in his palmy days would have called a 'monolithic 'party."[1] The CPC had survived in the Comintern world largely without praise or blame from Moscow because the leadership had never been seriously divided, because its variations on Comintern policy were never widely divergent from the original line, and because the party was small, and, in the Kremlin's eyes, of minor importance. After Spector was cast out, party life altered rapidly. A widespread and vitriolic campaign against Trotskyism was inaugurated, marked by large scale party meetings in Toronto, Montreal, Winnipeg, Edmonton, and Vancouver. According to the party such measures were highly successful. *The Worker*, January 26, 1929, for example, claimed that 99 per cent of the Toronto members had voted against Trotskyism and listed seven who had been expelled from the party. Two were suspended for six months. At the same time, the party's trade union and political policies were subjected to critical examination based, it must be added, on the shifts which had taken place at the Fourth Profintern and Sixth Comintern Congresses. The full import of these was not felt until after the initial excitement over the Trotsky issue had subsided, and until Stewart Smith, who returned from Moscow in November 1928, became the leading theoretician in the Canadian party. With Spector gone, Tim Buck, in alliance with Smith, became the focal point of the growing opposition to MacDonald's policies and leadership.

The reversal of policy formulated at the Ninth Plenum of the ECCI (February 9–25, 1928) which became evident at the Profintern's spring congress, manifested itself even more clearly at the Comintern's Sixth Congress, where the right-wing policy of alliance with non-communist parties was jettisoned. According to the Congress resolutions the main enemies singled out were the right-wing reformists inside communist parties, and social democrats, especially those with left-wing views who, while pretending to form a common front with the communists, were in reality working against them.

The shift of policy which was endorsed at the Comintern's Sixth Congress had been preceded by bitter and protracted dissension within the Russian party.[2] The quarrel between Bukharin and Stalin, the chief protagonists, soon spilled over into the Comintern, revealing the extent to which the Third International was affected by internal developments in the CPSU. Publicly, nothing was said about the dissensions, and at the Sixth Congress rumours of a split were officially denied. But the whispering campaign against Bukharin at the Congress, together with the resolutions passed at that gathering, effectively undermined Bukharin's prestige within Comintern, and by thus isolating him, played directly into Stalin's hands.

In the months following Spector's expulsion, a continuous stream of articles drumming home the danger of war, with Canada singled out as the prospective battleground between British and American capitalists, filled the communist press and increasingly occupied the CEC's attention. In stressing the nearness and inevitability of war, the CPC admitted that it had underestimated the danger of imperialist conflict. The first real indication of the reassessment presaged by the Comintern congress was put forward in a long statement prepared by MacDonald, entitled "Draft Thesis on Canadian Perspectives."[3] In future, the statement contended, the party must utilize the slogan of class against class to expose reactionary nationalism, to rally the poor farmers still suffering from pacifist delusions, to work more effectively among the French-Canadian population, and to make the class struggle a basis for building up a "mass non-party anti-imperialist organization."[4] The search for right deviations within the CPC had begun.

Reassessment of the party's ideological position, however, did not much modify the general pattern of its day-to-day activities. MacDonald, Buck, and R. Shoesmith,* under the colours of the Canadian Labor Party's Toronto Council, spent most of December 1928 campaigning unsuccessfully for aldermanic seats for Wards Five, Six, and Eight in the annual civic elections.[5] Their lack of success was offset by the re-election of W. Kolisnyk to the Winnipeg city council, and that success was hailed in the communist press as a victory over Ukrainian nationalists, and the ILP in the Manitoba capital.[6] The arrest of A. Vaara,† the editor of *Vapaus*, on a charge of seditious libel, momentarily diverted the CEC from its examination of the party's past actions, and provided the Canadian Labor Defence League with another opportunity to swing into action.[7]

Essentially these were secondary issues. The party line increasingly absorbed the leadership's attention, especially that of Buck and Stewart Smith, whose efforts began to coalesce into opposition to MacDonald, Florence Custance, and William Moriarty. A tacit alliance—it could not be described as formal or co-ordinated according to Smith—between Stewart Smith and Tim Buck gradually developed, with Smith, the Lenin School graduate, assuming the role of theoretician, and Buck applying the doctrine to trade union and labour matters.‡

Once Spector was out of the party the dissatisfaction with MacDonald's leadership soon reasserted itself more strongly than ever. At the end of November, MacDonald began a national tour to alert the party membership of Spector's Trotskyite activities, and to report the decisions of the Sixth Comintern Congress. He found supporters of Buck and Smith in party posts openly prepared to counter his views. Sensing the danger in leaving the party centre too long, he cut short his tour. Buck's version of this period, though inaccurate and weighted against MacDonald, reveals the ferment and manoeuvring that went on behind the scenes.

He [MacDonald] got no further than the head of the Lakes when reports came back to Toronto that the political line he was advocating against Spector was not the line of the world Communist movement but Lovestone's line of "American exceptionalism". In Winnipeg, Tom McEwen, district organizer of the party, was compelled to take public exception to elements of MacDonald's report. MacDonald did not complete his tour. He returned suddenly to Toronto where several members

---

*Shoesmith, a Toronto party member, was expelled from the party for right-wing deviation a year later.

†Vaara was fined $1,000 and imprisoned for six months. All sections of the communist movement raised a hue and cry declaring Vaara to be a class-war prisoner.

‡Smith, like most of the Lenin School students, became acutely aware of the controversy over industrialization and collectivization. He acknowledged that Bukharin had been singled out for criticism at the Sixth Congress, and that by the time he left Moscow to return to Canada, the Comintern's decision to fight the right-wing danger within its parties had been applied to the CPSU.

of the national leadership [Buck and Smith in particular] confronted him with the question as to his fundamental political position. That issue dominated all party discussion, the life of the party in fact, from then until the Sixth National Convention held in May, 1929.[8]

Once Lovestone promulgated his heresy by openly declaring his support for Bukharin, and once MacDonald revealed that he had been in touch with Lovestone over the Cannon-Spector correspondence, MacDonald became the prime target for Buck's and Smith's attacks.*

Following Spector's removal from the CPC a new factor intruded itself into the unsettled party situation: the Comintern began to "chivvy" the party into conformity. After Scott's departure, and until 1929, the Comintern exercised control and direction of the CPC through letters and instructions brought back by delegates returning from Comintern congresses and ECCI plenums. It was left to the discretion of the Canadian party leaders to work out specific details and to implement Comintern policy. Although the party at times had been taken to task, there had never been any need to despatch a Comintern representative to Toronto, or to bombard the Canadian CEC with cables and added instructions, as had been necessary in the case of the American party. The Trotsky issue and Stalin's rise to power altered the situation completely. In January Moscow emphasized to the Canadian party "how important it was for the Revolutionary Wing of the TU [trade union] movement to increase agitational activities in connection with the new war danger."[9]

Two articles, one by Smith and one by Buck, quickly complied with the Comintern's suggestion. Smith, in his examination of "Leninism and the Position of Canada" repeated many of the arguments put forward in the CEC's earlier draft thesis, but concluded with these words:

The struggle against imperialism for the Canadian working class is essentially a struggle against the Canadian bourgeoisie itself, every section of which is reactionary and counter-revolutionary in relation to the imperialist powers.[10]

For his part, Buck harnessed the war danger, as suggested in the Comintern letter, to the trade union policy first proclaimed at the Profintern's Fourth Congress:

It is in the revolutionary struggle against the war danger that the communist parties of the world, including our own, will be called upon to prove their Leninist understanding and firmness. Our work in the trade union movement, for the building of the New Industrial Unions,† to which we have set our hands in the unorganized industries, our work for the development of independent working class political action, defence of the Soviet Union, etc., must all be linked firmly with the struggle against imperial war, and must be clearly understood as preparatory steps in the work of mobilization. . . . Reformism and pacifism are the main enemies of our party in the struggle to mobilize the masses of the workers against capitalist war . . . .[11]

---

*Buck compresses the origin and development of the Lovestone controversy in the Canadian party. Lovestone did not publicly affiliate himself with Bukharin until December 1928, during a plenum of the American party. Smith, newly returned from Moscow, undoubtedly knew of Lovestone's close contacts with Bukharin, and may have become suspicious of the views Lovestone expressed in Moscow. In addition, Spector, in his first speech at the Sixth Congress, referred to the tendency in the Canadian party of some members to consider that the period of capitalist stabilization did not apply to North America, obviously a reference to MacDonald's views. At any rate, the Lovestone controversy in Canada did not reach any proportion until after the new year. The CPC's Sixth National Convention was held in Toronto May 31 to June 6, 1929, not "in May," as Buck says. One of the reasons MacDonald cut short his tour was that Florence Custance, one of his main supporters, was ill and Moriarty, more inclined to administration than controversy, could not hold his own against the Buck-Smith faction.

†The idea of dual unions, the "New Industrial Unions" specified by Buck in his article, had been accepted by the CPC's Central Committee, if not wholeheartedly, at least sufficiently to permit a tentative announcement in the party's leading organ. The policy had caused some friction between the Buck and MacDonald factions, though the rift had not yet become serious.

L

By the beginning of March, as the CPC controversy deepened, doubts about the exact time for the party's convention began to intrude into the CPC's inner circles. Originally scheduled for the beginning of April and with preparations, including a public call for pre-convention discussions on the situation and the tasks of the party well in hand, the CPC's plans were rudely disrupted by the cold winds of controversy blowing from the Comintern and from that perennial source of dissension and unrest, the American party. In Moscow, Molotov, quietly and without fanfare, replaced Bukharin as titular head of the Third International. With Bukharin's fall a shadow was cast over Jay Lovestone, the leader of the American communist party, who, having supported Bukharin, was left isolated by the Comintern's swing to the left. By the time the American communist party's Sixth Convention met in New York at the beginning of March 1929, Lovestone was aligned with Bukharin's view, proclaimed at the Comintern's Seventh Plenum in 1926, that North American economic development was still continuing to rise, and that therefore it was exceptional to the trend throughout most of the rest of the world.[12] The controversy was bound to spill over the border and affect the Canadian party, and the Comintern cabled the CPC suggesting that it postpone its own convention.

More important, the Comintern's request for a postponement of the CPC convention dovetailed with developments within the CPSU. There, matters had been brought to a head in February 1929, and Bukharin had been labelled a defender of the Kulak. His indictment by the Central Committee in April—it coincided with the concerted attack upon Lovestone of the American party—completed Stalin's triumph.[13] The breach between Stalin's supporters and the right was not publicized, but since Stalin was aware of developments, it was clearly in his interests to cut Bukharin off from any support which he might have obtained within the Comintern. Postponement of the Canadian party's convention was therefore in Stalin's interest.

At first the Canadian party, unaware of the true motivation behind the request, resisted the idea, and MacDonald, acting on the Political Committee's advice, "cabled [the] Anglo-American Secretariat on Feb. 24th in reply to their cable suggesting postponement of our Party Convention until late in May that we believed it unadvisable, because of advanced arrangements, etc., of our convention, to postpone same unless absolutely necessary."[14] The resistance was short-lived. Within a few days of MacDonald's report to the Political Committee the CPC received a further cable from Moscow in which the party was urged to "postpone Party Congress till third week in May" and to send "any conference materials prepared."[15] After considerable discussion the Political Committee, meeting on March 8, 1929, agreed to postpone the CPC's Sixth Convention until May 24, and despatched the convention materials which the Comintern requested.*

Among the documents submitted were copies of The Worker for February 23 and March 9, 1929, in which the Canadian party's position in terms of organizational tasks, trade union policy, and general conditions were discussed in a pre-convention review. These were part of a CEC decision taken on February 2 to carry out an intensive airing of party affairs in order to arrive at "concrete solutions to all of the major political problems [confronting] the Party . . . and to raise the general understanding of the members of the problems before the Party."[16] The first of these, a "Draft Thesis on the Situation and Tasks of the Party," written by MacDonald, was a lengthy statement which reviewed the general world situation, dividing it into the

*The convention actually opened on May 31, 1929.

three periods Bukharin had put forward at the Sixth Congress. The "Draft Thesis" called for a united front from below, and singled out Trotskyism and the right danger, with emphasis on the latter, as the chief dangers confronting the Canadian party.[17]

The same themes were taken up and amplified in the seventh anniversary edition of *The Worker* which contained long statements on the CPC's trade union policy and tasks. With the exception of Stewart Smith's contribution, the submissions made by MacDonald, Buck, and Beckie Buhay were repetitive, summarizing views and feelings previously put forward. Smith's views on the struggle against Trotskyism and the danger from the right stood apart because they contained the opening salvo of an attack upon MacDonald, and because they brought into the open the mounting criticism which had manifested itself from the time of Spector's expulsion.

Smith began his attack on MacDonald's views by claiming that in the past the CPC had never subjected its shortcomings and errors to close analysis, and ruthlessly criticized deficiencies in party work. MacDonald's presentation, he complained, was marked by an almost total absence of self-criticism, although the leadership in the past had admitted that, organizationally and politically, great mistakes had been made. In his "Draft Thesis" MacDonald had quoted at length from the views approved by the Sixth Comintern Congress. What he failed to mention, Smith submitted, were "those sections of the Comintern Thesis which attack in the most emphatic manner the 'right mistakes' committed by many sections of the Communist International."[18] In addition, Smith* continued, MacDonald had "left out any reference to the most important tendencies and events in the Communist International since the Sixth Congress—the struggle against the right danger in the Communist Party of the Soviet Union, and the intensified struggle against the right in the German Party."[19]

Because the danger was from the right, MacDonald's "Thesis" represented a false interpretation of the Comintern's views. The Canadian party could not brook any softening or modification of the struggle on both fronts: against Trotskyism on the one hand, and against right deviations on the other. Smith buttressed this general argument with two points: (*a*) that the CPC was wrongly organized; and (*b*) that the structure of the party as reflected by the CEC where the Finnish, Ukrainain, and Jewish members were appointed and not elected from the convention floor, was social democratic and therefore incorrect. The Central Committee, he charged, did not lead the party but merely acted as a central authority in settling any differences which arose within the party.

Smith's attack was calculated and deliberate. In one page of close print he identified MacDonald, the Party Secretary, as his chief antagonist, labelled him a right-wing deviationist favouring the theory later known as "North American exceptionalism," and pinpointed MacDonald's principal supporters within the CEC: Florence Custance and William Moriarty. In addition, by collaborating with Buck in formulating a draft resolution on the party's stand towards the CLP, the alliance between Smith and Buck was formally announced.

MacDonald rebutted Smith in the following issue of *The Worker* saying that the Political Committee had agreed to the publication of the analysis he had incorporated into the draft article in order to facilitate discussion prior to a Toronto district party

---

*Smith's charges constituted a public criticism of Bukharin before the latter was himself openly attacked by Stalin. The implication of Smith's connections in Moscow, and of his being forewarned, are inescapable.

convention, and that it was by no means the final amended version of what could be considered as constituting the party's views.[20] He repeated a charge made earlier at the Toronto convention that Smith's activities within the party constituted a "dishonest political intrigue." A. E. Smith, although a partisan observer, nevertheless catches some of the feeling pervading the party at the time.

The struggle against Trotskyism and MacDonald's right wing policies dominated the district and national conventions of the party. I remember well the meetings of the Toronto district convention to which I was a delegate. MacDonald delivered a lengthy speech in which he made a bitter attack upon Stewart [Smith]. He also attacked Maude and me . . . .
I felt compelled to speak immediately after he sat down. I was followed by Tim [Buck]. Stewart was absent in Montreal. The convention continued the following week with every delegate in place. Having returned from Montreal, Stewart was given an opportunity to reply. He characterized MacDonald's attack upon him as an attempt to divert attention from the main issue of his right-wing ideas to non-political personal abuse. A prolonged discussion ensued.[21]

The ensuing debate, which filled *The Worker*'s pages with charge and counter-charge, thesis and counter-thesis, publicly aired the differences between the two camps.[22] The tasks of drumming up support and countering charges dominated party life. The result, however, did not lead to clarification of the issues dividing the two groups, but instead succeeded in splitting the CPC. This, unquestionably, was Buck's and Smith's object.

As the differences were being taken up throughout the party, the Comintern, in a closed pre-convention letter to the CEC, specified its own views on the problems facing the CPC, and the course of action it expected its Canadian section to follow. The directive repeated that the Sixth World Congress had diagnosed the main danger in all parties as the "right danger," adding that Canada was in no way excepted.

Indeed, from a close study of our Canadian brother party, we see numerous manifestations of Right tendencies, persistence of Social Democratic forms of organization (federalism and independent language groups), underestimation of radicalisation of the masses, insufficient attention to trade union work and activity amongst unorganized, subordination of Party to [the Canadian] Labour Party, no agrarian programme, underestimation of war danger.[23]

These general criticisms were supplemented with specific examples, the most pointed of which centred around the CPC's leadership and the party's failure to modify its structure and organization according to the bolshevization programme.

That an outstanding leader of the Party and a member of the ECCI [Spector] could, for years, harbour leanings towards Trotskyism, according to the admission of the CEC, without the issue being raised sharply before the Party, is a sign of the weakness of the Party leadership.[24]

The CPC was warned not to separate entirely the struggle against Trotskyism from that of correcting the "right danger" which, in Comintern eyes, constituted the greatest threat for the party. On the other hand, the Comintern letter warned the party to guard against a mere mechanical expulsion of proletarian elements who were confused by Trotskyites.

Turning from leadership to the nature of the CPC, the Comintern felt that the CPC was largely an immigrant party weakly connected with what it termed the basic sections of the Canadian working class. Almost 95 per cent of the party membership was confined to three language groups, Finnish, Ukrainian, and Jewish, and the composition was a serious barrier between the party and the masses. The Canadian party was further handicapped in its development because it did not yet function as a centralized Communist party, but as a group of federated parties.

A large percentage of the Party membership still restricts its activities to the respective language organizations, and language forms of organization are still perpetuated within the Party itself. This is demonstrated by the federated system of the City Central Committee, by the predominance of language speaking units and by the lack of shop nuclei in the Party.[25]

These features, together with the complete absence of French-Canadian members in the party and the low percentage of Anglo-Saxon members—the figures listed by one member were Finnish, 65 per cent; Ukrainain, 25 per cent; Jewish, 5 per cent; and others, 5 per cent—clearly revealed the party's weakness and isolation.[26]

The party's industrial programme came in for similar treatment. In converting from the old trade union policy of burrowing from within existing unions, to one of separating Canadian unions from the AF of L and advocating a completely Canadian trade union movement as an alternative, serious "right mistakes" had weakened the party's influence among the Canadian working class. The CPC, according to the Comintern's reading of the party's progress, had leaned too much towards the idea of unity from the top rather than working for unity from below through the use of concrete slogans or taking the part of the workers in actual strikes. The glaring deficiency was that practically nothing had been done to organize the French-Canadian workers, the majority of whom received lower wages than workers in other parts of the country, and who were largely unorganized.

The Comintern's criticisms of the CPC's performance were tempered by its assessment of the party's convention programme. According to the letter, the ECCI's Political Secretariat had "carefully studied the materials for the Congress in the issues of '*The Worker*,' for February and March 9th 1929."[27] MacDonald's article on the "Situation and Tasks of the Party," Moscow felt, contained needless repetition of the Comintern's Sixth Congress, was overloaded with statistics, and avoided facing the problems confronting the party. Such a view was a clear signal of support to those members of the CPC opposed to MacDonald, and encouraged them to increase their attacks.

The Comintern based its analysis within the wider context of the general world situation. Canada, Moscow believed, was one of the main battle grounds between British and American imperialism. The Canadian party's duty was to lead the struggle on two fronts: the struggle against British and American imperialism, and the struggle against the capitalist world's desire to wage war against the Soviet Union. The stabilization within the Canadian economy was a temporary phenomenon, and all indications pointed to a coming crisis within the Dominion as well as throughout the world. Accordingly, the CPC was directed to concentrate upon a programme which would rally the poorer farmers and, together with the party's trade union work, would sharpen class antagonisms in all sectors of the national economy. Since Canada had developed into a definite capitalist country, the party was specified to emphasize that the Canadian bourgeoisie was the Canadian proletariat's main enemy. Only through a government of workers and poor farmers, it was argued, could the Canadian proletariat achieve real independence.

Touching upon the party's position with the Canadian Labor Party, the Comintern grudgingly admitted that the "reformists" had broken the united front despite the communists' efforts to prevent the rupture. The variable conditions prevailing in each Canadian province, while peculiar, had led to a number of mistakes in party policy towards the CLP, chief of which was the CPC's attempt to maintain the Canadian Labor Party as a screen for the communist movement in the belief that the Communist Party could become a mass party only through the medium of the Canadian Labor Party. But the object, according to the Comintern view, was to build a powerful Communist Party, thus eliminating any need for a national labour party. This could be achieved only by emphasizing the independent role of the CPC without hiding it behind the label of a labour party. The CPC was urged also, though in briefer terms, to step up its work among youth and women, to strengthen the party press by bringing the language papers more directly under its control, and to increase its anti-militarist propaganda.

The Comintern letter provided a comprehensive review of the ECCI's thinking and was explicit in its directions to the Canadian party. Within the party its themes were taken up at length by the contending factions, with MacDonald forced into a defensive role, and Buck and Smith attacking.[28]

The postponement of the Sixth National Convention to the end of May "at the unanimous request of the E.C.C.I.," publicly announced in *The Worker*, March 23, 1929, prolonged the controversy within the party, exacerbated jealousies, and, because of developments within the American party, stifled any chances MacDonald might have had of crushing the opposition. By that time many of the Districts had held their conventions and selected their delegates for the national meeting. News of the American dissensions which were openly revealed at the American party's Sixth Convention held at the beginning of March, and of the mass exodus of American party leaders to Moscow, quickly reached the Canadian party. In Toronto MacDonald was singled out for increased attack because of his connection with Lovestone of the American party. The after-effects of the American convention, followed by the news that Lovestone and Gitlow had fallen, toppled from their positions of pre-eminence in the American party while in Moscow, coming as it did at the height of the controversy in the CPC and just prior to its Sixth Convention, highlighted MacDonald's isolated position.[29]

As the time for the CPC's convention drew near, the issues dividing the party leadership centred more frequently upon the Bukharin-Lovestone heresy.

In the public debates that were held, as well as in executive discussions, the Lovestonites, of whom MacDonald was the leader and the main spokesman, tried to win support for the theory that the Canadian economy, by virtue of its close ties with the United States economy, was immune to the danger of capitalist crisis and, therefore, it was wrong to base the line of the party upon the prospect of economic crisis and increased radicalization of the masses. A minority of the members of the party leadership opposed that point of view. They based themselves upon the economic laws of motion of capitalism as revealed by Marx and the thesis adopted by the Sixth World Congress of the Communist International.[30]

The conflict, much more complicated than the view put forward by Buck, dominated the Canadian party's Sixth National Convention.*[31]

Its agenda formally covered four major points: the current situation and the party's tasks, which were reported by MacDonald; the inner party and organization report presented by Mike Buhay; trade union matters covered by Buck; and the communist programme and situation in the Comintern dealt with by Stewart Smith.[32] The reports and their allocation sparked controversy, which in turn was reflected in the discussions and resolutions eventually adopted. In the end, the convention unequivocally adopted the Comintern's letter to the party, acknowledging Moscow's criticisms, and accepting its suggestions. By endorsing the Comintern's letter, together with an organizational bulletin from Moscow, the party felt it had laid down "the basis for true bolshevik

*Six commissions were set up to deal with the party's problems in agrarian matters, women's work, youth, mass organizations, press, and the party constitution. These were headed respectively by W. Wiggins, Beckie Buhay who replaced Florence Custance because of the latter's illness, Oscar Ryan, Matthew Popowich, Michael Buhay, Annie Buller, and A. T. Hill.

unity" in its ranks. The new line, accepted by the CEC and the convention, it was felt, embodied a call for intensifying the fight against all forms of social reformism, and for exposing the reformist and fascist character of those elements of the working class both in the trade unions and in the political parties.

As the convention proceeded, the efforts of Buck and Smith to dislodge MacDonald from the party leadership failed. Their successes were more marked in the resolutions the convention adopted and, more important, in swinging some of the delegates to their side. According to A. E. Smith:

It was a time of high feeling and much distress of mind. Our Party was in the midst of a severe struggle leading the workers. . . . The delegates brought out those things in their speeches. They appealed to MacDonald to clarify his mind and to associate himself with the correct line of the Communist Party. I heard Tim Buck and Stewart [Smith] make this appeal to MacDonald. They and the comrades associated with them in the fight for correct policies wanted MacDonald to stay with the party, but they waged an uncompromising struggle against Trotskyism and the right-wingism which, under Lovestone, had split the Communist Party in the United States.[33]

At the end of the convention MacDonald, together with a majority of his supporters, still dominated the Central Executive Committee. Buck, Smith, and Malcolm Bruce, representing the dissident minority, were also elected, and the convention adjourned with the battle seemingly won by the party Secretary. One of the earliest casualties however, was Michael Buhay, editor of *The Worker*, who had resisted the Comintern line.* With his withdrawal from the party, and thus from the struggle, MacDonald lost a valuable ally. The loss was underlined all the more because Buhay's place was taken by Stewart Smith, who acted as editor of the paper until Malcolm Bruce took over at the end of July.[34]

Smith's assumption of the editorship of *The Worker* was a key factor in the subsequent developments within the party. Ostensibly defeated when the majority of the CEC supported MacDonald, the smaller group continued to manoeuvre after the Sixth Convention had dispersed. Control of the paper was thus a major asset. Buck writes:

The position of the minority was supported by the whole leadership of the Young Communist League [which Buck controlled]. The membership of the party was recognizing that the minority was fighting for a correct communist position. . . . As a result MacDonald found his position so contradictory that, six weeks after the [Sixth] convention, he called a special meeting of the new Central Committee (July 12, 1929).[35]

Before the CEC convened, the YCL,† reflecting Buck's control, had continued to emphasize the right danger within the Canadian communist movement, particularly singling out William Moriarty for attack.[36]

The meeting of the CEC, which began on July 12, 1929, originally intended to deal with organizational matters such as the appointment of party functionaries to various posts in order to carry out the Sixth Convention directives. By that time, however, news of Bukharin's removal from the chairmanship of the Comintern's ECCI had

---

*The Worker June 22, 1929, is the first issue without Buhay's name on the masthead. His action was one of the reasons why the paper did not come out for a fortnight. Malcolm Bruce, one-time business manager of *The Worker*, was appointed editor in July after MacDonald had lost his primacy in the party. Buhay, following the example of Zinoviev and others in the CPSU, returned to the party in 1930. During his period of disaffection he was at variance with his sister Rebecca who supported Smith and Buck throughout.

†The YCL held its Fifth National Convention in Toronto, June 28 to July 1, 1929. It was led by Oscar Ryan and Fred Rosenberg, more commonly known as Fred Rose, who later achieved notoriety because of his conviction during the "spy trials" in Canada in 1946. Rose was elected national secretary.

been made public.* With the news of Bukharin's downfall, the meeting, instead of confining itself to the routine business scheduled on its agenda, quickly developed into a four-day debate which again brought out all the differences within the party. Much of the discussion stemmed from a statement on the "Present Situation and Tasks of the Party," which had not been fully taken up by the convention, and presented as a joint effort by MacDonald and Stewart Smith.

When the time came to elect the party secretary, MacDonald made a statement in which he asked to be released from full-time duties with the CPC. The plenum accordingly approved a motion which let MacDonald stand down from election, and which, in addition, enabled him to be granted "at least one year's leave of absence, said leave of absence to commence as soon as possible, upon a date decided by the Pol-Bureau."[37] Until the newly-elected party officials were able to assume full-time duties in their respective departments, a temporary three-man secretariat made up of Buck, MacDonald, and Smith, was appointed to co-ordinate and direct CPC work. A similar preponderance of Buck-Smith supporters dominated the Political Bureau (Politburo)† and the departments created at the meetings to carry out reorganization and other changes decided upon by the convention.[38]

Buck's version of those eventful days in July 1929 and the subsequent impact upon the CPC are illuminating.

Right at the opening of the meeting, he [MacDonald] informed the Central Committee that, due to the conflict within the party, his position was untenable, and he had therefore decided to resign. In the same statement he nominated for the office of general secretary Tim Buck, who opposed Trotskyite tendencies within the Central Committee since Spector first revealed them in 1925, and who had been the main spokesman for the minority through the pre-convention discussion and the convention debates. All except three of the members of the Central Committee were ardent supporters of MacDonald yet, after some perfunctory debate, his resignation was accepted and Comrade Buck elected general secretary. The following day, a carefully prepared statement over the name of MacDonald appeared in papers edited by his supporters, calling upon the workers to abandon the Communist Party of Canada and establish a new organization.

It is evident that MacDonald's resignation and the election of a new secretary had been carefully staged in the belief that it would help to isolate the minority and tend to encourage members to follow MacDonald out of the Party. . . . Within a relatively short time, the organization that he established and the organization established earlier by Spector were compelled to join forces in an attempt to maintain an appearance of strength.[39]

The analysis, with its deliberate compression of time and blurring of events, is a revision of history in the best traditions of Stalinism. The same note is struck by A. E. Smith who, in his autobiography, regards Buck's rise to primacy within the CPC as "an important event in Canadian history."[40]

What Buck omits—Smith makes no attempt to cover the events in any detail—is that shortly after the plenum meeting he went on leave of absence on grounds of health and did not return to active party work until October.[41] During the interval

---

*Bukharin was ousted on July 3, 1929. The CPC may have been forewarned of the events within the Soviet party and of Bukharin's expulsion by Leslie Morris, who was then at the Lenin School.

†The Political Bureau consisted of Buck who acted as Executive Secretary, Rebecca Buhay, Malcolm Bruce, Albert Graves, MacDonald, S. Smith, A. Vaara, and Fred Rosenberg, the YCL representative. The department heads were: Agit-Prop, Stewart Smith; Organization, A. Vaara; Industrial, Tom Ewen; Women, Becky Buhay; Co-Operative, A. T. Hill; Agrarian, J. M. Clarke; French-Canadian, Stewart Smith. The report also announced Bruce's appointment as editor of *The Worker*. Rebecca Buhay replaced Florence Custance who died on July 13, 1929, when the plenum was meeting. *The Canadian Labour Monthly* was placed under the jurisdiction of the Agit-Prop department. This list of District Organizers reveals a distinct weighting of the offices in favour of the Buck-Smith faction. District One, J. Barker; Two, Charles Marriot; Three, Charles Sims; Four, A. G. Neal; Five, M. Parker; Six, A. T. Hill; Seven, L. Morris; Eight, H. Murphy; Nine, James Litterick.

MacDonald continued to head the party as Acting Secretary, which enabled him to muster some support. Nevertheless, his position was precarious, for every decision or move he made was regarded with suspicion.

Matters soon came to a head. The unrest and dissension manifested at the party's Sixth Convention broke out in the Finnish Organization of Canada. The decision taken at the CEC plenum to place A. Vaara, who had just come out of prison after serving six months for sedition, on the Political Bureau was regarded in the FOC as an attempt to prevent his returning to the editorship of *Vapaus*. Instead of taking up his Politburo duties, Vaara, through the efforts of John Ahlqvist, the Finnish Organization leader, was reinstated as *Vapaus'* editor, and A. G. Neal, who had occupied the post in Vaara's absence, was deposed. The result was the suspension of Vaara, Ahlqvist, and J. Wirta, by the CPC's Political Bureau on the grounds that they had resorted to splitting tactics, the tactics they had adopted under MacDonald's leadership at the Sixth Convention.[42] Suspicion over MacDonald's motives deepened at once, triggered by Stewart Smith, who accused MacDonald of using his position on the Political Bureau to promote factional activity.

Smith's accusation was not a quick reaction designed to stir up controversy. It was prompted by the Comintern which, in a post-convention letter to the Canadian party, had taken the new leadership to task for not having made a firm stand against the resignations of Buhay and MacDonald. The refusal of "the old leading group" to carry on its work amounted, practically, in Moscow's estimation, to desertion of their "communist responsibilities," and had resulted in a weakening of the Party apparatus at the centre during a very critical period. The attitude of the new Political Bureau "should and must be one of severe criticism." According to the instructions,

The Party must emphatically condemn such non-communist acts as an integral part of the fight against the Right danger, and for the further education of the Party membership. The Party must demand from those comrades who have resigned that they unreservedly accept and work for the decisions of the Convention and the CI letter, failing which decisive measures must be taken against them.[43]

In whirling once more upon MacDonald, Smith merely conformed to Comintern instructions. The instructions were based on an examination of the reports of the Sixth Convention and the plenum of the Central Executive sent to Russia by the CPC. By suspending the four Finnish comrades, the party had taken decisive action against them.

MacDonald's intransigence in refusing to devote himself to party tasks following the upheaval among the Finnish membership could not last indefinitely, a point emphasized by a further Comintern letter which reminded the CPC that paragraph 13 of the famous 21 conditions, which demanded that all communist parties should periodically purge their ranks, was still in force.[44] Within a few weeks of its receipt the party's Political Committee, meeting on February 25, 1930, suspended MacDonald from its membership for his refusal to disassociate himself from the Workers' Recreation Club, an organization the CPC claimed had been created by right-wing saboteurs and disrupters wishing to crystallize their anti-party views. In suspending MacDonald the Political Committee reviewed his anti-party activities for the previous year, cataloguing them in some detail.[45] His suspension was further highlighted by the expulsion of six right-wing advocates from the party, including F. J. Peel who had edited *The Workers' Guard*, and R. Shoesmith, a former CEC member of the Toronto City Committee.[46]

Subsequent attempts to get MacDonald to reconsider his position and to reconcile himself with the new leadership simply exacerbated the Party crisis. In a letter to "The Secretariat" of the CPC dated May 24, 1930, MacDonald made his position clear:

> I was invited by phone message on Friday evening May 23, by Stewart Smith to attend a Political Bureau meeting held on Monday evening May 26. At this meeting I was informed [that] the questions of "suspensions" will be considered. I was also invited to make a "statement" if I desired.
>
> Comrades; I can see no useful purpose to be served by me attending this meeting. . . . I have no knowledge of the numerous suspensions and expulsions that have taken place since I was suspended from the Pol-Bureau. I have received two copies of minutes of the Pol-Bureau meetings in recent weeks, but from my suspension until recently I have received no official communications and am therefore in the dark concerning the suspensions that will probably be dealt with at the projected meeting of the Pol-Bureau.
>
> Furthermore, I believe that many important questions have been considered by the Pol-Bureau and the commission from the C.I., questions that owing to my years as Secretary of the Party I might have been of considerable service in their consideration. . . .
>
> The Pol-Bureau has indulged in a campaign of lies and slander concerning me, distributed through the columns of the Party Press, while at the same time refusing me the privilege of making a statement or repudiating same, either publicly or through the Party Press.
>
> I have absolutely no confidence in the outcome of any "discussions" with the present Pol-Bureau . . . .[47]

There was no turning back for either side.

Suspension was one matter, expulsion another. The break, when it came, was not made cleanly nor quickly. Once again the Comintern intervened, forcing the Canadian party to take action. A cable in November from the German communist Fritz Heckert, then Secretary of the Anglo-American secretariat in Moscow, instructed Buck to give MacDonald an ultimatum that:

> . . . he, as a member of the Party and C.C. [Central Committee] must openly admit and abandon Right opportunist position, unconditionally agree to carry on resolute struggle against all Right elements in Party, against Lovestonites as well as Trotskyites, unconditionally accept C.C. and Party line and discipline, informing him that failure to accept these conditions of the Tenth [E.] C.C.I. Plenum [July 3–19, 1929] means expulsion from the Party. In case he does not comply with this demand C.C. should take action publishing statement on his position.[48]

It was too much for MacDonald. He refused to comply with the Comintern's conditions, and ten days later—the cable was dated November 22, 1930—was expelled from the Canadian party.

MacDonald's expulsion marked the end of an era in the history of the CPC. His exodus, while lacking the drama of Spector's stand or Lovestone's flight from Russia, completed the cycle, for with his departure from the communist movement the Canadian party lost the last vestige of its independence. The new leaders, Buck, Smith, Morris, Ewen, Bruce, Sam Carr, and Fred Rose, faithfully followed the Comintern line, and implicitly obeyed Moscow's orders. The new generation produced no leaders of the same calibre as MacDonald or Spector. MacDonald had the common touch which inspired confidence in the working man; Spector, a highly-developed political acumen and considerable eloquence. Indeed, as late as the spring of 1931 no one in the Canadian party had replaced Spector on the ECCI, and Stewart Smith represented the party at the ECCI Eleventh Plenum* held that year.[49] Thus, when Weinstone of the American party cabled the CPC asking if anyone were coming to the plenum in place of Spector, Buck replied: "Unable to send alternative to Spector. Smith will represent us." The reply underlined the triumph of Stalinism in Canada.

*The Eleventh Plenum was held in Moscow, March 26 — April 11, 1931. Buck was elected to the ECCI at the Seventh and last Comintern Congress held July 25 — August 20, 1935. During that interval the Canadian party was not represented on the body.

EPILOGUE

THE LEADERSHIP crisis within the CPC, dramatized by Spector's expulsion and high-lighted by MacDonald's suspension, caused the Comintern to scrutinize the Canadian party with unusual care. In the process the CPC's failure to bolshevize itself, that is, to transform itself into a strongly centralized unit after the model of the CPSU, became very clear. Accordingly, after the Sixth Comintern Congress, the Orgburo began to hector the Canadian party, pointing out its weaknesses and re-emphasizing the concepts upon which the orders and advice were based. A similar campaign was launched against the American party which had been as delinquent as the CPC in not carrying out a thorough-going reform.

In the Dominion, according to the Orgburo, the chief function of the ULFTA, the FOC, and other communist-controlled language units, was to become mass organizations that were to draw the foreign-born workers into the general stream of the Canadian labour movement. The failure of the CPC's language units to do so was, in Moscow's eyes, signal. Thus, in the autumn of 1929, with the unsettlement caused by Spector's defection and MacDonald's displacement still permeating the Party, the ECCI's Political Secretariat, in a letter addressed to "the comrades who now have the leadership of the Political Bureau" (i.e. Buck, Stewart Smith, Leslie Morris, and their supporters), the new men were again reminded that their chief task was still "that of converting the CPC from a federation of language groups into a genuine Bolshevist centralized Party."[1]

The failure of the displaced leadership to transform the CPC into the cohesive disciplined body Moscow desired was heightened by the international situation and by Canada's own domestic condition. According to the Comintern's diagnosis the danger of an imperialist war between the United States and Britain was increasing, while within Canada the class struggle had sharpened perceptibly. As the long shadow of the depression began to sweep across the Dominion, and as Buck, Smith, and their supporters clearly were unable to take advantage of the economic deterioration, the ECCI, in a resolution on the Canadian party's tasks, revealed the magnitude of the party's unpreparedness.

The ECCI emphasizes that the Communist Party of Canada still remains mainly a propagandist organization with small membership with weak connections with the broad masses of the Canadian workers. The membership of the Party despite its recent increase is only about four thousand, only a very minor percentage of which are native born, and the Party is divided ideologically and organizationally by a deep-rooted federalism. It has still very weak roots in the decisive industries and factories and practically no shop nuclei. . . . The ECCI . . . categorically insists that its instructions be carried out and that the Party and Ukrainian and Finnish comrades in particular undertake every measure in order to realize these instructions. . . . the work in the language mass organizations MUST BE COORDINATED with the tasks of the Party in the general class struggle . . . . The Political Secretariat of the ECCI has deemed it necessary to draw up a special resolution in regard to the tasks of the Party in the Ukrainian mass organizations which sets the relations of the work of the Party members in language organizations with that of the Party tasks as a whole . . . . Owing to the great importance of developing the work of the Party among the French Canadian masses, the Party leadership must give still greater attention to this question . . . . The main task of organizing the economic struggles and revolutionary unions must be concretized [*sic*] for the large factories and industries where the French workers, who are the most exploited section of the Canadian working class, are employed.[2]

Rarely had the weakness of the CPC been put more precisely or frankly. Such exhortations, however, written at tedious length in the jargon that characterized most Comintern instructions and publications, did little to assist the Canadian party. In turn, the party's attempts to implement Comintern policies put it increasingly out of touch with the realities of Canadian political, social, and economic life. After 1929, in conditions that ostensibly were ideally suited for a proletarian movement, the CPC made no lasting impact upon the Canadian people.

Inevitably, the failure of the Canadian party to become a political force within the Dominion must be attributed to the Comintern, and ultimately, to the Communist Party of the Soviet Union. Because the CPSU alone had succeeded in seizing power the Russian party and its leaders commanded extraordinary prestige within the International. As a result, leaders of Comintern auxiliary parties or nominees who were seconded for duty in Moscow, were all too prone to accept advice and instructions from Russian party sources to an extent that often cut across local conditions or flew in the face of common sense. After 1926, as the leadership struggle within the CPSU intensified, the parties making up the Comintern were increasingly caught up in that struggle. In the process, they became pawns in the struggle, with the contending factions in the Soviet party manoeuvring to obtain the support of the communist parties abroad. The parties abroad also became factionalized, and soon lost whatever independence they may have retained after accepting the 21 conditions of admission into the Comintern.

Certainly, such was the case with the Canadian party. During the first years of its existence the CPC had been relatively independent, a condition which briefly held true for the Comintern. During the interval between the Comintern's Sixth Congress and the time MacDonald was finally drummed out of the CPC, those who assumed party leadership became irrevocably committed to the Soviet party leader, Joseph Stalin. The willingness of Buck, Smith, Leslie Morris, and others to adopt similar tactics and to accept and reflect the same slogans used so readily by Stalin and his supporters in Russia not only reflected the decline in quality and stature of the Canadian party leaders, but also reflects the malaise that began to grip the Comintern. After the Sixth Congress the Comintern's policy of class against class, faithfully trumpeted by the CPC, alienated orthodox labour throughout the Dominion, thus further isolating the Canadian communist movement from the workers. By persisting with that policy through the depression years, and by insisting upon dual unionism—the organization of the left wing in old established bodies such as the AF of L, which was labelled as an agent of Wall Street—the CPC killed any possibility of co-operation with the labour movement in Canada when the Comintern eventually launched its united front movement in the mid-1930's. Equally, the legacy of the TUEL's failure to make any headway within Canadian labour did little to assist its successor, the Workers Unity League. As the CPC entered into the dark decade of the 1930's, an interval which coincided with the Comintern's "third period" and which has been described by one authority as "that peculiarly Stalinist alloy of logic and lunacy," the Canadian communist movement began a new phase of its development.[3] In the process the Canadian party became a mere satellite firmly in the orbit of the CPSU.

APPENDIX A

BIOGRAPHICAL NOTES
(party pseudonyms are given in brackets)

AHLQVIST, JOHN WERNER

Ahlqvist, sometimes called the"grand old man" of the Finnish communist movement in Canada, was born in Finland in 1881. It is not known when he came to Canada or what education he received. By trade he was a tailor. He became active in the Finnish Social Democratic Party (which was later transformed into the Finnish Organization of Canada) from its inception in 1911, and during the years 1918–1921 was also a member of the Independent Labour Party of Ontario. In January 1919, because of his association with the Finnish Social Democratic Party and the radical Finnish newspaper *Vapaus*, he was arrested in Sudbury for being in possession of prohibited literature and was sentenced to one month's imprisonment or a fine of $50 and costs. Following this clash with authority, Ahlqvist moved to Toronto, and became chiefly responsible for collecting money in Canada for the Refugees from Finland Fund. The donations were transmitted by Ahlqvist to Santeri Nuortava, 110 West 40th Street, New York, the office of Ludwig C. A. K. Martens, the Soviet representative in the United States.

Once made, Ahlqvist's contact with the international communist movement was never broken. He became a founding member of the Canadian Communist Party when it was formed in May 1921, and as the chief Finnish representative attended the conference which led to the formation of the overt Workers' Party of Canada in February 1922. Throughout the 1920's Ahlqvist was the lynch pin between the Finnish Organization of Canada and the Communist Party of Canada, and much of the success achieved by the communists among the Finnish population stemmed from his efforts. His easy-going personality enabled Ahlqvist to retain the confidence of the Finnish membership without diminishing his strong belief in the revolutionary movement. He was suspended temporarily from the Communist party in November 1929 on the grounds that he had supported John MacDonald at the party's Sixth Convention, and that he had resorted to splitting tactics within the Finnish membership. His exclusion was of short duration, and he returned to the party fold in 1930, remaining an active, loyal member until his death in June 1940.

BELL, THOMAS J. [Gregg; Frank Hope; D. Paul]

Tom Bell, the stormy petrel of the Canadian party's early history, was born in 1895, though exact details of time and place are not known. (Spector recalls Bell as an Ulsterman; other reports state that he was born in England.) He was a lithographer and engraver. Bell's influence on the party's origin was considerably greater than his subsequent role in its development. He became active in the revolutionary-minded groups which crystallized in Toronto in 1919, and a prime mover in bringing about the unification of dissident groups in 1921.

After the CPC's formation Bell, for a short time, became a party organizer in Toronto, as well as a member of the City Central Executive Committee of both the underground CPC and later, the overt Workers' Party. From September 1921 until March 1923 Bell was the District Four party organizer in Winnipeg. Manitoba. He was then transferred by the party to Glace Bay, Nova Scotia, the scene of a bitter labour struggle between coal miners and steel workers, and the British Empire Steel Company, where he became the business manager of the vociferous and outspoken *Maritime Labour Herald*.

Bell remained in Glace Bay only until April 1924 when he returned to Toronto before drifting to the United States. Browder recalls that Bell, for a time, worked for the American party press in Chicago. That contention is borne out by the publication in Chicago in 1925 of a booklet, *The Movement For World Trade Union Unity*, written by Bell. Ultimately, the United States party sent Bell to the Lenin School in Moscow. Before fading out of the communist movement in North America Bell wrote a commentary on the Sixth Comintern Congress, *Nakanune Epokhi Novyk Voin (Itogi VI Kongressa Kominterna)*, which was published in Moscow in 1928.

Bell was a pleasure-seeker with a strong penchant for drink, and it was largely on this score that the Canadian party lost confidence in him despite his marked abilities in doctrinal argument and his revolutionary fervour. Because of his taste for intrigue, he applied his talents in organizing factions, causing considerable ferment and uncertainty within the CPC. He was particularly at loggerheads with Florence Custance, who epitomized the dedicated puritan revolutionary, and those in the party who sided with her.

Bell was a cardinal figure in bringing about the formation of the CPC. Through his contact with Gustav and Hedda Ewert, through his uncompromising stand for the need for violent change characterized by such phrases as "we must smash the capitalists"—the terror side of Bolshevik action according to Spector—and through his ability to organize in an underground fashion, Bell was one of the agents who, taking advantage of the social conditions which existed in Canada following the First World War, made it possible for the party to come into being.

BOYCHUK, JOHN

Boychuk was born in the Ukraine on November 15, 1892, came to Canada at an early age, and was naturalized in 1910. He was a tailor by trade. Although his education was elementary, Boychuk, from the beginning of the First World War, became active in socialist circles. According to Misha Cohen, "He started boosting the socialist press in the coal towns of the Crow's Nest Pass 'way back in 1908 soon after he came to this country."* Despite being arrested in August 1918 for possessing prohibited literature, Boychuk's radicalism did not diminish, and he began to write in the *Ukrayinski Rabotnychi Visty* with considerable effect. Until the formation of the Communist party, Boychuk's revolutionary activities were confined entirely to the work of organizing the Ukrainian Labour Temple Association and, in 1920, collecting money for "Medical Help for Soviet Russia." For a short time Boychuk became a member of the One Big Union, but that connection withered away when he moved to Toronto in 1920 and gravitated to the more militant revolutionary groups then springing up in that city.

Boychuk, from the start, was a member of the Communist Party of Canada, but he is most important for his faithful work in helping to maintain the close connection between the Ukrainian group and the CPC. An able administrator, he was counted upon by the party leadership to deliver money and to obtain support for party policies from the Ukrainian membership. At the convention at which the Workers' Party of Canada was formed (February 17–19, 1922) Boychuk served as the Ukrainian representative on the Central Executive Committee. He attended all of the WPC conventions, all comparable gatherings of the Ukrainian organizations (the ULTA and after 1924, the ULFTA), and was chiefly instrumental in the building of the Ukrainian Labour Temple in Toronto in 1927. Boychuk's talents lay chiefly with practical details: the Ukrainian press; organizing schools; obtaining building funds.

BRUCE, MALCOLM LOCHIN [F. J. Masson]

Born March 30, 1881, at Seal River, Prince Edward Island, of Highland Scot parents, he was one of the few native-born and educated Canadians to become prominent in the early Canadian communist movement. Bruce, a carpenter, took up his trade at the age of 15 (he did not proceed beyond public school, i.e., about fifth grade). During his early years he followed a variety of occupations, including that of mining in the western United States: Montana, Colorado, Arizona, Nevada. At Butte he obtained his first experience of militant trade unionism when he took part in the hard-fought, bloody strikes led by the Western Federation of Miners.

On returning to Canada in 1910 he resumed his trade in the province of Saskatchewan, joining the United Brotherhood of Carpenters (AFL) in Regina, and became active in the Socialist Party of Canada. Bruce often spoke for the Socialist Party, opposing the war and the despatch of Canadian troops to Siberia. Like so many Socialist Party members in western Canada, Bruce became caught up in the initial enthusiasm which accompanied the organization of the One Big Union, and he was an active worker on its behalf. The decline of the OBU left Bruce, a sharp-tongued, outspoken, bitter left-wing socialist, isolated and frustrated, and he welcomed the rise of the more revolutionary Workers' Party of Canada. After attending the initial WPC convention in February 1922 he returned to Toronto in November 1922 to become the editor of *The Worker*. Bruce was selected for this important post because he was held to be reliable and because Spector went to Moscow to attend the Fourth Comintern Congress.

Bruce remained editor until the end of March 1924, when he left with Buck to attend the Fifth Comintern Congress. On his return Bruce replaced Bell on the Central Executive Committee, and in 1925 took over duties as the Business Manager of *The Worker*, replacing W. Moriarty. He resigned from the party at the end of October 1925 and returned to western Canada before proceeding to California to take up residence. Because of radical activity in the United States Bruce was deported from the United States in September 1927. He remained in Vancouver until 1929 when he returned to the party headquarters in Toronto following MacDonald's dismissal as a Lovestonite. Bruce resumed as editor of *The Worker*, replacing Michael Buhay who had assumed the post briefly after Spector's expulsion.

Although he was often in trouble because of his inability to handle drink, Bruce has never deviated

The Canadian Tribune, April 30, 1962.

from the party line. Like Buck, Hill, and other leading party members, Bruce was imprisoned during the early 1930's.

BUCK, TIMOTHY [G. Page]

Tim Buck, the former leader of the Communist Party of Canada, was born at Beccles, Suffolk on January 6, 1891. One of eight children, he began to work in a machine shop at the age of twelve, and became an engineering apprentice. When he turned fifteen Buck joined the Amalgamated Society of Engineers and for the first time came into contact with trade union theory and practice. It was at this time that he heard Keir Hardie, whose views and presence made a profound impression on him. At nineteen Buck emigrated to Canada, arriving in Toronto in May 1910, where he found employment as a machinist. He also began to attend night classes in order to supplement his meagre education, and simultaneously became active in trade union circles. From 1912 until 1919 Buck held many jobs as a machinist in both Canada and the United States. With the formation of the Independent Labour Party of Ontario in 1916 he became an active member, and collaborated with the editor, James Simpson, in producing a weekly labour paper called *The Industrial Banner*.

With the end of the war and the rise of revolutionary parties in the United States, branches of which were formed in Toronto, Buck became a member of the Communist Party of America. He attended the secret unity convention held at Guelph in May 1921, at which the Canadian extensions of the two American communist parties were fused under Comintern pressure. Because of his trade union experience Buck became a district organizer for the underground Communist Party of Canada. As the Workers' and later Communist party's industrial director, Buck headed the Canadian section of the Trade Union Educational League, and as a result was in frequent contact with W. Z. Foster, Earl Browder, and other American communist leaders.

In 1924 Buck attended the Fifth Comintern Congress, representing Canada on the Agrarian Committee and the Commission which dealt with the woman's role in the world communist movement. The following year, in October 1925, Buck produced a long pamphlet entitled *Steps to Power*. in which the Canadian party's trade union policies were clearly put forward. He attended the Comintern Executive Committee meeting held in December 1926, a meeting at which he and Matthew Popowich, the other Canadian delegate, upheld the Canadian party's trade union policies in the face of severe criticism from the United States party delegates. Because of his connection with the Canadian party, and because of his efforts in the trade union field to disrupt orthodox work, Buck was expelled from the International Association of Machinists in 1928.

Throughout the twenties Buck was extremely active, and the great distances he covered in connection with his party work testify to his complete dedication to the Communist party cause. In addition to trade union work Buck was responsible for the confidential underground missions which were required of all parties by the Comintern. These included handling money from abroad during the early period following unification; making arrangements for the passage through Canada of Comintern representatives destined for the United States, or assisting in obtaining travel documents for party members (both American and Canadian) proceeding abroad.

At the time of Spector's expulsion from the CPC in 1928 Buck sided with the majority. During the ferment which followed he allied himself with Stewart Smith, who had just returned from two years at the Lenin School, and the two were instrumental in displacing MacDonald from the party leadership. Buck, after a further period of manoeuvring, assumed leadership of the CPC, which he retained despite imprisonment for three years, 1931–1934.

Despite his later assumption of the role of party historian, accuracy and Marxist theory have never been Buck's strongest points, and the ideological disputes which characterized all parties during the twenties did not at the time make any great impression upon him. Buck's strength, both during his initial years in the party and after he became its leader, was his ability to divine what policies or practices were acceptable to the party, to the Comintern, and later, to Stalin. Browder, Murphy, Spector, Stewart Smith, Bertram Wolfe, and other contemporaries agree that Buck was a dedicated, hard-working party member of pleasant, amiable personality who, above all, could be trusted by Moscow. Indeed, he is one of the few communist party leaders who never lost his grip on leadership throughout the fluctuations which marked Soviet policy during Stalin's later years and the years following his death. In January 1962, after 32 years as Secretary of the CPC, Buck was made National Chairman of the party, a position which has been described as "largely honorary."

BUHAY, MICHAEL

Buhay was born in London, England, on November 30, 1890. Before emigrating to Canada in 1913 he and his sister Rebecca were members of the Socialist Party of Great Britain, and belonged to the same branch as V. J. Jerome, who later became editor of the American Marxist magazine *Political Affairs*. On arriving in Montreal Buhay became a member of the Canadian Socialist Party and plunged into trade union affairs. During the latter part of the First World War he took part in the anti-conscription rallies sparked by the nationalism of the French-Canadian leader Henri Bourassa. Early in his trade union career Buhay was elected Secretary of the Cloakmakers' Union, and during the early 1920's became an organizer for the Amalgamated Clothing Workers' Union.

With the decline of the Socialist Party of Canada and the One Big Union, in which he took a passing interest because of his sister's activities, Buhay turned to the more radical groups then springing up in central Canada. Together with his sister and other like-minded individuals such as the Gaulds, he played a leading role in the formation of the Montreal Labour College in 1920. From the foundation of the Labour College to the formation of the Communist Party of Canada was but a step, and Buhay became a founding member. He also soon became a key figure in laying the basis of the communist movement in French Canada.

In 1925 Buhay, who was Jewish, was appointed editor of the CPC's monthly Yiddish paper, *Der Kampf*. Because of his trade union activities, and because he was a reliable party man, Buhay represented the CPC at the Profintern's Fourth Congress held in Moscow during the spring of 1928. Buhay's loyalty to the party was unaffected during the turmoil which followed Spector's expulsion for supporting Trotskyism. Indeed, Buhay was appointed editor of the Canadian communist movement's most important mouthpiece, *The Worker*, in Spector's place. His tenure of office, however, was short-lived, for he in turn supported the party secretary John MacDonald who, like Jay Lovestone of the American party, contended that North America was immune to the periodic crises of capitalism.

Shortly after the CPC's Sixth National Convention in 1929 Buhay left the party. He returned to it within a year, remaining a faithful member until his death on August 9, 1947. In 1942 he was elected to the Montreal city council on a communist ticket, and in 1947 he stood unsuccessfully for the federal riding of Cartier, replacing Fred Rose, the only member of the CPC ever elected to the House of Commons, who had been convicted in 1946 of espionage for the Soviet Union.

BUHAY, REBECCA

Born on February 11, 1896, in London, England, Rebecca Buhay, familiarly known as "Becky" Buhay in party circles, came to Canada in 1912 and became active in socialist circles during the First World War. Her interest and activity increased while she was at the Rand School of Social Sciences in New York in 1918 and early 1919. There she met some of the better-known socialists such as Scott Nearing, and for a time was secretary of a Socialist Party of America group in the Bronx. Initially, after her return to Montreal, a return that was in part hastened by the Lusk committee investigations, she became a One Big Union organizer, and was particularly active within the Amalgamated Clothing Workers of America and the Ladies' Garment Union, becoming English secretary of the Montreal executive. At the same time, she played a leading role in the formation of the Montreal Labour College.

With the decline of the OBU and the rise of the Communist Party of Canada, Becky Buhay shifted her allegiance to the new revolutionary body, and in March 1922 was elected to the executive of the Workers' Party of Canada. In that capacity she toured the country lecturing and taking part in various labour actions in western Canada, later writing about her experiences for the Comintern's bulletin *International Press Correspondence*.

Her principal activities during the twenties consisted of militant organizational and speaking tours on behalf of the CPC and its press. Because of her ability to "expound the doctrine," her intense and overriding seriousness, she was entrusted with such responsibilities as organizing and directing party schools, and acting as business manager of the party paper, *The Worker*, at the beginning of 1926. During the upheaval within the party following Spector's expulsion and MacDonald's fall from power, Buhay remained loyal to the party and to the new leadership which followed, and has remained so.

BULLER, ANNIE

Annie Buller's background is obscure. Along with Rebecca Buhay and Alice Gauld she studied for a time at the Rand School of Social Sciences in New York, where she became well posted on socialism. On returning to Montreal Buller immediately became active in trade union and radical circles, becoming vice-president of the One Big Union's Montreal Executive in 1920, as well as a keen supporter of the Montreal Labour College. She shifted quickly to the Workers' Party of Canada when it was formally organized, and became an organizer in the Montreal area. Later, Buller became the business manager of *The Worker*, a post she held throughout the twenties. A dedicated, serious woman, she could be counted upon by the party to fulfil whatever tasks were allocated to her. She was content to follow doctrinal disputes, and although she admired Spector, she remained loyal to the party throughout the disputes which marked the years 1928–1930.

CUSTANCE, FLORENCE ADA [F. Johnston]

A rather prim woman, puritan in her habits and an idealist in outlook, Florence Ada Custance was born on December 31, 1881, at Dartford, Kent, and trained as a school teacher. Married to a prosperous contractor who shared her views, Custance, a militant socialist, devoted herself to the revolutionary cause soon after the end of the First World War. Together with Spector, Bell, and Moriarty she became one of the leading spirits in forming the Plebs League and the Ontario Labour College, two organizations which preceded and accelerated the rise of the Communist Party in Canada. As Secretary of the Plebs League, Custance was in contact with the counterpart English organization, as well as other radical groups, and received and distributed their literature,

After the formation and regrouping of American communist parties, Custance became a member of the United Communist Party of America wing which existed briefly in Toronto in 1921. She attended the unity convention held near Guelph in May, and in October 1921 she became Secretary of the Canadian Friends of Soviet Russia, the first of a long line of similar front organizations.

During the early days of the underground party's existence Custance became the focus of a faction which opposed the group led by Tom Bell and William Moriarty. The breach between the two groups, mostly caused by personal animosities, was healed when Bell was transferred for organization work to western Canada.

Custance attended the conventions at which the Workers' Party came into existence as the legal party organization in December 1921 and February 1922, and in April became Secretary of the open party's Women's Bureau. As Secretary-Treasurer of the Canadian Friends of Soviet Russia she was sent as a delegate to the International Workers' Aid (MRP) conference held in Berlin in 1922, and from Germany proceeded to Moscow as an extra Canadian party delegate to the Fourth Comintern Congress. The trip to Moscow succeeded in healing the breaches within the party, and raised her prestige. Following her return to Canada, Custance resumed her work as Secretary of the Women's Bureau, attended the Workers' Party of the United States—the American communist party—convention held in Chicago at the end of December 1923, and spoke about her experiences abroad in various places in Canada.

In October 1925 Custance became Secretary of the Canadian Labour Defence League, a party front organization intended to assist party and other left-wing radicals who were victims of the class war. Through the League and the party she took part in various Sacco-Vanzetti demonstrations and continued in her work in the Women's Bureau. At the 1929 party convention Custance was attacked for holding and displaying right-wing tendencies, and on the strength of the attack lost her seat on the National Executive Committee. Before she had time to organize her defence or to counter-attack, she died on July 12, 1929.

While she was in many ways rigid and uncompromising in her attitudes towards individuals, Custance was an outspoken energetic militant. She devoted herself completely to the revolutionary cause, and undoubtedly was one of the original driving forces which helped to co-ordinate and bring about the communist movement in its earliest days.

HILL, AMOS TOBIAS

Hill was born on October 12, 1897, at Polvigauvi Knopio, Finland, and came to Canada in 1912 or 1913. Although an electrician by training, Hill did not regularly follow his occupation and was soon attracted to the radical Finnish groups which began to spring up following the Russian revolution. In 1920 he became a manager of Finnish co-operatives in the Sudbury area, and the same year was elected secretary-treasurer of the revolutionary Finnish Organization of Canada, a post which he held until June 1924. During this period Hill also became active in the Workers' Party of Canada, attending both the preliminary and formal conventions at which the party was born.

In 1922 Hill became secretary of the Young Workers' Party of Canada, and in 1924 went to Moscow to attend the Fifth Comintern Congress as a delegate to the Young Communist International. After his return he became a Communist Party organizer and toured the country on behalf of both the Party and the Finnish organization. Hill resumed his duties as Secretary of the Finnish Organization in 1927 and retained this post until 1929. A staunch party man, he suffered imprisonment in 1927 for his part in a Sacco-Vanzetti demonstration, and during the early 1930's. A reliable worker, Hill was noted for his loyalty, which he maintained throughout the troubled 1928–1929 period, and for his his reliability in translating party policy and practice to the Finnish members.

KAVANAGH, JACK

Kavanagh was born in Liverpool, England, in 1882, where he learned his trade of tile-setting. He emigrated to Canada in 1907, settling in Vancouver and working as a longshoreman. He was active in trade union and political circles from the time that he settled on the west coast and joined the Socialist Party of Canada when it was formed in 1910, becoming a party organizer. By the end of the war Kavanagh had become President of the British Columbia Federation of Labour, an organization through which he made his ultra left-wing views widely known in Western trade union circles. Kavanagh was a member of the committee elected at the Western Labour Conference held in Calgary in March 1919 at which the OBU came into being.

With the decline of the OBU Kavanagh turned to the WPC, whose revolutionary views and organization coincided more nearly with his own thoughts and experiences. At the WPC's first convention Kavanagh was elected to the party's National Executive Committee. He also became a member of

M

the underground Communist Party, and as an organizer for the overt WPC frequently toured the country speaking on the party's behalf. In 1924, Kavanagh attended the annual Trades and Labour convention held in London, Ontario, where he nominated Tim Buck, the CPC's industrial organizer, for president, a tactic which squared with the Comintern's united front policy. His attitude at the meeting is exemplified by the remark that "the trouble [was] that the Communist Party [was] doing the work and the Trades [and Labour] Council [was] getting the credit."

Kavanagh left for Australia in April 1925 with another man's wife and two children, an action which became a mild cause célèbre in labour circles throughout Canada. He became active in the Australian Communist Party but was expelled in 1931. Kavanagh's chief contribution to the Canadian party's early development was that he brought trade union experience with him when he joined the party, and through his efforts both before the revolutionary groups amalgamated and after, he helped to create the climate of opinion which attracted so many of the militant labour men into the revolutionary party.

Like so many of his contemporaries Kavanagh fused his British trade union experiences into prevailing Canadian labour conditions and institutions. He differed openly with the party leaders on one matter only, for he advocated shifting the CPC's headquarters from Toronto to Winnipeg. The idea was not new and reflected western labour's traditional suspicion of any authority permanently located in central Canada. Kavanagh died in Australia in 1964.

KNIGHT, JOSEPH R.

The date of Knight's birth is not known, but he emigrated to Canada from England around 1907, and became a Socialist Party of Canada organizer in Edmonton, Alberta, before the First World War. A carpenter, he joined the Carpenter's Union local and was active in the city Trades and Labour Council. Knight was caught up in the ferment which followed the Armistice, and was drawn into the One Big Union movement. At the Western Labour Conference he was elected to the Executive Committee charged with forming the OBU, and afterwards became an active OBU organizer, ranging over eastern as well as western Canada in 1919 and 1920. Early in 1921 Knight was selected by Atwood [Caleb Harrison] and Ella Reeve Bloor to attend the initial congress of the Red International of Labour Unions (Profintern) held in Moscow in July. He also attended sessions of the Comintern's Third Congress which preceded the Profintern meeting, the first Canadian to do so, even though his position in relation to the Canadian Communist Party, which was formed after his departure, had not yet been defined. At Moscow however, Knight's actions and his approval of both Comintern and Profintern policies (in which he was in complete agreement with the American delegation) clearly showed where his sympathies lay. On his return to Canada Knight toured the country speaking about his experiences in Russia on behalf of the Canadian Friends of the Soviet Union. With the emergence of the WPC Knight became an organizer, and toured Nova Scotia in 1922, and northern Ontario in 1923.

During the period following his return from abroad Knight became caught up in the factionalism which marked inner party affairs. His failure to get the One Big Union to affiliate with the Profintern when he became a party member, invoked the Central Executive Committee's hostility and suspicion. Knight, in turn, was not averse to allowing his emotions and feelings towards MacDonald, Spector, and other Central Committee members to intrude into his party work. Such differences curtailed his activities, and curbed his effectiveness. Knight left the Canadian party early in 1924, emigrating to the United States.

MACDONALD, JOHN [J. Lawrence]

The son of a patternmaker, MacDonald was born in Falkirk, Scotland, on February 2, 1888. Despite indications of academic promise while at primary school—he was awarded various prizes including a gold medal and books for obtaining high marks—he was obliged by family circumstances to take up a trade, and like his father became a patternmaker, eventually joining the local Pattern Makers' Association. Through his family and the Pattern Makers' Association MacDonald's interest in socialism and in trade union matters was aroused. He joined the Socialist Party of Great Britain soon after, and remained an active member until he emigrated to Canada in 1912. In 1910 he was elected to the district executive of the Social Democratic Federation, and for two years, 1910–1912, he was president of the Falkirk Workers' Federation.

Soon after coming to Toronto MacDonald joined the local unit of the Pattern Makers' Lodge of North America, in which he quickly advanced to a leading position. During the Toronto metal trades strikes in 1919, for example, he was vice-president of the Metal Trades Council. MacDonald, in addition, became active in the Independent Labour Party of Ontario after its foundation in 1916, and by 1919 had been elected vice-president. The same year he stood as labour candidate for the provincial legislature in South West Toronto, but was defeated. Through his trade union and political activity MacDonald became a well-known and popular figure in Ontario labour ranks. When he openly espoused the communist cause in 1921 he brought with him the support and approval of many trade unionists and radically-inclined labour men who otherwise would have remained indifferent to the

Third International's call. In turn, because of his trade union experience and his personal prestige, MacDonald was the logical person to lead the new party, and he was elected Secretary of the WPC when it emerged in February 1922, and after it changed its name to the Communist Party of Canada in 1924. He retained that post until the autumn of 1929 when he was labelled as a supporter of Jay Lovestone, the United States party leader, and a right deviationist.

MacDonald, together with Spector, attended the Comintern's Fourth Congress in 1922. After his return from Russia he was arrested during the Nova Scotia miners' strike during the summer of 1923, tried, and acquitted by a jury of a charge of sedition brought against him by the provincial authorities. In 1924 he became president of the Canadian Labor Party, and in that capacity attended the British Commonwealth Labour Conference held in London in 1925, a gathering which only served to convince him further that revolutionary means were the only ones which would bring about social and political change in capitalist countries. MacDonald attended the Sixth Comintern Congress in 1928, and that autumn took a leading part in the expulsion of Maurice Spector, Chairman of the CPC, who had come out openly in support of Trotsky and the "oposition" group within the Russian party. When, in a matter of months, MacDonald in turn was identified as a Lovestonite, he was not immediately cast out of the Canadian party, but was given leave of absence, an indication of his general prestige within the Canadian communist movement. He was only expelled in November 1930 after refusing to conform with a Comintern directive which stipulated that he was to take an active stand against "right deviationists" as well as Trotsky supporters in order to remain in the party. After his break with the CPC, MacDonald and Spector joined forces in attempting to form an opposition Communist Party more in keeping with their views. The enterprise failed for lack of support, and ended when Spector left to settle in New York in 1936. MacDonald, though he remained a dedicated Marxist, never again resumed political activity. He died in Toronto on November 8, 1941.

McLACHLAN, JAMES BRYSON
The son of a Scottish miner, J. B. McLachlan was born on February 9, 1869, at Ecclefechan, Dumfrieshire. At the age of 11, after four years of elementary schooling, he went into the pits. McLachlan emigrated to Canada in 1902, taking up residence in Glace Bay, Nova Scotia, where he found employment as a coal miner. One of his earliest acts was to join the United Mine Workers of America, and in 1909 he became Secretary of District 26, holding that post until the District's charter was withdrawn in 1915. During the interim period until the District was reconstituted in 1919, McLachlan was active in organizing the miners into a new organization called the Amalgamated Miners of Nova Scotia. When the new District 26 emerged after the war, McLachlan again became its secretary, holding the post until July 1923, when he was deposed by John L. Lewis.

McLachlan joined the Communist Party of Canada soon after it was formed in 1921, and attended both the CPC and the WPC conventions held in February 1923. Through his position as Secretary of District 26, UMWA, McLachlan was able to exert considerable influence upon the miners and steelworkers in Nova Scotia. He was charged with sedition by the provincial authorities in 1923 and was sentenced to two years imprisonment. In keeping with the CPC's united front policy, McLachlan played an active role in the Canadian Labor Party, and in 1923 became president of the Nova Scotia provincial section. After leaving prison in 1924 he once more became editor of the radical *Maritime Labour Herald*, replacing Tom Bell. By then, however, both the party's and McLachlan's influence in the Nova Scotia labour scene had waned, never to be regained. He died in 1936.

MORIARTY, WILLIAM [Cuthbert]
Few details are known about Moriarty, one of the CPC's founding members. Born in London, England, Moriarty, a draughtsman by training, came to Canada in 1913. Together with MacDonald, Custance, and others in Toronto he drifted from the local socialist groups into the rising communist movement, serving first in the underground movement, and then as Secretary of the WPC during the first year of its existence. In the early days of the communist movement in the Dominion Moriarty, along with MacDonald, Spector, Annie Buller, and J. Sutcliffe, a wealthy supporter, served on the board of directors of the Proletarian Film Company, one of the initial propaganda organizations set up by the CPC. Until he went to Moscow in 1925 to represent the Canadian party at the Comintern's Fifth Plenum, Moriarty served as *The Worker*'s business manager. After his return he was made National Organizer, a post which suited his talent for administrative detail. He remained loyal to the party throughout the upheavals of 1928–1929, and died on May 14, 1936.

POPOWICH, MATTHEW [Volynec and Rabytnyk]
Popowich was born on August 21, 1890, in Lubyantisi in the Zabarazh district of the Ukraine. Before coming to America in 1910, he taught school. After his arrival in Canada in 1911, he edited and wrote for the Ukrainian radical papers *Rabochy Narod* and *Holos Praci*, and later *Ukrayinski Rabotnychi Visty*. Popowich was one of the pioneer Ukrainian communist leaders in Canada. His activities, which began before the First World War, crystallized in the formation of the Ukrainian Labour Temple Association, of which he became the national secretary in 1921, and the formation

of the Communist Party of Canada. He attended the meeting of communist leaders held in Toronto in December 1921 which preceded the emergence of the overt WPC in February 1922, and before that party came into being, helped to make arrangements for John MacDonald's organization tour across the country.

In addition to being actively connected with the Ukrainian communist press, Popowich was the Communist Party's standard-bearer in the Manitoba provincial elections in 1922, and in the Winnipeg civic elections of 1924 and 1925. At the CPC's behest, Popowich was brought to Toronto to be the permanent Ukrainian representative at the party centre, and in 1926 accompanied Buck to Moscow for the Comintern Seventh Plenum. Throughout his career with the communist party Popowich pressed for greater recognition of the Ukrainian membership by the party leadership, but that view never became an obstacle to party policy or practice. He devoted his entire energies to the revolutionary movement, including his talents as a concert singer, which were employed for raising funds. Popowich remained a staunch member throughout the upheavals caused by the expulsions of Spector and MacDonald, and was one of the main reasons why the differences within the party did not have a greater effect upon the Ukrainain party membership. He died on July 17, 1943.

SMITH, REV. ALBERT EDWARD

Of solid British stock, A. E. Smith was born at Guelph, Ontario, on October 20, 1871. As a boy he worked as a messenger and an apprentice bookbinder before undergoing training to become a Methodist minister. He subsequently served as a pastor in various western Canadian parishes ranging from Winnipeg, Manitoba, to Nelson, British Columbia. It was while at the latter in 1910 that Smith came into contact with the radical American organizer, Jack Johnstone, who first interested him in militant socialism. After returning to Manitoba just before World War I, he became president of the provincial Methodist Conference. His socialist views were stimulated by the Russian revolution, and were translated into active participation in the Winnipeg General Strike in 1919. Smith helped to prepare strike bulletins, he spoke at open air meetings, and organized a People's Church in Brandon (one of the earliest of the labour churches which flourished briefly in western Canada after the war). Such activities were incompatible with his position in the Methodist Church, and he resigned in June 1919, becoming, in effect, one of the earliest of clerical communists.

Smith was elected labour member in the Manitoba provincial legislature on June 29, 1920, representing the constituency of Brandon until 1923. In 1921 he attended the annual Trades and Labour Congress meeting held in Winnipeg, at which the Canadian Labor Party came into existence. After moving from Brandon to Toronto in 1923 Smith formed a People's Church and became active in the Labor Forum, a body sponsored by the Toronto branch of the Canadian Labor Party which organized classes in economics, sociology, politics, and similar subjects. The central issue which dominated the talks and discussions held by the Labour Forum was communism and what Smith himself termed "social-reformism." One result was that Smith chose the revolutionary as opposed to the democratic method of bringing about social and political change in Canada, and in January 1925 he joined the Communist Party, becoming an organizer in District Three and later a member of the party's Toronto city committee. In the federal elections of October 1925 and September 1926 Smith unsuccessfully stood as labour candidate for Port Arthur. In 1925 too he became President of the Canadian Labor Party's Ontario section, one of five communist members on an executive of 13.

The same year, with the formation of the Canadian Labor Defence League, a communist front organization ostensibly established to aid victims of the class war, Smith became one of the League's principal officers. After the death in 1929 of Florence Custance, who had headed the League from its inception, Smith became General Secretary, a post he held until the organization was banned in June 1940. Throughout the general unrest within the Canadian party during 1928 and 1929 caused by the expulsions of Maurice Spector, the party chairman, and John MacDonald, the party secretary, Smith remained steadfastly loyal to Moscow and to the new leadership headed by Tim Buck. He remained an active party member until his death in Toronto on May 11, 1947.

SMITH, STEWART OSBORNE [G. Pierce]

The son of Rev. A. E. Smith, and a third-generation Canadian, Stewart Smith was born in Portage la Prairie, Manitoba, on August 18, 1908. Brought up in an atmosphere of evangelical socialism, it was almost inevitable that young Smith should reflect some of that background. He did so by joining the Young Workers' League (YWL) of Canada after his family moved to Toronto in 1923. A year later, on October 20, 1924, he became the YWL's National Secretary. His activities with the League and with the CPC ranged from editing *The Young Worker* to speaking at forum meetings and rallies. His militancy is indicated by his arrest for disorderly conduct in Toronto on July 24, 1925. Smith's performance and his abilities impressed MacDonald, the CPC's Secretary, and other party leaders and when the Canadian party was allotted a place at the Lenin School in Moscow, Stewart Smith was selected as the first Canadian student. When he reached Moscow in the autumn of 1926 Smith was barely eighteen.

During his two-year stay in Moscow, Smith did not confine himself to the passive role of student, but took an active and increasing part in formulating the Comintern's directives to the Canadian party. On his return to Toronto in November 1928, Smith, with the prestige of Moscow behind him, took on the role of prosecuting counsel against the party chairman, Maurice Spector, who had declared his Trotskyite views in 1928. Later, in 1929, he combined with Tim Buck in forcing Mac-Donald out of the party leadership. Smith represented the Canadian party at the Comintern's Eleventh ECCI Plenum held in 1931, where he was strongly criticized by Piatnitsky for some of his actions during the CPC's period of crisis. In 1939 he was elected to the Toronto city council as alderman, but was defeated the following year. When the CPC and its front organizations were banned in June 1940, Smith went into hiding. On emerging from underground in 1942, he was re-elected alderman in the 1943 civic elections, and crowned that success by being elected to the Board of Control in January 1945. Smith broke with the Canadian Communist Party in May 1957. Still a dedicated Marxist, he was, for a time, secretary of a body called the Labour Progressive Party (the name adopted by the CPC in 1943 and retained until October 1959) Minority Group.

SPECTOR, MAURICE [G. Stanley]

Maurice Spector was born of Jewish parents in Nicolaev, a small town near Odessa, on March 19, 1898. Soon after, the family emigrated to Canada, settling in Toronto where Spector's father became a hardware merchant. Maurice Spector obtained all of his formal education at Strathcona Public School, Humberside Collegiate Institute, and finally at the University of Toronto. Spector's interest in socialism was first aroused while he was still at high school, when one of his teachers introduced him to *The New Age*, the guild-socialist publication produced in England by A. R. Orage. At university he continued to read widely, ranging through the writings of Bernstein, Sorel, Shaw, the Webbs, and others. After the Russian revolution he was given some pamphlets written by Lenin which were being circulated among socialist groups. During the war too, Spector had read avidly Trotsky's despatches on the Balkans which were reproduced in the *Mail and Empire*, fascinated even then by their content and style.

After the October revolution in Russia, Spector began to attend local meetings held by Social Democratic Party groups, and the Independent Labor Party. It was at this time that he learned Yiddish and first made contact with many of the individuals who later formed the nucleus of the Canadian communist movement: John MacDonald, Florence Custance, Tom Bell, William Moriarty, Tim Buck, F. J. Peel, Joseph Knight and, before they were deported, the Ewerts. Through these contacts, and with the formation of the Plebs League and the Ontario Labour College in 1920, both of which were started in order to educate the working man in terms of the class struggle, the need for a Canadian Communist Party became clear. When the two Canadian units of the United States parties, the Communist Labor Party of America, and the United Communist Party of America, were formed in Toronto, Spector joined the latter at the beginning of 1921. In May he attended the secret unity convention at which both organizations were fused into the Communist Party of Canada under Comintern pressure, under the supervision of Caleb Harrison or "Atwood," the Pan American Agency's representative. At the convention Spector was appointed to a three-man press committee, and he subsequently edited the first issue of *The Communist*, the party's underground paper which appeared in June. He was also elected to the CPC's Executive Committee.

With the emergence of the overt Workers' Party of Canada in February 1922, Spector, despite his comparative youth, was made party chairman, and in the autumn accompanied MacDonald, the party secretary, to the Comintern Fourth World Congress. On his return he toured Canada, describing his experiences and observations in Russia. At the end of 1923, Spector, his trip made possible by one of the communist movement's wealthy "angels," went to Germany to obtain first-hand experience from the revolution then expected to break out there. When the revolt failed to materialize, Spector continued to Moscow for discussions with Comintern leaders. It was from this trip that he began to harbour reservations and doubts about the Comintern and the Russian party's policies. From these initial doubts developed his conviction that Trotsky's views were being suppressed, and that attitude emerged openly when, in reply to a cable from Moscow in the spring of 1925, Spector was chiefly responsible for the Canadian party's refusal to take a firm stand against the "opposition group" within the Russian party. Spector was not condemned for his stand because of his own prestige within the Canadian communist movement, and because the party secretary, MacDonald, felt that the Canadian party should not concern itself with the controversy. Later in 1925 Spector accompanied MacDonald to the British Commonwealth Labour Conference held in London in July.

As the CPC's leading political thinker, and as editor of *The Worker*, the CPC's most important publication in Canada, Spector took a leading part in planning the party's policies towards the Canadian Labor Party. The effectiveness of the communists' efforts was demonstrated in terms of the number and nature of the resolutions passed by provincial section conventions, and by the number of party members elected to the national as well as to the provincial bodies. With the breakup of the Canadian Labor Party in 1927 the CPC lost its greatest opportunity to make itself a truly effective political force in the Dominion.

In 1928 Spector attended the Comintern's Sixth World Congress. There he renewed his contact with the American party leader, James P. Cannon. Both men, after reading a portion of Trotsky's *Draft Programme of the Communist International: A Criticism of Fundamentals*, agreed to take up the cause of Trotskyism, and to disseminate the exiled leader's views in Canada and the United States. Circumstances, however, never permitted them to do as they had hoped and planned. Instead, Cannon's exposure and expulsion a short time after his return to New York triggered Spector's ejection from the CPC in November 1928. After his expulsion from the Canadian party Spector became an assistant editor of *The Militant*, a Trotskyite opposition journal founded by Cannon. After John MacDonald was eventually expelled from the CPC in 1930, Spector combined with him in attempting to form an opposition Trotskyist party in Canada but the attempt failed for lack of support. Spector emigrated to New York in 1936.

A tall, well-built man with a shock of thick black hair, Spector, during his party career, was a highly effective speaker, an efficient organizer, and certainly one of the most politically minded of the Canadian communist leaders. At the same time he was one of the few intellectuals who joined the party during its first decade, and that, as much as any other factor, contributed both to his rise and to his fall.

APPENDIX B

CPC REPRESENTATION AT COMINTERN AND PROFINTERN CONGRESSES AND PLENUMS

Congress	ECCI Plenum	Date	Place	Canadian Delegates or Representatives
FIRST		Mar. 2–6, 1919	Moscow	None
SECOND		July 19, 1920 July 23 — Aug. 7, 1920	Petrograd Moscow	None
THIRD		June 22 — July 12, 1921	Moscow	Joseph Knight
	FIRST	Feb. 24 — Mar. 4, 1922	Moscow	None
	SECOND	June 7–11, 1922	Moscow	None
FOURTH		Nov. 5 — Dec. 5, 1922	Petrograd Moscow	Florence Custance John MacDonald Maurice Spector
	THIRD	June 12–23, 1923	Moscow	Charles E. Scott
	FOURTH	June 12 & July 12–13, 1924	Moscow	None
FIFTH		June 17 — July 8, 1924	Moscow	Malcolm Bruce Tim Buck A. T. Hill
	FIFTH	Mar. 21 — Apr. 6, 1925	Moscow	William Moriarty
	SIXTH	Feb. 17 — Mar. 15, 1926	Moscow	None
	SEVENTH	Nov. 22 — Dec. 16, 1926	Moscow	Tim Buck Matthew Popowich
	EIGHTH	May 18–30, 1927	Moscow	None
	NINTH	Feb. 4–25, 1928	Moscow	None
SIXTH		July 17 — Sept. 1, 1928	Moscow	John MacDonald John Navis A. G. Neal Maurice Spector
	TENTH	July 3–19, 1929	Moscow	None
	ELEVENTH	Mar. 26 — Apr. 11, 1931		Stewart Smith

Congress	ECCI Plenum	Date	Place	Canadian Delegates or Representatives
		Profintern Congresses		
FIRST		July 3–19, 1921	Moscow	J. Knight [Gordon Cascaden]
SECOND		Nov. 19 — Dec. 2, 1922	Moscow	John MacDonald Maurice Spector
THIRD		July 8–22, 1924	Moscow	Tim Buck [Malcolm Bruce?] [A. T. Hill?]
FOURTH		Mar. 17 — Apr. 3, 1928	Moscow	Michael Buhay

BIBLIOGRAPHY

Interviews

Aitken, George, London
Browder, Earl, New York
Lovestone, Jay, New York
Murphy, J. T., London
Smith, Stewart, Toronto
Spector, Maurice, New York
Wolfe, Bertram D., New York

Manuscript Sources

Attorney General's Department, Province of Ontario, Record Group. Department of Public Records and Archives, Toronto.
Borden, Sir Robert L. Papers. Public Archives of Canada, Ottawa.
Cahan, C. H. Papers. Public Archives of Canada, Ottawa.
Department of Militia and Defence. Files, 1917–1921. Public Archives of Canada, Ottawa.
Foster, Sir George. Papers. Public Archives of Canada, Ottawa.
Governor General's Office. Papers. Public Archives of Canada, Ottawa.
Kemp, Sir Edward. Papers. Public Archives of Canada, Ottawa.
Meighen, Arthur. Papers, Public Archives of Canada, Ottawa.
Milner, Alfred (Lord). Papers. New College, Oxford.
White, Sir Thomas. Papers. Public Archives of Canada, Ottawa.
Woodsworth, J. S. Papers. Public Archives of Canada, Ottawa.

Manifestos, Reports, Resolutions, Theses, and other Documents

Bolshevizing the Communist International. London, 1925.
Canada. House of Commons. *Debates*. Ottawa, 1924 and 1928.
Canada. Royal Commission to Investigate Disclosures of Secret and Confidential Information to Unauthorized Persons. *The Report of the Royal Commission Appointed under Order in Council P.C. 411 of February 5, 1946 to Investigate the Facts Relating to and the Circumstances Surrounding the Communication, by Public Officials and Other Persons in Positions of Trust of Secret and Confidential Information to Agents of a Foreign Power. June 27, 1946*. Ottawa, 1946.
Canada. Senate. *Debates*. Ottawa, 1925 and 1928.
Canadian Suomalainen Jarjesto 25 Vuotta. Sudbury, 1936.
Communist International. *Fifteen Years of the Communist International; Theses for Instructors*. New York, 1934.
Communist International. 3rd Congress. Moscow, 1921. *Protokoll des III. Kongresses der Kommunistischen Internationale (Moskau 22. Juni bis 12. Juli 1921)*. Hamburg, 1921.
Communist International. 3rd Congress. Moscow, 1921. *Report of Meetings held at Moscow June 22– July 12*. Communist Party of Great Britain [London, 1921]. "Reprinted from 'Moscow,' the special organ of the Congress."
Communist International. 3rd Congress. Moscow, 1921. *Theses and Resolutions Adopted at the Third World Congress of the Communist International (June 22nd–July 12th, 1921)*. New York, 1921.
Communist International. 4th Congress. Petrograd and Moscow, 1922. *Bericht über den IV. Kongress der Kommunistischen Internationale; Petrograd-Moskau, vom 5. November bis 5. Dezember, 1922*. Hamburg, 1923.
Communist International. 4th Congress. Petrograd and Moscow, 1922. *Bulletin*. Moscow, 1922.
Communist International. 4th Congress. Petrograd and Moscow, 1922. *Fourth Congress of the Communist International; Abridged Report of Meetings Held at Petrograd and Moscow, Nov. 7– Dec. 3, 1922*. London [1923].

Communist International. 4th Congress. Petrograd and Moscow, 1922. *Protokoll des vierten Kongresses der Kommunistischen Internationale, Petrograd-Moskau, vom 5. November bis 5. Dezember 1922.* Hamburg, 1923.

Communist International. 4th Congress. Petrograd and Moscow, 1922. *Resolutions and Theses of the Fourth Congress of the Communist International, Held in Moscow Nov. 7 to Dec. 3, 1922.* London [1923].

Communist International. 4th Congress. Petrograd and Moscow, 1922. *Thesen und Resolutionen des IV. Weltkongresses der Kommunistischen Internationale, Moskau, vom 5. November bis 5. Dezember 1922.* Hamburg, 1923.

Communist International. 5th Congress. Moscow, 1924. *Fifth Congress of the Communist International; Abridged Report of Meetings Held at Moscow, June 17th to July 8th, 1924.* [London], Communist Party of Great Britain [1924].

Communist International. 5th Congress. Moscow, 1924. *Protokoll des 5. Kongresses der Kommunistischen Internationale.* [Hamburg, 1924]. 2 vols.

Communist International. 5th Congress. Moscow, 1924. *Symposium on the Programme Question.* London, 1924.

Communist International. 6th Congress. Moscow, 1928. *Protokoll. Sechster Weltkongress der Kommunistischen Internationale, Moskau, 17. Juli-1. September 1928.* Hamburg [1928–29]. 4 vols.

Communist International. Enlarged Executive. *Protokoll der Konferenz der Erweiterten Exekutive der Kommunistischen Internationale, Moskau, 12–23. Juni 1923.* Hamburg, 1923.

Communist International. Enlarged Executive. *Protokoll; Erweiterte Exekutive der Kommunistischen Internationale, Moskau, 21. März–6. April 1925.* [Hamburg, 1925].

Communist International. Enlarged Executive. *Protokoll; Erweiterte Exekutive der Kommunistischen Internationale, Moskau, 22. November–16. Dezember 1926.* Hamburg [1927].

Communist International. Executive Committee. *ECCI Letter to the Central Committee Communist Party of Canada, October 3, 1929.* [Moscow].

Communist International. Executive Committee. *XIth Plenum of the Executive Committee of the Communist International; Theses, Resolutions and Decisions.* London [1931].

Communist International. Executive Committee. *From the Fourth to the Fifth World Congress. Report of the Executive Committee of the Communist International.* London, 1924.

Communist International. Executive Committee. *Protokoll der Erweiterten Exekutive der Kommunistischen Internationale, Moskau, 12.–23. Juni 1923.* Hamburg, 1923.

Communist International. Executive Committee. *Protokoll. X. Plenum des Exekutivekomitees der Kommunistischen Internationale, Moskau, 3. Juli 1929 bis 19. Juli 1929.* Hamburg [1929].

Communist International. Executive Committee. *Report on the Activities of the Executive Committee of the Communist International (for the period March-November 1926). Compiled by the Secretariat of the E.C.C.I.* [London], 1926.

Communist International. Executive Committee. *Report on the Activity of the Executive Committee of the Communist International (for the period March-November 1926).* [Moscow, 1926].

Communist International. Executive Committee. *Resolutions of the Canadian Commission. Fifth Plenum ECCI, to the CEC Communist Party of Canada.* Moscow [1925].

The Communist International Between the Fifth and Sixth World Congresses, 1924–8. London, 1928.

Communist Party of Canada. *Report of the National Convention, February 1923.* Toronto, 1923.

Communist Party of Canada. Central Executive Committee. *Report of the Central Executive Committee to the Fifth National Convention of the Communist Party of Canada.* Toronto, 1927.

Communist Party of the Soviet Union. XVth Congress. *Report of the XV Congress of the Communist Party of the Soviet Union.* London, 1928.

Great Britain. Cmd. 2874. *Documents Illustrating the Hostile Activities of the Soviet Government and Third International against Great Britain.* London, 1927.

How to Organize the Communist Party. London, 1924.

Instructions Sent to the Canadian Communists by the Third International. [Moscow, 1925].

Kommunisten Internationale. Stockholm, 1919.

Labour Organization in Canada, 1912–1932. Ottawa, 1913–1933.

New York (State) Legislature. Joint Committee Investigating Seditious Activities. *Revolutionary Radicalism, Its History, Purpose, and Tactics ... Report of the Joint Legislative Committee Investigating Seditious Activities, Filed April 24, 1920, in the Senate of the State of New York.* [The Lusk Report]. Albany, 1920. 4 vols.

On the Road to Bolshevization. New York [1929].

Ontario. Court of Appeal. *The King versus Buck and Others. The Judgement of the Court of Appeal of Ontario Concerning the Communist Party of Canada.* Toronto, 1932.

Ontario. Supreme Court. *The King v. Buck et al; Record of Proceedings.* Toronto, 1931.

Ontario. Supreme Court. *Rex v. Buck et al. Transcript of Evidence Heard before the Supreme Court of Ontario, November 2–12, 1931.* Toronto, 1931.

Propamyatna Knyha Ukrayinskoho Narodnoho Domu v Winnipegu. Winnipeg, 1949.

Red International of Labor Unions. 1st Congress. Moscow, 1921. *Resolutions and Decisions of the*

Red Labor Union International. Adopted at the First World Congress, Moscow, June 1921. New York [1921].
Red International of Labor Unions. 2nd Congress. Moscow, 1922. *Resolutions and Decisions Second World Congress of the Red International of Labor Unions Held in Moscow, November, 1922.* Chicago [1924].
Red International of Labor Unions. 2nd Congress. Moscow, 1922. *Second World Congress.* London [1923].
Red International of Labor Unions. 4th Congress. Moscow, 1928. *Protokoll über den 4. Kongress der Roten Gewerkschafts-Internationale, abgehalten in Moskau, vom 17. Marz bis 3. April 1928.* Moskau, 1928.
Red International of Labor Unions. 4th Congress. Moscow, 1928. *Stenograficheskii otchet, rezoliutsii i postanovleniia, 17 marta-3 aprelia 1928.* Moskva, 1928.
Red International of Labor Unions. 5th Congress. Moscow, 1930. *Resolutions of the Fifth World Congress R.I.L.U. Held in Moscow, August, 1930.* London, 1931.
Slavs in Canada: Vol. 1, Proceedings of the First National Conference on Canadian Slavs, June 9–12, 1965. Edmonton, 1966.
United States Congress. House of Representatives. Committee on Un-American Activities. *Hearings Regarding Communist Espionage: Hearings Before the Committee on Un-American Activities, House of Representatives, 81st Congress.* Washington, 1951.
United States Congress. House of Representatives. Special Committee on Un-American Activities. *Investigation of Un-American Propaganda Activities in the United States: Hearings Before the Special Committee on Un-American Activities (Dies Committee), 75th–76th Congresses.* Washington, 1939–1940.
United States Congress. Senate. Committee on Foreign Relations. *Recognition of Russia; Hearings before a Subcommittee, 68th Congress, 1st Session. . . .* Washington, 1924.
United States Congress. Subversive Activities Control Board. *Hearings Before the Subversive Activities Control Board: Official Report of Proceedings Before the Subversive Activities Control Board: Attorney General of the United States versus Communist Party of the United States of America.* Washington, 1951–1953.
Workers' Party of Canada. *Report of the Proceedings of the Conference called by F. J. Peel, editor of "The Workers' Guard."* Toronto, 1921.
Workers' Party of Canada. 1st National Convention. Toronto, 1922. *Report of the Workers' Party Convention, February 1922.* Toronto, 1922.
Workers' Party of Canada. 2nd National Convention. Toronto, 1923. *Report of the Proceedings of the Second Annual Convention of the Workers' Party of Canada, Toronto, February 22–25, 1923.* Toronto, 1923.
Workers' Party of Canada. 3rd National Convention. Toronto, 1924. *Report of the Third National Convention Workers' Party of Canada, April 18–20, 1924.* Toronto, 1924.
Young Communist International. *The Results of Two Congresses. The Fifth Congress of the Communist International and the Fourth Congress of the Y.C.I.* Stockholm, 1924.
Young Communist International. 3rd Congress. Moscow, 1922. *Resolutions and Theses Adopted by the Third Congress Y.C.I.* Berlin, 1923.
Young Communist International. 4th Congress. Moscow, 1924. *Resolutions Adopted at the 4th Congress of the Young Communist International.* Stockholm, 1924.
Young Communist International. Enlarged Executive. *Resolutions of the Enlarged Executive of the Young Communist International, November 1926.* London, 1926.
Young Communist League of Canada. National Executive Committee. *Report of the National Executive Committee from the Period of the Third to Fourth National Conventions of the Young Communist League of Canada.* Toronto, 1927.

Reference Publications

American Press Directory. New York, 1925.
American Labor Who's Who. New York, 1925.
American Labor Year Book, Vol. IV, 1921–1922, to Vol. VIII, 1927. New York, 1922–1927.
Canadian Annual Review of Public Affairs, Toronto, 1918–1931.

Newspapers and Periodicals

Alberta Labour News
British Columbia Federationist
Calgary Herald
Canadian Historical Review
Canadian Journal of Economics and Political Science

Canadian Labour Monthly
Canadian Tribune
Communist (New York)
Communist (Toronto)
Communist International
Confederate (Brandon, Manitoba)

Daily Worker (Chicago and New York)
Farmereske Zhitya
Globe (Toronto)
Hamilton Daily Times
Industrial Banner
International Press Correspondence (Inprecorr)
International Presse-Korrespondenz (Inprekorr)
Labor Herald
Labor Leader (Toronto)
Left Wing (Toronto)
Manitoba Free Press
Maritime Labour Herald
Marxist Quarterly
Marxist Review
Militant
National Affairs Monthly
New York Times
Observer (London)
Ost-Probleme
Ottawa Evening Citizen
L'Ouvrier canadien
Pacific Tribune

Pravda
Queen's Quarterly
Rand School News
Red Flag
Die Rote Fahne ("Red Flag")
Saturday Night
Sun (Toronto)
Sunday Worker (London)
Toiler
Toronto Daily Star
Toronto World
Ukrayinski Rabotnychi Visty
Ukrayinski Zhitya
Vancouver Sun
Western Clarion (Vancouver)
Western Labour News
Winnipeg Free Press
Worker
Workers' Guard
World Marxist Review
Young Worker

Books, Theses, and Articles

Allen, W. E. D. *The Ukraine: A History*. Cambridge, 1940.
Anonymous. "Leslie Morris." *The Marxist Quarterly*, No. 12, Winter, 1964.
Anonymous. "In Memoriam: Leslie Morris." *World Marxist Review*, December, 1964.
Balabanoff, Angelica. *My Life as a Rebel*. New York, 1938.
Balawyder, Aloysius. "Canadian-Soviet Relations, 1920–1935." Unpublished Ph.D. thesis, McGill University, 1966.
Bell, Tom. *Pioneering Days*. London, 1941.
―――― *The British Communist Party*. London, 1947.
Bloor, E. R. *We are Many*. London, 1941.
Borden, Henry (ed.). *Robert Laird Borden: His Memoirs*. London, 1938.
Borkenau, Franz. *The Communist International*. London, 1938.
Brady, Alexander. *Democracy in the Dominions*. Toronto, 1958.
Brody, David. *Labor in Crisis: The Steel Strike of 1919*. New York, 1965.
Browder, R. P. *The Origins of Soviet-American Diplomacy*. Princeton, 1953.
Bryant, Louise. *Mirrors of Moscow*. New York, 1933.
Buck, Tim. *Steps to Power*. Toronto, 1925.
―――― *Thirty Years 1922–1952*. Toronto, 1952.
―――― *1917–1957: Forty Years of Great Change*. Toronto, 1952.
―――― *Our Fight For Canada. Selected Writings (1923–1959)*. Toronto, 1959.
Bukharin, N. and Preobrazhensky, E. *The A.B.C. of Communism*. London, 1922.
Cahan, Jacqueline Flint. "A Survey of Political Activities of the Labour Movement, 1850–1935". Unpublished M.A. thesis, University of Toronto, 1945.
Cannon, J. P. *The Struggle For a Proletarian Party*. New York, 1943.
―――― *The History of American Trotskyism*. New York, 1944.
Careless, J. M. S. *Brown of the Globe: Statesman of Confederation 1860–1880*. Toronto, 1963.
Carr, E. H. *A History of Soviet Russia.*
    Vol. I.   *The Bolshevik Revolution 1917–1923*. London, 1950.
    Vol. II.   „   „   „   „   London, 1952.
    Vol. III.   „   „   „   „   London, 1953.
    Vol. IV. *The Interregnum 1923–1924*. London, 1954.
    Vol. V. *Socialism in the One Country 1924–1926*. Vol. I. London, 1958.
    Vol. VI.   „   „   „   „   Vol. II. London, 1959.
    Vol. VII.   „   „   „   „   Vol. III, Part One and Part Two. London, 1964.
Cascaden, Gordon. *Shall Unionism Die*. Windsor (Ontario), 1921.
Chamberlin, W. H. *The Ukraine: A Submerged Nation*. New York, 1944.
―――― *Blueprint For World Conquest as Outlined by the Communist International*. Washington, 1946.
Coates, W. P. and Zelda, K. *Armed Intervention in Russia 1918–1922*. London, 1935.
Coser, L. and Howe, I. *The American Communist Party*. Boston, 1957.

Creighton, D. G. *John A. Macdonald: the Old Chieftain*. Toronto, 1955.
Crook, W. H. *The General Strike*. Chapel Hill, 1931.
Crosser, Paul K. *Ideologies and American Labor*. New York, 1941.
Dallin, D. J. *Soviet Espionage*. Binghampton, 1955.
Davies, R. A. *Canada and Russia, Neighbours and Friends*. Toronto, 1944.
Dawson, R. M. *William Lyon Mackenzie King*. Toronto, 1958.
Degras, Jane (ed.). *Soviet Documents on Foreign Policy*. London, 1952.
———   *The Communist International 1919–1943*. Vol. I. 1919–1923. London, 1956.
———   *The Communist International 1919–1943*. Vol. II. 1923–1928. London, 1960.
———   *The Communist International 1919–1943*. Vol. III. 1928–1943. London, 1965.
Deutscher, Isaac. *Stalin: A Political Biography*. London, 1949.
———   *The Prophet Armed: Trotsky, 1879–1921*. London, 1954.
———   *The Prophet Unarmed: Trotsky, 1921–1929*. London, 1959.
———   *The Prophet Outcast: Trotsky, 1929–1940*. London, 1963.
Draper, Theodore. *The Roots of American Communism*. New York, 1957.
———   *American Communism and Soviet Russia*. New York, 1960.
Eayrs, James. *In Defence of Canada: From the Great War to the Great Depression*. Toronto, 1964.
England, Robert. *The Central European Immigrant in Canada*. Toronto, 1929.
———   *The Colonization of Western Canada*. London, 1936.
Fay, E. R. "The Early Years." *Marxist Quarterly*, Vol. I, No. 1.
Ferns, H. S. and Ostry, B. *The Age of Mackenzie King*. London, 1956.
Fischer, Louis. *The Soviets in World Affairs, 1917–1929*. London, 1931.
———   *Men and Politics*. New York, 1946.
Fischer, Ruth. *Stalin and German Communism*. London, 1948.
Florinsky, M. T. *World Revolution and the U.S.S.R.* New York, 1933.
Footman, David (ed.). *International Communism*. London, 1960.
Foster, W. Z. *From Bryant to Stalin*. New York, 1937.
———   *History of the Communist Party of the United States*. New York, 1952.
———   *History of the Three Internationals*. New York, 1955.
Freeman, Joseph. *An American Testament*. London, 1938.
French, Doris. *Faith, Sweat, and Politics*. Toronto, 1962.
George, David Lloyd. *War Memoirs*. London, 1936.
Gitlow, Benjamin. *I Confess*. New York, 1939.
———   *The Whole of Their Lives*. New York, 1948.
Glazebrook, G. P. deT. *A History of Canadian External Relations*. Toronto, 1951.
Graham, Roger. *Arthur Meighen: The Door of Opportunity*. Vol. I. Toronto, 1960.
Graves, W. S. *America's Siberian Adventure, 1918–1920*. New York, 1931.
Hecht, David. *Russian Radicals Look to America, 1825–1894*. Cambridge, Mass. 1947.
Hulse, J. W. *The Forming of the Communist International*. Stanford, Cal., 1964.
Ironside, Edmund. *Archangel 1918–1919*. London, 1958.
Kai-shek, Chiang. *Soviet Russia in China*. Revised, abridged ed. Toronto, 1965.
Kaye, V. J. *Early Ukrainian Settlements in Canada 1895–1900*. Toronto, 1964.
Kennan, George F. *The Decision to Intervene*. London, 1958.
———   *Russia and the West Under Lenin and Stalin*. Boston, 1960.
Kennedy, D. R. *The Knights of Labor in Canada*. London (Ontario) 1956.
Kirkconnell, Watson. *Seven Pillars of Freedom*. Toronto, 1944.
Kolisnyk, W. N. "In Canada Since the Spring of 1898." *Marxist Review*. January – February, 1961.
Kollontai, Alexandra. *The Workers' Opposition in Russia*. London, 1920.
Komor, I. *Ten Years of the Communist International*. London, 1929.
Kornbluh, Joyce L. (ed.). *Rebel Voices: An I.W.W. Anthology*. Ann Arbor, 1964.
Kublin, Hyman. *Asian Revolutionary: The Life of Sen Katayama*. Princeton, 1964.
Lefaux, W. W. *Winnipeg, London, Moscow: A Study of Bolshevism*. Winnipeg, 1921.
Lenin, V. I. "The Third International: its place in history," *Living Age*, Ser. 8, Vol. XVIII, Boston 1920.
Lipton, Charles. "Canadian Labor and Peace—Some Historical Notes," *Marxist Quarterly*, No. 5, Spring 1963.
Logan, H. A. *Trade Unions in Canada*. Toronto, 1948.
Lower, A. R. M. *From Colony to Nation*. Toronto, 1946.
Lysenko, Vera. *Men in Sheepskin Coats*. Toronto, 1947.
MacFarlane, L. J. *The British Communist Party*. London, 1966.
MacInnis, Grace. *J. S. Woodsworth: A Man to Remember*. Toronto, 1953.
MacKenzie, Kermit E. *Comintern and World Revolution 1928–1943*. New York, 1964.
Martens, L. *Information Respecting the Russian Soviet System and its Alleged Propaganda in North America*. Montreal, 1920.
Marx, Karl and Engels, Frederick. *Letters to Americans*. New York, 1953.
Masters, D. C. *The Winnipeg General Strike*. Toronto, 1950.

McNaught, Kenneth. *A Prophet in Politics*. Toronto, 1959.
Morris, Leslie. *The Story of Tim Buck's Party 1922-1939*. Toronto, 1939.
Morton, W. L. *The Progressive Party in Canada*. Toronto, 1950.
——— *The Kingdom of Canada*. Toronto, 1963.
Murphy, J. T. *New Horizons*. London, 1941.
——— *The "Reds" in Congress: Preliminary Report of the First World Congress of the Red International of Trade and Industrial Unions*. London, n.d. [1921?].
Nollau, Gunther. *International Communism and World Revolution*. London, 1961.
O'Neal, James. *American Communism*. New York, 1927.
Ormsby, Margaret A. *British Columbia: A History*. Vancouver, 1958.
Ostry, Bernard. "Conservatives, Liberals, and Labour in the 1870's," *Canadian Historical Review*, Vol. XLI, June 1960.
——— "Conservatives, Liberals, and Labour in the 1880's," *Canadian Journal of Economics and Political Science*, Vol. XXVII, May 1961.
Pelling, Henry. *The British Communist Party*. London, 1958.
Pirker, Theo. (ed.). *Komintern und Faschismus 1920-1940*. Dokumente zur Geschichte und Theorie des Faschismus. Stuttgart, 1965.
Popov, N. *Outline History of the C.P.S.U. Vols. I. and II*. London, n.d.
Robin, Martin. "Registration, Conscription, and Independent Labour Politics, 1916-1917," *Canadian Historical Review*, Vol. XLVII, No. 2, June 1966.
Roy, M. N. *The Communist International*. Bombay, 1943.
——— *The Russian Revolution*. Calcutta, 1949.
Schapiro, L. B. *The Origin of the Communist Autocracy*. London, 1955.
——— *The Communist Party of the Soviet Union*. London, 1960.
Scheffer, Paul. *Seven Years in Soviet Russia*. London, 1931.
Scott, F. R. "The Trial of the Toronto Communists." *Queen's Quarterly*, Vol. XXXIX, 1932.
Selver, Paul. *Orage and the New Age Circle*. London, 1959.
Shannon, D. A. *The Socialist Party of America*. New York, 1955.
Sheridan, C. *Russian Portraits*. London, 1921.
Skelton, O. D. "Trotsky." *Queen's Quarterly*, Vol. XXV, 1918.
Souvarine, Boris. *Stalin*. London, 1939.
Smith, A. E. *All My Life*. Toronto, 1949.
Steeves, Dorothy G. *The Compassionate Rebel: Ernest E. Winch and His Times*. Vancouver, 1960.
Symons, Julian. *The General Strike*. London, 1957.
Trotsky, L. D. *Sochinenya*. Moscow, 1927.
——— *The Real Situation in Russia*. London, 1928.
——— *The Third International After Lenin*. New York, 1936.
——— *Stalin*. New York, 1946.
——— *The First Five Years of the Communist International*. New York. 1953.
Valtin, Jan. *Out of the Night*. London, 1941.
Wade, Mason. *The French Canadians*. London, 1955.
Wangenheim, Elizabeth. "The Ukrainians: A Case Study of the 'Third Force'," in Peter Russell (ed.). *Nationalism in Canada*. Toronto, 1966.
Wheare, K. C. *Federal Government*. London, 1955.
Wiggins, Walter. "Hired Man in Saskatchewan." *Marxist Quarterly*, No. 8, Winter, 1964.
Wittke, Carl. *A History of Canada*. New York, 1928.
Wolfe, Bertram D. *The Trotsky Opposition*. New York, 1928.
——— *Three Who Made a Revolution*. New York, 1948.
Woodsworth, J. S. *On the Waterfront*. Ottawa, 1925.
Yuzyk, Paul. *The Ukrainians in Manitoba*. Toronto, 1953.
Zeigler, Olive. *Woodsworth, a Social Pioneer*. Toronto, 1934.

NOTES

CHAPTER ONE

1. Doris French, *Faith, Sweat, and Politics* (Toronto, 1962), p. 3.
2. D. G. Creighton, *John A. Macdonald: The Old Chieftain* (Toronto, 1955), pp. 123–24.
3. J. M. S. Careless, *Brown of the Globe: Statesman of Confederation* 1860–1880 (Toronto, 1963), pp. 288–89.
4. French, p. 21.
5. Carl Wittke, *A History of Canada* (New York, 1928), p. 286.
6. French, p. 64.
7. G. P. de T. Glazebrook, *A History of Canadian External Relations* (Toronto, 1950), p. 218.
8. Creighton, p. 123.
9. *Ibid.*, p. 125.
10. *Labour Organization in Canada* (Ottawa, 1924), p. 218.
11. See D. R Kennedy, *The Knights of Labor in Canada* (London, Ontario, 1956), p. 14–17.
12. *Ibid.*, p. 122.
13. *Labour Organization in Canada* 1913 (Ottawa, 1914), p. 43.
14. *Labour Organization in Canada* 1927 (Ottawa, 1928), p. 221.
15. *Ibid.*
16. Tim Buck, *Thirty Years*, 1922–52 (Toronto, 1952), p. 11.
17. Karl Marx anu Frederick Engels, *Letters to Americans* (New York, 1953), p. 177.
18. *Ibid.*, p. 204.
19. Buck, pp. 11–12.
20. D. C Masters, *The Winnipeg General Strike* (Toronto, 1950), p. 6.
21. R. M. Dawson, *William Lyon Mackenzie King* (Toronto, 1952), pp. 138–39, and 141–42. Also Glazebrook, p. 160.
22. Buck, pp. 11–12.
23. *Labour Organization* 1913, p. 28.
24. *Labour Organization in Canada* 1912 (Ottawa, 1913), p. 16.
25. *Labour Organization* 1913, p. 28.
26. Theodore Draper, *The Roots of American Communism* (New York, 1957), p. 16.
27. *Ibid.*, p. 32.
28. Buck, p. 12.
29. P. Yuzyk, *The Ukrainians in Mantitoba* (Toronto, 1953), pp. 24–25.
30. *Report on the Seventh Census of Canada* 1931, Vol. I (Ottawa, 1936), lists the following figures for Ukrainian immigrants (pp. 214, 710–11):

Year	Total Population	Total Ukrainian Population
1881	4,324,810	—
1891	4,833,239	—
1901	5,371,315	5,682
1911	7,206,643	75,432
1921	8,787,949	106,721

31. *Ibid.*, (pp. 717–20):

	1901	1911	1921
Manitoba:			
Rural	460	15,467	21,705
Urban	174	2,117	2,112
Saskatchewan:			
Rural	1,075	20,985	25,290
Urban	19	1,291	2,807
Alberta:			
Rural	3,893	25,740	35,587
Urban	1	5,313	8,542

Winnipeg and Edmonton were the main urban centres in which Ukrainians settled. Yuzyk, p. 194, estimates that about 6,000 were living in Winnipeg in 1911, but his figure is not borne out by census returns. His estimates for 1916 and 1921 are "about 10,000," and "over 12,000." According to Masters p. 7, the total population in Winnipeg in 1911 was 128,000 and for 1919 just under 180,000, of which two thirds were Anglo-Saxon. Of the latter estimate, some 6,000 were alleged to be Ukrainians. For further details of early settlement see *Propamyatna Knyha Ukrayinskoho Narodnoho Domu v Winnipegu* ("Memorial Book of the Ukrainian National Home in Winnipeg") (Winnipeg, 1949); V. J. Kaye, *Early Ukrainian Settlements in Canada 1895–1900* (Toronto, 1964); and Vera Lysenko, *Men in Sheepskin Coats* (Toronto, 1947).

32. Yuzyk, p. 78.
33. Buck, p. 17.
34. Draper, p. 160.
35. *Canadian Annual Review* 1909 (Toronto, 1910), p. 283.
36. Joseph Freeman, *An American Testament* (London, 1938), p. 257.
37. Draper, pp. 14–15.
38. H. A. Logan, *Trade Unions in Canada* (Toronto, 1948), p. 4.
39. A. E. Smith, *All My Life* (Toronto, 1949), pp. 38–39.
40. Buck, p. 18.
41. *Labour Organization in Canada* 1917 (Ottawa, 1918), p. 40.
42. Masters, p. 5.
43. Logan, pp. 5–6.
44. A. R. M. Lower, *From Colony to Nation* (Toronto, 1946), p. 469.
45. Sir Robert Borden Papers, OC519, September 14, 1918.
46. Borden Papers, OC391, August 8, 1917.
47. Bowell Papers, Series A, Privy Council Memorandum, February 20, 1919.
48. *Victoria Daily Times*, September 14, 1918. See also *Report of the Canadian Economic Commission (Siberia)* (Ottawa, 1919), pp. 9–10.

CHAPTER TWO

1. Tim Buck, 1917–1957: *Forty Years of Great Change* (Toronto, 1957), p. 7.
2. *Labour Organization in Canada* 1917 (Ottawa, 1918), p. 13 and pp. 40–42.
3. *Labour Organization in Canada* 1919 (Ottawa, 1920), p. 56.
4. Buck, p. 8.
5. *Ibid.*, p. 9.
6. G. P. de T. Glazebrook, *A History of Canadian External Relations* (Toronto, 1950), pp. 329–30. The estimate of the Russian Party strength is taken from L. B. Schapiro, *The Communist Party of the Soviet Union* (London, 1960), pp. 170–71.
7. Theodore Draper, *The Roots of American Communism* (New York, 1957), p. 101.
8. A. E. Smith, *All My Life* (Toronto, 1949), pp. 43–44.
9. P. Yuzyk, *The Ukrainians in Manitoba* (Toronto, 1953), p. 98.
10. Buck, p. 10.
11. Department of Militia and Defence Headquarters file C 2051, Vol. I, Ottawa, March 14, 1918.
12. *Ibid.*, Cable dated London, March 29, 1917, and letter, Halifax, Nova Scotia, April 1, 1917. Also Military District Six File 73–1–15, Vol. II. For Trotsky's account of his experiences in Amherst, see *Observer* (London), September 8, 1929.
13. Borden Papers, OC 498, Winnipeg, February 14, 1918.
14. Borden Papers, OC 515, February 23, and March 21, 1918.
15. Borden Papers, OC 519, May 19, 1918.
16. *Ibid.*, July 20, 1918.
17. *Ibid.*, September 14, 1918.
18. *The Canada Gazette* (Extra), November 27 and December 7, 1918. See also *Borden Papers*, OC 519, October 22, 1918, and Henry Borden (ed.). *Robert Laird Borden: His Memoirs* (2 vols., Toronto, 1938), II, p. 857.
19. Yuzyk, p. 98.
20. *Borden Papers*, OC 518, Borden to White, London, July 25, 1918.
21. *Ibid.*, Mewburn to Borden, London, August 13, 1918.
22. David Lloyd George, *War Memoirs* (London, 1936), Vol. VI, pp. 3171–72. Also, Borden Papers, OC 518, Devonshire to Long, Ottawa, October 24, 1918.
23. *Borden Papers*, OC 518, Crerar to White, Ottawa, November 22, 1918.
24. *Ibid.* Also, White to Sir Edward Kemp, November 14, 1918.
25. Grace MacInnes, *J. S. Woodsworth: A Man to Remember* (Toronto, 1953), p. 123.
26. Edmund Ironside, *Archangel 1918–1919* (London, 1953), p. 14.
27. Borden Papers, OC 518, S. D. Scott to Borden, Vancouver, October 22, 1918.
28. File C 2832, Telegram G.O.C. Military District 11, Victoria, B.C., November 18, 1918, and C.G.S. Memorandum, Ottawa, December 4, 1918.

29. Borden Papers, OC 559, Borden to White, London, December 2, 1918.
30. File C 2940, telegrams and letters from the Provost Marshal of Canada to White, Vancouver, January 31, 1919. Also, File C 2051, Vol. I, Victoria, B.C., December 17, 1918; Vancouver, December 30, 1918; Vol. II, Victoria, January 9, 1919. Also, *Ottawa Evening Citizen*, December 6, 1918; *Sun* (Toronto), December 11, 1918; *Hamilton Daily Times*, December 12, 1918; *Hamilton Herald*, December 13, 1918; *Daily Colonist* (Victoria), December 17, 1918; *Vancouver Sun*, December 30, 1918.
31. C 2514, Vol. I, Letter U.F.O. to Mewburn, Toronto, January 4, 1919.
32. Glazebrook, pp. 329–30.
33. H. A. Logan, *Trade Unions in Canada* (Toronto, 1948), p. 304. Also, Kenneth McNaught, *A Prophet in Politics* (Toronto, 1949), p. 137.
34. C 2051, Vol. II, Cahan to Minister of Justice, Ottawa, January 10, 1919. See also *Ottawa Evening Citizen*, January 9, 1919 and *Saturday Night*, January 11, 1919.
35. *Ibid.*, January 11 and 17, 1919.
36. C 2051, Vol. III, Assistant Director of Military Intelligence to British Control Officer in New York, Ottawa, April 1, 1919. Also, C 2051, Vol. V., A. Bowen Perry to Comptroller, RNWMP, Regina, February 18, 1919.
37. Borden Papers, OC 559, White to Borden, April 16, 1919
38. Logan, pp. 306–308.
39. *Ibid.*, p. 304.
40. MacInnes, pp. 131–32.
41. McNaught, p. 137.
42. Jane Degras (ed.), *The Communist International* 1919–1943, Vol. I, 1919–1923 (London, 1956), p. 34.
43. Draper, pp. 148–53.
44. Borden Papers, OC 518. See the exchange of views between Borden and Churchill, March 17 and May 1, 1919. Also Borden to Lloyd George, May 18, 1919, concerning withdrawal of Canadian troops from Archangel. See also James Eayrs, *In Defence of Canada: From the Great War to the Great Depression* (Toronto, 1964), Ch. I.
45. Logan, p. 308.
46. *Proceedings of the Western Labour Conferences* held at Calgary, Alberta, March 13, 14, 15, 1919 [Calgary, 1919], p. 5.
47. Borden Papers, OC 515, Perry to Comptroller, RNWMP, Regina, April 2, 1919.
48. Logan, p. 319.
49. Mason Wade, *The French Canadians* (London, 1955), p. 773.
50. Borden Papers, OC 564, Kavanagh to Borden, Vancouver, May 27, 1919.
51. *Ibid.*, GOC Military District 13, Calgary, to Ottawa, May 26, 1919.
52. Henry Borden (ed.), *Robert Laird Borden: His Memoirs* (2 vols., Toronto, 1938), II, p. 972.
53. Borden Papers, OC 559, Borden to White, London, December 2, 1918.
54. Smith, pp. 48–49.
55. Borden Papers, OC 515, Ottawa, July 28, 1919.
56. Yuzyk, p. 98.
57. Borden *Memoirs*, II, p. 972.
58. C 2051, Vol. V, Chicago, May 27, 1919. For details about Spolansky see Draper, pp. 368–69.
59. C 2051, Vol. V, Chicago, September 27, 1919.
60. Borden Papers, OC 515, Ottawa, July 28, 1919.
61. Woodsworth Papers, MG27, III, C7, Vol. II, Winnipeg, August 25, 1921.
62. Borden Papers, OC 515, Ottawa, July 28, 1919. See also W. W. Lefaux, *Winnipeg, London, Moscow: A study of Bolshevism* (Winnipeg, 1921), p. 76.
63. Borden Papers, OC 559, Milner to Governor General, London, July 23, 1919.
64. Buck, p. 25.
65. Smith, pp. 50–51.
66. Tim Buck, *Thirty Years* 1922–52 (Toronto, 1952), p. 19.

CHAPTER THREE

1. For details see Paul Selver, *Orage and the New Circle* (London, 1959).
2. Joseph Freeman, *An American Testament* (London, 1938), pp. 478 and 455.
3. *The American Labor Year Book*, Vol. VI (New York, 1925), pp. 209–10. See also *Rand School News*, March 1918 and April 1919.
4. *Hearings before a Subcommittee of the Committee on Foreign Relations, United States Senate, Sixty-Sixth Congress, Second Session* (Washington, 1920), p. 279. Buhay's letter, dated April 21, 1919, is also reproduced in New York (State) Legislature . . . *Revolutionary Radicalism: Report of the Joint Legislative Committee Investigating Seditious Activities*, Vol. I (Albany, 1920), p. 639. The investigation is sometimes referred to as the Lusk Report, or the Lusk Committee.

N

5. Borden Papers, OC 559, Ottawa, January 21, 1920.

6. Tim Buck, *Thirty Years*, 1922–52 (Toronto, 1952), p. 28. Also Tim Buck, 1917–1957: *Forty Years of Great Change* (Toronto, 1957), pp. 26–27.

7. Theodore Draper, *The Roots of American Communism* (New York, 1957), pp. 178–84.

8. Jane Degras (ed.), *The Communist International* 1919–1943, Vol. I, 1919–1923 (London, 1956), p. 73.

9. Draper, p. 197.

10. Buck, *Thirty Years*, pp. 19–20.

11. For details of the unification of American factions which occurred in May 1921, see Draper, pp. 267–70.

12. Buck, *Thirty Years*, p. 21.

13. P. Yuzyk, *The Ukrainians in Manitoba* (Toronto, 1953), p. 98.

14. See *Canadian Suomalainen Jarjesto 25 Vuotta* (Sudbury, 1936).

15. Borden Papers, OC 519, September 14, 1918.

16. *The Canada Gazette*, November 8, 1923, p. 1491.

17. Alexander Brady, *Democracy in the Dominions* (Toronto, 1958), p. 129.

18. *Recognition of Russia: Hearings Before a Sub-Committee On Foreign Relations, United States Senate*, January 21–23, 1924 (Washington, 1924), p. 356. The communication was signed by Charles Edward Scott, identified as one of the three members of the Pan American Bureau.

19. Draper, pp. 268–69.

20. *Ibid.*

21. *Recognition of Russia*, p. 372. The document was among the papers seized at 170 Bleeker Street, New York, on April 29, 1921.

22. *Ibid.*, p. 373.

23. Draper, p. 270.

24. *Ibid.*, pp. 336, 342, and 450.

25. *The Marxist Quarterly* (Toronto), Vol. I, No. 1, pp. 23–25.

26. *Communist*, Vol. I, No. 1, June 1921.

27. *Rex* v. *Buck et al.: Transcript of Evidence Heard Before the Supreme Court of Ontario 2–12 November* 1931 (Toronto, 1931), p. 384.

28. Gordon Cascaden, "How the Red Trade Union did Business at Moscow," in *Alberta Labour News*, February 11, 1922. Cascaden also attended the Moscow meetings. Also, interviews with Earl Browder and Maurice Spector. Draper, p. 316, lists the delegates together with their pseudonyms, but incorrectly attributes the cover name "Emmons" to Knight. George Williams of the IWW who attended the Congress, and later wrote a pamphlet "The First Congress of the Red Trade Union International at Moscow, 1921," correctly notes that "Emmons" was Ella Reeve Bloor's cover name. See also J. T. Murphy's *The "Reds" in Congress* (London, n.d. [1921?]), p. 6.

29. *Communist*, No. 1.

30. *Ibid.*

31. *Ibid.* Buck, in *Thirty Years*, p. 21, and in 1917–1957, p. 27, states incorrectly that the constituent convention was held in June. In his testimony before the Supreme Court of Ontario, however, he specifically confirmed that the meeting was held in May. See also *Rex* v. *Buck et al.*, p. 384. In both of these works Buck omits any mention of the part played in the formation of the CPC by the Comintern through its American Agency, or the presence and role of Atwood at Guelph. Yuzyk, p. 101, correctly notes that "three well-financed Soviet agents" were instrumental in bringing the Canadian Party into being, but he does not indicate the nature and extent of their role, and he is wrong in stating that the party born at Guelph was the Workers' Party of Canada, a body created "as a facade for the underground 'Communist Party of Canada'." That did not take place until six months later when the Workers' Party was formed in February 1922. *Bol'shaya Sovetskya Entsyclopedya*, Vol. 22 (Moscow, 1953), p. 256, omits any mention of the early party development in Canada. According to its version, the Canadian communist movement began with the formation of the Workers' Party in 1922. The same error is perpetuated in the article "Entwicklung des Kommunismus in Kanada," in *Ost-Probleme*, No. 24, November 15, 1960, pp. 752–60. H. B. Mayo's article, "Communist Party" in the *Encyclopedia Canadiana*, Vol. III, (Toronto, 1958), p. 54, is a superficial account.

C. W. Harvison, former Commissioner of the Royal Canadian Mounted Police, states that the secret founding meeting was "attended by a sergeant of the RCMP working undercover." See Clifford W. Harvison, "The Spies in Our Midst" in *Weekend Magazine*, January 21, 1967, p. 14.

32. *Communist*, No. 1, See also Draper, pp. 244–45 and 269–70.

33. *Ibid.*

34. *Ibid.*

35. *Ibid.*

36. *Ibid.*

37. *Ibid.*

38. *Rex* v. *Buck et al.*, p. 386.

39. *Ibid.* See also Degras, pp. 168–72.

CHAPTER FOUR

1. *The Communist*, Vol. I, No. 1, June 1921.
2. *Ibid.*
3. Tim Buck, *Thirty Years* 1922–52 (Toronto, 1959), pp. 26–27. Leslie Morris, *The Story of Tim Buck's Party* 1922–39 (Toronto, 1939), pp. 11–12, claims that the *Workers' World* began publication in June 1921, but that after "some police raids" it was renamed *The Workers' Guard.* See also Tim Buck, *Our Fight for Canada. Selected Writings* (1923–1959) (Toronto, 1959), pp. 32–33.
4. For details of the "Workers" opposition in Russia, see L. B. Schapiro, *The Origin of the Communist Autocracy* (London, 1955), Ch. VIII.
5. *Labour Organization in Canada* 1922 (Ottawa, 1923), p. 241. Tim Buck, 1917–1957: *Forty Years of Great Change* (Toronto, 1957), p. 36, claims that the pamphlet was the first of Lenin's works published in Canada, and provided workers with a programme of action which countered the syndicalist tradition of secession from existing labour organizations.
6. Jane Degras (ed.), *The Communist International* 1919–1943, Vol. I, 1919–1923 (London, 1956), p. 283.
7. Theodore Draper, *The Roots of American Communism* (New York, 1957), p. 278.
8. *Third Congress of the Communist International Report. Report of Meetings Held at Moscow* (London, 1921), p. 145. Knight's speech was published in *Moscow*, the Congress's special organ, which was reprinted by the Communist Party of Great Britain in its *Report* on the meeting. He also wrote an article entitled "The Canadian Movement," which appeared in *Moscow*, June 23, 1921.
9. *Alberta Labour News*, February 18, 1921.
10. *Labour Organization in Canada* 1921 (Ottawa, 1922), p. 43.
11. *Ibid.*, p. 48. See also Gordon Cascaden, *Shall Unionism Die* (Windsor, 1921), pp. 1–4, and *Hearings Before a Special Committee on Un-American Activities, House of Representatives*, Vol. VII (Washington, 1940), p. 4541.
12. *Labour Organization in* 1922, p. 174. See also *Globe*, December 12, 1921, and *Workers' Guard*, January 14, 1922.
13. *Labour Organization* 1922, p. 175.
14. *Ibid.*
15. *Ibid.*, pp. 176–77.
16. *Rex* v. *Buck et al.: Transcript of Evidence Heard Before the Supreme Court of Ontario* 2–12 *November* 1931 (Toronto, 1931), p. 123. The text of the letter, dated December 23, 1921, is given on pp. 209–10.
17. *Ibid.*, p. 125.
18. E. R. Fay, "The Early Years," in *Marxist Quarterly*, Vol. I, No. 1, pp. 19–20.
19. *Workers' Guard*, December 24, 1921.
20. Fay, p. 20.
21. *Ukrayinski Rabotnychi Visty*, January 7, 1922, expressed similar optimism.
22. Gordon Cascaden, "How the Red Trade Union Did Business at Moscow," in *Alberta Labour News*, January 14–February 25, 1922.
23. *Alberta Labour News*, January 14, 1922.
24. *Ibid.*, January 21, 1922.
25. *Ibid.*, February 4, 1922.
26. *Labour Organization* 1922, p. 173.
27. *Ibid.*, p. 174.
28. *Ibid.*, p. 177.
29. Draper, pp. 314 and 320–22.
30. *Labour Organization* 1922, pp. 178–79.
31. *Ibid.*, p. 180.
32. Draper, pp. 341–43.
33. *Rex* v. *Buck et al.*, p. 422.
34. *Ibid.*, p. 457.
35. Buck, *Thirty Years*, p. 23.
36. *The Worker*, March 15, 1922. The Central Executive Committee listed in Tim Buck's *Thirty Years*, pp. 23–24, is at considerable variance with that listed in *The Worker*. For example, Buck lists Florence Custance, Mr. and Mrs. J. Knight, Tom Bell, M. Buhay and others, and makes Spector editor of *The Worker*.

CHAPTER FIVE

1. *Rex* v. *Buck et al.: Transcript of Evidence Heard Before the Supreme Court of Ontario*, 2–12 *November* 1931 (Toronto, 1931), pp. 134–37.
2. *Ibid.*

3. For details of Valetski's entry and role in settling disputes within the CPSU, see Theodore Draper, *The Roots of American Communism* (New York, 1957), pp. 363–75.

4. *Rex* v. *Buck et al.*, pp. 134–37.

5. *Ibid.*, p. 163.

6. *Ibid.*, p. 206. For details of the Bridgeman convention, see Draper, pp. 369–72.

7. *Ibid.*, pp. 130–31.

8. *Report of the Proceedings of the Second Annual Convention of the Workers' Party of Canada, Toronto, February 22nd–25th 1923* (Toronto, 1923), p. 2.

9. *Ibid.*

10. *Rex* v. *Buck et al.*, p. 139.

11. Attorney General's Office Papers, Box Eight, Envelope 4. The breakdown of monies received and expended was as follows:

Receipts		*Payments*	
dues	$5,377.28	office	$736.75
literature	1,158.52	wages	3,805.70
supplies	329.96	travelling expenses	1,531.81
sundry	1,396.60	convention 1923	945.10
convention quota	1,182.15	literature	620.03
convention assessment	1,677.01	sundry	2,883.03
special	1,128.10		
		TOTAL	$10,522.42
	$12,249.62	transfer petty cash (April)	25.00
balance, January 31, 1923	624.01		$10,497.42
		balance, March 31, 1924	2,548.21
TOTAL	$13,045.63		
	[*sic*]	TOTAL	$13,045.63

Figures in MacDonald's report showing details of assessments and dues from the party's sections and districts confirm the numerical domination and financial importance of the Finnish and Ukrainian groups.

	Special	*Convention*	*Dues*
Finnish Section	$666.95	$1,104.91	$3,014.86
Ukrainian Section	272.00	381.25	1,149.98
District One	20.40	22.50	59.15
District Two	14.00	7.50	186.00
District Three	38.80	64.75	329.60
District Four	60.35	33.95	278.25
District Five	18.80	47.65	175.25
District Six	36.80	14.50	178.10
Members at large			6.00
TOTAL	$1,126.10	$1,677.01	$5,377.19

12. *Ibid.*, Box Eight, Envelope 7, Buck's speech, February 7, 1930, *Plenum Report*, p. 16.

13. Theodore Draper, *American Communism and Soviet Russia* (New York, 1960), p. 208.

14. *Spector Interviews*, October 17–22, 1959.

15. *Ibid.* Also *Report Second Annual Convention*, p. 2ff.

16. Benjamin Gitlow, *I Confess* (New York, 1939), p. 440.

17. *Hearings Before a Special Committee on Un-American Activities, House of Representatives, Investigations of Un-American Propaganda Activities in the United States* (Washington, 1939), p. 4540. Gitlow, *I Confess*, pp. 388–89, states that when Arcos, the Russian trading mission in London, England, was first established, money destined for the United States and Canada was transmitted through the mission. The arrangement ceased when the mission was raided in 1927.

18. *Rex* v. *Buck et al.*, p. 187.

19. Jane Degras (ed.), *The Communist International 1919–1943*, Vol. I, 1919–23 (London, 1956), pp. 168–72.

20. *Report of the Royal Commission* (Ottawa, 1946), p. 14.

21. Draper, *American Communism*, p. 149.

22. Jan Valtin [R. J. H. Krebs], *Out of the Night* (London 1941), pp. 98–100. See also pp. 209, 274, and 318 for further disclosures about couriers and transmission of Comintern funds.

23. *Official Report of Proceedings Before the Subversive Control Board. Attorney General U.S.A.* vs. *Communist Party U.S.A.* 1951–52 (Washington, 1952), pp. 82–83.

24. Gitlow, *I Confess*, pp. 418–19, and see the inside covers for facsimile reproductions of the document.

25. Benjamin Gitlow, *The Whole of Their Lives* (New York, 1948), p. 147. Bertram Wolfe in an interview described Mendelsohn as a "man of confidence" for the Canadian party, a point corroborated by Spector.
26. Governor General's Office Papers. MG7, G21, Vol. 637, File 34691, Vol. I (b), October 3 and 19, 1923 and September 24, 1924.
27. Vol. 638, File 34691, Vol. II (b), Secretary of State for Dominions to Governor General, London, May 16, 1927.
28. Cmd. 2874. *Documents illustrating the Hostile activities of the Soviet Government and Third International against Great Britain* (London, 1927), pp. 20-21 and 28.
29. Vol. 638, File 34691, Vol. II (b), Governor General to Secretary of State for Dominion Affairs, Ottawa, May 30, 1927.
30. *Hearings Un-American Activities* 1939, p. 4678.
31. Gitlow, *The Whole of Their Lives*, pp. 150–51. See also *Hearings Un-American Activities* 1939, pp. 4677–79, and R. N. Carew Hunt, "Willi Muenzenberg," in *International Communism*, David Footman (ed.) (London, 1960), pp. 76–77. In the same connection it is worth noting that Trotsky's assassination was made possible through the use of an illegally acquired and deliberately falsified Canadian passport. For details, see William Rodney, "Leon Trotsky and Canada," in *Queen's Quarterly*, Autumn 1964.

CHAPTER SIX

1. *The Labor Herald*, September 1922, pp. 9–10.
2. *The Worker*, 1 May, 1922.
3. R. N. Carew Hunt, "Willi Muenzenberg," in *International Communism*, David Footman (ed.) (London, 1960), p. 76.
4. *The Worker*, June 1, 1922.
5. Kavanagh to Rodney, January 11, 1962.
6. *Labour Organization in Canada* 1922 (Ottawa, 1923), pp. 185–86.
7. *Spector Interviews.*
8. *The Worker*, August 1, 1922.
9. *The Worker*, October 16, 1922.
10. *Rex* v. *Buck et al.: Transcript of Evidence Heard Before the Supreme Court of Ontario*, 2–12 *November* 1931 (Toronto, 1931), pp. 141–42. The Report of the International Delegation was signed by "Stanley," the cover name used by Spector.
11. *Ibid.*, p. 142.
12. *Ibid.*, p. 709. *The Worker*, December 15, 1922, is the first issue on which Bruce's name appears as editor. The editorial board of Kavanagh, Peel, and Spector was replaced by a single editor, Spector, within a little more than four months. Spector formally headed the paper from the issue dated August 1, 1922.
13. *Labour Organization in Canada* 1922, p. 171.
14. *Bulletin of the Fourth Congress of the Communist International* (Moscow) No. 13, November 23, 1922, Report of the Credentials Committee, p. 4.
15. *The Worker*, October 2, 1922. Custance's visit was reported in some detail in the *Globe*, January 6, 1923, the day after her return to Toronto.
16. J. MacDonald, "Die Gewerkschaftbewegung in Kanada," in *Internationale Presse-Korrespondenz* (Inprekorr), II, No. 209, October 31, 1922, pp. 1443–44. The article was much the same as the one written by MacDonald for *The Labor Herald*, July 1922. The German edition of *Internationale Presse-Korrespondenz* commenced publication on September 24, 1921, and at first appeared weekly. The English-language edition, *International Press Correspondence* (Inprecorr), began October 1, 1921, and the French-language edition on October 13, 1922. Subsequent articles written by Canadian communist leaders appeared in complete form in the English edition, and mostly in abridged form in the German edition. See, for example, W. Moriarty, "The Origin and Growth of the Canadian Communist Party," in *Inprecorr*, III, no. 36, May 9, 1923, which appeared in condensed form as "Die Entwicklung der Kommunistischen Partei in Kanada," *Inprekorr*, III, no. 79, May 11, 1923, p. 675.
17. *The Worker*, December 15, 1922. See also *Bulletin Fourth Congress*, p. 1. Theodore Draper, *The Roots of American Communism* (New York, 1957), p. 382, mistakenly states that the Congress opened in Moscow.
18. *The Fourth Congress of the Communist International Abridged Report of Meetings Held at Petrograd and Moscow Nov. 7–Dec. 3, 1922* (London, n.d. [1923?]), p. 288.
19. *Protokoll des Vierten Kongresses der Kommunistischen Internationale* (Hamburg, 1922), p. 366. See also *The Fourth Congress Abridged Report*, p. 292. The American party in contrast received 10 invitations and nine delegates came. During the period between the Third and Fourth Congresses, Canada was discussed once by the Executive Committee of the Communist International (ECCI), Great Britain twice, United States five times, and Germany nine times.

20. *Rex* v. *Buck et al.*, p. 144.
21. The *Globe*, January 6, 1923. Custance spoke about the church in Soviet Russia on January 26, 1923 at the Labour Temple.
22. Theodore Draper, *The Roots of American Communism* (New York, 1957), p. 382.
23. *Bulletin Fourth Comintern Congress*, p. 14.
24. *Ibid.*
25. *Red International of Labor Unions, Second World Congress, Resolutions and Decisions* (London, n.d. [1923?]), p. 14. Resolutions 37–39 dealt with the TUEL.
26. *Ibid.*, resolution no. 38.
27. *Bulletin Fourth Comintern Congress*, p. 5.

CHAPTER SEVEN

1. *Rex* v. *Buck et al.*, *Transcript of Evidence Heard Before the Supreme Court of Ontario, 2–12 November* 1931 (Toronto, 1931), pp. 185–86.
2. *Ibid.*, Spector confirmed that a canvass of party opinion was made.
3. *Ibid.*, p. 184.
4. *Ibid.*, p. 459.
5. *Ibid.*
6. *Ibid.*, pp. 134 and 137.
7. *Ibid.*, p. 139.
8. *The Worker*, March 15, 1923.
9. *Rex* v. *Buck et al.*, p. 184.
10. *Report Second Workers' Party of Canada Convention*, p. 1.
11. *The Worker*, March 15, 1923. See also *Labour Organization in Canada* 1923 (Ottawa, 1924), p. 158.
12. *The Worker*, March 15, 1923.
13. *Ibid.*
14. *The Worker*, December 1, 1922.
15. *The Worker*, March 15, 1923.
16. *International Press Correspondence* (Inprecorr), III, No. 24, March 8, 1923, p. 187.
17. *Report Second WPC Convention*, p. 6. This figure corresponds closely with the 4,810 listed in *The Fourth Congress of the Communist International, Abridged Report of Meetings Held at Petrograd and Moscow Nov. 7–Dec. 3, 1922* (London, n.d. [1923?]), p. 292.
18. *Report Second WPC Convention*, p. 23.
19. *Labour Organization in Canada* 1923, p. 16.
20. *Report Second WPC Convention*, pp. 20 and 23.
21. *The Worker*, April 2, 1923.
22. *The Worker*, April 18 and 25, 1923; May 1, 9, 16, 23, and 30, 1923.
23. *Labour Organization in Canada* 1923, p. 204.
24. *The Worker*, June 6, 1923.
25. *The Worker*, June 27, 1923, featured writings about the campaign by MacDonald and James Simpson, secretary of the Canadian Labor Party.
26. *The Worker*, July 4, 1923.
27. For details of the UFO and the National Progressive Party, see W. L. Morton, *The Kingdom of Canada* (Toronto, 1963), pp. 434–50.

CHAPTER EIGHT

1. *Internationale Presse-Korrespondenz* (Inprekorr), III, No. 11, January 15, 1923, p. 75. Also, *The Worker*, February 15, 1923. For a detailed account of the German affair, see E. H. Carr, *A History of Soviet Russia. The Interregnum 1923–1924* (London, 1954), ch. IX; Ruth Fischer, *Stalin and German Communism* (London, 1948), chs. XV and XVI; and Jan Valtin, *Out of the Night* (London, 1941), Ch. VI.
2. For similar articles on the German situation see *The Worker*, April 11, May 16; June 6 and 20; August 1 and 30; September 12, 19 and 26; October 10, 17, and 31; November 14; and December 1, 1923.
3. E. H. Carr, *Socialism in One Country*, Vol. III, Part I (London, 1964), pp. 976–86.
4. For details of Trotsky's attitude and the opposition's impact within the Soviet party, see Isaac Deutscher, *The Prophet Unarmed* (London, 1959), pp. 140–60; and L. B. Schapiro, *The Communist Party of the Soviet Union* (London, 1960), pp. 280–86. The relevant Comintern documents are most easily available in Jane Degras (ed.), *The Communist International 1919-1943*, Vol. II, 1923–1928 (London, 1960), pp. 62–65 and 68–78.
5. The *Globe*, March 18, 1924. The paper's designation of the conference as "the Second All-Russian Congress" is misleading. See Schapiro, p. 226.

6. *Report of the Third National Convention Workers' Party of Canada*, 18–20 April 1924 (Toronto, 1924), p. 8.

7. Jane Degras (ed.), *The Communist International 1919–1943*, Vol. II, 1923–1928 (London, 1960), pp. 79–82.

8. *From the Fourth to the Fifth Congress: Report of the Executive Committee of the Communist International* (London, 1924), pp. 80–81.

9. *Ibid.*, p. 118.

10. *Ibid.*, p. 81.

11. *The Worker*, December 22, 1923. Also, *Labour Organization in Canada 1923* (Ottawa, 1924), pp. 79–82.

12. *The Manitoba Free Press*, December 18, 19, 20, 21, 22, 24, 25, 27, 28 and 29, 1923.

13. *The Worker*, March 8, 1924.

14. *Report Third WPC Convention*, p. 11.

15. *Ibid.*, p. 8.

16. *Ibid.*,

17. *Ibid.*, p. 9.

18. *Ibid.*

19. E. H. Carr, *Socialism in One Country*, Vol. III, Part II (London, 1964), p. 897.

20. Theodore Draper, *American Communism and Soviet Russia* (New York, 1960), Chap. V.

21. *Report Third WPC Convention*, p. 1. See also *Labour Organization in Canada 1924* (Ottawa, 1925), p. 151.

22. *Report Third WPC Convention*, p. 2.

23. *Ibid.*, p. 4.

24. *The Worker*, May 3, 1924.

25. *Ibid.* Spector's summary of the convention also appeared in *International Press Correspondence* (Inprecorr), IV, No. 31, pp. 311–12.

26. *Report Third WPC Convention*, p. 4.

27. *Ibid.*, p. 12.

28. *Inprecorr*, IV, 31, p. 311.

29. Draper, *American Communism*, pp. 160 and 403.

30. *Rex v. Buck et al.: Transcript of Evidence Heard Before the Supreme Court of Ontario*, 2–12 November 1931 (Toronto, 1931), p. 187.

31. Carr, Vol. III, Part II, pp. 909–10.

32. *The Daily Worker* (Chicago), April 22, 1924.

33. Draper, *American Communism*, chs. II–IV.

34. *Rex v. Buck et al.*, p. 709.

35. *The Worker*, August 23, 1924.

36. *Report Third WPC Convention*, p. 4.

37. *Ibid.*, p. 5.

38. *The Worker*, March 1 and 15, 1923. See also *The Worker*, April 27, 1924, for Leslie Morris' views on the second convention's tasks, and *World Marxist Review*, December 1964, p. 42, for biographical details.

39. *The Worker*, May 3, 1924. See also *Labour Organization in Canada 1924*, p. 152.

40. *Rex v. Buck et al.*, pp. 188–89.

41. *The Worker*, May 3, 1924, is the first issue to carry Spector's name on the mast head.

42. *Ibid.*

43. *Ibid.* See also *Inprecorr*, IV, 31, pp. 311–12.

CHAPTER NINE

1. Jane Degras (ed), *The Communist International 1919–1943*, Vol. II, 1923–1928 (London, 1960), pp. 79–82.

2. E. H. Carr, *Socialism in One Country*, Vol. III, Part II (London, 1964), pp. 900–901.

3. *Spector Interviews*.

4. Theodore Draper, *American Communism and Soviet Russia* (New York, 1960), pp. 157–58.

5. *Ibid.* See also *How to Organize the Communist Party* (London, 1924), pp. 90–109.

6. *Fifth Congress, Communist International: Abridged Report Published by the Communist Party of Great Britain* (London, 1924), pp. 92–93 and 268–69.

7. *The Worker*, April 11, 18, 25, May 2 and 9, 1925.

8. *The Worker*, July 18, 1925. The proposed draft of an amended constitution promulgating factory units as the basic element in the CPC's organization and structure was published in the August 22, 29 and September 5 issues.

9. *Resolution of the Canadian Commission, Fifth Plenum ECCI, to CEC, Communist Party of Canada* ([Moscow?], 1925), p. 9. Draper, pp. 190–92, deals with the American party's difficulties.

10. *Rex* v. *Buck et al.: Transcript of Evidence Heard Before the Supreme Court of Ontario,* 2–12 *November* 1931 (Toronto, 1931), p. 422.

11. *Labour Organization in Canada* 1925 (Ottawa, 1926); p. 148.

12. *Ibid.* See also *Labour Organization in Canada* 1926 (Ottawa, 1927), p. 157; and *Labour Organization in Canada* 1927 (Ottawa, 1928), p. 182.

13. *Report of the Central Executive Committee to the Fifth National Convention of the Communist Party of Canada* (Toronto, 1927), p. 3.

14. *Ibid.*

15. *The Worker,* January 25 and March 27, 1926.

16. A. E. Smith, *All My Life* (Toronto, 1949), p. 99. For biographical details of Kolisnyk and his entry into the Ukrainian radical movement, see W. N. Kolisnyk, "In Canada Since the Spring of 1898," in *Marxist Review,* January–September 1961, p. 37.

17. *Labour Organization in Canada* 1927 (Ottawa, 1928), p. 170.

18. *CEC Report Fifth Convention,* p. 3.

19. *Ibid.*

20. *Ibid.,* p. 4.

21. *Rex* v. *Buck et al.,* p. 693.

22. *Ibid.,* p. 477

23. Carr, p. 936.

24. *Rex* v. *Buck et al.,* trial exhibit 49, p. 1, Letter from the Political Secretariat ECCI to CEC, Communist Party of Canada, dated Moscow, April 8, 1929.

CHAPTER TEN

1. *Interview,* Bertram Wolfe, October 28, 1959.

2. Theodore Draper, *American Communism and Soviet Russia* (New York, 1960), pp. 108 and 169–70. For details and comments about the Hotel Lux on Tverskaya Street, see Ruth Fischer, *Stalin and German Communism* (London, 1948), pp. 541–42.

3. *The Worker,* July 12 and 17, 1924.

4. Jane Degras (ed.), *The Communist International* 1919–1943, Vol. II, 1923–1928 (London, 1960), pp. 94–98.

5. Paul Scheffer, *Seven Years in Soviet Russia* (London, 1931), p. 218.

6. *Rex* v. *Buck et al.: Transcript of Evidence Heard Before the Supreme Court of Ontario,* 2–12 *November* 1931 (Toronto, 1931), p. 711.

7. *The Worker,* August 30, 1924.

8. *Labour Organization in Canada* 1924 (Ottawa, 1925), p. 177.

9. *The Worker,* November 29, 1924. It is now known that the Zinoviev letter was a forgery. See *Sunday Times* (London), December 18, 1966, and *New York Times,* December 19, 1966.

10. *Labour Organization* 1924, p. 193. See also *The Worker,* November 22, 1924.

11. *The Worker,* December 13, 1924. See also *Manitoba Free Press,* December 1, 1925.

12. *The Worker,* December 13, 1924.

13. The article was reprinted in *International Press Correspondence* (Inprecorr), V, 18, March 5, 1925, pp. 254–55. See also Kenneth McNaught, *A Prophet in Politics* (Toronto, 1959), Ch. XI.

14. *The Worker,* March 21, 1925, Tim Buck "Canada and the British Empire"; April 4, 1925, K. Radek, "The British Empire, its Organization and Policy," are but two examples.

15. For the origin and importance of the Minority Movement, see Henry Pelling, *The British Communist Party* (London, 1958), pp. 26–27 and 32.

16. *The Worker,* July 18, 1925.

17. Draper, pp. 133–40.

18. *Ibid.* Also, Degras, pp. 183–200.

19. *Rex* v. *Buck et al.,* p. 422.

20. Isaac Deutscher, *The Prophet Unarmed* (London, 1959), p. 162–63.

21. *Protokoll der Erweiterte Exekutive der Kommunistischen Internationale, Moskau,* 21 *März–6 April* 1925 [Hamburg, 1925], pp. 290–311.

22. *Spector Interviews.*

23. *The Worker,* August 1, 1925.

24. Articles by Moriarty describing "Ivano-Vosnesenk" (*sic*) [i.e., Ivanovo-Vosnesenk] were featured in *The Worker,* August 8 and 22, September 5, 12, and 19, and October 10, 1925.

25. *Ukrayinski Rabotnychi Visty,* June 4, 1925.

CHAPTER ELEVEN

1. *Bericht über den IV Kongress der Kommunistischen Internationale* (Hamburg, 1923), p. 12.

2. Theodore Draper, *The Roots of American Communism* (New York, 1957), pp. 314 and 320–22.

3. *Labour Organization in Canada* 1922 (Ottawa, 1923), p. 222.

4. *Ibid.*
5. *Ibid.*, p. 27
6. *The Worker*, December 1, 1922.
7. *The Worker*, March 15, 1923.
8. *Ibid.* The letter was also reproduced in *Labour Organization in Canada* 1923 (Ottawa, 1924), p. 158.
9. *The Worker*, May 30, 1923.
10. *Labour Organization* 1922, p. 27.
11. *The Worker*, November 24, 1923.
12. *Report of the Third National Convention Workers' Party of Canada* 18–20 *April* 1924 (Toronto, 1924), p. 8.
13. *Labour Organization in Canada* 1923 (Ottawa, 1924), p. 207.
14. *Ibid.*, p. 206.
15. *The Worker*, November 24, 1923.
16. *International Press Correspondence* (Inprecorr), IV, No. 13, February 21, 1924, p. 101.
17. *Ibid.* See also Theodore Draper, *American Communism and Soviet Russia* (New York, 1960), Chs. II and V.
18. *The Worker*, April 5, 1924. See also *Labour Organization in Canada* 1924 (Ottawa, 1925), p. 194.
19. *The Worker*, April 26, 1924.
20. *Report Third WPC Convention*, p. 8.
21. *Ibid.*, p. 9.
22. *The Worker*, May 3, 1924.
23. *Labour Organization* 1924, p. 49.
24. *The Worker*, October 4, 1924.
25. *The Worker*, April 25, 1925.
26. *Labour Organization in Canada* 1925 (Ottawa, 1926), p. 187. See *The Worker*, March 28, 1925 for the text of the cable, and *Labour Organization* 1925, p. 208, for the subsequent use of the funds.
27. *Labour Organization* 1925, p. 188. See also *The Worker*, April 25, 1925, and A. E. Smith, *All My Life* (Toronto, 1949), pp. 76–81.
28. *Labour Organization* 1925, p. 189.
29. On his return Spector wrote an article for the British communist publication, *Labour Monthly*, September 1925, pp. 448–52. See also *The Worker*, September 19, 1925, for an interview Spector had with A. J. Cook, Secretary of the Miners' Federation.
30. *The Sunday Worker* (London, England), August 2, 1925. Also *The Worker*, August 29, 1925, and September 19, 1925.
31. *The Worker*, September 12 and 19, 1925. Also *Labour Organization* 1925, pp. 186–87.
32. *The Worker*, December 5, 1925.
33. *Ibid.*
34. *Ibid.*
35. *Labour Organization in Canada* 1926 (Ottawa, 1927), p. 196. See also Smith, p. 88.
36. Smith, p. 88. Also *The Worker*, April 17, 1925.
37. *Labour Organization* 1926, pp. 199–201.
38. *Ibid.*, pp. 194–95. See also *The Worker*, December 18, 1926.
39. *Labour Organization in Canada* 1928 (Ottawa, 1929), pp. 173–76. Also *Labour Organization in Canada* 1927 (Ottawa, 1928), p. 222.
40. *The Worker*, April 30. 1927,
41. *Report of the Central Executive Committee of the Fifth National Convention of the Communist Party of Canada* (Toronto, 1927), p. 6. See also Kenneth McNaught, *A Prophet in Politics* (Toronto, 1959), pp. 204–14, which discusses in general terms the role of the ILP in Manitoba and the changes then taking place in Canadian politics.
42. *Labour Organization* 1927, p. 179.
43. *Report of the Central Executive Committee to the Fifth National Convention of the Communist Party of Canada* (Toronto, 1927), p. 7.
44. *Ibid.*, p. 6.
45. *The Worker*, October 22 and November 6, 1927.
46. *The Worker*, November 12, 1927.
47. *The Worker*, November 26, 1927.
48. *Labour Organization* 1927, p. 221.

CHAPTER TWELVE

1. *The Labor Herald*, September 1922, p. 9. The paper began publication in Chicago in March 1922.
2. *Ibid.*, p. 10. Also, *The Worker*, October 16, 1922.
3. *The Labor Herald*, September 1922, p. 10.

4. Theodore Draper, *The Roots of American Communism* (New York, 1957), pp. 320–22; and *American Communism and Soviet Russia* (New York, 1960), pp. 70–72.

5. *Labour Organization in Canada* 1922 (Ottawa, 1923), pp. 21 and 27. See also *The Labor Herald*, September 1922, p. 9.

6. *Ibid.*, pp. 169 and 181.

7. *Ibid.*

8. *Maritime Labour Herald*, August 26, 1922. See Draper, *Roots*, p. 316, for Browder's role in Profintern and TUEL.

9. *The Labor Herald*, September 1922, pp. 9–10.

10. *Ibid.* Draper, *Roots*, p. 372, only notes that Foster and Browder were arrested at a meeting (undated) in Chicago, and does not deal at all with the TUEL convention. Benjamin Gitlow, *I Confess* (New York, 1939), p. 174, notes that the "Editorial Committee [of *The Labor Herald*] consisted of Knudsen, Carney, Wortis, Buck and Foster—all Communists. . . . the Profintern's Commissar at the conference—was Carl B. Johnson, alias Scott."

11. *Bulletin of the Fourth Congress of the Communist International* (Moscow, 1922), p. 10.

12. *Red International of Labor Unions, Second World Congress Resolutions and Decisions* (London, n.d.), p. 14. Nos. 37–39 deal with the TUEL.

13. *Labour Organization in Canada* 1923 (Ottawa, 1924), p. 160.

14. *Ibid.*, p. 159.

15. *Ibid.*

16. *The Worker*, April 2 and 25, 1923.

17. *Spector Interviews.*

18. Jane Degras (ed.), *The Communist International* 1919–1943, Vol. II, 1923–1928 (London, 1960), p. 26. See also *The Worker*, February 2, 1924.

19. Draper, *American Communism*, p. 108.

20. *The Maritime Labour Herald*, April 21, 1923. The letter dated Moscow, March 19, 1923, and signed by G. Slucky, Secretary of the International Propaganda Committee of Revolutionary Miners, and A. Kalnin, Acting General Secretary, RILU, was reprinted in *The Worker*, May 9, 1923. It was also quoted at length in an analysis of the Nova Scotia situation by John Dorsey, "The R.I.L.U. and the U.M.W.A.," which appeared in the TUEL's mouthpiece, *The Labor Herald*, May 1923, pp. 17–19.

21. *The Worker*, May 23, 1923.

22. *The Worker*, August 8, 1923. See also *The Worker*, October 31 and November 7, 1923, and *Labour Organization* 1923, p. 195.

23. *The Worker*, August 8, 1923.

24. *Ibid.* See also *The Labor Herald*, September 1923, pp. 11–12.

25. *International Press Correspondence* (Inprecorr), IV, 13, February 21, 1924, p. 101.

26. *Ibid.*

27. *The Worker*, August 22, 1923. A condensed report of the conference, entitled "Canadian League Eastern District Conference," written by Buck, appeared in *The Labor Herald*, September 1923, p. 24.

28. *The Worker*, August 22, 1923.

29. *The Labor Herald*, September 1923, p. 24.

30. *The Worker*, August 29, 1923.

31. *The Labor Herald*, October 1923, p. 12.

32. *Ibid.*, p. 13.

33. *The Worker*, September 19, 1923. Draper, *American Communism*, pp. 38–51, does not touch upon the TUEL conference held in Chicago in 1923.

34. *The Labor Herald*, November 1923, p. 26.

35. *Ibid.*

36. *Ibid.*

37. Draper, *American Communism*, p. 76. Also, *The Worker*, October 17 and 24, 1923.

38. *Report of the Third Convention Workers' Party of Canada* 18–20 April 1924 (Toronto, 1924), p. 4.

39. *Labour Organization in Canada* 1924 (Ottawa, 1925), p. 146.

40. *The Worker*, August 23, 1924.

41. *The Worker*, May 10 and 17, and June 14, 1924.

42. *Labour Organization in Canada* 1924 (Ottawa, 1925), pp. 152–53. See also *The Worker*, September 13, 20, and 27, 1924.

43. *Ibid.*, p. 146.

44. *The Left Wing*, November 1924.

45. Tim Buck, *Steps to Power*, (Toronto, 1925), p. 1.

46. Draper, *American Communism*, pp. 215–23.

47. *The Worker*, October 9, 1926. Also *Labour Organization in Canada* 1926 (Ottawa, 1927), p. 210.

48. *Labour Organization in Canada* 1927 (Ottawa, 1928), p. 169.

49. *Ibid.*, p. 170.

50. *The Worker*, July 9, 1927. Also *Labour Organization* 1927, p. 177.
51. *The Worker*, July 9, 1927.
52. *The Canadian Labour Monthly*, January 1928.
53. Degras, pp. 423–24. Also A. Losovsky, "Results and Prospects of the United Front," in *The Communist International*, March 15, 1928.
54. *Protokoll über den Vierten Kongress der Roten-Gewerkschafts Internationale* (Berlin, 1928), pp. 174–78, and 354.
55. *Ibid.*, p. 667. Also M. Buhay, "The Fourth Congress of the R.I.L.U.," in *The Canadian Labour Monthly*, July 1928.
56. *Rex v. Buck et al.: Transcript of Evidence Heard Before the Supreme Court of Ontario, 2–12 November* 1931 (Toronto, 1931), p. 567.
57. *Ibid.*
58. *Inprecorr*, IV, February 13, 21, 1924, p. 101. Also *Spector Interviews*.

CHAPTER THIRTEEN

1. *Resolution of the Canadian Commission, Fifth Plenum ECCI, to the CEC, Communist Party of Canada* (Moscow, 1925), p. 1.
2. *Ibid.*, p. 2.
3. *Ibid.*
4. *Ibid.*, pp. 7–8.
5. *Ibid.*, pp. 8–11.
6. *The Worker*, September 26, 1925.
7. *Labour Organization in Canada* 1925 (Ottawa, 1926), pp. 145–46.
8. *The Worker*, September 26, 1926.
9. *Labour Organization* 1925, pp. 144–45.
10. *Ibid.*
11. Theodore Draper, *American Communism and Soviet Russia* (New York, 1960), pp. 140–49. Browder, in interview, stated that Gusev wired the American party from Montreal.
12. A. E. Smith, *All My Life* (Toronto, 1949), pp. 83–84. See also Draper, *American Communism*, pp. 180–82.
13. *Labour Organization* 1925, p. 208.
14. *Ibid.*
15. See *The Calgary Herald*, January 26, 1926; *The Worker*, July 17, 1926; *Labour Organization in Canada* 1926 (Ottawa, 1927), p. 211; and Smith, p. 98.
16. *The Worker*, October 10 and 17, 1925.
17. *Labour Organization* 1925, p. 190. repeats figures which are confirmed in *The Parliamentary Guide*, 1926, and other sources. See *The Worker*, December 12, 1925, for details of the Winnipeg civic elections.
18. Draper, *American Communism*, pp. 226–29. Ruthenberg was also elected to the ECCI at the Plenum.
19. Jane Degras (ed.), *The Communist International* 1919–1943, Vol. II, 1923–1928 (London, 1960), pp. 245–48. See also Ruth Fischer, *Stalin and German Communism* (London, 1948), Ch. XXV.
20. *Internationale Presse-Korrespondenz* (Inprekorr), VI, 68, May 6, 1926, p. 1071.
21. *Stewart Smith Interviews*. Also *The Young Worker*, June 12, 1926.
22. Interviews with Smith, J. T. Murphy, and George Aitken (Levack). See also E. H. Carr, *Socialism in One Country*, Vol. III, Part II (London, 1964), pp. 1018–1019.
23. Stewart Smith, *The Red Bogey* (Toronto, n.d. [1947–1948]), p. 18.
24. *The Worker*, June 19, 1926.
25. *The Worker*, August 21, 1926. See also L. B. Schapiro, *The Communist Party of the Soviet Union* (London, 1960), pp. 299–301.
26. *The Worker*, November 6, 1926.
27. *Ibid.*
28. *Ibid.* For the best and most succinct account of Trotsky's defeat see Schapiro, Ch. XVI.
29. *The Worker*, November 13 and 20, 1926. See also Schapiro, Ch. XVI.
30. *The Worker*, December 18, 1926.

CHAPTER FOURTEEN

1. *Labour Organization in Canada* 1927 (Ottawa, 1928), pp. 170–72.
2. *International Press Correspondence* (Inprecorr), VII, January 6, 20, 1927, p. 110.
3. *The Worker*, April 23, 1927.
4. *The Worker*, April 16, 1927.
5. *The Worker*, April 23, 1927.

6. *The Worker*, December 25, 1926, and March 26, 1927.

7. *The Worker*, January 29, and June 4, 1927. For the ECCI Eighth Plenum statement on China see *Internationale Presse-Korrespondenz* (Inprekorr), VII, 41, April 16, 1927, p. 859. Also, Jane Degras (ed.), *The Communist International 1919-1943*, Vol. II, 1923-1928 (London, 1960), pp. 357-65. The Comintern's denunciation of Chiang Kai-shek was reproduced in *The Worker*, May 14, 1927.

8. *The Worker*, February 12, 1927 for the report of the District Nine convention held January 22; May 14, 1927, for District Eight proceedings on April 17-19; May 21, 1927 for Toronto City convention held May 8; June 4, 1927 for District Three convention held May 21-22; and June 11, 1927 for report of District Four meeting held May 14-15.

9. *Labour Organization* 1927, p. 167. Also *The Worker*, July 2, 1927.

10. *Report of the Central Executive Committee to the Fifth National Convention of the Communist Party of Canada* (Toronto, 1927), p. 2.

11. *Ibid.*

12. For details of this aspect of Canadian politics see Kenneth McNaught, *A Prophet in Politics* (Toronto, 1959), Ch. XIV, and W. L. Morton, *The Progressive Party in Canada* (Toronto, 1950), Ch. V.

13. *CEC Report Fifth Convention CPC*, p. 8. See also *Labour Organization* 1927, p. 181.

14. Paul Yuzyk, *The Ukrainians in Manitoba* (Toronto, 1953), p. 100. There is considerable evidence to suggest that the majority of Ukrainians in Canada, particularly those in rural areas, were politically quite unsophisticated and joined the ULFTA or subscribed to the Ukrainian communist press because of the cultural contacts they provided. See Elizabeth Wangenheim, "The Ukrainians: A Case Study of the Third Force" in Peter Russell (ed.), *Nationalism in Canada* (Toronto, 1966), p. 82.

15. *CEC Report Fifth Convention CPC*, p. 9.

16. *Ibid.*, p. 10.

17. For the Comintern resolution, see Degras, pp. 382-90. For the effect on the struggle between Trotsky, Stalin, Zinoviev and Bukharin within the CPSU, see L. B. Schapiro, *The Communist Party of the Soviet Union* (London, 1960), p. 303. For a Chinese Nationalist view of these events see Chiang Kai-Shek, *Soviet Russia in China* (revised abridged edition, Toronto, 1965), pp. 27-38.

18. *CEC Report Fifth Convention CPC*, p. 11.

19. *Ibid.*

20. *Ibid.*

21. *Ibid.*

22. *Spector Interviews.*

23. *The Worker*, July 9, 1927.

24. *Ibid.*

25. *Labour Organization* 1927, p. 182.

26. *Report of the National Executive Committee from the Period of the Third to Fourth National Conventions of the Young Communist League of Canada* (Toronto, 1927), p. 2.

27. *Ibid.*

CHAPTER FIFTEEN

1. *The Worker*, August 6, 1927.

2. *The Worker*, September 17, 1927, for example, printed an abridged version of Rykov's views on the opposition's misdemeanours, which was delivered at a meeting of Moscow party functionaries—no date given—as well as an opposition declaration signed by Avdyev, Bakayev, Yevdokimov, Kamenev, Lisdin, Muralov, Petersen, Pyatkov, Rakovski, Smilga, Trotsky, and Zinoveiv. The statement which announced Trotsky's and Vuyovitch's expulsion from the Executive of the International was printed on October 15.

3. The Fifteenth Party Congress decisions were summarized in *The Worker*, January 7 and 14, 1928.

4. *The Worker*, December 24, 1927 and January 14, 1928. Also *Labour Organization in Canada* 1927 (Ottawa, 1928), p. 225.

5. Theodore Draper, *American Communism and Soviet Russia* (New York, 1960), p. 363.

6. *The Daily Worker* (New York), February 6, 1928. These views were put forward earlier in an editorial written by Spector in *The Worker*, January 7, 1928. The American plenum was reported in *The Worker*, February 14, 1928.

7. *The Worker*, March 24 and 31, and April 21, 1928.

8. *Debates of the Senate of the Dominion of Canada* 1928 (Ottawa, 1928), pp. 166-76, and 415-35. Also *Labour Organization in Canada* 1928 (Ottawa, 1929), p. 174. See also *Labour* (Washington, D.C.), September 29, 1928 for the results of Buck's appeal.

9. *The Worker*, May 26, 1928. See also Tim Buck, *Thirty Years 1922-1952* (Toronto, 1952), pp. 86-87.

10. *Protokoll über den Vierten Kongress der Roten-Gewerkschafts Internationale* (Berlin, 1928), pp. 174-78, and 667. The Congress was held March 17 to April 3, 1928. See also *Canadian Labour*

Monthly, July 1928. Buhay gave his impressions of the meeting in an article entitled "The Fourth Congress of the R.I.L.U."

11. *Ukrayinski Zhitya*, November 12, 1927.

12. The route was mentioned in a passing reference in *The Worker*, July 14, 1928.

13. *Labour Organization* 1928, p. 182. *The Worker*, July 14, 1928, reprinted a statement by James Simpson published in the Toronto *Globe*, June 30, 1928, which repudiated Spector and MacDonald as possible delegates to the Commonwealth conference.

14. *The Worker*, September 22 and 29, 1928.

15. Spector Interviews.

16. For Bukharin's report to the Congress see *International Press Correspondence* (Inprecorr), VIII, 41, July 30, 1928. For the theses which were put before the Sixth Congress on August 24, 1928, see *Protokoll des VI Weltkongresses der Kommunistischen Internationale, Moskau, 17 Juli–1 September* 1928 (Hamburg, 1928), Vol. IV, p. 13, These dealt with the fight against imperialist war, and the Comintern's tasks. See also Draper, *American Communism*, pp. 306–307; Benjamin Gitlow, *I Confess* (New York, 1939), p. 507; L. B. Schapiro, *The Communist Party of the Soviet Union* (London, 1960), pp. 366–67. For an assessment of Neumann, see Ruth Fischer, *Stalin and German Communism* (London, 1948), pp. 445–46.

17. *International Press Correspondence* (Inprecorr), VIII, No. 63, September 12, 1928, pp. 1139–40. Navis, whose name is incorrectly given in the English edition as "Nairs," signed a declaration on behalf of the CPC which confirmed the correctness of the "decisive measures" taken by the ECCI against Trotsky and his allies inside as well as outside the Soviet Union. Also *Inprecorr*, VIII, No. 64, September 19, 1928, p. 1156; and *Inprecorr*, No. 81, November 21, 1928, pp. 1531–32. Canada received four decisive votes, which ranked her with Hungary, Belgium, Austria, and Roumania.

18. *Inprecorr*, VIII, No. 44, August 3, 1928, p. 779. MacDonald spoke at the sixth session, July 23, 1928.

19. *Inprecorr*, VIII, No. 50, August 16, 1928, p. 882. Spector spoke at the 11th session on July 26, 1928.

20. *Ibid.*, pp. 883–84.

21. *Inprecorr*, VIII, No. 64, September 19, 1928, p. 1150.

22. *Inprecorr*, VIII, No. 62, September 14, 1928, p. 1107. See also Degras, pp. 574–75.

23. *The Worker*, July 28; August 4, 18, 25; September 1 and 8, 1928, covered the Congress in general terms only, as did the Finnish and Ukrainian papers.

24. *Pravda*, August 24, 1928.

25. J. P. Cannon, *The History of American Trotskyism* (New York, 1944), p. 49. Spector and Cannon read only the first and third portions of the document, and it was this version which was first published in *The Militant*, the semi-monthly Trotskyite organ started by Cannon and subsidized by royalties from Max Eastman's book *The Real Situation in Russia*. The complete version was published in Trotsky's *The Third International After Lenin* (New York, 1936).

26. *The Worker*, January 19, 1929. The correspondence between Cannon and Spector was reproduced in part in an article signed by MacDonald. *The Militant*, January 1, 1929, reported that Cannon's flat was burgled on December 23, 1928, and copies of the correspondence between the two men were sent to MacDonald by Jay Lovestone.

27. *The Worker*, November 10, 1928.

28. *The Worker*, January 19, 1929. The meeting was advertised for Friday, October 26 in *The Worker*, October 27, 1928.

29. A. E. Smith, *All My Life*, (Toronto, 1949), p. 94.

30. Tim Buck, *Thirty Years* 1922–1952 (Toronto, 1952) p. 64.

31. *The Worker*, January 19, 1929.

32. Draper, pp. 370–71.

33. Spector, *Letter to the Political Committee, CPC*, Toronto, November 6, 1928, pp. 1–2. A nine-page document, Spector's letter was reproduced in abridged form in the second issue of *The Militant*, December 1, 1928, p. 6.

34. *The Worker*, January 19, 1929.

35. *The Worker*, November 24, 1928. The CEC statement was published in *Inprecorr*, VII, No. 85, November 30, 1928, pp. 1608–09. *Inprecorr*, IX, No. 38. August 9, 1929, p. 818, announced the Tenth Plenum's decision to expel Spector from the ECCI. On the same page was the notice that Jay Lovestone had been cast out of the Comintern.

36. *The Globe* (Toronto), November 13, 1928.

37. *The Worker*, December 1 and 8, 1928. The meeting was held on November 23, with a claimed attendance of over 400. A. E. Smith, p. 95, claims that over 800 were present.

38. *The Worker*, December 1, 1928.

39. *The Militant*, December 15, 1928, p. 3, listed Spector as Associate Editor of the publication.

CHAPTER SIXTEEN

1. *The Militant*, June 1, 1929.
2. For details see L. B. Schapiro, *The Communist Party of the Soviet Union* (London, 1960), Ch. XX.
3. *The Worker*, December 22, 1929.
4. *The Worker*, December 29, 1928. The same issue carried a reprint from *International Press Correspondence* (Inprecorr) of extracts of Stalin's speech delivered to a plenary session of the Central Committee CPSU dealing with Soviet problems. In the CPC's draft thesis a reference was made to the four points which Stalin, in earlier days, had put forward as characteristics of a nation: culture, language, territory, and economic unity.
5. *The Worker*, December 16, 1928.
6. *The Worker*, December 8, 1928. Also *Ukrayinski Rabotnychi Visty*, December 1, 1928.
7. *The Worker*, January 5, 12, and March 2, 1929.
8. Tim Buck, *Thirty Years 1922–1952* (Toronto, 1952), p. 65. For details of Lovestone's actions, see Theodore Draper, *American Communism and Soviet Russia* (New York, 1960), p. 388.
9. *Rex* v. *Buck et al.: Transcript of Evidence Heard Before the Supreme Court of Ontario* 2–12 November 1931 (Toronto, 1931), pp. 262–63. The January Comintern communique was referred to in a letter from Moscow dated May 1929.
10. *The Worker*, January 26, 1929.
11. *Ibid.*
12. Draper, pp. 268–72.
13. Schapiro, pp. 366–77. Also Draper, pp. 398–429.
14. *Rex* v. *Buck et al.*, p. 260. MacDonald reported cabling Moscow at a Political Committee meeting held March 1, 1929. At the time no reply had been received from the Comintern.
15. *Ibid.*, p. 261.
16. *The Worker*, February 23, 1929.
17. *Ibid.*
18. *The Worker*, March 9, 1929.
19. *Ibid.*
20. *The Worker*, March 16, 1929.
21. A. E. Smith, *All My Life* (Toronto, 1949), pp. 95—96. Stewart Smith was advertised to speak in Montreal on March 3, 1929, in *The Worker*, March 2, 1929.
22. *The Worker*, March 23 and 30; April 13 and 27; May 4, 11, and 25, 1929, featured articles by Rebecca Buhay, Leslie Morris, John Weir, Buck, MacDonald, Smith, and newcomers such as Sam Carr. The debate also spilled over into the Finnish and Ukrainian communist press, but on a smaller scale and with parochial overtones.
23. *Letter, Political Secretariat ECCI to CEC, Communist Party of Canada*, Moscow, April 8, 1929, p. 1. Parts of the letter, a nine-page document, were quoted at the trial *Rex* v. *Buck et al.*, where it appeared as Exhibit 49. Receipt of the special letter is confirmed in J. Williamson's article on the CPC's Sixth Convention, *International Press Correspondence* (Inprecorr), IX, 38, August 9, 1929, pp. 815–16.
24. *ECCI Letter*, p. 7.
25. *Ibid.*, p. 8.
26. J. Williamson, "CPC's Sixth Convention," *Inprecorr*, IX, 38, August 9, 1929, pp. 815–16.
27. *ECCI Letter*, p. 1.
28. *The Worker*, March 16, 23, 1929; April 27; May 4, 11; and June 8, 1929. Also Leslie Morris, "Zum VI Parteitag der K P Kanadas," in *Internationale Presse-Korrespondenz* (Inprekorr), IX, 40, May 10, 1929.
29. Draper, pp. 399–404 for the American party convention held March 1–9, 1929, and pp. 423–25 for Lovestone's and Gitlow's downfall. The news of their fall from power was first published in *Pravda*, May 18, 1929. It was reported in a despatch from Walter Duranty in *The New York Times*, May 19, 1929. *The Daily Worker* (New York), published news of the Comintern's action on May 20, 1929.
30. Buck, pp. 65–66.
31. *Labour Organization in Canada* 1929 (Ottawa, 1930), p. 161, states that 67 delegates, 42 with decisive votes and 25 with consultative voice, attended. Buck, p. 66, states that there were 78 accredited delegates.
32. *The Worker*, June 1 and 8, 1929.
33. Smith, p. 96.
34. See *The Worker*, July 27, 1929, for Bruce's appointment. Also *Vapaus*, August 12, 1947; *Ukrayinski Zhitya*, August 19, 1947; and *The Canadian Tribune*, September 3, 1947.
35. Buck, p. 67. See also *The Worker*, July 13, 1929.
36. *The Worker*, July 6, 1929, published a statement from the National Executive Committee of the YCL which rebutted the arguments Moriarty put forward in a letter to the Comintern.
37. *The Worker*, July 27, 1929.

38. *Ibid. Labour Organization* 1929, p. 161, lists Tom Ewen as a member of the Political Bureau, but Ewen was not co-opted until after MacDonald became inactive.

39. Buck, pp. 67–68.

40. Smith, p. 97.

41. Both Bertram Wolfe and Stewart Smith independently corroborated Buck's absence and illness. *The Worker*, October 5, 1929, contains a CEC statement signed by MacDonald in his capacity as "Acting Secretary."

42. *The Worker*, November 16 and 30, and December 7, 1929. Also, A. G. Richman, "Die Reaktion in Kanada," in *Inprekorr*, XI, No. 98, October 18, 1929, pp. 2343–44; Stewart Smith, "The Struggle against Opportunism in the C.P. of Canada," in *Inprecorr*, IX, No. 69, December 13, 1929; and John Porter, "The Struggle Against the Right Danger," in *The Communist International*, VI, No. 23, October 15, 1929, pp. 944–54.

43. *Letter, Political Secretariat ECCI to CEC, Communist Party of Canada*, Moscow, October 3, 1929, p. 2.

44. *The Worker*, March 8, 1930, published the communication which was dated Moscow, December 30, 1929.

45. *The Worker*, March 15, 1930.

46. *The Worker*, March 1, 1930.

47. Attorney General's Department Record Group, Box One, Envelope 14, Toronto, May 24, 1930.

48. *Rex* v. *Buck et al.*, pp. 600–10, and 746–47.

49. *Ibid.*, pp. 344–345.

EPILOGUE

1. Attorney General's Department Record Group. Box Nine, Envelope 15. Letter, Political Secretariat ECCI to Central Committee, CPC, Moscow, October 3, 1929.

2. *Ibid.* Resolution of the Political Secretariat of the ECCI on the Situation and Tasks of the Communist Party of Canada, Moscow, n.d. [1930].

3. Alexander Dallin, "Comintern," in *Survey*, No. 59, April 1966, p. 118.

INDEX

Except where indicated party pseudonyms are given in brackets.

Lightning Source UK Ltd.
Milton Keynes UK
UKHW051622071222
R3232500001B/R32325PG413199UKX00001B/1